The Early Years Foundation Stage

Theory and Practice

Second

Edited by **Ioanna Palaiologou**

The Early Years Foundation Stage

Theory and Practice

Second Edition

Los Angeles | London | New Delhi
Singapore | Washington DC

Los Angeles | London | New Delhi
Singapore | Washington DC

SAGE Publications Ltd
1 Oliver's Yard
55 City Road
London EC1Y 1SP

SAGE Publications Inc.
2455 Teller Road
Thousand Oaks, California 91320

SAGE Publications India Pvt Ltd
B 1/I 1 Mohan Cooperative Industrial Area
Mathura Road
New Delhi 110 044

SAGE Publications Asia-Pacific Pte Ltd
3 Church Street
#10-04 Samsung Hub
Singapore 049483

Commissioning editor: Jude Bowen
Development editor: Robin Lupton
Assistant editor: Miriam Davey
Production editor: Nicola Marshall
Copyeditor: Elaine Leek
Proofreader: Neil Dowden
Marketing manager: Catherine Slinn
Cover design: Naomi Robinson
Typeset by: C&M Digitals (P) Ltd, Chennai, India
Printed by: MPG Books Group, Bodmin, Cornwall

First edition published 2010
Second edition published 2013

Library of Congress Control Number: 2012944558

British Library Cataloguing in Publication data

A catalogue record for this book is available from the British Library

ISBN 978-1-4462-5697-8
ISBN 978-1-4462-5698-5 (pbk)

Contents

Essential book for every student interested in the Early Years. Up-to-date information and good examples of practices.

Paivi Valtonen, Education, Grimsby Institute of Further and Higher Education

A book that is very appropriate for students engaged in the study of early years policy and practice. Clear, well focused and enables students to reflect on practice.

Michael Reed, Institute of Education, Worcester University

An accessible and practical guide for students working in the Early Years. The layout ensures that the reader can access relevent material quickly. A very good resource book for practice.

Judy Gracey, Education, Canterbury Christ Church University

This book is an essential text for all students undertaking a degree or foundation degree in early childhood studies. It is informative, readable and undeniably the practitioner's bible to gaining insight into the theory, policy and application of this distinct phase of education. Excellent read.

Joanne Hall, Health, Care and Early Years, Blackpool and the Fylde College

The text encourages a critical approach to existing and new frameworks that is essential for current practitioners to extend their understanding and awareness of the influences at work within early years and education.

Chelle Davison, Education, Leeds Metropolitan University

Acknowledgements

This book would have never been completed without the help of the people who gave us permission to use observations of their children or material from their settings. We would like to thank the following people:

Anastasia, David, George and Harry Hollings
McMillan Nursery, Hull
Aspire Trust, Merseyside
Creative Partnerships, Hull
Croxteth Children's Centre, Liverpool
Jude Bird

Andrew Shimmin and the staff in
Melvin King Childminders, Liverpool
Ruth Spencer Nursery School, Hull
The Lemon Tree Nursery at Bude
Children's Centre, Hull
Childhaven Nursery School, Scarborough

I would also like to thank all the authors for their contribution. Without them this book would have not happened.

A great thank you as always to the team at Sage for their support and help: Jude Bowen, Robin Lupton and Miriam Davey.

The publisher would like to thank all those who provided feedback and suggestions for this new edition:

Jonathan Glazzard, FHEA Course Leader Primary ITT Courses School of Education and Professional Development, University of Huddersfield

Patricia Cunningham, Senior Lecturer in Education & BED Early Years Programme Leader, University College Plymouth

Chelle Davison, Senior Lecturer Early Years Professional Practice, Leeds Metropolitan University

Stephanie Evans, Programme Leader 3Yr QTS Primary, University of Cumbria

Annabel Dawson, Curriculum Leader, New College Durham

Jane Beniston, Senior Lecturer Early Childhood Education and Care, Newman University College

Denise Reardon, Senior Lecturer, Canterbury Christ Church University

Helen Sutherland, Senior Lecturer in Early Years Education, Kingston University

Katherine Goodsir, Senior Lecturer in Early Years, Bath Spa University

Contributors

Ioanna Palaiologou

 Ioanna Palaiologou (BA (Hons), MA, MEd, PhD, PGCHE, Chartered Psychologist) is a lecturer and researcher in the Centre for Educational Studies, University of Hull. After completing her PhD, Ioanna worked as a researcher and lecturer on Early Childhood Studies degree courses in the University of Wales Swansea and Nottingham Trent University. In 2004 she joined the University of Hull and worked as Programme Director of BA (Hons) Educational Studies. Ioanna currently is leading the Masters in Early Childhood Studies and is the Academic Coordinator for Research Students Support within the Faculty of Education. She is a Chartered Psychologist of the British Psychological Society with specialism on child development and learning theories. Her books include: *Child Observation for the Early Years* (Sage, 2012) and *Ethical Practice in Early Childhood* (Sage, 2012).

About the Contributors

Jane Arnott

Jane Arnott is a Senior Lecturer at Canterbury Christ Church University. She has worked as a nurse, midwife and health visitor and has worked as a Senior Lecturer at Christ Church for the past eight years. Jane's main area of interest lies within the early child years. She is particularly interested in the role of empathy in professionals working with parents and children. Jane is part of the Specialist Community Public Health Nursing team at Canterbury who are responsible for the development and delivery of student health visiting and school nursing programmes.

Jane is also seconded to the Kent Surrey and Sussex GP Deanery and works with GP training. She is particularly interested in supporting trainees in developing good communication skills and understanding the role of empathy in general practice.

John Bennett

John Bennett is currently a lecturer in education at the University of Hull. He is the programme director for the BA (Hons) Learning and Teaching (Primary Education) and works mainly in primary initial teacher education, including the postgraduate and undergraduate routes. In his work in the Faculty of Education, he also contributes to the masters level provision as a module leader and assists in the supervision of doctoral students. His PhD included a significant focus on the potential impact of the original National Curriculum on personal, social and moral education in primary schools and his research interests have continued to be around those areas, alongside primary English, curriculum policy and curriculum design in primary schools. Before moving to work in higher education, he was a primary school headteacher and in his 25 years working in primary schools he also acted as a curriculum support teacher, working with many different settings.

Gary Beauchamp

Gary Beauchamp is Director of Research and Professor of Education in the School of Education at Cardiff Metropolitan University. After many years working as a primary school teacher, Professor Beauchamp moved into higher education where he has led undergraduate and postgraduate courses in education. His research interests focus on ICT in education, particularly the use of interactive technologies in learning and teaching. He has published widely in academic journals, as well as books, book chapters and research reports. In addition, he is Additional Inspector for Estyn, chair of governors in a primary school and has served as external examiner for many universities.

David Coates

David Coates has taught children between the ages of 5 and 18 in a variety of schools. He has been involved in teacher education and associated research for a number of years, teaching on undergraduate and postgraduate programmes. David's most recent research has focused on the education of gifted and talented pupils and supporting teachers to meet the needs of these pupils.

Elizabeth Dunphy

Elizabeth Dunphy teaches and coordinates a range of pre-service and in-service early childhood education courses in her role as Senior Lecturer in Early Childhood Education at St Patrick's College (Dublin City University), Ireland. Her research interests include young children's mathematics, early childhood pedagogy and the assessment of early learning. She is the author of 'Supporting early learning through formative assessment: a research paper' (National Council for Curriculum and Assessment (NCCA), 2009), one of four background papers commissioned to inform the development of Aistear: The Framework for Early Learning (NCCA, 2009). Forthcoming publications include the co-authored *Literacy in Early Childhood and Primary Education (Children Aged 3–8 Years),* Commissioned by NCCA. The report can be accessed in full on www.ncca.ie.

Cheryl Ellis

Cheryl Ellis, PhD, is a principal lecturer on the Educational Studies and Early Childhood Studies degree at Cardiff Metropolitan University. She is a member of the university's outdoor learning team and regularly works with children and students within Forest School. Her key areas of research interest include outdoor learning and play, inclusion and additional learning needs. Having previously worked as a primary school teacher, Cheryl has experienced the 'practical realities' of classroom life.

Michiko Fujii

Michiko Fujii is an artist and creative practitioner based in the North West of England. She has worked on a number of creative learning projects in schools, children's centres and galleries since 2005. She completed her MA Art & Design in Education at the Institute of Education, London, in 2008, where she underpinned her practice as an artist working with young children, while also carrying out a two-year action research project working in children's centres in Manchester. Her masters research focused upon the role of the artist as both an outsider and collaborative educator within the early years. Michiko continues to fuse her practice as a visual artist with her ongoing work as a creative practitioner working with different learner groups. She is focused upon the interplay between participants, materials and space and spends much of her time developing creative learning environments that are designed to excite and engage young children and their adults.

Laura Grindley

Laura Grindley is a qualified early years professional with a BA Hons degree in Early Childhood Studies and has subsequently worked in nursery settings in children's centres in Merseyside. She has taken on many additional roles, including Early Years Professional Coordinator and Early Years Professional Mentor and has been published in *Nursery World* and *Impact* magazine. She has a wealth of experience implementing early years training, including lecturing for Edge Hill University and Hull University. She was seconded into the role of Early Years Pedagogue for the Midas Touch Creative Recycling Project in February 2010 and has always been passionate about open-ended creativity and international perspectives on early childhood, in particular the Reggio Emilia approach. She continues to promote awareness of the project through her current role as Senior Children's Development and Leaning Officer for Knowsley Children's Centres. She is currently working towards achieving an MA in Education with Early Years at Edge Hill University.

Laura Harkin

Laura Harkin has worked as a nursery nurse, a class teacher, a children's centre teacher, an EYP assessor and moderator, and an early years standards and improvement officer. Laura is currently working as a class teacher in a pupil referral unit for children at risk of exclusion, or permanently excluded due to their behaviour. She is currently studying for her masters in early childhood education. Laura moderates early years practitioners end of foundation stage assessments as part of the local authority moderation team.

Chantelle Haughton

Chantelle Haughton joined Cardiff Metropolitan University in 2008 as a lecturer in Early Childhood Studies and Educational Studies. Previously, Chantelle worked supporting children and families in a range of settings. Coordinating a number of community projects and relative school initiatives has provided Chantelle with the basis for her research interests, which reflect on real life practice through engagement with stakeholders. As an early career researcher Chantelle has participated in capacity-building research and enterprise projects funded by WERN, ESRC and HEFCW. Chantelle also coordinates and delivers Outdoor Learning and Forest School Programmes at the university. Chantelle is a trained Forest School Leader and often works in collaboration with Forestry Commission Wales. Chantelle runs regular Forest School projects on campus for visiting school children and practitioners; these sessions are supported and observed by students. Chantelle is undertaking PhD research into contemporary understandings and interpretation of the Forest School ethos.

Claire Head

Claire Head is a lecturer in Primary English and Early Years Education on undergraduate and postgraduate degree programmes at the University of Hull, Scarborough Campus. Her research interests centre on dialogic teaching approaches to early reading, early literacy, the multilingual classroom, collaborative approaches to learning, and early years pedagogy and practice. Claire has taught at the University for eleven years and particularly enjoys working in partnership with teachers and students in the community. Claire formerly worked as a primary school teacher in Bradford where she assumed leadership responsibility for English and assessment across the curriculum and was the coordinator for special educational needs, early years and Key Stage 1.

Sally Howard

Sally Howard is currently a senior lecturer at Warwick University on the Primary PGCE and Early Years programme. Prior to this she was a primary headteacher, school inspector, educational consultant and senior lecturer in other UK universities. Among her publications, she co-authored *Inside the Primary Black Box: Assessment for Learning in Primary and Early Years Classrooms* (GL Assessment, 2008). Her career in education builds on her earlier life as a nurse and midwife which gives her a depth of understanding of child development and effective management of learning from birth into adulthood.

Angie Hutchinson

Angie Hutchinson graduated from the University of Hull with a First Class BA (Hons) in Educational Studies, specialising in Early Childhood Studies. She went on to attain an initial teacher training PGCE with a focus on the 3–7 age range and subsequently worked as a Foundation Stage teacher, primarily with Foundation Stage 1 children. Still working in a Hull primary school, she is currently a Foundation Stage Leader, a teacher of Foundation Stage 2 children and a member of the school's Senior Leadership Team. She has lectured in the Centre for Educational Studies on the BA (Hons) Education and Early Years Programme and is a current masters (MEd) student at the University of Hull.

Anna Knowles

Anna Knowles has worked in early education for a number of years and currently works as a teacher at McMillan Nursery School in Hull. When working with families in a family support role she developed a particular interest in effective engagement of parents. Working closely with parents and carers to support the learning and development of the child is a continuing area of research interest. She has lectured in the areas of child observation and working with young children at the University of Hull and has worked as a placement mentor for degree students. She has spoken at the annual ISC conference in the areas of 'Boys and Gunplay' and 'Gender and Play'. She continues to research to support her role as a teacher and has recently considered the role of peer observation and supporting boys in observed rough and tumble play.

Paulette Luff

Paulette Luff is a Senior Lecturer in the Department of Education at Anglia Ruskin University (in Chelmsford and Cambridge) where she leads the MA in Early Childhood Studies and teaches on other early years degree courses. For the past ten years much of Paulette's implementation and evaluation of early childhood curricula. She has spoken and written on this subject for different audiences, including co-authoring two books, and is now engaged in a new project examining understandings and uses of pedagogical documentation in different types of early years settings. Paulette has worked in the field of early childhood throughout her career, as a teacher, foster carer, school–home liaison worker, nursery practitioner and adviser, and as a lecturer in further and higher education.

Sarah MacQuarrie

Sarah MacQuarrie is a research associate within the Centre for Rural Childhood, University of the Highlands and Islands. Prior to this, her PhD (at the University of Strathclyde) investigated the role of group work within secondary school classrooms, and devised a group work programme aimed at strengthening productive interaction. She is currently developing a research-based toolkit that incorporates outdoor learning for the early years and primary sectors and is working in conjunction with the educational consultancy Mindstretchers (www.mindstretchers.com). Sarah's research looks at the relationship between theory and practice in education, in particular investigating ways to support the implementation of research-based practice. Wider research interests span topics such as peer interaction (inside and outside the classroom), teachers' professional development, bilingual learners, and children's social and emotional welfare. Sarah is a Chartered Psychologist, accredited by the British Psychological Society.

Trevor Male

In previous careers Trevor Male has been a teacher, an LEA officer and a tutor for the Open University. He has been employed full-time in higher education since 1993 and held lecturing and managerial posts at Brunel University and the University of Lincoln before joining the University of Hull in 2002. Trevor's PhD thesis investigated the career transition issues facing newly appointed headteachers which was subsequently developed and published as a book entitled *Being an Effective Headteacher* (2006), – published by Sage. In addition he has been published widely in books and journals nationally and internationally and is a regular contributor to research conferences. He was Head of the Centre for Educational Studies from 2011 to 2012 and is currently Course Leader for the MEd in Leadership and Learning with responsibility within the Faculty of Education for International Development.

Alison Murphy

Alison Murphy is the programme director for the BA Educational Studies programme and is a senior lecturer in Educational Studies and Early Childhood Studies at Cardiff Metropolitan University. As a former primary school teacher Alison has had experience of teaching in England and Wales, both in the mainstream and special education sector. She has also worked in further education as well as lecturing at other higher educational establishments including Swansea University and the University of Glamorgan.

Alison obtained her masters degree in 1996 with research that focused on the social composition of special educational needs units in Birmingham. She is currently studying for a PhD and this is a study of children's perceptions of national identity in Wales. The aim of this research is to look at the issue of national identity and its construction and importance in the world of the young child

David Needham

David Needham's learning journey within the field of education has taken place in schools, further education and universities. His early work focused upon the influence of pedagogies and methods within the classroom with an underpinning philosophical emphasis, but in recent years he has looked at the influence of reflexivity upon the development of professionals within the formative years of their career development.

Nick Owen

Nick Owen MBE is Director of the international arts education organisation the Aspire Trust, and has spent over 30 years developing arts education practice in community and cultural contexts across the UK and internationally. He was the first Head of Community Arts at the Liverpool Institute of Performing Arts (LIPA) between 1994 and 2002. Here, he initiated and developed the UK's first full-time performing arts course in higher education for disabled people. Recent publications include *Placing Students at the Heart of Creative Learning* (Routledge, 2012) and 'Outsiders insiders: becoming a creative partner with schools', in *The Routledge International Handbook of Creative Learning* (Routledge, 2011). Recent theatre directing credits include *Closing Schools for the Future* at the Tête-a-Tête Experimental Opera Festival, Riverside Studios, London. He was awarded Honorary Fellowships in Education at both the University of Hull and University of Tasmania in 2012.

Theodora Papatheodorou

Theodora Papatheodorou (PhD, MEd, BEd, PGDip(SEN) and MBPsS), an early childhood educator and researcher, is visiting Professor of Early Childhood at the University of the Free State University in South Africa. Prior to that she was Professor of Early Childhood and Director of Research at Anglia Ruskin University. She trained as a pre-school teacher and worked in mainstream, special education and bilingual early years settings. Her teaching and research are in the areas of pre-school curriculum and pedagogy, educational and social inclusion, behaviour problems, multicultural pedagogy and bilingualism, and early childhood programme evaluation. She is the author of *Behaviour Problems in the Early Years* (Routledge, 2005); co-author of *Child Observation for Learning and Research* (Pearson, 2011), editor of *Debates on Early Childhood Policies and Practices* (Routledge, 2012); and co-editor of *Learning Together in the Early Years: Exploring Relational Pedagogy* (Routledge, 2009) and *Cross-Cultural Perspectives on Early Childhood* (Sage, 2012).

Donna Potts

Donna's interest in early years began in 1987 when she became mother to her son, followed by a daughter in 1989. She was fortunate to enjoy their pre-school years as a full-time parent, and still considers this to be the best job she has ever had. Her interest in early years grew into a passion and she volunteered to help in their classes when her children started school. This led to the offer of a teaching assistant job and after ten fulfilling years she was encouraged to consider a career in teaching. With no degree, no maths GCSE and a background as a 'free school meals child' who had been raised single-handedly by her father from the age of 13, she thought this was beyond her but in 2004 she graduated with a First Class BA Honours Degree in Early Childhood Education. She qualified as a teacher in 2006 and is currently teaching as a qualified Reading Recovery Teacher. She hopes her story can inspire others to see that anyone can beat the odds stacked against them with determination and desire.

Wendy Thompson

Wendy Thompson was Programme Director for the Early Years at the University of Hull before her retirement. She led the PGCE Early Years (3–7 age phase) for a number of years and has a great deal of experience in preparing students for qualified teacher status (QTS). Her research interests were in child development and child pedagogy.

Glenda Walsh

Glenda Walsh (BEd (Hons), PhD, ALCM) is a Principal Lecturer at Stranmillis University College, Queen's University Belfast, where she is Head of Early Years Education. She has a particular interest in young children's learning and development, especially researching play and pedagogy in early childhood settings. Her own doctoral thesis concentrated on the play versus formal debate in early childhood education in Northern Ireland and Denmark and for the past ten years she has been involved in the longitudinal evaluation of the Early Years Enriched Curriculum Project in primary schools in Northern Ireland. Her recent projects include 'Examining Pedagogy in Early Childhood' for the Department of Education in the Republic of Ireland, 'Making it Work for Two Year Olds', funded by Atlantic Philanthropies, and 'Translating a Developmentally Appropriate Curriculum into Practice', sponsored by the Northern Ireland Council for the Curriculum, Examinations and Assessment and Sesame Tree Northern Ireland for Sesame Workshop. She is currently joint-leading an Evaluation of the All Ireland Centre of Excellence Award throughout Ireland for Early Childhood Ireland and Early Years, the organisation for young children.

Jane Waters

Jane Waters, PhD, is the Head of Initial Teacher Education and Training at Swansea Metropolitan University; part of the South West Wales Centre of Teacher Education. Having worked initially as a classroom teacher and, more recently, as a director of an undergraduate Early Childhood Studies programme she now works most closely with postgraduate students training to be teachers. She is passionate about the potential in Wales for innovative engaging early years education as a result of the Foundation Phase framework, introduced across Wales from 2008. Jane's research interests lie in early childhood education, young children's experiences of outdoor spaces. Current research projects include working with international colleagues to consider pedagogical intersubjectivity in early education contexts in different countries. This project is an extension of Jane's doctoral research that focused on adult–child interaction, sustained shared thinking and the affordance of different educative spaces.

Free online material to accompany the book

To gain **free access** to selected SAGE journal articles related to key topics discussed in this book please visit: www.sagepub.co.uk/Palaiologou2e

Preface

In the first edition of this book we explored issues around the Early Years Foundation Stage (EYFS), drawing upon its key elements, such as planning, play, assessment, partnerships with parents/carers and others in the context of the new statutory guidance. EYFS opened to public debate the questions around what constitutes effective practice, quality in early years education and care, and how the optimum programme should be delivered in order to meet the Early Learning Goals. As will be demonstrated in Chapters 1 and 2 of this second edition, there was a long period when the early years education and care of young children from birth to 5 years of age was left with little attention and few regulations. Consequently the introduction in 2008 of EYFS as a framework of good practice was welcomed as proving a coherent and consistent framework across the sector to support young children's learning and development. In the first edition a number of authors shared their experiences, knowledge and thoughts about what was then the 'new' Early Years Foundation Stage. That book reflected the variation of these experiences around key themes to celebrate the manner in which expertise in early years education and care had developed in recent years in terms of research, legislation, policy, pedagogy and practice.

The Tickell Review of March 2011 concluded that EYFS should continue to provide a coherent and consistent framework that supports young children's learning and development. It further recommended a flexible, less bureaucratic and more inclusive EYFS with clear distinctive learning areas. The publication of the review was followed by a number of consultations about the future of the nature of EYFS and its implementation, which led to the publication of the revised version of EYFS in March 2012 (DfE, 2012). The revised EYFS was implemented from September 2012 in all maintained schools, non-maintained schools, independent schools and all providers on the Early Years Register (DfE, 2012).

The revised EYFS continues the vision of improving quality of children's education and care and has been welcomed by practitioners and other key personnel in the early years sector. Throughout this book key aspects of the revised EYFS, such as pedagogy, play-based learning, assessment, transitions, welfare and safeguarding children, as well as the Early Learning Goals, will be discussed.

Although EYFS has been generally welcomed as an overarching framework of guidance for early years practice there is still some scepticism around its implementation and especially with its inherent emphasis on 'school readiness'. Some contributors to this book draw attention to the statutory nature of the EYFS assessment profile, the inspection of early years settings and the emphasis on school readiness, and argue this is not so much demonstrating a culture of framework and guidance as displaying characteristics of a central, prescribed and standardised curriculum. The EYFS, it is argued, thus continues to represent a totality and control of the learning and development assistance provided through education and care to support children from birth to 5 years of age and is underpinned by a raft of statutory and non-statutory guidance that forms the framework for inspection and accountability. In the light of these developments, this edition of the book aims to offer a critical examination of the revised EYFS through political, social and pedagogical lenses. Continuing with the tone of the first edition, this book does not aim to become a guide of how to implement EYFS; rather it aims to offer an in-depth understanding of key issues in early years education and care and consider how these can be applied. This edition is based, therefore, on the belief that early years practitioners need to develop a theoretical understanding and in-depth knowledge of key issues of early years pedagogy and practice in order to be able to reflect and mirror these in their practice.

The way forward in early years education and care is to raise the quality of provision, which may be achieved in a plethora of ways. Thus this book aims to bring a number of voices through the authors' chapters. It is essential that the early years practitioners 'listen' to a plethora of 'voices' in order to make informed decisions and not just simply accept practices that meet government requirements. Thus the tone of each author's 'voice' has not been changed. Similarly to the first edition, it was decided to interfere minimally with the author's personal style in order to allow pluralistic interpretations of EYFS.

Consequently, the collective focus of the book suggests that early years practitioners could make the revised EYFS work in an effective way in order to create a learning environment for young children where play is central, rather than as a preparation for school. While the current policy in which early childhood education and care is situated is both exciting and challenging, it remains imperative that practitioners rise to the challenge of critically reflecting upon how they are positioned, and how they seek to position themselves to construct their pedagogical practices.

The second edition is divided into four parts.

Part 1 discusses the policy context from which EYFS emerged and offers an overview of the national picture. It comprises three chapters:

Chapter 1   Historical developments in policy for early years education and care
Chapter 2   The implementation of the Early Years Foundation Stage
Chapter 3   The national picture

Part 2 deals with key issues on pedagogy of early years education and care. Chapter 4 discusses the essence of the concept pedagogy, Chapter 5 explores the role of play in early years, Chapters 6 and 7 focus on the key aspects of early years pedagogy observation and assessment. Chapters 8, 9 and 10 explore key issues of early years practice around the use of learning stories as an example of effective practice, effective transitions and, finally, an example of how EYFS outcomes can be met outside the classroom using local communities.

The first edition of the book included in Chapter 8, 'Meeting EYFS outcomes outside of the early years setting', discussion of the work of the Museums, Libraries and Archives (MLA) Council. This was the strategic non-departmental public body in England working with and for the museums, libraries and archives sector and making a major contribution to communities. MLA worked towards fostering learning and skills, supporting community cohesion and local identity, and playing a role in strengthening local economies. They claimed that 'by helping to create a "sense of place" they [made] a difference to the quality of people's lives and the success of communities' (http://living-places.org. uk/culture-and-sport-planning-toolkit/tools-and-guidance/museums-libraries-and-archives-council.html). Owing to a number of cuts in central funding from the coalition government, on 26 July 2010 it was announced that the MLA would be abolished and its functions were subsequently transferred on 1 October 2011 to Arts Council England and the National Archives. Consequently it was decided to leave the original chapter in this second edition (where it now appears as Chapter 10) as it is an excellent example of multi-agency work and meeting EYFS outside of the classroom. This chapter provides an example to be translated to other contexts as it demonstrates how early years practitioners can be creative with the opportunities offered from local or national bodies and create links with their community. As MLA's documentation was mapped to EYFS as introduced in 2008, we have decided not to make any changes as a result of the revised EYFS.

Part 3 focuses on key aspects of implementing EYFS that are related to the multi/inter-agency ethos. There are a number of books discussing multi-agency working, such as:

Davis, J. (2011) *Integrated Children's Services*. London Sage.

Davis, J. M. and Smith, M. (2012) *Working in Multi-professional Contexts: A Practical Guide for Professionals in Children's Services*. London: Sage.

Edmond, N. and Price, M. (2012) *Integrated Working with Children and Young People*. London: Sage.

Gasper, M. (2010) *Multi-agency Working in the Early Years*. London: Sage.

We therefore decided not to include a chapter specifically on multi-agency work in this edition as the key themes of multi-agency work are addressed in the five chapters that constitute this part of the book:

Chapter 11   Working in partnership with parents
Chapter 12   Working together to safeguard children
Chapter 13   Children's health
Chapter 14   Inclusion in the early years
Chapter 15   Leadership in the Early Years Foundation Stage

Finally, Part 4 explores the prime and specific areas of the Early Learning Goals within EYFS. All seven chapters offer a theoretical approach to these areas of development:

Chapter 16   Personal, social and emotional development
Chapter 17   Communication and language
Chapter 18   Literacy
Chapter 19   Mathematics
Chapter 20   Understanding the world
Chapter 21   Physical development
Chapter 22   Creative development

The contributors hope you will find the second edition of this book not only useful, but also significant in guiding you towards developing a critical understanding of the Early Years Foundation Stage as well as a theoretical understanding of key issues of early years pedagogy and practice.

Ioanna Palaiologou

Part 1
Policy Context

Historical Developments in Policy for Early Years Education and Care

Trevor Male and Ioanna Palaiologou

Chapter roadmap

The Early Years Foundation Stage (EYFS), described by the Department for Children, Schools and Families (DCSF) as 'a comprehensive framework which sets the standards for learning, development and care of children from birth to five' (DfE, 2012), became a requirement for early years providers and schools from September 2008. The introduction of EYFS thus ended a history of nearly 200 years of discussion and debate surrounding the philosophy, purpose and provision for early years education and care in the UK, a period when policy had been advisory rather than statutory. The discussion regarding the appropriateness of EYFS still continues (as will be seen elsewhere in this book), but government policy has at last been clarified and ratified.

There have been several key reports and Acts of Parliament through the last two centuries which have shaped the nature of provision for children up to the age of 5 years, with most of those elements still evident at the time this book is published. The 1870 (Forster) Education Act, the series of reports from the Hadow Committee between 1923 and 1933 and the Plowden Report of 1967 together constitute the main influences, but other legislation and reports have also contributed to the current situation.

(Continued)

(Continued)

This chapter aims to help you develop an understanding of:

- the three key issues that have emerged in the development of mass education in general and specifically in pre-school education:

  - education of the masses should be undertaken for the benefit of the national economy

  - education that liberated children or was child-centred was not always popular with those in privileged positions

  - educational settings should provide nurture and care for children in addition to that provided by the family and serve as a safety net for society

- the historical developments in policy in early childhood education and care

- the policy context in which early years education and care is based

- the antecedents that have led to the introduction of EYFS.

Policy context

The government of education and care in Great Britain and Northern Ireland is complicated, as four countries together form the United Kingdom (UK). As a consequence of the development of the union, separate regulations apply to Scotland and Northern Ireland than to England and Wales, with further complications arising from devolution to national assemblies during the latter stages of the twentieth century. The commonalities and differences are explored in more detail in Chapter 3, while the discussion in this chapter will not seek to highlight differences between the countries. Instead, the exploration of policy conducted here will consider the UK as a single entity, particularly in regard to developments during the nineteenth century. It was during this century that the major elements of discourse emerged.

The EYFS, as will be explored more fully in Chapter 2, establishes a framework for children up to the age of 5 years, an age at which the UK required children to participate in compulsory education following the passing of the 1870 Education Act. Provision for younger children was thus non-compulsory, although there is ample evidence of education and care outside of the home and family environment since the first infant school was established by Robert Owen in New Lanark, Scotland, in 1816. In this instance children were admitted at the age of 2 and cared for while their parents were at work in the local cotton mills. As the century progressed the label attached to provision for children younger than 5 years changed, but was generally referred to as 'nursery schools or classes', albeit with some examples of 'kindergarten' and 'babies'. The key factor here was to distinguish between the provision offered for older children for whom 'infant' (generally 5–7 years of age) and 'junior' (over the age of 7 years) schools were established as part of the drive to universal education that took place in the latter stages of the nineteenth century.

The driving forces for nursery provision were twofold: the desire for providing education appropriate to age and the desire to provide alternative care systems for young children than could be found in some social settings. These two driving forces subsequently have been features of state-maintained provision and are ones that have also affected the private sector. While at various times and in certain circumstances one or other of these driving forces has been uppermost in terms of policy determination, an examination of this history shows there to be consistent recognition of the centrality of the family (and mostly the mother) as being the most significant feature in the health, well-being and education of a young child. Early years education and care was considered supplemental to the family, therefore, and is probably best described by the joint circular on children under school age from the Ministry of Health and the Board of Education issued in 1929 to maternity and child welfare agencies and local education authorities:

> The purpose of a nursery school is to provide for the healthy physical and mental development of children over two and under 5 years of age.

The purpose was thus twofold – 'nurture' and education – and these two driving forces have seldom been separated subsequently.

Influences on 'pre-school' provision prior to the 1870 Education Act

As indicated above, the first recorded attempt to establish an early years education and care setting in Lanark was posited on the need to provide care while parents were at work. At this time, the instruction of children under 6 years of age was to consist of 'whatever might be supposed useful that they could understand, and much attention was devoted to singing, dancing, and playing' (Hadow Report, 1931: 3). Such schools were thus at first partly 'minding schools' for young children (mostly) in industrial areas, but they also sought to promote the children's physical well-being, to offer opportunities for their moral and social training and to provide some elementary instruction in basic educational functions so that the children could make more rapid progress when they entered school.

At this time mainstream education was being geared to the needs of the industrial revolution, with schools for older children reflecting the immediate need of this rapidly growing economy. 'Schools of Industry' were established, which focused on providing the poor with manual training and elementary instruction, soon to be rivalled by 'Monitorial Schools', which involved the use of monitors and standard repetitive exercises so that one teacher could teach hundreds of children at the same time in one location. In both types of school the curriculum comprised basic literacy and numeracy plus practical activities related the occupations of the age. Provision for children too young to enter these elementary schools tended, however, to mirror this curriculum rather than offer something more appropriate to their age and capability. Owen's model of infant schools was copied, notably by Samuel Wilderspoon, although these schools were later criticised as having 'a mistaken zeal for the initiation of children at too early an age to formal instruction' (Hadow Report, 1931: 3). By 1836 a child-centred approach to infant education, based on the work of Pestalozzi (the Swiss educational reformer), was being promoted through the newly initiated Home and Colonial Society. Here the curriculum specifically rejected rote-learning and was based on providing the child with a secure emotional environment and allowing their development through their senses.

Neither the utilitarian approach to schools, whereby children were trained for industry, nor the emancipatory approach envisaged within the child-centred approach was universally popular, however, with key figures in society speaking out against the education of the 'poor'. Educating children, suggested one MP in 1807, would lead, 'them to despise their lot in life, instead of making them good servants in agriculture and other laborious employments to which their rank in society had destined them and ... would [eventually] render them insolent to their superiors'.

Nevertheless, calls for more and better education were increasing in number and volume and were endorsed by school inspectors (Hadow Report, 1926: 8). From around 1830, national funds began to be made available for school building and five Acts of Parliament were passed between 1841 and 1852, designed to facilitate the purchase of land for school buildings and to provide grants for the education of the poor with the consequence that schools were being built and school attendance was rising.

Unfortunately, and as Gillard carefully documents, successive governments had allowed a divided school system to develop in line with its class structure, a situation further exacerbated by three national education commissions, whose reports – and the Acts that followed them – each related to provision for a particular social class (Gillard, 2011). Only one of these, the Newcastle Report of 1861 (and the subsequent 1870 Elementary Education Act), made provision for schools for the masses, while the other two continued to support the more privileged middle and upper classes. It was not until well into the second half of the twentieth century, following the 1944 Education Act and the move to comprehensive education in the 1960s, that universal education for the masses superseded the interests of the upper and middle classes (although even now there are many who would disagree with that statement).

The Newcastle Commissioners commented, however, that infant schools for children up to the age of 7 were 'of great utility', providing places of security as well as of education, since 'they were the only means of keeping children of poor families off the streets in town, or out of the roads and fields in the country' (Gillard, 2011). They distinguished two types of infant schools: the public infant schools, which often formed a department of the ordinary day school, and the private or 'dame' schools, which were very common in both town and country but were frequently little more than nurseries in which 'the nurse collected the children of many families into her own house instead of attending upon the children' (Hadow Report, 1933: 17). The subsequent Education Act of 1870 (the Forster Act) effectively saw the demise of dame schools, however, as infant schools became a permanent part of the public elementary school system. The age of 5 years was established by the Act as the lower limit for obligatory attendance at public elementary schools, with separate provision to be made for infants within the school buildings.

Building regulations

Up to the 1860s the main objective in separating the infants had been to ensure that the teaching of the older children should not be 'unduly disturbed' (Galton et al., 1980: 31). After 1870, building regulations required distinction between the infant school or department and the rest of the elementary school. Infants should always be on the ground floor, with a separate room for 'babies', and have their own outdoor playground (or exclusive use at certain times) which should have direct access to playground and latrines without the necessity of passing through the schoolroom. Thus it was established that provision for nursery school or classes should recognise the distinctive needs of younger children and the need for play, features that can still be seen in the twenty-first century.

The rationale underpinning these regulations appears to stem from a growing knowledge of child development whereby formal 'lessons' should be short in length and be followed by intervals of rest, play and song. In instructions issued to school inspectors it was advised that the 'subjects of lessons should be varied, beginning with familiar objects and animals, and interspersed with songs and stories appropriate to the lessons' (Revised Instructions to Inspectors, February 1891, cited in Haddow, 1933: 27). The guidance also noted that cooperation between the children was judged to be a key factor in their learning.

In a similar vein, the first London School Board appointed a committee chaired by Professor Huxley to review the system of school organisation (Hadow Report, 1931: 11). The Huxley Committee was convinced of the importance of infant schools, arguing that they protected children from evil and corrupt influences and disciplined them in proper habits, and recommended introducing Froebel's kindergarten methods into infant schools. Two leading principles were to be regarded as a sound basis for the education of early childhood:

1 The recognition of the child's spontaneous activity, and the stimulation of this activity in certain well-defined directions by the teachers.
2 The harmonious and complete development of the whole of the child's faculties. The teacher should pay especial regard to the love of movement, which can alone secure healthy physical conditions; to the observant use of the organs of sense, especially those of sight and touch; and to that eager desire of questioning which intelligent children exhibit. All these should be encouraged under due limitations, and should be developed simultaneously, so that each stage of development may be complete in itself. (Hadow Report, 1933: 27)

We can therefore see the emergence of the learning process in early childhood settings we are familiar with in the twenty-first century, whereby young children intersperse formal lessons with play and other activities that sustain and stimulate their natural interest in the world around them.

Understanding child development into the twentieth century

By the early 1900s the environmental conditions needed for the proper physical and mental development of young children were better understood than before, and the training of children below the age of 5 was discussed by both educationists and doctors. Educationists argued that the elementary schools were not providing a suitable type of education for under-5s, while doctors suggested that attendance at school was actually prejudicial to health, since it deprived young children of sleep, fresh air, exercise and freedom of movement at a critical stage in their development (Hadow Report, 1933: 30–1). The newly formed local education authorities (LEAs), formed as a consequence of the 1902 Education Act, sought guidance on the issue. Consequently the national Board of Education asked five Women Inspectors to conduct an inquiry regarding the admission of infants to public elementary schools and the curriculum suitable for under-5s. The inspectors were agreed that children between the ages of 3 and 5 did not benefit intellectually from school instruction and that the mechanical teaching which they often received dulled their imagination and weakened their power of independent observation (Board of Education, 1905). Kindergarten teachers were praised, but kindergarten 'occupations' – when taught mechanically in large classes – were condemned as being contrary to the spirit of Froebel, the originator of the kindergarten system, which placed emphasis on play, play materials and activities.

CASE STUDY

Extracts from: *Reports on Children under 5 Years of Age in Public Elementary Schools by Women Inspectors of the Board of Education (1905)*. London: HMSO.

Miss Munday's Report

In the schools visited for the purpose of this inquiry in London all except four have a separate room or in some cases two rooms for the use of the children under five. This is so far satisfactory, though in some cases the rooms are very small. In situation and aspect, however, they leave much to be desired. Many are due north, or north-east, thus practically sunless.

> The furniture of our infant babies' room still chiefly consists of a huge gallery constructed to hold nominally forty to sixty children, but often containing as many as eighty at the end of the educational year, or if classes have to be put together owing to the lack of sufficiency of staff.
>
> Arrangements for sleeping, either cots or frames, are provided in a few schools, but in some are never used owing to the danger of spreading dirt, infectious and contagious diseases through their use. Four head mistresses informed me that they used to have arrangements for sleeping in the baby rooms, but that they had to have them removed for sanitary reasons. One head mistress told me that she would like a cot in the baby room, but when I asked her if she would put her own little girl, present at school, to rest in it after certain other children had used it, she replied rather indignantly and inconsistently, 'most certainly not'.

The discourse thus continued on the purposes of schools for children under the age of 5, with some prominent campaigners promoting the benefits of formative education, while some sought closure of such provision as it damaged health, and others suggesting that the nursery school was the best place to bring up young children as:

> All observers agree that children attending school are better looked after by their parents, kept cleaner and tidier, than they would be if they stayed at home. ... One capable, motherly, experienced woman, with a suitable number of trained assistants, can superintend the tending and training of a large number of infants; while one woman with a house to clean, a family to feed and clothe, and the washing to do, cannot properly care for one. (Townshend, 1909: 4–5)

Greater clarity on purpose was thus sought throughout the proceeding period, which included the Great War of 1914–18 and the economic depression of the 1930s, which caused immense poverty.

Shaping early years provision through the twentieth century

Through the 1921 Education Act LEAs were empowered to provide or aid nursery schools for 2–5-year-olds, although these schools were to attend to the 'health, nourishment, and physical welfare' of children attending such schools, including, in one memorable phrase, the 'cleansing of verminous children'. Even though the Board of Education would make grants for such schools provided they were inspected by the LEA there was no obligation to do so and a survey undertaken by the Consultative Committee in 1908 showed that from the 327 LEAs in England and Wales 32 wholly excluded children under 5 from their elementary schools, 154 retained all children between 3 and 5, while the remaining 136 took a middle course, retaining some and excluding others (Board of Education, 1908). Thus the pattern was set for the next 100 years in that government seemed convinced of the need for nursery education, yet it was not until the twenty-first century that funding matched this desire, a situation perhaps best summed up in the Plowden Report, which noted 'Nursery education on a large scale remains an unfulfilled promise' (CACE, 1967: 116).

While there was still an active debate at this time about the nature of primary education, there was growing interest in the works of Froebel, Dewey, Montessori, Edmond Holmes, Margaret and Rachel McMillan and Susan Isaacs. Consequently the key influential factors at this time were:

- the growth of developmental psychology
- Dewey's emphasis on liberation from traditional thought
- the Kindergarten movement, based on Froebel's theory and practice from the 1890s
- the work of Dr Maria Montessori in the early 1900s, with its emphasis on structured learning, sense training and individualisation
- the work of Margaret and Rachel McMillan and their emphasis on improving hygienic conditions, overcoming children's physical defects and providing an appropriate 'environment' for young children;
- condemnation of emphasis on examinations, which 'controls education ... arrests the self-development of the child, and therefore strangles his inward growth' (Holmes, 1911: 8)
- Susan Isaacs' two books on the intellectual and social development of children in 1930 and 1933.

The Hadow Committees of 1931 and 1933, which focused on the needs of young children, can be accredited with most successfully taking account of these influences, while still recognising the need for children's health and thus defining the purpose and desired processes of early years education and care (Hadow Report, 1931 and 1933). The reports made recommendations that would shape the national education system for the rest of the century; Lady Plowden herself confirmed that 'we did not invent anything new' (Plowden, 1987: 120). In its conclusion, the Hadow Committee of 1933 urged the provision of early years education and care for children between the ages of 2 and 5 years, stating:

> it is a desirable adjunct to the national system of education; and ... in districts where the housing and general economic conditions are seriously below the average, a nursery school should if possible be provided. (Hadow Report, 1933: 187–8)

The series of reports from the Hadow Committee between 1926 and 1933, together with the Spens Report from 1938, which focused on secondary schooling, formed the basis of the discussion around educational provision undertaken by the coalition government during the Second World War of 1939–45.

From war to prosperity: 1944–1967

Planning for a post-war society began in 1940 and was based on the desire, stated by the war-time coalition leader Winston Churchill, to '[establish] a state of society where the advantages and privileges which hitherto have been enjoyed only by the few, shall be far more widely shared by the men and youth of the nation as a whole' (Taylor Report, 1977: 158). This was to lead to the provision of free universal education for all children and young people aged 5–18 through the 1944 Education Act. This was intended to be the establishment of a tripartite educational system consisting of compulsory primary and secondary education, with further, non-compulsory, education beyond the age of 15. Significantly, however, nothing was included about pre-school provision, although in 1948 the Nurseries and Child-Minder Regulation Act was published which required local health authorities to register and monitor premises where children under the age of 5 years were looked after for a substantial part of the day. Once again we can see, therefore, the continued engagement of the education and health authorities in the management of pre-school provision.

A Labour government was elected in 1945 and pursued a series of initiatives, including the establishment of the National Health Service, which together sought to create a welfare state to reduce poverty and the influence of social class. But when a Conservative government under the leadership of Churchill came to power in 1951, it immediately cut spending on education. In the ensuing 13 years of Conservative government, however, they accepted the notion that increased investment in education led to national economic growth. Consequently public expenditure on education rose from 3 per cent of GDP (gross domestic product) in 1953–4 to 4.3 per cent in 1964–5 with a concomitant huge improvement in educational provision (Gillard, 2011).

This investment in education was not directed to the under-5s, however, despite a growth in demand that was driven both by the greater number of women entering employment and increasing numbers of parents desiring some pre-school education for their children. In fact, nursery education during the 1950s faced a long period with no expansion even though this was a time of relative government prosperity. The answer to greater provision, the government signalled through Circular 8/60, lay in the private and voluntary sectors as there was to be no expansion of local authority nursery school provision (Cleaveet et al., 1982). Day nurseries provided only a very small number of places, however, and in their absence the Playgroup Movement was started. In 1961 a young London mother, Belle Tutaev, wrote to the *Guardian* newspaper about how, in the absence of a state nursery place for her young daughter, she had set up a group of her own. The idea proved attractive and groups grew in number dramatically, not only providing necessary care for children but also becoming valuable places of nurture through the direct involvement of parents. By 1973 the Secretary of State for Social Services, Sir Keith Joseph, described the family support they offered as 'an essential social service' (Pre-School Learning Alliance, 2012).

Belle Tutaev and the birth of playgroups

As a young mother and teacher living in London, Belle Tutaev started the Playgroup movement in 1961 by writing a letter to the *Guardian*. In the letter, published on 25 August 1961, she asked the Education Minister for more nursery schools and play facilities for children under 5 and encouraged mothers to start their own provision for under-5s.

What happened next?

The response was overwhelming, from people wanting to establish such groups and from some already running them. Belle borrowed a typewriter, set up a duplicator in her garage and started to put people in touch with one another. Within a year, 150 members attended the first AGM of the Pre-school Playgroups Association, which was to become a major educational charity.

By 1966 membership had increased to 1,300 and the new organisation opened its first office, with a staff of two. Within the next year membership almost doubled again, to 2,200, and the Department for Education and Science provided the charity with a grant to employ its first national adviser.

The Pre-school Learning Alliance continued to grow and now supports more than 800,000 children and their families in England through its membership network of more than 14,000 day nurseries, sessional pre-schools, and parent and toddler groups. It directly manages 493 early years settings, including 113 registered childcare and early years settings, predominantly in socially and economically disadvantaged areas.

Belle was awarded the OBE in the Queen's Birthday Honours in 2012 for services to children and families.

Plowden Report

Most commentators recognise the investigation carried out by the Central Advisory Council for Education (CACE: The Plowden Report) in 1967 as being the defining moment for child-centred primary education. Prior to this, and despite the intentions underpinning the 1944 Act, there had been little progress in changing the secondary selection system. Most primary education had been geared to the examination culture of the Eleven Plus, the entrance test that determined whether children in the state-maintained sector went to grammar, technical or secondary modern schools, with selection all too often becoming the main determinant of life chances. The newly elected Labour government sought to change this inequity and published Circular 10/65, which began with the bold declaration that it intended 'to end selection at eleven plus and to eliminate separatism in secondary education' (DES, 1965: para. 1). This was the first call for comprehensivisation of the secondary sector and it was in the spirit of the time that the Plowden Committee was established to review primary education and was described as 'a welcome push in the direction of solving the central problem of educational inequality through its concern with the mainstream of state-provided schools for the vast majority' (Halsey and Sylva, 1987).

The Plowden Report was the first thorough review of primary education since Hadow (1931) and was commissioned at a time of great change in educational policies. The essence of the findings from the enquiry document was that at 'the heart of the educational process lies the child' (CACE, 1967, 1: 7), a philosophy that

> espoused child-centred approaches in general, the concept of 'informal' education, flexibility of internal organisation and non-streaming in a general humanist approach – stressing particularly the uniqueness of each individual and the paramount need for individualisation of the teaching and learning process. (Galton et al., 1980: 40)

While not focusing specifically on the under-5s, the committee agreed that nursery provision on a substantial scale was desirable, not only on educational grounds but also for social, health and welfare considerations (CACE, 1: 296). There should be a large expansion of nursery education which, however, they considered, should be part-time, as young children should not be separated for long from their mothers.

> In the words of Susan Isaacs: the nursery school is not a substitute for a good home: its prime function ... is to supplement the normal services which the home renders to its children and to make a link between the natural and indispensable fostering of the child in the home and social life of the world at large. (1: 301)

In a list of 13 recommendations, the committee determined that, in addition to sentiments already expressed, nurseries should be: for children aged 3–5, the responsibility of education rather than health authorities and under the ultimate supervision of qualified teachers. Such provision should be funded as non-profit-making nursery classes in primary schools or separate nursery centres and to be subject to inspection in similar manner to all other educational provision (1: 343). The Plowden Committee thus set the standard for nursery provision for the next 50 years.

Austerity rules

The impetus provided by the Plowden Report led to plans for a ten-year expansion of facilities for the under-5s in the government White Paper that withdrew Circular 8/60 entitled *Education: A Framework for Expansion* (DES, 1972). Places were to be available for half of all 3-year-olds and 90 per cent of all 4-year-olds by 1982 and investment was also to be made into playgroups and the training of specialist teachers and assistants, principally through the National Nursery Examination Board (NNEB). The 1970s were a period of economic depression, however, shaped by labour disputes and the oil crisis of 1971–3, which together saw the demise of the 'post-war [welfare] consensus' (Chitty, 2004: 31). In the absence of continued prosperity, further investment leading towards universal pre-school education was suspended.

The following years featured successive Conservative and Labour governments wrestling with difficult economic conditions, which eventually led to application to the International Monetary Fund (IMF) for financial support and the 'Winter of Discontent' in 1978, both of which paved the way for the election of Margaret Thatcher as Prime Minister in 1979. The ensuing period was based on a market-driven policy whereby businesses and public services were to survive, thrive or die according to their use and popularity. The twin-track policy in education was to transfer power from local to central government and to transform schooling from a public service to a market economy. With a drive to reduce inflation proving unpopular and producing increasing social unrest over the ensuing years, Thatcher eventual lost power in 1990, by which time investment in education had slumped dramatically in terms of proportion of gross domestic product. In short, there had been no focus of attention on pre-school education with most effort, discourse, policy and legislation focusing on compulsory schooling.

Resourcing issues

Seemingly the only emergent policy issue during the period of austerity described above that was relevant to children of pre-school age was the prospect of 'school vouchers'. The prominent Conservative politician Sir Keith Joseph, also Secretary of State for Education from 1981 to 1986, was a champion of the market-place philosophy based on the belief that more provision by the independent sector would increase competition and provide more choice for parents. During the 1990s a number of government policies were introduced that encouraged the use of formal childcare, based on the notion of attracting people to work rather than remaining on social welfare. Tax relief for employer-provided workplace childcare was introduced in 1990, for example, followed by the reform of the Family Credit programme for working parents in 1994, which allowed some earners to claim deduction of childcare costs in income assessment. When vouchers for all parents of 4-year-olds to buy part-time nursery school or playgroup places were introduced in 1996, it was on the back of a long debate relating to the marketisation of education.

The incoming Labour government of 1997 brought radical changes, however, to the field of early years education and care. In a similar manner to the previous government, it was high on the Labour government's agenda to minimise poverty and increase quality in early childhood education and care by modernising the services. The new government demonstrated its commitment to raising quality in early years education and care by investing money in the sector, as well as in research. The voucher scheme was replaced in 1997 with a Nursery Education Grant (NEG) which was paid to providers rather than parents. This was followed by the launch of the National Childcare Strategy in 1998 based the notion of a mixed economy under the banner of 'partnership'. This was the first time in British history that government recognized the need for a national childcare policy (Lewis and Lee, 2002). Childcare provision became the responsibility of the Department for Education and Employment, who introduced the first Childcare Unit in 1998.

Consequently the administrative boundary between childcare and early years education has been eroded through the funding mechanisms provided by government. Funding channelled through local government, the *supply* side of funding, has often been allied to funding received by parents, the *demand* side, in a way that has led to most working parents in the UK constructing 'packages' of childcare, by using both (Lewis and Lee, 2002). For pre-school providers, and notably playgroups, it created a radical shift as many state-maintained schools were attracted by additional funds and either lowered admission ages for reception classes or opened new nursery units. By 2001 parents in the UK were spending over £3 billion on childcare, including £1.33 billion on day nurseries – 15 per cent more than in 2000. This was an increase fuelled by a steady rise in employment rates of women with pre-school children, an increasing preference for nursery provision over other forms of childcare and increasing government support to help parents meet the costs (DfES, 2001).

Into the new millennium

At the beginning of the new millennium childcare categorised as *education* could take place in: nursery schools (public or private); nursery classes in schools or reception classes in schools; playgroups and pre-schools; and occasionally with suitably qualified and registered childminders in private homes. Childcare categorised as *care* could take place in: playgroups and pre-schools (in the voluntary sector); out of school clubs on school sites, day nurseries, family centres and Early Excellence Centres (in the state sector); day nurseries and community day nurseries, out of school clubs (in the independent sector); with childminders, nannies and au pairs (in the private sector). Childcare provision designated as education must meet different standards, and is differently regulated from childcare provision that is designated as care. Thus, provision for the education of 3- and 4-year-olds can be offered by childcare centres that register as education providers (Lewis and Lee, 2002).

By this time, government policy intentions had shifted to aiming to provide a better start in life for deprived children, using education as a tool. Pre-school education was seen as a key aspect of helping children to break the 'cycle of deprivation' (Baldock et al., 2013). This did not translate into a long-term coherent policy unless the practitioners and local politicians acted upon breaking this circle, taking advantage of any opportunities that were available (Baldock et al., 2013). The government's commitment to improving early years education and care was shown by the launch of the Excellence in Schools programme (DfEE, 1997). In this White Paper the targets within early childhood education and care for the year 2002 were set out. There was an emphasis on improving quality in early years for all children from the age of 4 years, to meet the local needs of childcare and education, and to improve good practice in early years. Cohen et al. (2004), in their studies of early childhood education and care systems of national governments in three countries – England, Scotland and Sweden – and on the types of children's services found there, summarised the key features of the post-1997 period regarding children's services as: 'split departmental responsibility between welfare (DoH), responsible for daycare/childcare services, and education (DfEE), responsible for nursery and compulsory schooling' (Cohen et al., 2004: 55). This dichotomy of responsibilities between childcare services and formal schooling had an impact on funding, the structuring of provisions and, of course, upon different levels of the workforce. As a result this led to a 'fragmented body of services ... low levels of publicly funded childcare and early education ... a growing marketisation of all services ... and an increasing role for central ... controlling government' (Cohen et al., 2004: 55–6).

It was evident by this stage that the government was seeking to decentralise children's services by delegating the concomitant responsibilities and implementation to local authorities. It was clear, however, that the government intended to remain in control by setting targets with specific measurements, with the focal point for measurement to be the assessment of all children. Subsequently the decentralisation of early years education and care began with the requirement of all local authorities to set up an Early Years Development and Childcare Partnership (EYDCP) with responsibility for delivering the National Childcare Strategy (DfES, 2001). The aim of EYDCP was to operate independently of local authorities to expand childcare provision. This service was later replaced by Children's Trusts in 2004.

Towards integrated provision

The Early Excellence Centres programme had been set up in 1997 to develop models of good practice in integrating early education, care and family support services. The government's aim was to establish a network of holistic, one-stop services for children and parents that were to be run under local control and in the context of local need. The commitment to 'lift families out of poverty' and improve educational outcomes for all children was translated into an ambitious and well-funded intervention programme, Sure Start, which commenced in 1998. Sure Start was designed to be a ten-year programme for children under 4 years of age and for families living in deprived and disadvantaged conditions. Glass (1999), influenced by the Head Start intervention programme in the USA, founded Sure Start as an intervention programme to help tackle poverty and offer a good start in life to disadvantaged and deprived children.

Sure Start local programmes were transferred into Children's Centres in 2006, a somewhat precipitate move as the action was taken before the evaluation of Sure Start was complete (as will be discussed further in Chapter 2). It appeared that the government was determined to implement changes and sometimes these changes were probably too hasty. Local authorities felt they were unable to apply these in practice and early years practitioners were left with uncertainty as to how best to proceed. As part of the continued process of devolution, however, local authorities were given the responsibility to develop the Children and Young People's Plan by 2006, establish the Children's Trust and appoint Directors of Children's Services. They were also responsible for the unification of inspection systems across all children's services. A ten-year strategy for childcare (DfES, 2004) was developed which aimed to provide out-of-school childcare for all children aged between 3 and 14 years. In consequence, by the end of the first decade of the new millennium expectations and minimum standards for provision of early childhood education and care had been established and consolidated through the statutory framework of the EYFS, with appropriate advice available through the accompanying non-statutory guidance. The evolution and effectiveness of EYFS, including the revised version of 2012, will be reported and evaluated in the next chapter.

Summary

The policy context explored in this chapter has focused on the legislation and administrative arrangements framing provision over the last 200 years for pre-school children in the UK, and specifically in England and Wales. This process of policy evolution has consistently featured the dichotomy of provision for education and care, with evidence of government intent often matched by a failure to provide adequate funding. By the beginning of the new millennium, however, there were clear indications (by successive governments) that the policy intention was to break the cycle of deprivation and provide a better start in life by using early years education and care as a tool. Despite the introduction of a national childcare strategy, however, this has not yet developed into a wholly coherent policy, although the discussion emanating from recent research has informed the development and amendment to EYFS, which will be explored in greater depth in the next chapter.

Key points to remember

Table 1.1   Historical developments in policy in early years education and care

Date	Policy	Key changes
1816	First infant school established in Scotland	Children aged 2 years and above cared for while parent(s) worked in local cotton mill
1836	Home and Colonial Society promotes Pestalozzi approach to child-centred education	Early years curriculum rejects rote-learning and promotes learning through use of senses
1841–52	Five Acts of Parliament related to building of schools	Provision and standardisation of school buildings for 'education of the poor'
1861	Newcastle Report	Provision of schools for the masses with infant schools up to age of 7 years 'of great utility ... to keep children of poor families off the streets'
1870	(Forster) Education Act	Education for under-5s was non-compulsory, but where provided was to have separate building requirements
1890s	Kindergarten Movement	Based on Froebel's theory and practice
1891	Revised Instructions to Inspectors	Formal 'lessons' should be short in length and be followed by intervals of rest, play and song
1900s	Work of Dr Maria Montessori	Emphasis on structured learning, sense training and individualisation
1902	Board of Education appoints five Women Inspectors to conduct an inquiry regarding the admission of infants to public elementary schools and the curriculum suitable for under-5s.	1905 Report indicates children between the ages of 3 and 5 did not benefit intellectually from school instruction and that the mechanical teaching which they often received dulled their imagination and weakened their power of independent observation
1921	Education Act	LEAs were empowered to provide or aid nursery schools for 2–5-year-olds
1923–33	Series of reports from Hadow Committee(s)	Defining the purpose and desired processes of early years education and care
1929	Ministry of Health and the Board of Education issues Joint Circular on maternity and child welfare to local authorities	Care and education were the two driving forces
1930/33	Work of Susan Isaacs	Two influential books on the intellectual and social development of children
1944	Education Act	Expansion of education to the masses, but still not early years provision
1948	Nurseries & Child-Minder Regulation Act	Local health authorities to register and monitor premises for children under the age of 5 years
1960	Government Circular 8/60.	Greater provision for nursery school provision to be in the private and voluntary sectors

Date	Policy	Key changes
1961	Bella Tutaev letter to the *Guardian*	First playgroup established
1967	The Plowden Report	Part-time nursery provision confirmed desirable on both educational grounds and for social, health and welfare considerations
1990s	Government policies on tax relief for employers and Family Credit programme for working parents	Principle of educational vouchers established
1997	New Labour government	Introduction of Nursery Education Grant
1998	National Childcare Strategy	Notion of a mixed economy under the banner of 'partnership' (i.e. integrated services)
2001	Establishment of Early Years Development and Childcare Partnerships (EYDCP)	Decentralisation of early years education and care
2006	Children and Young People's Plan	Establishment of the Children's Trust and appointment of Directors of Children's Services
2008	Early Years Foundation Stage (EYFS) introduced	Framework of standards for learning, development and care of children from birth to 5 years of age

Points for discussion

- With reference to Table 1.1, which summarises the key historical developments, can you identify any similarities and differences in the policy changes among them?
- Central to recent government policies is the integration of services, the development of a skilful early years workforce and parental involvement. How have these changes affected your practice?
- Discuss the role of the economy in policy formation.

Reflective tasks

- Reflect on the current economic situation. With reference to the section 'Austerity Rules', can you identify any similarities and differences?
- Reflecting on the ideology of each government, can you identify whether their policies reflect their ideology?
- Drawing on the key policies and reports that have led to EYFS becoming statutory, reflect on how the political landscape has changed our views of childcare.

Further reading

Baldock, P., Fitzgerald, D. and Kay, J. (eds) (2013) *Understanding Early Years Policy*, 3rd edn. London: Sage.

Miller, L. and Hevey, D. (eds) (2012) *Policy Issues in the Early Years*. London: Sage.

Pugh, G. and Duffy, B. (eds) (2010) *Contemporary Issues in the Early Years*, 5th edn. London: Sage.

For an overview of the social constructions of childhood and education:

Blundell, D. (2012) *Education and Constructions of Childhood*. London: Continuum.

Useful websites

For more information on government policies and documents:
www.education.gov.uk/publications

To gain **free access** to selected SAGE journal articles related to key topics in this chapter visit:
www.sagepub.co.uk/Palaiologou2e

2

The Implementation of the Early Years Foundation Stage

Ioanna Palaiologou and Trevor Male

Chapter roadmap

The field of early years education and care has been transformed over the last two decades and is still witnessing a number of changes. As of September 2008, the Early Years Foundation Stage (EYFS) was implemented for all children aged 0–5 years in England. It was recognised 'that a child's experience in the early years has a major impact on their future life chances' (DCSF, 2008, Statutory Framework, p. 7). It was also recognised that 'families [of children] will be at the centre', in terms of helping them to meet their responsibilities and support them in their involvement in their children's education and care, emphasising the important role of families within early years (DCSF, 2007). In March 2012 the government published the revised version of EYFS, which was implemented in September 2012. The field of early years has welcomed these developments as the recognition of the significance of early years education and care. As was detailed in Chapter 1, at the policy level the early years field is now receiving positive attention and appreciates the government's commitment to early years education and care becoming a policy priority, after experiencing many years of either low status care for young children or a lack of coherent policies and legislation.

(Continued)

(Continued)

This chapter aims to help you to develop an understanding of:

- the development In EYFS in England
- the impact of contemporary research in the developments of the early years curriculum
- the main principles and learning goals of EYFS
- issues relating to the children's workforce, how roles and responsibilities have been changed and what challenges are now faced by practitioners.

Curriculum historical developments

As was demonstrated in Chapter 1, the field of early years education and care has not always received an appropriate degree of attention. The study by Bertman and Pascal (2002) revealed that early years education and care policies in England were dominated by the short-term priorities of government and local authorities, outcomes that were also demonstrated in the previous chapter. It has taken many years to reach this level of recognition of the importance of early years education and care.

Earlier research had emphasised the key role of the early years in children's and their families' lives, yet a successful synergy between policy developments and research findings was not then established and it was only in the 1990s that the situation began to change. The introduction of Early Childhood Studies or Early Years Education degrees as university subjects in their own right led to the qualification of graduates outside traditional teacher training. Students on these courses found themselves studying a number of child-related subjects, such as psychology, the history of childhood, sociology and pedagogy, while their career intentions remained unclear. At the same time there was a boost in academic research within the field of early years education and care. A number of academics started looking at the early years provision and services of other countries (Hennessy et al., 1992; David, 1993; Goldschmied and Jackson, 1994; Smith and Vernon, 1994; Pugh, 1996; Penn, 1997; Anning, 2009). This was in addition to looking at the international context of the United Nations Convention on the Rights of the Child (1989) (Nutbrown, 1999), and comparing early years education and care in England with those of other European countries. There was an attempt to compare systems and services (Moss and Pence, 1994; Penn, 1997, 2000; Moss, 2000, 2001) and then to reflect on the current practices in this country.

There was also a vast quantity of research on the impact of early years education and care on children's development and learning (Moyles, 1989, 2007; Athey, 1990; Alexander et al., 1992; Nutbrown, 1999; Moyles et al., 2001; Sylva et al., 2001; Devereux and Miller,

2003; Penn, 2008). All of these findings strongly argued in favour of improvement in the early years sector, raising the need for further policy and curriculum development.

As reported in Chapter 1, policy in the field of early years education and care was often designed as a way to reduce levels of poverty and to help children to have better prospects in life. The impact of the research by Mortimore et al. (1998) showed that the quality of teaching and management of schools play a central role in children's quality of learning; it was not, as then thought, the socio-economic and educational background of children that brought about changes. The government of the time took on board the findings of this research and introduced the notion of Effective Schools and School Improvement. A number of developments followed within the school context, including curriculum changes, as well as alterations regarding inspections. These changes were not implemented, however, in early childhood provision.

It was the attempt to analyse poverty and deprivation that motivated the government to turn its attention to early years education and care. It was high on the agenda of the incoming Labour government in 1997 to minimise poverty and increase quality in early years education and care by modernising the services. The commitment of the new government to raising quality was demonstrated by financial investment in the sector, including research and the evaluation of its projects. This can be seen as a positive attempt to bring synergy between research and policy developments and occurred at a time when there was an urgent need for the government not only to improve practice but also to investigate in depth, through research findings, the effectiveness of its initiatives and policies.

The impact of research

The most influential study during this period has been the Effective Provision of Pre-School Education (EPPE) Project (Sylva et al., 2001). This government-funded research programme, which lasted for nearly seven years (1997–2003), was further extended until 2008 and followed these children into secondary school, looking at what effect early years education and care had on young children's lives. The project had some interesting findings in terms of the quality of training of people in the early years sector, as it was clear from the results that adult and child interactions had a decisive impact on children's development and learning. Also, there was an emphasis on creating relationships with parents and the key role that parent involvement can play within the early years. It was encouraging that it seemed, at the time, that the government was taking into account research findings in the context of policy. Research continued to raise issues about the quality of provision and training in early years education and care.

Alongside the EPPE project, research by Anning and Edwards (2006) into what constitutes quality in pre-school education offered important evidence regarding the quality of experiences for young children before they start school. They added to the EPPE project and emphasised the effectiveness of early years provision. They found that to raise quality in early years required a partnership between parents and staff in educational settings. They also proposed an expansion of services for young children to meet the changing needs and lifestyles of modern families and employers. One of the key findings in their research was that pre-school children's experiences are determined by the commitment demonstrated by practitioners. These, in turn, determine the quality of the relationships and interactions with children and parents. The research by Anning and Edwards further showed that children attending pre-school education benefited in many ways, most importantly in their cognitive, social and emotional development, and were thus better prepared for the demands of formal schooling. They also argued, however, that their findings demonstrated that poor quality of day care could result in high levels of aggression and poorer social skills when children come to enter formal schooling. Finally, and equally importantly, they found that children from less privileged backgrounds achieve better results during formal schooling if the pre-school education they have experienced is of a high standard and is delivered by well-trained day carers. Key findings to both research projects and additional independent research strongly suggested that to improve quality in early years education and care, a careful consideration of policy, funding, structuring, staffing and delivering services for young children – and the inclusion of parents – were integral.

In the reforms that followed these findings appeared to have been embraced to a certain degree by new government policy and there was a commitment to translating this into practice. In their first term of office the incoming Labour government of 1997 demonstrated a positive attitude towards improving quality in early years provision. Policy and implementation in this first term of power, however, was characterised by haste. For example, the government, despite funding the EPPE project, did not wait for the full report of the Sure Start evaluation, and moved into creating Children's Centres, leaving Sure Start staff uncertain of what was to follow and the new roles and responsibilities that would subsequently emerge. To some extent this haste continued in their second term, after 2001. It appeared that the government was determined to implement changes. This was translated into the creation of policies, and in changes to services and structures for children and young people. A number of reforms followed with important changes in policy, and sometimes these changes were deemed to be too hasty. Local authorities felt they were unable to apply these in practice, as it left professionals with an uncertainty as to how best to proceed. This period can be characterised as a time when early years practitioners, as well as local authorities, were trying to incorporate these restructuring and reshaping issues within children's services.

Integrated services and the children's plan: building brighter futures

Central to all these changes to improve quality of life for children and families, and to promote a welfare concept, was the creation of the 'joined-up' thinking of the integration of services. In a commitment to modernise public services, the government aimed to restructure and reshape services so that they would become flexible, immediate and proactive in their responses and would meet local needs.

At a time when the government was advocating these changes and supporting the ways in which the new integrating services would improve the life of children, a young girl – Victoria Climbié – was killed by her carers. This was a shocking case as the child had been abused over a period of time; it seemed that all children's services had an awareness that this was happening, but had failed to communicate information effectively and none of the services had wanted to take the necessary responsibility to act. The Laming Inquiry that followed revealed problems regarding the structure and management of these services. The government then appeared to act decisively and the principles of joined-up thinking and working in a multi-agency, multi-professional and multi-departmental mentality were reflected by two Green Papers: Every Child Matters (DfES, 2003) and Every Child Matters: Change for Children (DfES, 2004a). These led to the Children Act of 2004.

Children's services now had to respond to five outcomes for all children from birth to 18 years of age: being healthy, being protected from harm and neglect, being enabled to enjoy and achieve, making a positive contribution to society, and contributing to economic well-being (DfES, 2004a). Central to the ECM agenda is the protection of children's well-being.

Every Child Matters was followed by *Choice for Parents, The Best Start for Children: A Ten Year Strategy for Childcare* (DfES, 2004b) and the Childcare Act of 2006 identified the need for high-quality, well-trained and educated professionals to work with the youngest child groups.

In December 2007 *The Children's Plan: Building Brighter Futures* (DCSF, 2007) was published. The document emerged in response to the urgent need of the government to demonstrate that it planned for children and families and that its plans were long term in order to produce effective outcomes. The Children's Plan strategy suggested that government 'strengthen support for all children and for all families during the formative early years' (DCSF, 2007). The government's vision was to create world-class schools and provide an excellent education for every child; creating partnerships with parents, helping young people to enhance their interests and find interesting activities outside the school, and the creation of safe areas for children to play were all incorporated.

There was a clear emphasis on the role of integrated services as facilitators for families and children's needs, and it is suggested that 'traditional institutional and professional structures' would be challenged and reshaped to accommodate these needs. One of the first targets was the creation of new leadership roles for the Children's Trust in every area: in there were new roles for schools as part of communities, and effective links between schools, the National Health Service (NHS) and other children's services, to achieve the engagement of parents in order to tackle problems with children's learning and the health and happiness of every child. Such a method of services working together was viewed as the beginning of integration, not only to meet government targets, but also to demonstrate to the world how England was meeting the United Nations Children's Rights Convention (DCSF, 2007: 159–61).

The Children's Plan was a principled approach to children's services. There are five key principles:

- parents should be supported in bringing up their children
- all children to have the potential to achieve and succeed in life if they are given the right opportunities
- children and young people need to enjoy their childhood while at the same time becoming prepared for adult life
- services need to be shared and responsive to children
- professional boundaries have to become flexible and adopt a proactive and preventative role. (DCSF, 2007)

Within this document, the new targets for 'lifting children and families from poverty' were announced:

> Poverty blights children's lives, which is why we have committed to halve child poverty by 2010 and eradicate it by 2020. (DCSF, 2007)

The new joint Department for Children, Schools and Families (DCSF) and the Department for Work and Pensions Child Poverty Unit were to coordinate work across government to break the cycle of poverty from generation to generation.

The government also went ahead with the commitment to children's safety by introducing the Staying Safe Action Plan, 2008, and the Staying Safe consultation. As part of this plan the government intended to continue the flow of money to improve services for children. The government announced that £225m – with a potential increase to £235m – would be invested in creating playgrounds nationally and making accessible play areas for children with disabilities. In July 2008 a national Play Strategy was published: 'Fair Play'. It stated that research findings had been taken on board, as well as consultation with parents, play experts and children, for transforming the quality of children's play.

Curriculum context in England

These wide changes to policy had an impact in terms of quality in provision and were reflected in the shape of alterations to the curriculum. In September 2000 the Qualifications and Curriculum Authority (QCA) introduced the Foundation Phase, which aimed to become the 'recognised stage of education relating to children from 3 years old to the end of reception year in primary school'. The Desirable Learning Outcomes introduced by the Conservative government in the 1990s were replaced with the Early Learning Goals and all providers of early years education and care followed the *Curriculum Guidance for the Foundation Phase* (QCA/DfEE, 2000). In 2002, in an attempt to include provision for children under the age of 3 years, the *Birth to 3 Matters* paper was published by the DfES (Sure Start Unit, 2002). Concerns were raised, however, as to how these connected with the Foundation Phase and the transition to the National Curriculum. Young children attending informal (*Birth to Three Matters*) and formal (Foundation Phase) education were progressing to formal schooling at the age of 6 years and were working under the National

Curriculum. This presented transitional problems, as well as problems in the continuity of assessment. The desired continuity appeared not to be implemented. Moreover, in 2003 came the publication of the *National Standards for Under 8s Day Care and Childminding*. This set out requirements for all children attending sessional childcare, and formed part of the Ofsted inspection.

As mentioned earlier, Every Child Matters was implemented as a law, and consequently all children's services and settings – including early years settings – had to demonstrate that they met the *five* outcomes of the ECM agenda. In *Birth to Three Matters*, as well as in the Foundation Phase, it was not clear how the early years workforce could meet the ECM outcomes. Moreover, the Children's Plan was setting new targets and principles for children's services.

At a time when practitioners, teachers and professionals in early years education and care were trying to adapt to these changes and translate policy into practice, the government moved by introducing the Early Years Foundation Stage (EYFS) in 2007, to be implemented in all early years settings from September 2008. The statutory document aimed to ensure a 'coherent and flexible approach to care and learning so that whatever setting parents choose, they can be confident that [their children] will receive a quality experience that supports their development and learning' (DfES, 2007: 7).

First period of implementation of EYFS (2008–2012)

EYFS was introduced by the government to bring together and replace the existing documents Every Child Matters, Curriculum Guidance for the Foundation Stage and the Full Day Care National Standards for Under 8s Day Care and Childminding. It was introduced as a cohesive, statutory framework for early years education and care, and from September 2008 the implementation of EYFS was a legal requirement for all early years settings for children from birth to 5 years of age. EYFS 2008 comprised the *Statutory Framework for the Early Years Foundation Stage* (DCSF, 2008), which explained its purposes and aims, the learning requirements and assessment processes, and *Practice Guidance for the Early Years Foundation Stage*, which described in detail how EYFS was to be implemented. There were also supportive resources for providers and early years practitioners in the form of CD-ROMs, posters and 'Principles into Practice' Cards.

The stated central aim of EYFS was to help all in the early years sector to meet the outcomes of the ECM imperative. This would be achieved through five key procedures:

1 EYFS would to set the standards for children's learning and development, and these standards would be met by all children.
2 EYFS would be committed to cultural diversity and anti-discriminatory practice.
3 EYFS would place emphasis on bridging the gap between parents and childhood settings. Commitment to such integration would be a step towards creating a framework for the 'working together' practice, and parents would constitute its focus.

4   There would not be a distinction between 'care' and 'education' and the early years sector would work towards improving quality and consistency with a universal set of standards (DCSF, 2008). As discussed in Chapter 1, childcare and education had been separated under the respective responsibilities of two different departments, i.e. the Department of Health and the Department for Education (in its various guises). Although in early 1998 departmental responsibility for childcare was transferred to Education, the distinction between childcare and education had been evident across the early years sector. Investment in the early years workforce training and qualifications had failed to bridge the gap between childcare and early years education. EYFS set an ambitious and positive standard, however, as it now eliminated at policy level the division between childcare and education. Consequently it was recognised that an important aspect of providing quality in the early years is that care and education are synonymous. In the early years these two aspects of provision should happen together and be indivisible (DCSF, 2008). In practice, however, it was likely to take a while to change the attitudes towards these two concepts, as variations in training, standards and wages would be obstacles to be overcome.

5   Important procedures within EYFS were to be observation and assessment of children. Through ongoing observation and assessment the early years workforce would be asked to plan children's learning and development, in order that individual needs and interests were met. Based on observations and assessments, the early years workforce would provide a diverse range of play-based activities designed to support children's development.

The principles of EYFS

Similarly to the Children's Plan (published in 2007), EYFS represents a principled approach to young children's care and education. Four key principles, which still remain after revision in 2012, illustrate the commitment to an emphasis on integration and parental involvement:

- *A Unique Child* recognises that every child is a competent learner from birth who can be resilient, capable, confident and self-assured. The commitments are focused around development, inclusion, safety, health and well-being.
- *Positive Relationships* describes how children learn to be strong and independent from a base of loving and secure relationships with parents and/or a key person. The commitments are focused around respect, partnership with parents, supporting learning and the role of the key person.
- *Enabling Environments* explains that the environment plays a key role in supporting and extending children's development and learning. The commitments are focused around observation, assessment and planning, support for every child, the learning environment and the wider context, i.e. transitions, continuity and multi-agency working.

- *Learning and Development* recognises that children develop and learn in different ways and at different rates, and that all areas of learning and development are equally important and are inter-connected.
  (DCSF, 2008: *Statutory Framework*, p. 9)

These principles reflect the commitment of the Labour government to viewing early years education and care as an important part of the community; the EYFS recognises the individuality of each child and the diversity of learning in the early years, and the importance of partnerships with parents and other services for better provision.

First came the developmentally driven Early Learning Goals: personal, social and emotional development; communication, language and literacy; problem solving, reasoning and numeracy; knowledge and understanding of the world; physical development; and creative development. All of these goals need to be covered across the early years sector and become part of the overall educational programme, this being the second element for an effective implementation of EYFS. To support the early years workforce in meeting these goals, EYFS provided a number of guidelines concerning how an educational programme needs to be created, in the *Practice Guidance for the Early Years Foundation Stage* (DCSF, 2008). This document offers detailed examples of what constitutes effective practice, with suggested activities according to the developmental age and abilities of each child.

The role of assessment in EYFS

Central within EYFS are the assessment processes. Considerable emphasis is placed upon the ongoing assessment of children, and this is viewed as an integral part of the learning and development process. Providers must ensure that practitioners are observing children and responding appropriately to help them to make progress from birth towards the early learning goals. It is expected that all adults who interact with the child should contribute to that process, thus information provided from parents would be taken into account. An essential feature in EYFS in terms of parental involvement is an ongoing dialogue, based on observations and the assessment of children. The ongoing dialogue takes the form of a formal, formative assessment, used as evidence to identify learning priorities for children, and to plan relevant and motivating learning experiences for each child. It is also required that for each child an EYFS profile is completed. Formulating a profile is a way of summing up each child's development and learning achievements at the end of EYFS. Using 13 assessment scales derived from the Early Learning Goals an e-portfolio has to be completed for each child.

The important role played by observation and assessment in the early years in improving practice constantly and in monitoring children's progress cannot be underestimated. However, a concern exists that the EYFS assessment scales will overtake practice, and the early years workforce may feel the need to tick boxes rather than to create the innovative practice so important for the early years.

Inspection in EYFS

EYFS providers will be inspected by Ofsted. All settings are now required to register with Ofsted, in respect of all provisions for children from birth to 5 years of age. August 2008 saw the publication of *Early Years Leading to Excellence*, a two-part report on how providers should promote the ECM outcomes for children. Part One reviews childcare and early years provision at the end of the three-year cycle of inspections. Part Two describes how providers organise, lead and manage their settings in partnerships, and sets the standards of how providers should develop and improve the quality of their work with children (www.ofsted.gov.uk/ofsted-home/Leading-to-excellence/).

Although EYFS is a detailed and descriptive practical guide to play-based activities for young children, the government did not intend it to be seen as part of the National Curriculum (DCSF, 2007). This has created a contradiction between policy and practice; perhaps in name EYFS is not a curriculum, yet in practice it is a detailed description of what should be done in each early years setting. Moreover, there is also an emphasis on meeting standards and goals. Ofsted, the same body that inspects schools, is responsible for its implementation.

The role of local authorities

Crucial to the implementation of EYFS are the role and responsibilities of the local authorities. As was demonstrated in Chapter 1, there has been a clear attempt by central government to delegate the responsibilities of the implementation of early years provision to local authorities. Central government maintains overall control, however, with the Ofsted inspection reports serving as a measurement tool for effective practice. Local authorities have responsibilities for assessment, training, staff support and collecting the documentation from all early years providers; they are also required to play a key role in meeting the needs of EYFS, as well as the individual needs of each child, in a proactive and protective way, so that cases such as that of Victoria Climbié can be prevented in the future. Although all these policies were introduced to protect children, more recent events, such as the case of Baby P (in Haringey) and the Doncaster Children case have shown that there is still an inability to protect children at risk. Among the main duties of the local authorities is to visit the settings regularly in order to make sure that each provider is completing an effective early years self-evaluation form to ensure that local needs are met (Ofsted, 2008).

To summarise, from a period where the early years sector was left with no coherent policy, practices or legislation, and there were boundaries between childcare and education, with the implementation of EYFS the situation has now moved to focusing on children's development, with clear age ranges, stages and goals 'in an attempt to make clear that there are no clear boundaries, and to value the unique progress made by every child' (Devereux and Miller, 2003: 2). These standards reflect an urgent attempt to raise quality in the early years sector. Consequently, there has been increasing public debate about the meaning of quality in early years education and care. The sceptics have been concerned that raising standards can be achieved in a plethora of ways other than by investing all of our efforts into meeting outcomes and outputs targets in the bureaucratic way that underpinned EYFS, and the limitation on fixed standards around development and learning has been challenged as allowing no space for autonomous, creative and constructive early years practice.

A revised EYFS

The new coalition that took office in 2010 has set out a programme for government until the next elections, scheduled for 2015. The Secretary of State for Education, Michael Gove, has led the proposed changes, with the main message being to 'drive up education standards'. The economic crisis that has affected Europe, however, has not left England without problems. One of the main aims of the coalition has been to reduce the ongoing deficit of the UK government. As a result a plan to cut expenses has led to the closure of a number of public bodies, among them the General Teaching Council for England, the Qualifications and Curriculum Development Agency and the Children's Workforce Development Council.

Additionally, the government commissioned a number of reviews to be undertaken of the policies related to early years education and care. This resulted in the publication of Frank Field's (2010) review *The Foundation Years Parenting: Poor Children Becoming Poor Adults*, examining poverty in England and ways to support poor families to get out of a cycle of social deprivation, Graham Allen's (2011) *Early Intervention: The Next Steps*, Michael Marmot's (2011) *Fair Society, Healthy Lives* and *The Munro Review of Child Protection Report* (DfE, 2011). All these reports aimed to bring changes in the early years sector and to investigate ways in which we can address issues of child poverty and safeguarding of children

One of the most important reviews in the field of early years education and care was the Tickell Review, which examined the implementation of EYFS. In Dame Clare Tickell's review *The Early Years: Foundations for Life, Health and Learning*, published in May 2011, the key points raised were that there is a need to continue providing good quality care and support for early learning as a key to later success of children and a way of helping them to overcome disadvantage. Tickell (2011) suggested a clear, accessible, flexible and less bureaucratic EYFS; that the government increase the emphasis within EYFS on the role of parents and carers in their children's learning; that the learning and development areas be reduced and there be an added emphasis on welfare and safeguarding of children.

Just before the release of the Tickell Review Ofsted published, in February 2011, a report on *The Impact of Early Years Foundation Stage*. This survey aimed to evaluate EYFS in the embryonic stages and investigate whether in the first stages of its implementation outcomes for children have been improved. The key findings demonstrated that there was an improvement in the children's outcomes on the key learning and development areas, but what is interesting in the report is that Ofsted emphasised that in settings where early years practitioners had achieved qualifications above the minimum requirement, the outcomes were better.

The revised EYFS (March 2012 to the present)

In March 2012 a slimmed-down version of EYFS was published by Children's Minister Sarah Teather. In introducing the revised EYFS she said:

> What really matters is making sure a child is able to start school ready to learn, able to make friends and play, ready to ask for what they need and say what they think. These are critical foundations for really getting the best out of school. It is vital we have the right framework to support high quality early years education. Our changes, including the progress check at age two, will support early years professionals and families to give children the best possible start in life.
>
> People working in the early years, teachers, parents, and other professionals, support our proposals, which keep the best of the existing framework but slim it down. This is the first part of our reforms to the early years. Where we find examples of regulation and paperwork that are not necessary to safeguard children, drive up quality or promote child development, we will remove them. We will continue to help practitioners to focus on children's healthy development.

The key changes of the revised EYFS are focusing on:

- reducing paperwork and bureaucracy
- strengthening partnerships between parents and professionals
- changes in the learning and development areas, with emphasis on the health and safeguarding of children alongside their readiness for future learning
- a simplified assessment and a progress check at age 2.
  (www.education.gov.uk/schools/teachingandlearning/curriculum/a0068102/early-years-foundation-stage-eyfs)

The revised curriculum reduces the number of Early Learning Goals from 69 to 17, gives more focus to the main areas of learning that are most essential for children's healthy development and simplifies assessment at age 5 (DfE, 2012). With a progress check at age 2, it also provides earlier intervention for children who need extra help.

In the revised EYFS it is stated that it seeks to provide:

- quality and consistency in all early years settings, so that every child makes good progress and no child gets left behind;
- a secure foundation through learning and development opportunities which are planned around the needs and interests of each individual child and are assessed and reviewed regularly;
- partnership working between practitioners and with parents and/or carers;
- equality of opportunity and anti-discriminatory practice, ensuring that every child is included and supported.
  (www.education.gov.uk/schools/teachingandlearning/curriculum/a0068102/early-years-foundation-stage-eyfs)

In the light of this, although the principles of EYFS remained the same, the phrasing was slightly changed:

- every child is a unique child, who is constantly learning and can be resilient, capable, confident and self-assured;
- children learn to be strong and independent through positive relationships;
- children learn and develop well in enabling environments, in which their experiences respond to their individual needs and there is a strong partnership between practitioners and parents and/or carers; and
- children develop and learn in different ways and at different rates. (DfE, 2012: 2)

The framework covers the education and care of all children in early years provision, including children with special educational needs and disabilities.

The key areas of learning and development are now divided into prime and specific areas:

- Prime areas: communication and language; physical development, personal, social and emotional development.
- Specific areas: literacy, mathematics, understanding the world, expressive arts and design.

There is much emphasis in the revised version of EYFS on the welfare of children, such as child protection, safeguarding and welfare of children, suitable people and qualifications.

Overall, the revised version was received with conflicted feelings. On the one hand, the emphasis on play-based learning, inclusion and safeguarding children was welcomed, but on the other hand the emphasis throughout for readiness for formal education and learning contradicts an ethos among early childhood education that 'all children, at all stages, are ready to learn' (Whitebread and Bingham, 2011: 1). It appears that EYFS, in its approach to the child,

> places value on children in terms of their meeting future goals and standards and their learning outcomes. It assumes that children need to progress to the next stage of development, from lesser child to better child. The terms 'development', 'developmental goals' or 'learning goals' invoke a sense that children are not yet developed (whole/holistic) and thus need developing ('improving'), or that there is an existing, pre-determined place at which a child may arrive (presumably school). (Palaiologou, 2012: 137)

On the positive side, in June 2012 Professor Cathy Nutbrown published a review of early years practitioners' qualifications. The Labour government introduced EYFS with the ambition that by 2015 all early years settings would be graduate-led, with a requirement for all staff to have a minimum level three qualification. In *Foundation for Quality: Review of Early Education and Childcare Qualifications* Nutbrown suggests that the biggest factor in determining quality and delivering an effective curriculum in early years education and care lies with the qualifications of the early years workforce. In the report it is recommended that the skills, knowledge and understanding of those who work with young children needs to be improved if the sector wants to develop a positive early education and care experience for children to have the best start in life.

CASE STUDY

An early years setting manager's perspective on EYFS

Nicky is manager of a private day nursery within a Children's Centre set in a council estate in a city in North England. Although the area is considered one of social deprivation, the parent body has many parents who work, rather than live, locally. She considers Ofsted as central to her priorities and is pleased to have received a grade of 'Good' in a recent inspection. However, her main aim is to have 'Outstanding' in the next Ofsted inspection.

EYFS, to her and her team, is 'everything ... and central to what we do. Looking back [before the implementation of EYFS] to when I first started as a nursery nurse the aim wasn't the child, it was the parent. As long as the parent was happy it was fine and you didn't really spend much time with the child, it was all "let them do that". It was very much the parents are paying, so they are the main priority. Since the introduction of the EYFS practitioners' perspectives have changed and we are focusing more on the quality of planning activities for children. Now it does seem more child-centred and if the child is happy then the parent is going to be happy because it has a knock-on effect.'

Consequently the curriculum within this setting is now child-centred, based on the principle of play, and makes full use of indoor and outdoor facilities because 'if they are interested in it they are going to learn from it. If they're not interested they're not going to learn'. Staff within the setting are encouraged and trained to use children's individual and collective interests to establish appropriate learning experiences and assess learning outcomes mainly through observations. In thinking about the revised EYFS, however, she indicates concern about the administrative demands: 'in the setting it was supposed to be less paperwork, less formal writing things out and seems more, if anything. It seems more getting everything down, noting everything and writing, and having the evidence to prove it so you can send it to school. This is fine as you need to have evidence to prove that you're doing it, but I just think it's all paperwork.'

Summary

Chapter 1 and Chapter 2 seek to demonstrate the historical policy developments in early years education and care that led to the introduction of EYFS in September 2008. Alongside the changes in policy, research in the field of early years education and care was trying to establish an ethos whereby all children, families and early years practitioners were valued. As has been shown, early years education and care was not given due weight until the twenty-first century. The introduction of EYFS and the standards that were set within it reflect the government's urgent attempt to raise quality in the early years sector. Consequently, there has been growing public discussion about the meaning of quality in early years education and care. An examination of EYFS has revealed that, on the positive side, there is much-needed regulation of early years provision, it seems that there is a positive move towards increasing early years workforce qualifications and a significant amount of money had been invested towards that direction. Due to economic difficulties, however, this investment has now been withdrawn. Additionally, the revised EYFS seems to place emphasis on children's readiness for school. On the one hand, a major change brought by EYFS is that the welfare of children is seen to be 'nested' within the wider social context of the family and community. On the other hand, however, it seems that children are perceived as needing socialisation in preparation for their future role as adults, given that emphasis is placed on what the child will become rather than the child's current state of being.

Key points to remember

- The field of early years has experienced radical changes since the Labour government came to power in 1997. The most important policies are Every Child Matters, the Children's Plan and the Early Years Foundation Stage.

- Key to all government policies is the integration of services, the development of a skilful early years workforce, parental involvement and excellence in provision.

- All early years settings were required to implement the Early Years Foundation Stage from September 2008.

- The early years workforce has changed and new roles and responsibilities – as well as new standards – were introduced by the Children's Workforce Development Council (CWDC).

- There are also further changes in early years workforce after the publication of the 'Foundation for Quality: Review of Early Education and Children Qualifications'.

- In March 2012 the coalition government published the revised EYFS, which keeps the original principles of the first version and places emphasis on children's learning, development, well-being and safeguarding.

Points for discussion

- What, in your view, should a curriculum for young children be? Should it be appropriate to their stage of learning or should it be outcomes-driven?

- What are your views on the learning and development requirements in EYFS?

- In your view, what should be the purpose of early years education and care?

> ⭐ **Reflective tasks**
>
> - Reflect on the changes that the revised EYFS has brought. What do you think the implications of these changes will be in your practice, regarding its effective implementation, how local needs are met, or how the principles of the EYFS are achieved?
>
> - Reflect on what socio-constructions of childhood emerge from EYFS. How are children viewed? How does EYFS consider the children's participation?
>
> - Reflect on government policy and perspectives on 'school readiness' and what this term means. How and why should a child should be 'ready' for school? Is this the role of an early years curriculum?

Further reading 📖

Clark, M. and Waller, T. (2007) *Early Childhood Education and Care: Policy and Practice*. London: Sage.

Dahlberg, G. and Moss, P. (2012) *Contesting Early Childhood and Opening for Change*. London: Routledge.

Parker-Rees, R., Leeson, C., Savage, J. and Willan, J. (eds) (2010) *Early Childhood Studies*. London: Sage.

For a historical review on early childhood:

Cohen, B., Moss, P., Petrie, P. and Wallace, J. (2004) *A New Deal for Children? Re-forming Education and Care in England, Scotland and Sweden*. Bristol: The Policy Press.

Useful websites 🖱

The relevant documentation on EYFS and other information can be accessed at:

www.education.gov.uk/schools/teachingandlearning/curriculum/a0068102/early-years-foundation-stage-eyfs

www.foundationyears.org.uk

For the Nutbrown Review, *Foundations for Quality*: The Independent *Review of Early Education and Childcare Qualifications, see:*

www.education.gov.uk/nutbrownreview

To gain free access to selected SAGE journal articles related to key topics in this chapter visit: www.sagepub.co.uk/Palaiologou2e

3

The National Picture

Ioanna Palaiologou, Glenda Walsh, Sarah MacQuarrie, Jane Waters and Elizabeth Dunphy

Chapter roadmap

As was mentioned in Chapter 1, the education and care of young children in Great Britain and Northern Ireland is complex, as four countries together form the United Kingdom. As a result of the Union, separate regulations apply to Northern Ireland, Scotland and Wales. This book aims to discuss the Early Years Foundation Stage as it is applied in England. After reviewing the historical developments in early years policy in England and the implementation of EYFS, however, it is important to consider the bigger picture as a way to investigate what happens not only in the constituent parts of the UK, but also within the entire British Isles (which also include the Republic of Ireland). Thus this chapter examines early years education and care in the British Isles and aims to help you:

- develop an understanding of the implementation of different curricula
- develop an understanding of the role of policy in curricula implementation
- make comparisons via your own reflections.

Early years in Northern Ireland

Glenda Walsh

Historical perspective

Northern Ireland, the smallest of the four devolved nations within the United Kingdom, with a population of approximately 1.5 million, is a country slowly emerging from a troubled past, when from the late 1960s to the mid-1990s it was fraught with political and sectarian violence. Peace was finally restored as a result of the paramilitary ceasefires in 1994 and subsequently the Belfast Agreement of 1998, which provided Northern Ireland with its own devolved government and enabled it to start on a journey towards a peaceful society and a better future for its children and young people (Walsh and McMillan, 2010). Presently such power-sharing negotiations are stable, and despite the current climate of significant financial constraint, the Northern Ireland government appears committed to delivering the aims of the Ten Year Strategy (2006–2016), where each child and young person should be:

> Healthy, enjoying, learning and achieving, living in safety and with stability, experiencing economic and environmental well-being, contributing positively to the community and society and living in a society which respects their rights. (OFMDFM, 2006: 7)

Pre-school developments

3–4-year-olds

In 2012, while pre-school education still remains a non-compulsory phase of education, the government in Northern Ireland has committed to making available at least one year of pre-school education to every family that wants it, reiterating the requirements of the Pre-School Education Expansion Programme – PSEEP (DENI and DHSSPS, 1998) – designed as a partnership between the statutory and voluntary/private sectors. The strategy incorporates a number of features such as the adherence to a common curriculum in all settings in line with the Curricular Guidance for Pre-School Education (CCEA, DENI, DHSSPS, 2006)[1] and a quality assurance mechanism whereby all funded settings are inspected by the Education and Training Inspectorate.

---

[1] The Curricular Guidance for Pre-School Provision embraces a child-centred and play-based pedagogy, premised on six discrete themes, namely the arts; language development; early mathematical experiences; personal social and emotional development; physical development; and exploration of both the indoor and outdoor worlds. While the guidance recognises that children learn and develop in different ways, it emphasises the need for a programme where children get the opportunity to progress their learning and reach their full potential.

A review of the PSEEP, conducted by the Northern Ireland Audit Office (NIAO) in 2009, revealed that provision had risen to 97 per cent from a baseline of 45 per cent prior to the start of the PSEEP (a figure that has remained static in 2011/2012 (DENI, 2012) and the number of reception places in primary schools (considered to be a less suitable form of pre-school provision) had decreased from 2,547 in 1997 to 606 (NIAO, 2009). The Chief Inspector's Report for 2008–10 (ETI, 2010a) indicated that the overall quality of pre-school education has improved in just over 80 per cent of the pre-school settings inspected; the quality of provision was evaluated as good or better. It goes on to say that while the highest percentage of good to outstanding practice remained within the statutory nursery schools, an improvement is noted in the number of nursery units and voluntary/private settings falling into the higher categories.

Despite the success of the PSEEP in substantially increasing the availability and enhancing the quality of pre-school provision, a Review of the Pre-school Admissions Arrangements (DENI, 2012) has highlighted a number of actions for the Department in an effort to ensure greater equity across the sector, e.g. a withdrawal of the July/August birthdays criterion in the 1999 Regulations to prevent older children from having prec-edence to a free pre-school place; the definition of Free School Meal Entitlement (FSME) to be used as the main proxy measure of social disadvantage and some groups of children such as newcomer children, children of travellers and children with special educational needs to be given greater consideration in allocation of places.

0–3-year-olds

The government in Northern Ireland has also committed some funding to a Sure Start programme for 2-year-old children from socio-deprived backgrounds. This initiative began in March 2006 as part of the Children and Young People's Package and was devel-oped in February 2007 when Early Years: The Organisation for Young Children won DENI's tender to develop a suitable programme for 2-year-olds and accompanying train-ing for Sure Start practitioners to deliver the programme, commencing in 2008. According to the Education and Training Inspectorate (ETI) (2010b), there are currently 32 Sure Start programmes across Northern Ireland, covering a wide geographic area which has, in the main, a good urban and rural mix.

The Programme for 2 Year Olds (ETI, 2010b) is based on the overarching premise that all young children have potential and recognises the young child as an initiator, explorer and self-learner in a play-based environment that is physically safe, cognitively challeng-ing and emotionally nurturing. Active and respectful partnerships with parents are a core element of the programme.

Although evidence from an ETI evaluation (ETI, 2010b) showed that satisfactory to good progress has been made in the early development of the Programme for 2 Year Olds, there is still much work to be done in terms of strategic planning, better training, higher levels of qualifications, appropriate accommodation and resources, effective sup-port and access to specialist support when required and more developed collaborative working practices.

School developments

While the past five years have seen some developments in the field of pre-school education and, in the main, a commitment by the government at least to maintain the status quo, the early years of primary schooling have undergone significant change, at least in rhetoric, with the compulsory implementation of the Foundation Stage Curriculum (CCEA, 2007) for all 4–6-year-old children in Years 1 and 2 of primary school from September 2007 and September 2008, respectively. Northern Ireland has the youngest statutory school starting age of all the devolved nations, where young children, as a result of the Education Reform Order (Great Britain, 1989), are obliged to commence formal schooling in the September after their fourth birthday and until recently followed a statutory curriculum that was subject-based and assessment-led (Harland et al., 1999; Sheehy et al., 2000; Walsh et al, 2006). Concerns about the inappropriateness of this formal curriculum for young children led to a pilot study being conducted that espoused a child-centred and play-based approach known as the Early Years Enriched Curriculum. The findings from the Early Years Enriched Curriculum project were principally positive where the learning experience on offer in the play-based classrooms was much superior in terms of children's learning dispositions, social development and emotional well-being (Walsh et al., 2006). To ensure effective challenge and progression for young children, however, a more balanced and integrated pedagogy known as playful structure has been recommended where adults initiate and maintain a degree of 'playfulness' in the child's learning experience, while at the same time maintaining adequate structure to ensure that effective learning takes place (Walsh et al., 2010; Walsh et al., 2011).

These findings were pivotal in the subsequent and recent introduction of the Foundation Stage (FS) curriculum (CCEA, 2007), where children in their first two years of schooling should 'experience much of their learning through well-planned and challenging play' (CCEA, 2007: 9) and their learning should be supported by early years practitioners who are 'committed, sensitive, enthusiastic and interact effectively to challenge children's thinking and learning' (CCEA, 2007: 16).

This shift towards play as pedagogy in the early years has not been easy for teachers, where according to Hunter (2009), despite early years practitioners' enthusiasm for the principles of the FS curriculum, upskilling is required to ensure that the complexities involved in implementing high-quality challenging play are fully resolved.

The Early Years Strategy

In an effort to provide a more cohesive approach to early years education and care from birth to 6 years of age, the Department of Education (DE) launched a draft Early Years Strategy (0–6) for consultation in June 2010 (DENI, 2010). The vision that lies at the heart of the strategy is 'to enable every child to develop their full potential, by giving each one the best possible start' (DENI, 2010: 17). The key objectives are:

- To improve the quality of early years education and care thereby promoting for children better learning outcomes by the end of the Foundation Stage especially in language and number; and also in the child's personal and social development, physical and cognitive development, emotional well-being and readiness to learn;
- To recognise and respect the role of parents of young children and to raise the level of engagement by DE (and its partners) with families and communities;
- To improve equity of access to quality early years education and care; and
- To encourage greater collaboration among key partners to promote greater integration in service delivery. (DENI, 2010: 18)

The strategy is still under review and awaiting publication, but by the end of 2012 is expected to clearly signpost the way for an exciting and challenging future for early years care and education for children in Northern Ireland from 0 to 6 years of age.

Early years in Scotland

Sarah MacQuarrie

Historical perspective

Since devolution in 1999 education in Scotland is a devolved matter governed solely by the Scottish Parliament, meaning that the UK Parliament has no direct jurisdiction regarding Scottish education. The introduction of the 'Standards in Scotland's Schools Act' set out the guidelines for the free and compulsory schooling of all Scottish children between 5 and 16 years of age (Scottish Executive, 2000). Younger children were at that time covered in an earlier separate publication, *Education of Children under Five in Scotland* (SOED, 1994).

The philosophy of comprehensive education embedded in Scottish policy has long been recognised as a distinctive feature of education provision in Scotland (Humes and Bryce, 2003). Scottish schools are holistic in their approach to pupils' learning and development, exemplified by the revision and updating of inclusion policies (HM Inspectorate of Education, 2002, 2005a) and mirrored in the role and approach undertaken by Her Majesty's Inspectorate of Education in Scotland (HM Inspectorate of Education, 2009). Decision making in Scotland is less centralised as schools and stakeholders play a major role in their own organisation and management. The comprehensive philosophy is most recently evident in the creation of a single body, 'Education Scotland', which brought together Learning and Teaching Scotland (which provided advice, practical materials and resources to enhance the quality of learning and teaching) and Her Majesty's Inspectorate of Education (Education Scotland,n.d.a).

A further distinctive feature relates to the provision of Gaelic Medium Education (GME), which spans pre-school, primary and secondary education where the Scottish curriculum is delivered through the medium of Gaelic. According to a recent publication, an encouraging picture is evident, as during 2010–11 there were more than 2000 children in birth to 5 years of age provision within 60 primary schools in 14 education authorities. Considering that GME was only formally introduced in 1986 these figures can be taken as an indicator of the demand for GME (HM Inspectorate of Education, 2005b, 2011). A commitment to the provision of Gaelic within Scotland is noted by the publication of the first Gaelic Language (Scotland) Act in 2005, followed in 2007 by the National Plan for Gaelic[2] and the subsequent Gaelic plans of a wide range of local and national organisations.

A key strength of Scottish education is collaboration between practitioners that continues to be supported by the development of inclusion-orientated strategies. The New Community Schools Initiative (later Integrated Community Schools), began in 1998 as a component of the Scottish social inclusion strategy (HM Inspectors of Schools, 1999). Schools were obliged to introduce the child-centred strategy by 2007. It recommended that schools adopt an integrated approach, utilising a range of resources, including family support and health as priorities to pupils' education, managing an increased use of inter-agency working and resources available in their communities. The strategy continues as a central tenet of the Scottish Curriculum.

Curriculum and policy

Curriculum guidelines in Scotland support teaching with examples of good practice, in contrast to the prescriptive nature of the National Curriculum established by Parliament in England (Jenkins, 2000; Macnab, 2003). In 1991 the Scottish Office Education Department (later SEED) developed a series of curriculum and assessment national guidelines covering the curriculum for children aged 5–14, from the first year of primary school to the second year of secondary school. In Scotland these requirements and relevant support materials constituted a broadly agreed agenda for over a decade.

A curriculum review group was established in 2003 based on the findings of a national consultation on education where the consensus was that a more engaging

---

[2] A second National Plan is imminent; a draft version was published for public consultation between November 2011 and January 2012.

curriculum was needed (Education Scotland, n.d.b). An extended period of development ensued (2005–9), involving a wide variety of practitioners and research processes. Revised curriculum guidelines were published in 2009 ready for implementation. Scotland now has a single curriculum for ages 3–18 known as 'A Curriculum for Excellence'. Further developments (largely pertaining to qualifications) are ongoing. The purpose of the curriculum is represented within the 'Four Capacities': through the curriculum each child should be a successful learner, a confident individual, an effective contributor and a responsible citizen. Attributes and capabilities that underpin each of the four capacities are clearly signalled and provide a straightforward resource for educators, allowing them to make provisions for learners' progression. 'Experiences and outcomes' are used within the Curriculum for Excellence to describe the nature of learning (experiences) and how they ought to be recognised (outcomes). 'Experiences and outcomes' are referred to in four of the five levels of learning,[3] of particular relevance is the 'early' level that encompasses both pre-school and Primary 1. Educational settings are provided with guidance on how to ensure that all children in pre-school and primary school settings experience stimulating, effective learning in ways that are appropriate to their needs (Scottish Executive, 2007; Scottish Government, 2008a). Scottish schools and local authorities are encouraged to design a customised curriculum utilising input from stakeholders, teachers and parents as well as drawing on National Guidelines and support materials. Their aim is to meet the schools' and local communities' expectations and to ensure each child acquires the four capacities of the Curriculum for Excellence.

The Curriculum for Excellence spans the ages 3–18; children younger than 3 years of age are covered separately within the publication *Pre-birth to Three: Positive Outcomes for Scotland's Children and Families* (Learning and Teaching Scotland, 2010). This national guidance is in line with the principles and philosophy that underpin the Curriculum for Excellence and is supported by the Early Years Framework (Scottish Government, 2008b). The framework presents a ten-year strategy that aims to enable those caring for children younger than 3 to develop a child's social and interactive skills, so that a child is supported and able to achieve its full potential. The framework spans the interests of children from pre-birth to the age of 8 and proposes ten elements of transformational change, each supported by examples of good practice. These examples (taken from actual practice within Scotland) reflect key elements of the framework, including a focus on children's play, experiential and holistic approaches to learning and supporting children's progression and transition. The strength of the framework is its commitment to the promoting and upholding of children's rights as defined by the UN Convention on the Rights of the Child – UNCRC (United Nations, 1989). A series of vision statements refer regularly to UNCRC articles in order to illustrate the aims of the framework. Of particular relevance is the emphasis given to valuing the child's voice: 'Children and families are valued and respected at all levels in our

---

[3] The fifth level refers to qualifications (Scottish Executive, 2010).

society and have the right to have their voices sought, heard and acted upon by all those who support them and who provide services to help them' (Article 12 of UNCRC). This is coupled with the provision of a range of learning opportunities indoors and out: 'Children are entitled to take part in physical activities and to play, including outdoors, and have an opportunity to experience and judge and manage risk' (Article 31) (Scottish Government, 2008b: 11).

A final point to complete this section considering early years education and care in Scotland refers to the workforce within educational settings. A review of teacher education (focused on primary and secondary education) provided over 50 recommendations (Donaldson, 2010) and the positive response given by the Scottish Government is indicative of the commitment to the enhancement of initial teacher education as well as the long-term opportunities for continued professional development (Scottish Government, 2011). Recognition of the need to support teachers, educators and carers responsible for children forms a key part of the Curriculum for Excellence and early years framework if education is to meet the needs of learners. Such developments mean it is an exciting time for early years education and care in Scotland.

Early years in Wales

Jane Waters

Historical perspective

Wales is a small country with a population of just over three million in June 2010 (WG, 2012a). Of these, 18.2 per cent were children aged 0–15 years (548,000), meaning that for the first time there were more people aged over 65 (18.6 per cent) than children in Wales. In 2010, 24.8 per cent of the Welsh population reported being able to speak Welsh (WG, 2012b), although in the 2001 census 16 per cent of the population declared an ability to understand, speak, read and write Welsh (WG, 2012c). The development of Wales as a bilingual nation is a central WG policy focus (e.g. WalesOnline, 2012) and the study of Welsh is compulsory until the age of 16 years of age in all maintained educational settings.

The Welsh Government (WG)[4] came into being after the first Welsh general election on 6 May 1999, following a referendum on 19 September 1997 in which there was a narrow majority in favour of the devolution of Wales from UK central government. This signified the devolution of responsibility for education within Wales from the UK government in Westminster to the Welsh Government in Cardiff. Now administered by the Department

---

[4] Previously the National Assembly for Wales (NAfW) then the Welsh Assembly Government (WAG).

of Education and Skills (DES),[5] education policy for the first decade of devolution was informed by the vision document *The Learning Country* (NAfW, 2001) which set out the intention to 'build stronger foundations for learning in primary schools with a radical improvement for early years provision' (p. 12). The subsequent consultation document, *The Learning Country: Foundation Phase 3–7 Years* (NAfW, 2003), set out the specifics of the proposals for a Foundation Phase curriculum framework for children aged 3–7 years. This included developing a curriculum that linked and strengthened the principles and practice in ACCAC's document for children aged 3–5 years – *Desirable Outcomes for Children's Learning Before Compulsory School Age* (2000a) – with the programmes of study and focus statements in the National Curriculum for Wales Key Stage 1 (ACCAC, 2000b, providing for children aged 5–7 years), to 'create a rich curriculum under seven Areas of Learning for children in the Foundation Phase' (WAG, 2008: 3). This radical over-haul of early years education and care in Wales signalled a shift away from UK central government education policy. It was also predicated upon a concern, supported by research literature, about the 'detrimental' (NAfW, 2001a: 8) effect of an overly formal approach to early years education and care for children below the age of 6 years of age.

The Foundation Phase Framework for Children's Learning for 3–7 Year Olds in Wales

Following an evaluation of the two-year pilot period (Siraj-Blatchford et al., 2005), the Foundation Phase Framework (WAG, 2008a) was introduced for school children aged 3–7 years (Nursery, Reception, Year 1 and Year 2 classes) in an annual roll-out over the period from 2008 to 2011. The statutory curriculum document advocates the adoption of a play-based approach to early years education and care within the context of a balance of adult-directed and child-directed activity. Educational settings are required to provide children with access to 'indoor and outdoor environments that are fun, exciting, stimulating and safe' and to 'promote children's development and natural curiosity to explore and learn through first-hand experiences' (WAG, 2008: 4). In addition, children are to interact with adults with whom they should share episodes of sustained and shared thinking and adults are to 'build on what they [children] already know and can do, their interests and what they understand' (WAG 2008a: 6). The Foundation Phase Framework therefore requires that teachers, in part at least, engage flexibly and contingently with child-initiated activity in order to support learning indoors and outdoors. Baseline development is recorded on entry to the phase and end-of-phase achievement is assessed along a continuum of out-comes (see WAG, 2011a, 2011b). The central role of the practitioner within the Foundation Phase is to be a 'facilitator of learning' (WAG, 2008b: 12) and the curriculum is planned to

---

[5] Previously ACCAC (Awdurdod Cymwysterau Cwricwlwm ac Asesu Cymru: the Welsh Assembly Government department for curriculum and qualifications) and Department for Children, Education and Lifelong Learning and Skills (DCELLS).

meet 'the needs of the individual children and facilitate progress' (WAG, 2008a: 12). This requirement is situated within the broader context of the Welsh Government's overall vision for children and young people which is based around seven core aims developed from the United Nations Convention on the Rights of the Child (see WAG, 2006, 2008: 3). The Foundation Phase sits within this overarching and emancipatory vision for children with an emphasis on the personal development and well-being of the child.

> Children learn through first-hand experiential activities with the serious business of 'play' providing the vehicle. Through their play, children practice and consolidate their learning, play with ideas, experiment, take risks, solve problems, and make decisions individually, in small and in large groups. First-hand experiences allow children to develop an understanding of themselves and the world in which they live. The development of children's self-image and feelings of self-worth and self-esteem are at the core of this phase. (WAG, 2008a: 6)

Seven areas of learning are identified, the first of which is situated 'at the heart of the Foundation Phase' (WAG, 2008a: 16):

- Personal and social development, well-being and cultural diversity
- Language, literacy and communication skills
- Mathematical development
- Welsh-language development
- Knowledge and understanding of the world
- Physical development
- Creative development.

There is a specific directive for 'a greater emphasis on using the outdoor environment as a resource for children's learning' (WAG, 2008a: 4), although in the pilot stages research indicated that some schools may have missed the opportunities for children's learning that the policy initiative offered (Maynard and Waters, 2007).

Future developments

There is an implicit emphasis in the Foundation Phase documentation on 'proactive and intentional pedagogy' (Wood, 2007b: 127) and the Welsh policy has been recognised as providing the potential for practitioners to 'develop the integrated approaches that are advocated in contemporary play research' (Wood, 2007a: 313). The disappointing PISA scores for Wales (OECD, 2010; WG, 2010), however, heralded an intense focus on pupils' development in literacy and numeracy throughout the education system. One outcome of this is the imposition of national reading tests for 7-year-olds from summer 2012, with numeracy tests planned for 2013. Such a policy move may threaten the play-based, child-initiated aspects of the Foundation Phase initiative though the future direction of early years policy in Wales may actually depend upon the findings of a large-scale evaluation of the Foundation Phase due to report in 2014 (WISERD, 2012).

Early years education and care in the Republic of Ireland

Elizabeth Dunphy

Historical perspective

Ireland, one of the smallest countries in Europe (approximately 300 miles from north to south and 170 miles east to west), has a population of about four and a half million. The Republic of Ireland comprises 26 of the 32 Irish counties; the remaining six counties comprise Northern Ireland, which forms part of the United Kingdom. From the mid-1990s until about 2008 Ireland enjoyed a decade of unprecedented economic boom. This was also a period of rapid social, cultural and demographic changes. While Ireland is working its way out of the current recession, it can be anticipated that any developments in early childhood education and care services will be affected by economic constraints. Nevertheless, there have been a number of important developments in this sector in Ireland over the past five years.

Ministerial responsibility for ECEC in Ireland

The Department of Children and Youth Affairs (DCYA) was established in June 2011. The provision of high-quality early childhood education and care (ECEC) and the strengthening of support for all children to enable their full engagement in learning were identified at the outset as key issues for that department. The Early Years Education Policy Unit is co-located with the DCYA and the Department of Education and Science (DES).

Recent developments in ECEC provision

Statutory school starting age in Ireland is 6 years, though in practice traditionally about half of all 4-year-old children and almost all 5-year-old children have attended primary school. Within the primary school system the DES provides targeted provision for some (1,600) 3-year-old children identified as at risk because of economic and social disadvantage. The DES also provides various targeted support for young children with special educational needs. The Delivering Equality of Opportunity in Schools (DEIS) programme extends additional support for schools in areas of economic and social disadvantage, though there have been some recent cutbacks in this support. Pre-school education and care is to a large extent provided by community and voluntary agents and agencies, supported by grant aid from DCYA.

The free pre-school year

Prior to 2010, pre-school education was largely financed by parents, sometimes with support from community and voluntary organisations. The DES did give additional resources to enhance the educational dimension of existing childcare provision in areas of economic and social disadvantage. In January 2010 the government introduced an important structural change to the Irish Education System. A 'free pre-school' year is now available to all eligible children in the year before they attend primary school. According to the DCYA website the objective of the ECCE programme, which is open to both community and commercial service providers, is to benefit children in the key developmental period prior to starting school. In July 2011, speaking in the Dáil (the Irish Parliament), the Minister stated that 'in September 2010, the first full year of the programme, 63,000 children participated, amounting to 94% of all eligible children. Some 4,300 preschool services, or 95% of all services, are participating in the programme, thus ensuring that it is available to all children in all areas.'

Síolta: The National Quality Framework for Early Childhood Education

Síolta is the Irish word for 'seed'. *Síolta: The National Quality Framework for Early Childhood Education* (Centre for Early Childhood Development and Education, 2006) presents 12 principles related to quality. These include the value of early childhood; children's rights and needs; the importance of relations; the centrality of play; and the role of adults. The principles are articulated in a set of 16 standards and all services availing of the grant for the provision of the free pre-school year must demonstrate their engagement with the standards.

Aistear: The Early Childhood Curriculum Framework

Aistear is the Irish word for 'journey'. *Aistear: The Early Childhood Curriculum Framework* (National Council for Curriculum and Assessment, 2009) is a curriculum framework for children from birth to 6 years of age. It supports educators, including parents, in planning learning experiences for young children. It describes the learning that takes place in early years education and care in terms of the development of dispositions, knowledge, skills, values and attitudes. Importantly, it provides guidelines in four key areas: play, assessment, interactions and partnerships with parents. It also offers theoretical support in the form of research papers on each on these areas. The framework presents learning and development using four themes: well-being; identity and belonging; communicating; and exploring and thinking. The framework is based on 12 principles grouped in relation to: children and their lives in early childhood; children's connections with others; and how children learn and develop. There is no requirement for any specific content, programme or philosophy with the framework, rather the intention is that practitioners will judge how best to work with the themes to enable children to reach the goals of the curriculum. Educators can access resources, including examples of Aistear in practice, on the NCCA website. At present there is a programme of support for teachers using Aistear, working with 4–6-year-old children in primary schools. This is delivered by specially trained Aistear tutors through the network of Teachers' Centres. Unfortunately no such structure currently exists for pre-schools, so educators working in those settings cannot currently avail themselves of such assistance.

Developing the workforce

The Early Years Education Policy Unit, which is co-located with the DCYA and the Department of Education and Science (DES), was responsible for the development of what was termed 'a childcare training strategy' (www.dcya.gov.ie). This was deemed important in order to meet the target of providing 17,000 childcare training places by 2010. A workforce development plan for the early years education and care sector in Ireland (DES, 2010) identifies a range of flexible education and training opportunities for the development of the current workforce.

To summarise, the last five years have seen some important developments in relation to ECEC in Ireland. It is disappointing to note, however, that the old divide between education and care appears still to persist in the minds of policymakers at least. This is explicit in the fact that all details related to the pre-school year are currently located under the heading of childcare on the DCYA website, indicating perhaps some confusion amongst policymakers regarding the nature and purpose of the initiative.

The duration of the pre-school day (three hours) is a concern. Also of concern is the relatively late start for children attending pre-school, with no provision at all for children under 3 years 3 months. Perhaps one of the greatest concerns is that only about 15 per cent of early years practitioners working in these services have degree-level qualifications in ECE or equivalent. Most have much lower levels of qualifications, though the workforce development plan indicates that some progress is possible in this area.

The continued apparent lack of support at policy level for the long tradition of early years education and care in the primary education system is evidenced by poor structural support for ECE in primary schools. There is also a sense that public policy, particularly in relation to key areas of decision making such as early years practitioners competences, is not well aligned with the evidence base. A recent decision of DCYA to restrict recognition, on quality grounds, for higher capitation grants for pre-schools to only those holding an ECEC degree needs to be audited against the research about what constitutes quality in pre-school education. See, for example, the arguments on what early years practitioners in the United States need to know and do as presented by Pianta et al. (2009). See also the points made by Early and colleagues (2007), also in the United States, regarding findings from their review of the effects of teachers' education on classroom quality and young children's academic skills.

Significant levels of investment are needed in the years ahead if Ireland is to develop the high-quality early years education and care that all its youngest citizens deserve, but perhaps as a first step what is needed is a vision for an integrated, high-quality system of early years education and care. The recent announcement by DCYA of Ireland's first National Early Years Strategy which will address all aspects of children's experiences in their early years, including health, family support, care and education, is to be greatly welcomed as an important step in this direction.

CASE STUDY

Moving from England to Scotland: the voice of a mother

'When my husband changed jobs and we decided to move from the Midlands to Scotland I had concerns about our children's education. I have a daughter who was 4 years old at the time and she would have attended the Reception class in England, but when we moved to Scotland she spent another year in nursery and she only moved to what they call in Scotland P1 (equivalent to English Key Stage 1).

When we first moved to Scotland she used to spend two and half hours daily in the nursery. Now she attends P1 and I have found that it has been extremely helpful. What they do in her school is to mix children from different classes and they do a lot of shared activities and lessons. I found that very helpful as it has helped her social skills. I was concerned when we moved that my daughter would have been held back in not starting school as it would have happened if we had stayed in England, but I am so pleased about this now. She had an extra year of playing with no 'structured' learning [*laughter*] although her teacher said to me that they do have structured learning although it does not seem that they learn letters, reading and writing as in the Reception class in England. When she moved to P1 she did not have any problems to do the Jolly Phonics, read and write and I feel lucky that she had the extra year of play in nursery.

My son was 2 years old when we moved. He was assessed in Scotland with Complex and Severe Disabilities and required additional support needs. I am not sure what support I would have had in England, but I am grateful to the Scottish system. He attends a nursery for only children with Complex and Severe Disabilities where he is in a class with only four children, one teacher and two learning support assistants and has one-to-one support. In this school there are also occupational health professionals, psychotherapists and any other services that we might need. As a parent of a child with severe disabilities I was worried, but his nursery had offered us a lot of support, communicates with us regularly and I feel it has helped my son and us as parents. I feel as a parent that I am listened to and valued. Now my son's speech has improved, he has better interactions with others and I am very pleased with his progress. I am not sure I would also have this support in England, but I am pleased he goes to this nursery as I do not think he could have coped in a mainstream school. I have a friend in England that also has a child with disability and when we talk about what is offered to us it seems it is a struggle for her when I feel I am very lucky to have these services for my children.'

Summary

Examining the early years education and care provision in Northern Ireland, Scotland, Wales and the Republic of Ireland helps to put into perspective the developments in the sector. As can be seen in all four countries, there are attempts to develop a coherent policy and curriculum framework in an effort to improve quality in early years education and care. Quality as portrayed in the government policies, however, is 'fixed' and 'limited' to standardised outcomes and outputs. A common theme is that policies attempt to improve quality by placing emphasis on assessed standards. These standards appear to be the 'official approach' to quality, characterised by an objectivity reality that can be defined measured, evaluated, assured and inspected (Moss and Pence, 1994; Dahlberg et al., 2007). A key common element in early years curricula approaches is that these standards of quality are related to children's development. There is now a shift of concern on what is learned in terms of children's interests, as these will be translated into the child's assessment and children's performativity, outcomes or outputs in order that we can ensure that quality in early years education and care is achieved. On a positive note, all the countries examined here reflect the idea that there is now discourse taking place as to what constitutes good, effective practice in early years education and care.

Key points to remember

- Attitudes towards improving early years education and care can be identified in all countries of the British Isles. A common element is that these changes have resulted from political changes, and in the current era of economic instability we see a cut in funding across the early years sector.

- Key themes to all the curricular approaches are an emphasis on play and play-based activities, bridging the gap between parents and early years settings,

(Continued)

(Continued)

with observations as a tool to inform planning, inform assessment and to open communication with families and other services. Integration is the concept that all curricula seek to embody.

- Integration hides its problems, however, as there are complex issues to be overcome, such as the professional and financial boundaries, variations in training, the creation of a common work culture, and a lack of clarity in roles and responsibilities. Early years practitioners are asked to overcome these problems in order to meet the individual children's needs and to promote children's development and learning.

- The emerging role of the early years workforce across all curricula appears to be more complex than ever. Meeting standards or competences is not the only challenge they face. The role of early years practitioners in curricular implementation is becoming multi-dimensional, requiring a good understanding of the theoretical aspects of children's development, as well as its pedagogical aspects. It is also necessary to develop a good understanding of the curriculum.

- It is argued that it is equally important for early years practitioners to voice their own opinions about curricular implementation. These voices need to be informed not only by a knowledgeable, theoretically grounded workforce, but also by effective practice. Early years practitioners are required to develop a range of skills in order to be able to promote a pedagogy based on flexible planning, driven by children's interests, and informed by on-going observation of children and evaluation of practice. Dialogue requiring listening to children's interests and needs will become the starting point, in order to communicate with parents, staff and other necessary, related services.

- Another important aspect is recognition that in early years education and care effective practice cannot be seen in isolation from the community and the family environment. Considerable emphasis is placed on the role of parents in children's activities, assessment and observation.

Points for discussion

- Compare the early years education and care among these countries and try to identify the similarities and differences in their curriculum practices.

- What are your personal thoughts on curriculum developments in early years in the region in which you are studying/working?

- What do you think about the role of play in curriculum implementation in early years education and care?

Reflective tasks

- Reflect on the current emphasis in England to improve the skills, knowledge and understanding of those who work with young children. Do you identify similarities in Northern Ireland, Scotland, Wales and the Republic of Ireland?

- Reflect on the areas of learning and development of the EYFS in England and compare it with the curricula approaches in Northern Ireland, Scotland, Wales and the Republic of Ireland. Is there a dichotomy between officially, centralised, pre-described concepts of what quality is, on the one hand, and of what quality is at a local level, on the other, based on discussions between early years practitioners, parents or guardians and the child?

- It appears that the EYFS has brought a shift from the non-participant child to the child as a social actor, an individual who enacts agency, as well as the EYFS being a demand for the inclusion of the voices of children. Do you identify this trend in other curricula approaches that have been examined in the chapter?

Further reading

Nutbrown, C. (2011) *Key Concepts in Early Childhood Education and Care,* 2nd edn. London: Sage.

Papatheodorou, T. and Moyles, J. (eds) (2012) *Cross-Cultural Perspectives on Early Childhood.* London: Sage.

Reed, M. and Canning N. (eds) (2011) *Implementing Quality Improvement and Change in the Early Years.* London: Sage.

Useful websites

Northern Ireland early years provision:
www.deni.gov.uk
Scotland early years provision:
www.educationscot land.gov.uk
Wales early years provision:
www.wales.gov/uk
Republic of Ireland early years provision:
www.siolta.ie
www.ncca.ie

To gain **free access** to selected SAGE journal articles related to key topics in this chapter visit: www.sagepub.co.uk/Palaiologou2e

Part 2
Pedagogy

4

Pedagogy of Early Years

Theodora Papatheodorou and Donna Potts

Chapter roadmap

In this chapter the concept of pedagogy will be explored, by referring to different definitions, and consideration will be given to how different theories and policy requirements have informed and shaped pedagogical practice. A case study will illustrate the conscious and unconscious complex processes of reflection that take place during practice to reach a pedagogical approach that responds to children's individual needs and potential. It is concluded that early years practitioners need to espouse a pedagogy that is purposeful and intentional, appropriate and relevant to children's interest and potential, and is transformative and empowering.

This chapter aims to:

- develop a theoretical understanding of the concept of pedagogy
- understand key ideas that impact on pedagogy
- explore the impact of policy on pedagogy
- link current thinking and theory of pedagogy with practice in early years education and care.

Defining pedagogy

In the English context, pedagogy is often understood as being synonymous with teaching, defined as the act and performance of curricula delivery. Alexander (2000: 540), however, argues that 'Pedagogy encompasses the performance of teaching together with the theories, beliefs, policies and controversies that inform and shape it.' Within early years education and care Moyles and colleagues offer a similar definition, by stating that 'Pedagogy encompasses both what practitioners actually DO and THINK and the principles, theories, perceptions and challenges that inform and shape it' (Moyles et al., 2002: 5; original emphasis).

These definitions acknowledge *teaching* as being part of pedagogy, but it is the *thinking* behind teaching that is at the heart of pedagogy. Drawing upon Woodhead's (2006) work four major perspectives regarding child development and learning that have influenced pedagogical thinking and practice have been identified: developmental perspectives; socio-cultural perspectives; policy perspectives; and the rights perspective.

Developmental perspectives

The image of the developmental child has emerged mainly from biological and child development theories which understood development as a maturational process, taking place in different stages and ages. Notably, Piaget viewed children as progressing through a series of development stages with recognisable cognitive attributes. Through his studies Piaget demonstrated that young children are curious and intrinsically motivated to explore their environment and, through their doings, to work out the principles underpinning phenomena. Given suitable resources and an appropriate level of challenge, children are able to construct their own ideas and knowledge. Piaget's ideas have been particularly influential in creating learning environments that provide appropriate stimuli for investigation, experimentation and hands-on activities (Piaget, 1952).

In contrast to the Piagetian view, behaviourists saw learning as being the direct outcome of responses to environmental stimuli through a process of (positive or negative) reinforcement. According to this stimulus–response model, the child makes an association between a stimulus and the consequences which follow the triggered behaviour; a rewarding consequence is likely to increase the occurrence of the exhibited behaviour, while a punishing consequence would minimize it. The belief in the power and impact of behaviourism is better expressed in John Watson's (1930: 104) quotation below:

> Give me a dozen healthy infants, well-formed, and my own specified world to bring them up in and I'll guarantee to take any one at random and train him to become any type of specialist I might select – doctor, lawyer, artist, merchant-chief and, yes, even beggar-man and thief, regardless of his talents, penchants, tendencies, abilities, vocations, and race of his ancestors.

The unidirectional influence of the environment on individuals has been criticised from within behaviourism. Social learning behaviourists argued that environmental, biological, cognitive and other personal factors influence each other bidirectionally. Children are not passive in the learning process; instead their learning takes place within the social context and through observation, imitation, association and generalisation processes (Bandura, 1977).

Today the importance of the environment in which children live, and especially the early experiences they have there, cannot be disputed. Research in the field of neuroscience demonstrates that early stimulation and experiences shape the architecture of the brain and determine future development (SCDC, 2010). Lack of appropriate nutrition, health and care undermine children's survival, while adverse life experiences (such as care deprivation, chronic fear and anxiety, harsh punishment and mistreatment, and inadequate stimulation) affect negatively children's psycho-social and cognitive development. In contrast, early stimulation and positive experiences increase resilience and ameliorate negative effects (Shonkoff and Phillips, 2000; Fox and Shonkoff, 2011). The evidence from psychoanalytical theory, and mainly the work of Freud, as well as attachment theory (which will be discussed in Chapters 9 and 16), has been further supported by neuroscience which recognises the significance of early experiences with regard to children's attachment, emotional security and mental health in later life.

Child development theories raise awareness of early childhood as a discrete period of life that is characterised by certain needs and requires certain conditions for children to flourish. In many ways, these theories echo and further support the ideas of early pioneers, who had long before argued for age-appropriate resources to enable children's exploration through hands-on activities (e.g. Froebel's occupations and Montessori's learning resources) and the impact of environmental stimuli (e.g. John Locke, who claimed that children are *tabulae rasae*, blank slates, where environmental stimuli leave their imprint).

Some well-known ideas in the field of early childhood derive from developmental theories. For example:

- development takes place at certain stages and ages, determined by maturational processes
- children are viewed as being curious and intrinsically motivated and having enquiring minds
- children need access to resources that enable exploration, active experimentation, hands-on activities
- children thrive in stimulating, supportive and positively reinforcing environments
- early childhood is valued as a discrete period in life, where children's *being* itself is valued.

These ideas made significant contribution to pedagogical practice by:

- contesting traditional adult/teacher-centred pedagogical practice which focused on knowledge transmission
- introducing notions of child-centred, play-based, experiential and hands-on learning

- influencing the way learning environments are organised to offer rewarding and positive experiences
- contributing to the introduction of developmentally appropriate practice.

Socio-cultural perspectives

Socio-cultural theories have furthered our understanding of child development and learning as a social process. Vygotsky (2002) argued that development and learning take place within the social and cultural milieu: children are neither the lone scientists, isolated from their social environment (assumed in Piaget's theory), nor the product of direct stimuli of the environment and the process of positive or negative reinforcement (argued by behaviourists). Children are product of their socio-cultural milieu, its beliefs and values, and its customs and practices.

Socio-cultural theorists emphasise interdependence and relationships with others: how children learn to negotiate, problem solve and make meaning out of their experiences through the facilitation of knowledgeable others, be it parents, teachers or other children. Malaguzzi (1993: 10), the founder of Reggio Emilia pre-schools, saw children as being 'rich in potential, strong, powerful, competent and most of all, connected to adults and other children' and Bruner and Haste (1987) referred to them as *meaning makers*. Children reach their potential through adult *scaffolding* (Bruner, 2006), *guided participation* (Rogoff et al., 1993) and *sustained shared thinking* with knowledgeable others (Siraj-Blatchford et al., 2002), as they work within their *zone of proximal development* (Vygotsky, 1978).

Bronfenbrenner's (1979) ecological theory attempted to provide a broader framework for understanding children's development and learning. He highlighted the influence of dynamic interactions of many factors within and between different systems in which the children find themselves. It is not any single factor that is more important than others; instead it is the cumulative effect of the complex interactions of many factors, taking place over time, that influence and determine child development and learning.

Many contemporary theorists have also challenged the image of the *developmental* child in the light of the widespread diversity encountered in today's societies (e.g. of ethnicity, religion, social class, disability, linguistic) and the unspoken power of dominant ideologies and institutions. They have argued that notions such as stages and ages (the developmental child) assume distinct universal features that are applicable to all children, at all times and in all societies, and ignore social and cultural influences (Cannella, 2005; Dalhberg et al., 2007; Moss, 2008). Developmentally Appropriate Practice, in particular, was contested and became Developmentally and Culturally (or Contextually) Appropriate Practice (DCAP) to highlight that *what we learn* and *how we learn* are informed and influenced by the cultures of particular communities (NAEYC, 1996; Hyun, 1998).

These theories have furthered understanding of:

- the influences of the social and cultural milieu on child development and learning
- the significant role of cultural values and practices
- the role of knowledgeable adults/others in children's learning through processes of scaffolding, guided participation and sustained shared thinking
- the influence and power of dominant ideologies embraced by particular groups and institutions, and/or policies
- the importance of children's a sense of *belonging* in the context and place, where they find themselves.

These ideas have extended pedagogical thinking and practice to include:

- greater emphasis on social and contextual factors
- collaborative learning and group work, where children work together, support each other, encounter challenges, problem solve, cooperate, negotiate and arrive at shared meaning and action
- scaffolding, guided participation and sustained shared thinking to facilitate children's learning
- greater emphasis on the processes of learning (i.e. how and why we learn)
- acknowledgement of diversity and creation of cultures of inclusion and celebration of diversity
- forging relationships and a sense of belonging
- development of assessment and evaluation strategies that reflect diversity and capture contextual influences (e.g. introduction of documentation and learning journeys/stories; self-evaluation of early years settings).

Policy perspectives

Child-development theories have raised awareness of the importance of children's experiences and their being. These ideas became a double-edged sword, however. The notion of the *developmental* child, in particular, became the yardstick to measure children's development and progress according to universal standards, considered to be applicable to all children, ignoring contextual factors. Terms such as areas of development, desirable learning outcomes, stepping stones, benchmarking, standards, quality indicators and school readiness became the reference for defining indicators to measure/profile children's progress (Cannella, 2005; Dahlberg et al., 2007; Moss, 2008).

Developmental standards have been extensively used in the evaluation of early childhood programmes to demonstrate their immediate and lifelong impact (e.g. longitudinal studies such as EPPE in the UK – see Sylva et al., 2004; High/Scope and Head Start in the USA – see Schweinhart, 1994 and US Department of Health and Human Services,

2010). The accrued impact of early childhood on children, their families and societies, and the economic returns on investment for early years education and care became the cornerstone of international and national policies. As was demonstrated in Chapters 1 and 2, during the last two decades we saw a plethora of international policies that legally bind governments to make appropriate provisions for children to enjoy a certain level of living standards (for instance, the Millennium Developmental Goals – UNDP, 2000; Education for All – UNESCO, 1990, 2000; United Nations Convention on the Rights of the Child – UNCRC, 1989, 2006).

In the English context, since the mid-1990s there has been the introduction of curricula frameworks for the Foundation Stage and the Sure Start programme, plus the increase of external inspections and programme evolution (e.g. OFSTED inspections; National Evaluation of Sure Start). Both versions of the EYFS constitute a developmentally informed document. EYFS identifies language and communication, physical development, and personal, emotional and social development as its prime areas (DfE, 2012). Its specific areas focus on academic and cognitive development (e.g. literacy and mathematics) and offer opportunities for understanding communities and the world, and creativity and imagination.

Although it is located within a rights perspective (discussed in the next section), the EYFS highlights the importance of 'school readiness' and the need for acquiring a 'broad range of knowledge and skills that provide the right foundation for good future progress through school and life' (DfE, 2012: 2). It also requires that 'Each child's level of development must be assessed against the early learning goal' (DfE, 2012: 11), indicating that assessment remains child-centred and is the main factor for determining programme evaluation.

Policy has influenced thinking in:

- seeing the child *in the making, in becoming* tomorrow's productive citizen, by emphasising development and the acquisition of certain valued skills (e.g. the EYFS prime areas, literacy and numeracy)
- assessing and evaluating children's progress against identified learning outcomes
- viewing early years education and care as interventionist, especially for children and families experiencing disadvantage
- evaluating provision to measure its accrued impact.

The impact of policy on pedagogical practice is evident in:

- curricula frameworks that are learning outcomes-based/oriented (i.e. the EYFS)
- child assessment and profiling (e.g. Foundation Stage Profile)
- using developmental checklists for assessing children
- increased external evaluation of early childhood provision (e.g. Ofsted inspection)
- emphasising school readiness.

The rights perspective

The United Nations Convention on the Rights of the Child (UNCRC) has made an important contribution to understanding of young children as citizens of today rather than as individuals in the making (UNCRC, 1989). The UNCRC starts from the principle of acting in the best interest of the child and articulates specific rights that children are entitled to enjoy, including: adequate living standards (article 25), education (article 28), health (article 24), rest and recreational activities and enjoyment (article 31), social security (article 26), participation in decision making for matters that affect them (article 12).

The UNCRC discussed these rights in relation to young children (from birth to 8 years of age) in its fortieth session in 2005. It reiterated that these rights apply to young children too, and affirmed that children are 'rights holders' from birth. More importantly, it mandated that the quality of services for children should be evaluated to the extent that children's rights are observed (UNCRC, 2006). The UNCRC places the responsibility for ensuring that children enjoy their rights with parents and/or carers, but governments are held accountable in supporting parents for doing so.

The UNCRC has changed the landscape for early years education and care in many and different ways. At policy level, governments are expected to align aims, targets and priorities that meet children's rights. In the English context, for example, children's rights are reflected in the five outcomes of Every Child Matters, that is: being healthy; staying safe; enjoying and achieving; making a positive contribution; and achieving economic well-being (DfES, 2004). The revised EYFS is also positioned within a rights perspective by stating that children deserve 'the best possible start in life' and need support 'to fulfil their potential'. It acknowledges that: 'A secure, safe and happy childhood is important in its own right' (DfE, 2012: 2), ensured by adhering to four overarching principles: the unique child, positive relationships, enabling environments and that children develop and learn in different ways and at different rates (DfE, 2012: 3).

In terms of pedagogical practices, awareness of children's rights, and especially their participation in decisions that affect them, has raised awareness about listening to young children's voices. A growing body of research has enriched our understanding of the many ways that children can express their views and the attentive listening of adults that is required. This is reflected in Malaguzzi's (1993) idea of children's *hundred languages* and Rinaldi's (2001) concept of a *pedagogy of listening*. Children are natural communicators from birth, but adults need to invest in relational inter-subjectivity in order to capture and give meaning to children's many communicative signs (Trevarthen, 2011).

The UNCRC has:

- enriched our understanding of the child as a unique and potent individual, who is able to express her/his views and influence the care and education received
- recognised the importance of maturational factors (e.g. right to health and nutrition) and acknowledged the significance of the social and cultural context (e.g. right to education, leisure and enjoyment) for child development and learning

- explicitly articulated the obligations of families, communities and the state towards children.

As a result:

- policies are clearly aligned with the UNCRC
- pedagogical practices are gradually shifting to more participatory methods, enabling children's voices to be heard and listened to.

Pedagogy: a framework for practice

It is evident that the field of early years education and care draws upon a range of ideas from different theoretical perspectives and policy requirements to understand child development and learning and to inform pedagogical practice. In the next section this will be illustrated with reference to a case study.

CASE STUDY

Ben's story (through the voice of the teacher)

Ben spent two years in nursery and a full year in a Reception class. At the age of 6 years, he was admitted in Year 1. Due to his low Foundation Stage Profile score he was kept in a Year 1 class where he would continue the EYFS for the first two terms. There was concern for his low achievements in reading and writing and he was highlighted as a potential candidate for the Reading Recovery programme ... an expensive and intensive intervention programme for which Ben was assessed and qualified ...

Ben had very weak pencil control and was unable to form letters to write his name correctly. He was still undecided about his hand preference for writing. When he did attempt to put pen to paper he kept swapping hands, questioning the strength of his fine motor control. During initial assessments, Ben said, 'I can't read, I can't write.' 'I don't want to do it.' He had very low self-esteem and a poor concept of himself as a reader and writer and a negative disposition towards learning in general.

In the Reception year Ben would mostly 'choose' either the computer or to be outside on the bikes. At home, he spends his time playing on the computer.

I [the Reading Recovery teacher] called upon all of my known strategies trying to get Ben enthusiastic to articulate a sentence for writing. I tried to focus on his own experiences, but he just shrugged. I tried using playdough and paint to try to engage him in talking while developing his fine motor skills. Very, very slowly he began to gain trust in me and respond. I knew I needed to break through his attitude first and to get him to see what learning looked like. Finally, I found a picture of a boy sitting on the ground with a bleeding knee.

Me: What has happened to this boy?
Ben: *Shrug*
Me: Look at the picture and tell me what you see.
Ben: *Silent*
Me: I think he has fallen over and cut his knee. I bet you have fallen over and cut your knee before haven't you?
Ben: Yeah, but I ain't gonna write about it!

Reflection

I had a response and could see from it that he was sharp to be on to me so fast. It took 9 weeks – 22½ hours – of hard work and effort to build a relationship with Ben and get him to see that with my support he could begin to read and write and maybe even enjoy it. He suddenly started to see that he could do it for himself. I withdrew my support slowly as he gained in confidence. His attitude has turned around and he now sees himself more positively. When asked what he needs to do when he gets stuck he reels off the strategies he has learned (and has been taught!) in order to solve his problems more independently rather than wait and expect to be told.

Emerging issues

The case study above exemplifies what pedagogy looks like in practice and highlights the importance of reflection. It illustrates the importance of relationships, self-esteem and self-worth and the development of dispositions and skills. It raises awareness of the challenges and consequences of children's assessment and profiling against pre-identified learning outcomes and school readiness. It raises questions about interpretations and use of play for learning. The teacher's own response to Ben's needs and potential illustrates that pedagogy is not only a matter of skills and knowledge, but is an ethical stance.

Enacting pedagogy

The reported case study exemplifies the definition of pedagogy as the act of teaching and the thinking behind the teaching. Drawing upon 'known' strategies, the teacher started working with Ben in order to support his fine motor skills (concrete teaching strategy) required for pencil-control and writing (rationale). The teacher called upon ideas and notions from different theoretical and policy frameworks to inform her pedagogy. She employed, for example, a number of child-appropriate activities and materials, such as playing with playdough and painting, drawn from developmental perspectives. She drew upon Ben's possible experiences, such as falling from the bike and/or hurting his knee, adhering to principles of contextually appropriate practice. She tried to enthuse and enable Ben to enjoy learning, and to build up his confidence, self-esteem and self-worth, acknowledging developmental and rights perspectives, and she aimed at improving Ben's reading and writing skills (policy requirements). This, however, does not mean that the teacher's pedagogy was either arbitrary or selective. Instead, as is discussed in the following sections, this was a dynamic and ever-evolving process that was well reasoned against certain principles and substantiated with evidence and through reflection.

Reflecting on pedagogy

Confronted with Ben's refusal to engage with the tasks and his overall negative disposition to learning, the teacher embarked on a process of continuous reflection *in action* and *on action* (Schön, 1983). She became more aware of what she was doing when working with Ben (reflection in action) and stood back and looked at the whole experience to gain deeper insights (reflection on action) to inform her pedagogy. The teacher engaged in a process of what we might call *investigative* reflection, aiming at *seeing* the child behind the mask of observable behaviour and understanding the unspoken messages conveyed by such behaviour. This involved attentive listening and interpretation of Ben's overt messages (e.g. 'I can't read, I can't write', 'I don't want to do it.') and the effect of her strategies on him. Ben's refusal and avoidance techniques were interpreted in terms of his potential, not in the light of what he was lacking. She concluded that, while the concerns were about Ben's 'low achievement in reading and writing', the actual barrier was his 'low self-esteem and self-worth' and 'negative dispositions to learning in general'.

Building relationships

The teacher recognised that Ben's 'response' to and 'trust' in her and a 'relationship' with him were a prerequisite in order to engage him with reading and writing activities.

This required the teacher's attentive listening to Ben's explicit messages (e.g. I can't) and subtle cues (e.g. lack of confidence and self-esteem). The teacher took the time, watched Ben's responses and, in turn, modified her responses too. She waited and took the cues from Ben rather than applying her knowledge of what children need in general (Dahlberg and Moss, 2005).

It necessitated reflection on the impact of the teacher's planned learning activities on Ben and the subtle negotiation and renegotiation of activities that provided meaningful experience to both of them. Building a relationship with Ben meant that the teacher was in tune with him; she was able to think with him, not for him. Such a relationship made the teacher and the child co-travellers in the learning journey rather than the teacher trying to determine the learning journey and mould the child in dominant images.

Building self-esteem and self-worth

Building relationships is not an end itself; it is the building block for the child's self-awareness, self-worth and self-esteem, for these are attributes that derive from the ways others relate to the child and the acknowledgement of her/his efforts (Papatheodorou, 2006, 2009). The teacher noted, 'with my support he [Ben] could begin to read and write', 'started to see that he could do it for himself', 'I withdrew my support slowly as he gained confidence', 'his attitude has turned around and he now sees himself more positively'.

These strategies draw upon concepts of scaffolding, guided participation and sustained thinking, and the zone of proximal development. With the teacher's support Ben became aware of what he could do and this increased his self-worth and self-esteem. It gave him the confidence to engage with tasks that he might have thought of as being too challenging or beyond his skills.

Positive dispositions and skill development

Development of positive dispositions such as curiosity, creativity, independence, cooperativeness and persistence are at the heart of early years education and care. Katz (1993: n.p.) defines dispositions as patterns of behaviour 'exhibited frequently and in the absence of coercion … and that is intentional and oriented to broad goals'. Dispositions refers to all conscious and deliberate or habitual/automatic acts that seem to be intuitive and spontaneous. Carr (1995) suggests several ways of supporting the development of dispositions, namely valuing and modelling them, orchestrating interactions that support them, teaching them and providing support and affirmation to children.

Working with Ben the teacher herself demonstrated positive dispositions and modelled them (e.g. relating, trusting, showing perseverence and confidence). She created an environment where relationships and positive interactions were created; offered support and taught Ben skills and tools to use. The teacher noted that 'when he gets stuck he reels off the strategies he has learned (and has been taught!) in order to solve his problems'.

While skill training *per se* is questionable, provision of appropriate support and at the right time is necessary for the child to cross the threshold of challenge, gain confidence and persevere with the task at hand (Papatheodorou and Loader, 2009). Positive dispositions enable children to develop skills and competences, but supporting skills and competences can forge positive dispositions too. There is a dialectical and interactive relationship between the two, but it requires an insightful teacher with positive dispositions to learning to provide the right balance.

School readiness

School readiness figures highly in the revised EYFS, which also mandates children's assessment. The scores of the EYFS Profile are used to inform many decisions about individual children. Ben, for instance, 'was kept in a Year 1 class, where he would continue the EYFS for the first two terms' and was a 'candidate for the reading recovery programme … an expensive and intensive intervention programme'.

School readiness is a contested notion, much debated and challenged in terms of its definition (e.g. certain level of cognitive skills) as to whether the child or the school should be ready (Pre-school Learning Alliance, 2011). Caution must be also exercised about decisions made on the basis of the EYFS Profile, for it may indicate the child's challenges, but it says nothing about why these challenges exist. In Ben's case, reading and writing were seen as his main difficulties, but as the teacher realised these were secondary to his lack of positive dispositions and skill, and low self-esteem and confidence.

To ignore the requirement for school readiness, however, may mean that a potent child, like Ben, will be left behind by his peers and his self-esteem and self-worth further lowered, or will be placed on expensive interventions (e.g. Reading Recovery). To act in the best interest of the child and serve her/him well entails careful considerations of the pedagogical options and choices to be made.

Playful learning

Working with Ben the teacher employed a playful learning pedagogy that, initially, was mostly adult-led, aiming at the particular objective of improving skills and competences necessary for reading and writing skills. The teacher appreciated that Ben's previous play was mainly static and around solitary activities (e.g. spending time on the bike or the computer), so she invested in joined and interactive playful activities (e.g. playing with playdough, sharing reading). She provided space and made time for both of them to find common ground of understanding in order to develop purposeful and playful learning that would be owned by Ben. This was a flexible playful approach that gave Ben (and the teacher) the opportunity to draw upon his experiences and interests and exercise his agency.

Play is enshrined in the consciousness and practices of early years practitioners for its impact on all areas of development (e.g. physical, cognitive, emotional and social), positive dispositions and skill development (for more on play see Chapter 5). Play and the pedagogy of play are not without challenges, however. In a culture and context of outcomes-based curricula and children's profiling, even the discourse of play has changed. This has shifted from play to playful learning; from child-initiated play to balanced child-led and adult-led play (for an extensive overview of play, see Moyles, 2010). Practices – as the case study illustrates – are also variable. In some cases play may become so open-ended as to allow children to engage with limited preferred choices and refuse to extend their play repertoire. In other instances play may be narrowed down to the extent that it is mostly, if not exclusively, adult-led.

Considering Ben's challenges, it is important to remember that whatever play or playful approach to learning is chosen, this should:

- contribute to children's positive dispositions to learning
- develop an appropriate level of skill and competences that enable children to engage with challenging tasks and enjoy them
- enable children to interact, collaborate and work with others and to problem solve
- instil a sense of self-esteem and self-worth and confidence
- lead to independence and self-reliance.

Relational pedagogy

The teacher's playful approach was also informed by her/his view of Ben as the 'sharp' individual, who was able to exercise his agency 'to solve his problems', to be 'independent' and 'reel off the strategies he had learned', to 'see what learning is like', 'not to expect to be told'. This was a pedagogical stance that acknowledged the child as a strong, powerful and meaning-making individual, but it placed the responsibility of enabling the child to do so on the teacher. The teacher's practice reflected the principles of relational pedagogy, articulated by Brownlee (2004), namely:

- showing respect to the child as a knower
- providing learning experiences that related to her/his own experience
- articulating and facilitating an approach that emphasised meaning making rather than transmission and accumulation of knowledge.

The case study illustrates that well-known and good practice needs to be framed against an appropriate pedagogy that leads to a meaningful experience for both the child and the teacher. This requires, to recall Dahlberg and Moss (2005: 1), investment in 'a relation, a network of obligation' and 'infinite attention to the other'. Reciprocal relationships inform and enable a pedagogy that is purposeful and intentional; are appropriate and relevant to the child's interest and potential; are transformative and empowering.

By investing in relational inter-subjectivity – to recall Trevarthen (2011) – relational pedagogy bridges dichotomies and polarised discourses such as child-centred/led/initiated versus adult-centred/led learning; learning processes versus outcomes/competences-based education; or children's *being* versus children's *becoming*. In doing so it necessitates continuous negotiation of different, and often conflicting, influences and ongoing reflection for developing meaningful and worthwhile practices.

Summary

In conclusion, pedagogy offers a broad framework that informs the ways early years practitioners engage with children and the planning of learning activities. It is the springboard for conscious and unconscious reflections and forms the basis for evaluating whether these actions are responsive to children's interests and/or brought about by intended outcomes. It offers the lenses and filters by which theoretical perspectives, policy requirements and established good practices are critiqued and questioned in order to act in the best interest of children and in safeguarding best outcomes for them.

It is neither the child's being here and now (developmental perspectives) nor her/his becoming in some distant future (policy perspectives) that is more important than the other. There is a moral and ethical obligation to observe children's being and becoming and instil a sense of belonging through an appropriate pedagogy (Papatheodorou, 2010). For this, engagement is needed in a dialectical manner with theoretical perspectives and policy requirements, as both inform and shape each other (Papatheodorou, 2012). The ability to critique and negotiate different and often conflicting and polarised discourses can only enable creativity and flexibility of thinking and thus advance practice.

Key points to remember

- The concept of pedagogy has been influenced by developmental theories, as the way we learn is influenced by development and children thrive in stimulating, supportive and positively reinforcing environments.
- The concept of pedagogy is influenced by policy in terms of curricular approaches, child assessment and external evaluation bodies such as Ofsted.
- The introduction of UNCRC in 1989 has enriched the understanding of the child as a social actor who is able to express her/his views, and has influenced the care and education received and consequently has impacted on our views on pedagogy.
- Pedagogy in the field of early years education and care draws upon a range of ideas from different theoretical perspectives and policy requirements and is influenced by ongoing dialogue and reflection among early years practitioners.

Points for discussion

- To what extent do the concepts of scaffolding, guided participation and sustained shared thinking reflect similar ideas, and how might they be different?
- What are the characteristics, similarities and differences between play, playful learning, child-initiated and adult-led learning?
- What does it mean 'acting in the best interest of children' and 'safeguarding children's rights'?

Reflective tasks

Consider your own practice and context to reflect on:

- whether any particular perspective, discussed in this chapter, is more evident than others, and why
- the ways and methods you use to capture children's voices and how these might be improved
- whether children's formative assessment and EYFS profiling do evaluate whether children's rights are observed, and how this might be improved.

Further reading

Moyles, J. (2010) *The Excellence of Play*, 3rd edn. Maidenhead: Open University Press.
Papatheodorou, T. (2009) 'Exploring relational pedagogy', in T. Papatheodorou and J. Moyles (eds), *Learning Together in the Early Years: Exploring Relational Pedagogy*. London: Routledge.

Useful websites

United Nations *Convention on the Rights of the Child, General Comment No. 7: Implementing Child Rights in Early Childhood*: www2.ohchr.org/english/bodies/crc/docs/AdvanceVersions/GeneralComment7Rev1.pdf

To gain **free access** to selected SAGE journal articles related to key topics in this chapter visit: www.sagepub.co.uk/Palaiologou2e

5

Play in the Early Years Foundation Stage

Chantelle Haughton and Cheryl Ellis

Chapter roadmap

This chapter will highlight key features of play, acknowledging different forms of play, including child-initiated and adult-led play. It will identify how play experiences may impact on holistic child development. Recommendations for good practice will be explored, including the identification of some benefits and challenges for both adults and children which can result from a play-based pedagogy. Issues relating to the use of indoor and outdoor play spaces will be reflected upon.

This chapter aims to help you to:

- define play and its various forms
- identify and reflect upon elements of good practice in play provision, establishing links with the Early Years Foundation Stage
- develop an element of criticality by thinking about issues related to working within a play environment from differing perspectives.

Theoretical perspectives on play

Chapter 4 discussed the notion of pedagogy in early childhood education and care and suggested 'playful learning' as a key element that allows children to engage in meaningful sense-making of the world. Wood and Bennett (1997) acknowledge that support for the importance of play is based on a number of psychological theories, philosophies and educational principles from different eras and cultures. They suggest that there is broad agreement that young children need to play in order to find out more about themselves, their culture, roles and relationships. There is no unified theoretical or pedagogical base to guide practice in relation to play, however, which has resulted in 'conceptual confusion' regarding the role of play within an educational setting (McAuley and Jackson, 1992 cited in Wood and Bennett, 1997). Indeed, a review of literature by the BERA Early Years Special Interest Group (2003: 14) identified that 'Whilst play forms the bedrock of early learning, an agreed pedagogy of play is less well articulated, and play in practice is deeply problematic. The dominant ideology is not underpinned by systematic empirical research, and key studies both in preschool and statutory school settings have identified significant gaps between the rhetoric and the reality of practice.' BERA (2003: 13) identify four key areas of concern:

- There is little understanding of how play progresses in early childhood, and how progression can be supported.
- Practitioners tend to espouse an ideological adherence to the efficacy of free play, even though there is little empirical evidence to support this.
- Practitioners make assumptions about the competence and ability of young learners to benefit from a predominantly *laissez-faire* environment, in which they are expected to choose from a wide range of activities and experiences.
- Not all young children know how to play.

Many argue, however, that true play encourages children to engage in active discovery that is fluid and spontaneous. Bruner (2006: 91) acknowledges the creative freedom of children's play:

> It is not that children don't pursue ends and employ means to get them in their play, but that they often change their goals en route to suit new means or change the means to suit new goals. Nor is it that they do so only because they have run into blocks, but out of sheer jubilation of good spirits. It provides not only medium for exploration, but also for invention.

CASE STUDY

Pirates

Within a Reception class, a group of children aged 4–5 years move from bridge builders to pirates. (Creative freedom – changing goals in the course of play.)

Story time has just ended. A small group of children feel inspired to work at the craft table to build a bridge, 'just like the one the troll lives under'. The teacher agrees this would be a fantastic idea and the children quickly start searching through the 'crafty chest' for building materials. They come across a number of boxes and kitchen roll tubes which they think they could use. Katy suggests they use glue; in response Bessy says that 'glue takes too long'. Bessy works with the sticky tape to join two tubes together and Katy assists by holding them. Khalid and Tom work alongside them, building 'the tall bits'. Khalid takes the lead on building the bridge tower as Tom sits holding another tube. Tom peeps through the tube and says, 'This can be a troll telescope. Look.' All four of the children take turns to look through it as Tom holds the 'troll telescope'. Bessy says, 'We can use it to be troll pirates. We can be pirates and find the trolls and their treasure.' Tom jumps up and moves away from the table. 'Come on,' he says, skipping towards the role-play corner. Katy, Bessy and Khalid drop what they are doing at the craft table and follow excitedly. A game of 'troll-seeking pirates' begins, using the telescopes. The children select items from the costume box to dress as pirates and Katy runs back to the craft table to get herself a telescope. Soon, all four of the children have a telescope and others join in the search for trolls and treasure.

As the above case study demonstrates, within the first few years of life play develops from the 'physical' play of a small baby into more complex play which involves many sophisticated mental processes. Children use all of their senses during play. From a Piagetian perspective, this enables children to assimilate new information. This information is stored with existing ideas until something happens, i.e. until new information is assimilated which contradicts or questions this existing knowledge. This discomfort or disequilibrium of thought causes children to rethink the idea that they had assimilated (Pound, 2005). This re-thinking, known as accommodation, enables them to adjust or adapt their thinking to restore equilibrium. Pound (2005: 37) refers to the outcome of equilibrium as 'feeling comfortable with our own thinking'. Stephen (2010) identifies that Piaget's focus on the child's active exploration and movement through the processes of assimilation and accommodation can be seen in the emphasis that practitioners place on providing resource-rich play environments and ample opportunities for children to explore as they choose. These provide opportunities for children to experience novel situations and experiences that can trigger assimilation and accommodation (Pound, 2005). This can be viewed as a two-way relationship, whereby more complex forms of play can aid cognitive development and whereby cognitive development aids more complex forms of play.

Socially, play develops from the solitary play of a young child, to parallel play (where children play side by side but function separately) and then to socially interactive play where much of the play relies on the interactions with others. Avgitidou (1997) suggests that play with friends is characterised by specific qualities that encourage children's social, cognitive and affective development and that 'these qualities reflect patterns of interaction among friends which are duration, intensity, coordination and continuity of interaction, interdependence and the development of a shared knowledge of the relationship' (Avgitidou, 1997: 6). Play that facilitates the development of these qualities helps children to form positive attitudes towards others as they assist each other, share and exchange information. Play can therefore involve high levels of intellectual demand and creativity, particularly within reciprocal play as children sustain cooperative endeavour, a key feature of which is joint problem solving in a variety of forms (BERA, 2003).

While play may well be a powerful aid to learning within EYFS, it also has a crucial part to play in the wider, holistic development of individuals. As Walker (2005) acknowledges, the aim of education should be to equip individuals with self-determination and the development of a sense of self which enables active involvement in emotional, intellectual and professional relationships with others. Play within trusting and caring environments can help to foster this positive sense of self.

The meaningful business of play: What is it all about?

As we have seen, play has been studied from different theoretical approaches, but a common element to all studies about play is that it is an activity that children undertake for pleasure and is one of children's primary needs in their development. The Early Years Foundation Stage (DfE, 2012) promotes the use of play to help children develop a broad range of knowledge and skills that provide the right foundation for future progress through school and throughout life. There is, however, no concise or agreed definition of 'play'. Santer et al. (2007: xviii) acknowledge that 'Play is perhaps too profound and intangible a concept to neatly define in a way that brooks no argument.' Lindon (2001: 2) does suggest, however, that 'play includes a range of activities, undertaken for their own interest, enjoyment or the satisfaction that results'. Similarly, the DCMS (2004: 8) highlights that 'Play is what children and young people do when they follow their own ideas in their own way and for their own reasons.' A powerful element of this is that children have ownership of their play. From a child's perspective, play can be a satisfying and enjoyable occupation that can promote feelings of inner well-being.

The importance of the pleasure gained from play should not be underestimated both for psychological and physiological development. Children play because it is fun.

From a child's perspective, any learning that arises from play is likely to be incidental as it is often the process of play that is most satisfying. When choosing to bake a cake, for example, the business of mixing flour and eggs can be pleasurable and rewarding in itself. In some instances the actual finished product, the cake, may be of far less interest.

Where children choose and have control over their play, this can be viewed as 'free-play'. EYFS (DCSF, 2008) has embedded into its framework the 12 features of free-play identified by Bruce and since updated (Bruce, 2005, cited in Bruce and Ockelford, 2010: 113), which are summarised below. These features embrace a diverse approach to play cross-culturally and in relation to children with disabilities and learning difficulties and are considered to provide a 'birth throughout life' approach (Bruce and Ockelford, 2010: 113).

1 Children draw upon the first-hand experiences they have had in their play. The richer and deeper the experiences, in the way they bring into action all the senses as well as movement and the kinaesthetic feedback that accompanies it, the more the child's possibilities for rich play develop.
2 In play children make up their own rules.
3 Children make play props from found materials and sometimes from toys. Home-made play props are often thought to be most loved by children in their play rather than expensive toys, as they are more open ended and flexible to use, offering more play opportunities (see Bruce and Ockelford, 2010, for further detail).
4 One of the most crucial features of play is that children must choose to do it. They cannot be made to play. Children have to move into play in their own way, at their own pace.
5 Children rehearse future possibilities when they play (for example in role-play).
6 Play opens up opportunities to pretend.
7 Sometimes children play alone. This is in no way inferior to playing alongside or with others.
8 When children are playing with others they might play in companionship, which means they play in parallel, enjoying each other's company, but not wishing to interact directly, or they may play cooperatively with others.
9 It is easier to play in a larger group cooperatively if everyone is clear what the play theme is and has realistic props to use.
10 Quality free-flowing play means that children become deeply involved in their play.
11 When children are involved in their play, they often demonstrate their recent learning.
12 Free-flow play helps children to coordinate and bring together their learning.

It is important to acknowledge that play can be a highly personal and rewarding experience for all children. The BERA Early Years Special Interest Group (2003) question the efficacy of 'free play', however, and describe how play can be stereotypical and lacking in challenge. It is suggested here that this is more likely to be the case where the principles detailed above are not present. If we accept that 'free play' is socially and culturally constructed, however, we do need to consider the level of 'freedom' for each individual within it. As Wood and Bennett (1997) highlight, children's skills and competences as 'players' vary considerably.

Play as a platform for learning

It is crucial that adults appreciate the importance of play as a process and do not become overly focused on end results. While any learning that may result from 'free-play' is likely to be incidental, practitioners are also encouraged to develop 'purposeful play' with the aim of promoting learning. This can create a dilemma for practitioners as they endeavour to find a balance between child-initiated 'free-play' and adult-led play. Gaining a balance between 'free-play' and adult-led play can be a complex process that may be compounded by a need to meet explicit learning goals. One suggestion is that 'free-play' can be enriched when a more knowledgeable or experienced individual extends or enriches the play. From a Vygotskian perspective this refers to the difference between what a child can do on his/her own and what they can do when guided by someone else (either an adult or a more able child) (Vygotsky, 1978). The Effective Provision of Pre-school Education Project (EPPE, 1997–2004) identified 'sustained shared thinking' within adult–child interactions as a necessary prerequisite for excellent early years practice. They describe this as an episode in which two or more individuals 'work together' in an intellectual way to solve a problem, clarify a concept, evaluate activities and extend a narrative (Sylva et al., 2004). Both parties must contribute to the thinking in order to develop and extend thinking. More challenging forms of sustained shared thinking can be encouraged by using increasingly more sophisticated and abstract scaffolding props (Siraj-Blatchford, 2009).

Supporting learning through play: 'sensitive intervention'

One form of scaffolding can be provided by 'sensitive intervention' which is necessary to enable the child to maintain control of play while providing opportunities and ideas to develop it further. By scaffolding children's play experiences, young children can develop the skills they need to become successful learners – for example, building their confidence, developing their flexibility of thought and seeing problems from different perspectives (Tickell, 2011). This supports the use of play-based approaches for learning which combine instructional and playful teaching. It highlights the importance of techniques such as modelling, demonstrating and questioning while engaging in fun and active experiences. The EPPE Project (Sylva et al., 2004) identified that adult 'modelling' is often combined with longer periods of more focused thinking and that open-ended questioning is also associated with improved cognitive development. The Project identified that even in settings classed as 'excellent', however, the frequency of use of these approaches was very low.

Sensitive intervention may involve initiating particular activities with specific children: individually, in small groups or as a whole class or it may entail observing the activities chosen by children and then scaffolding their learning via prompts to extend the opportunities for learning. A key element of this may be to encourage children to verbalise what they are doing, to help develop linguistic and cognitive skills and confidence in their own abilities. Freely chosen play activities often provide the best opportunities for adults to extend children's thinking. Adults need, therefore, to create opportunities to extend child-initiated play as well as teacher-initiated group work, as both have been found to be important vehicles for promoting learning (Sylva et al., 2004). The skill of the practitioner may, therefore, be viewed as the ability to know how and when to intervene and collaborate within the play experience to nurture 'sustained shared thinking'. Moyles (2010) describes this process as a spiral which begins with free-play, continues with adult-directed play and then extends to enriched free-play as knowledge and abilities are acquired and consolidated.

The key element identified here is the use of a flexible approach to play-based learning, based on the level of development, needs and interest of the individual child. While in theory this may seem quite straightforward, in reality it may be difficult to judge when to intervene within a play scenario to further extend learning. Practitioners need to be aware of the possible detrimental impact of 'interrupting' young children who are involved and enthused within play Indeed, Wood and Bennett (1997) identified a common concern among practitioners that they may 'spoil' or 'intrude upon' children's play. As Lindon (2001) suggests, there may be a difference in perceptions between practitioners and children regarding the quality of play whereby some activities, games and play resources, important to children, may be misinterpreted and/or undervalued by practitioners. As a result, it is important to pause, observe and reflect before stepping into a play interaction. Practitioners need to become 'play partners', who participate within children's play with sincerity and enthusiasm. Some practitioners can do this with ease whilst others may find it more difficult to achieve (Smidt, 2010).

C A S E   S T U D Y

Play partnership and 'sensitive intervention' episode

Cassie is 2 years of age and attends full-time day care five days per week. Amina has been her key worker for over a year now and so Amina feels very in tune with Cassie's developmental progress. Generally, Cassie plays confidently on her own and alongside others. Across the week it has been noticed that Cassie usually chooses a variety of activities from those on offer, but often seems to prefer to join in with activities that involve the use of gross motor movements and she is particularly drawn to play in the garden when the doors are open during the free-play period. Amina has reflected upon her observations and decided to focus on developing Cassie's thinking skills and fine motor skills. Amina will engage in 'sensitive intervention' by working as a 'play partner'. The focus will be on explicitly extending Cassie's involvement in some of the play activities that focus on development of thinking skills and also hand–eye coordination. Amina has set these areas of development as specific targets for intervention and observation in play over the next few weeks.

On top of the grass mound Amina has positioned a play activity and herself, with the hope that Cassie will be enticed to join her. Amina sits on a blanket on the grass. A pile of small items are in one basket (such as pebbles, corks, acorns). Another basket holds a variety of containers (including small boxes, bottles with different-sized openings and jars).

The doors into the garden are opened by Sally, another child-care assistant, and the children are encouraged to look out to see what there is to play with in the garden today. Amina is already positioned sitting on the grass mound and can be seen by the eight children as they enter the garden.

Cassie hurries towards the small red tricycle and gets on. After a few minutes of using the tricycle, Cassie moves on to the grass area, climbs over the tyres and spends a moment laying quietly on her tummy on the grass. Before long, Cassie notices Amina playing. Playfully, Amina talks through her play actions. Picking up a pebble she says, 'Mmmm, I think I'll put this in here,' and tries to put it into the neck of a bottle. 'Oh no, that won't fit!' Amina uses a pole-bridging technique by reporting out loud to herself her every move and thought. Amina works through different items and containers. 'Ahh, this fits. What else can I put in here?' Cassie followed by Jak comes and stands alongside Amina. Amina welcomes the children and continues to play. Cassie is tempted to join in the game and starts by selecting a jam jar. Smiling to herself, after a little persistence, Cassie is able to remove the loose lid and picks pebbles to place in the jar. She smiles maybe at the sound of the small pebbles dropping into the glass jar. Amina continues to talk through her thoughts and actions. 'Ooh, that won't fit. Maybe it will if I try and move it this way? No, maybe I need to try something different. In it goes ... and in goes another.' Cassie puts down the jar, moves to sit down and shifts a little closer to Amina. Cassie picks up a different jar, but she has trouble opening it and holds it out to Amina. She encourages Cassie to twist the lid instead of pulling; Cassie is delighted when she succeeds. The side-by-side playing continues for some time and Cassie starts to join in talking through her actions: 'In ... No, too big ... In this one.'

Through reflection, simple planning and playful partnership, valuable and sensitive intervention can be achieved. In this episode, Cassie was encouraged subtly to choose to participate and continue with involvement in a play activity that had a specific link to developmental targets identified.

Early Years Foundation Stage and play

A key emphasis within EYFS (and in other educational systems, such as the Foundation Phase in Wales) is the use of play as a vehicle for learning. In this context, play may be viewed as a platform for desirable forms of learning rather than play for its own sake.

The EYFS (DfE, 2012) identifies three main characteristics of effective learning: *Playing and exploring,* which may include the children:

- investigating
- experiencing
- being willing to 'have a go'

Active learning, which may include the children:

- being involved and concentrating
- keeping on trying (even when encountering difficulties)
- experiencing achievement in what they set out to do

Creating and thinking critically, which may include the children:

- developing their own ideas
- making links between ideas, knowledge and experiences
- developing a range of strategies for doing things.

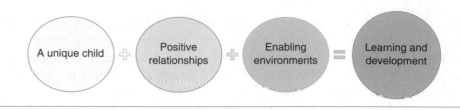

Figure 5.1   *The four themes of EYFS (DfE, 2012)*

An engaging and stimulating play environment provides opportunities for these characterics to be experienced and crafted. This can impact positively on holistic child development, enabling progress across the seven areas of learning and development. Possible benefits for learning and development within the EYFS as highlighted by Moyles (2010) include:

- Children have confidence in play activities and this has a positive effect on motivation, concentration and self-image.
- Play involves children in using imagination and creativity.
- Play requires experimentation and exploration.
- Children enjoy cooperating and collaborating with their peers in play activities.
- Children learn to make decisions and organise their own time and activities.
- Play exercises the mind and the body and aids motor and perceptual development.

As well as the importance of the play environment, it is also crucial to acknowledge that each child is unique and so practitioners will need to spend time to get to know each individual child. In addition, to facilitate learning and development through play, positive relationships and a sense of belonging within the setting will need to be nurtured and maintained. This interconnection is illustrated in Figure 5.1.

While play can help children to learn and develop, some practitioners question whether approaching their interactions with children from the perspective of supporting learning and development conflicts with what they see as their overarching caring role. For example, many playwork providers view it as against playwork principles to observe children with the intention of guiding them to their next level of development. Likewise, some childminders argue that they are there to provide a home-from-home environment, in line with parents' and carers' wishes, and feel they are not 'educators' (Tickell, 2011). Some practitioners consider their role to be more focused on caring for the child, which includes nurturing and developing individual play choices.

While this view may be more prevalent with carers or practitioners of very young children it does highlight possible tensions between the 'process' of play (i.e. inner well-being of the individual) versus the 'product'(i.e. to meet specific learning outcomes).

Outdoor play

One area of play that is growing in popularity in early years settings is outdoor play, which can provide a rich setting for children's imagination and fantasy. Indeed, Dowdell et al. (2011) found that exploration and discovery of nature were a significant part of children's play within an outdoor setting. For outdoor play to be at its most effective it should not be seen as an opportunity to take indoor activities outside. Rather it should be viewed as an opportunity for children to play in a context that allows them to combine play with sensorial experiences, talk and movement.

Opportunities to play with natural resources can stimulate children's natural curiosity and their intrinsic motivation, enabling them to develop a range of skills such as problem solving, negotiation and cooperation. Open access between the indoor and outdoor play spaces can empower young children to make choices about where, what and how to play. Equipping children and practitioners with appropriate clothing and footwear for all weathers can extend the use of the outdoor play environment across all seasons (Knight, 2009). Nevertheless, a challenge for practitioners is to identify opportunities for outdoor play in natural environments (Waller et al., 2010). This may require creative use of existing outdoor space or the use of community areas such as local parks. While the environment must be assessed to ensure that it is a safe place to play, it is also beneficial for young children's development to engage in 'risky' play as many children have an appetite for risk-taking (Gill, 2007; Little et al., 2011). If we are empowering children, this may entail children taking risks they consider acceptable. This can be a difficult and contentious issue for many practitioners, as their level of tolerance to risk within play can limit the opportunities for such play. Practitioners may also have fears of legal action if a child is injured while in their care (Waller et al., 2010). Ideally, children need to be supported to assess their own capabilities and regulate their own behaviours within a safe environment. This requires an underlying view of the child as competent rather than one of the child as vulnerable and in need of adult protection (Sandseter, 2009, cited in Waller et al., 2010).

Observation and reflective practice

This move to child-led play in a variety of settings makes assessment more challenging and, therefore, observational assessment is a key aspect of effective early years education and care – discussed further in Chapters 6 and 7. Practitioners can observe children while they act and interact in their play, everyday activities and planned activities. This can provide a valuable insight into individual children's achievements, interests and progress. As Chapter 6 will demonstrate, reflection on these observations can help practitioners to tailor their provision to support the emerging needs of each individual. It is essential that adequate time is taken to undertake and reflect upon these observations both as individual practitioners and, wherever possible, as a whole team.

Observations of play can provide:

- a comprehensive picture of each individual child in relation to knowledge and understanding, skills and attitudes
- opportunities for the progression of play via the varied use of strategies, resources and changes to the learning environment.

Planning for quality play experiences

It is important to note, however, that even apparently 'free-play' requires careful planning and skilled practitioners will keep children at the heart of the planning process. They will actively seek and engage with the interests, needs and ideas of children so that play can be fun, enticing and yet instructional. When play is a vehicle for learning, practitioner's knowledge and expertise combined with the creative thoughts of children can shape the planning process.

Some key aspects of good practice in this process to consider are:

- Each child is unique and will have his/her own individual interests, needs and ideas.
- Prior learning can be used to inform the 'next steps' for the enrichment of play.
- A responsive approach towards 'golden moments' (unanticipated learning opportunities) can lead to a spontaneous change in emphasis.

The role of the practitioner is central, therefore, to providing a supportive and stimulating environment with opportunities for free-play and more structured play. The practitioner is pivotal in providing themes for play and a range of resources, but should not be afraid to let children transform, extend or adapt play. Above all, although play can provide a valuable platform for learning, practitioners should not lose sight of the fact that play should be a valuable and enjoyable activity in its own right.

Summary

This chapter has discussed the role of play in early years education and care. It is encouraging to see that within EYFS the role of play is emphasised, both indoors and outdoors, and that the importance of the early years practitioner in facilitating children's play is acknowledged. Children need play opportunities to initiate their own learning, to develop social interactions, negotiate relationships with their peers and pursue their own interests. Theoretical perspectives on play conclude that children develop and learn through play both in an enjoyable, pleasurable way and at the same time in a challenging way. This learning can be both planned and unplanned and practitioners play a central role in facilitating opportunities to play, but also in providing the freedom for children to explore their own ideas. In doing so, play provides an opportunity for children to build communication skills, social and emotional skills, physical skills and creativity.

Key points to remember

- EYFS promotes the use of play as a vehicle for learning for holistic child development.
- Each child is unique and will have his/her own individual interests, needs and ideas in relation to play.
- Play is a valuable activity in its own right.
- Sensorial experiences, talk and movement can be woven together through play.
- 'Free-play' enables children to make choices and experience ownership.
- It is the process of play and not necessarily the product that is important.
- Sustained shared thinking provides opportunities to extend the learning that can result from play.
- Techniques such as modelling, scaffolding and open-ended questioning within play can result in enriched and extended play.
- Sensitive intervention requires practitioners to think carefully about how and when to intervene in child's play.
- Observation is a valuable tool for creating a comprehensive picture of each individual child in relation to knowledge and understanding, skills and attitudes.

Points for discussion

- Drawing upon the work of Bruce and Moyles, which is explored in the chapter, consider how you could improve play provision for a group of young children. Discuss how the use of play activities and resources could be enhanced within an early years setting.
- Discuss your own experiences of supporting 'sustained shared thinking' episodes within play.
- Undertake observation of children during play and try to analyse your observations of play focusing on the role of the adult, the play environment and the resources children used, together with the aspects of development that children demonstrated during their play.

⭐ Reflective tasks

- Good practice requires listening to children's own ideas as part of the planning process. Reflect on how the voice of individual children can be captured for the purpose of planning the play curriculum across different age ranges.

- Reflect on the scenarios below and identify possible positive and negative consequences of each. Try to reflect on both viewpoints and fill in a grid, like the one below.

Scenario	Practitioner perspective (positives and negatives)	Child perspective (positives and negatives)
Withdrawal of a young child from a 'free-play' situation to complete an adult initiated activity		
Long periods of time devoted to 'free-play' without adult intervention		
During 'free-play', a child chooses to remain in one area of the setting, e.g. the sand play area (for an extended period of time)		
During 'free-play' a child chooses to repeat the same activity consecutively over a number of sessions		

- A group of children aged 3–4 years are playing in a wooded spot at the end of the playing field. Shannon and Malik are busy giggling and running along the uneven pathway. The early years practitioner calls out a warning to the children to 'Take care and walk, not run.' A positive outcome of the warning may be to prevent the children from falling and hurting themselves. A possible negative outcome may be that they miss out on the chance to take a calculated risk of running on uneven ground which may help them to refine their gross motor skills. Reflect on the EYFS Section 3: Safeguarding and Welfare Requirements. Can you identify other possible consequences for their development?

Further reading

BERA Early Years Special Interest Group (2003) *Early Years Research: Pedagogy, Curriculum and Adult Roles, Training and Professionalism.* Southwell: BERA.

Smidt, S. (2010) *Playing to Learn: The Role of Play in the Early Years.* London: Routledge.

Sylva, K., Melhuish, E., Sammons, P., Siraj-Blatchford, I. and Taggart, B. (2004) *The Effective Provision of Pre-school Education (EPPE) Project Final Report: A Longitudinal Study (1997–2004).* London: DfES.

To gain **free access** to selected SAGE journal articles related to key topics in this chapter visit: www.sagepub.co.uk/Palaiologou2e

Observations: Recording and Analysis in the Early Years Foundation Stage

Paulette Luff

> ### Chapter roadmap
>
> Observation is of great importance within the Early Years Foundation Stage. Through using observations, present-day early years practitioners are following in the footsteps of pioneers such as John Dewey, Maria Montessori and Susan Isaacs. While these traditions continue to inspire our current practice, ideas are emerging about new ways to observe. There are differences between narrative observations, which are undertaken in order to get to know children and foster their development, and more objective, scientific approaches employed in making summative assessments. Whatever types of observations are used within EYFS, it is important to record, analyse and interpret these carefully in order to appreciate children's capabilities and to support and enrich meaningful learning.
>
> The aims of this chapter are to:
>
> - note the history of observation and its importance in early years education and care
> - emphasise the place of observation within EYFS
> - consider some ways of understanding and knowing young children through observations.

Observation in early years education and care – some historical influences

Observation has a long-held and important place in early years education and care. This is because the discoveries that arise from careful observation are well recognised as central to learning. In Maria Montessori's (1912) pedagogical method, for example, the child is encouraged to observe and his/her senses are trained to enable perception of geometric forms, colours and the features of the natural environment. Similarly for John Dewey (1933/1998), thoughtful observations provide a basis for the reflective enquiries that promote learning at every age.

Dewey and Montessori both stress that observations of children should form the basis of pedagogy. In his *Pedagogic Creed*, Dewey stated:

> I believe that … the constant and careful observation of interests is of the utmost importance for the educator … only through the continual and sympathetic observation of childhood's interests can the adult enter into the child's life and see what it is ready for and upon what material it could work most readily and fruitfully. (1897/1974: 436)

Montessori, similarly, explained that she developed and trialled her methods on the basis of numerous exact observations and advocated that teaching should stem from systematic observations of children acting freely in natural contexts. She stressed that observational study of children, within learning environments free from negative constraints, can yield 'great surprises and unexpected possibilities' (1912: 30).

As a scientist, Montessori emphasised the close observation of the external and visible world, highlighting the relationship between objective observation and logical thought. Yet observation, for Montessori, also went beyond scientific interest to the close relationships that can exist between the observer and the observed. She draws interesting parallels between the observant child and watchful adults:

> He stands with respect to the plants and animals in relations analogous to those in which the observing teacher stands towards him. Little by little, as interest and observation grow, his zealous care for the living creatures grows also and, in this way, the child can logically be brought to appreciate the care which the mother and the teacher take of him. (1912: 157)

Thus Montessori recognised that the attention and love of one human being for another can make observant teaching a deeply caring act.

As a trained psychoanalyst, Susan Isaacs also recognised the significance of undertaking and analysing observations for seeing, knowing and empathising with young children:

> by patient listening to the talk of even little children, and watching what they do, with the one purpose of understanding them, we can imaginatively feel their fears and angers, their bewilderments and triumphs; we can wish their wishes, see their pictures and think their thoughts. (Isaacs, 1929: 165)

Like Dewey and Montessori, Isaacs promoted an approach to learning based upon observing children in order to understand and meet their needs. From 1924 to 1927 she was head teacher at the Malting House experimental school in Cambridge, where children were offered a range of real-world experiences in order to stimulate their natural curiosity. Narrative observations of children engaged in these experiences formed a basis for provision of rich opportunities for learning. Isaacs' (1930, 1933) books about children's development were based upon her observations, and those who studied with her while she was head of the first Department of Child Development at the Institute of Education in London were encouraged to engage actively with observational enquiries (Podmore and Luff, 2012).

The place of observation within the EYFS

As proposed by Montessori and Dewey (see above), the Early Years Foundation Stage includes a requirement for children to observe and to become observant. In the understanding the world area of learning, for example, it is noted: 'They make observations of animals and plants and explain why some things occur, and talk about changes.' In the associated *Development Matters* document (Early Education/DfE, 2012) adults are advised to provide opportunities and materials to encourage close observation, to support children to discuss their observations, introducing relevant vocabulary, and to offer resources to enable children to represent what they have observed. For babies and toddlers, 'treasure baskets' and 'heuristic play' (Goldschmeid and Jackson, 2004) offer possibilities for observing objects with all the senses as adults watch; older children can engage with more structured explorations and observant adults may guide these early scientific investigations through a ' spiral of discovery' (Brunton and Thornton, 2010).

In order to support each 'unique child' practitioners are advised to 'understand and observe each child's development and learning, assess progress, plan for next steps' (Early Education/DfE, 2012: 2). Observation, of children's play and other activities, forms the basis for a cycle of formative assessment and curriculum planning. Being observant is crucial to the formation of 'positive relationships', in which the practitioner understands the child and sees and supports his or her interests. It also plays a part in the provision of 'enabling environments' where adults notice what resources and opportunities they could provide.

Practitioners are advised to look, listen and note what children are doing, when they play and interact and then analyse what they have observed to use their findings as the basis for planning. Once experiences and opportunities have been planned and implemented observation is used as a basis for evaluating the activity, taking note of children's progress and considering possibilities for enrichment and extension. Thus the cycle continues as a constant process designed to stimulate and support learning.

Observation is also central to the partnership working between parents and practitioners that is valued in EYFS (as discussed in Chapter 10). Sharing observations between home and early years settings offers opportunities for dialogue about the child in order to identify the progress he or she is making and create plans for further supporting and promoting learning and development. These shared observations may be informal anecdotes, photographs capturing particular moments, or more structured records. It is stated in the EYFS statutory framework document that 'Paperwork should be limited to that which is absolutely necessary to promote children's successful learning and development' (DfE, 2012: 10), so it is important that whatever is documented is necessary and meaningful.

There are two points within EYFS when summative assessments are made and recorded. The first is for 2-year-olds, reviewing their progress in the prime areas of learning (i.e. communication and language; physical development; and personal social and emotional development) and the second is the Early Years Profile, completed during the Reception year at the end of EYFS. In order for robust, accurate judgements to be made these assessments of children have to be underpinned by precise, systematic observations.

Approaches to seeing and knowing young children

For formative assessment and curriculum planning within EYFS, methods of observation are needed that will enable the observer to get close to and understand children. For this purpose narrative methods of observation are useful. These can be traditional written narratives, but may also involve photograph sequences and/or audio and video recordings to capture learning. The three approaches to observation and analysis suggested below are drawn from different theoretical perspectives and are, therefore, undertaken and evaluated in different ways. What they have in common is their basis in narrative, recognising the importance of stories in human lives and harnessing this for educative purposes (e.g. Goodson et al., 2010; Carr, 2001, 2012). The chapters that follow in this book about the use of pedagogical documentation for assessment in EYFS (see Chapter 7, for example) and the use of Learning Stories (see Chapter 8) provide further strong examples of approaches to observation that can be used to foster learning.

Possible Lines of Direction

Planning the curriculum on the basis of information about children's interests and abilities, gleaned from observations, is central within EYFS. It is, however, not always a simple process. Many educators have drawn inspiration from the work at the Pen Green Centre, including the use of Possible Lines of Direction (PLOD) charts (Whalley et al., 2007). Staff in several other early years settings have adapted this idea and created their own forms of PLOD chart. This method works by selecting different children from a class or group each week and concentrating upon those children when making observations. In a nursery group with 24 children attending each morning, for example, a focus upon four children each week will mean that every child will be targeted once each half-term throughout the year. Narrative observations will be made of the focus children, typically, two or three sustained ten-minute observations during the week. The following case study is an extract from one such narrative observation.

CASE STUDY

Observation of Chloe painting

Chloe, who is 3 years 5 months old, is in her first term in the nursery class of a village primary school.

Chloe walks over to the painting area. She takes an apron off the peg, without being reminded, and manages to put it on without any assistance. Chloe picks up a sheet of light-purple sugar paper from the centre of the painting table and places it in front of her. Tracy [teacher], who is sitting at the painting table, offers to write Chloe's name on the paper. Chloe nods and Tracy prints 'C-h-l-o-e', sounding each letter. Chloe is looking at the trays of red and yellow paint. She stretches out her right hand and puts it into the tray of yellow paint. She spreads her fingers and moves her hand backwards and forwards. Chloe then lifts her hand and places it down firmly on the piece of paper and raises it again. She looks at the clear hand print and smiles and then puts her hand back into the tray of paint. She then makes two more firm and clear prints on the paper. Tracy speaks to her, asking if she likes the colour yellow and how many fingers on her hand, but Chloe just nods and does not answer. Chloe reaches to put her right hand in the red paint but then changes her mind and reaches out her left hand instead. She presses her hand into the paint tray and then onto the paper, applying less pressure than when using her right hand. Chloe then rubs her hands together, looking quite intently at the red and yellow colours merging together. She then puts her right hand down on her paper again, choosing the remaining empty space on the page to place the print.

Table 6.1   Initial interpretation of observation of Chloe painting

Observation	Interpretation: observer's initial notes
Chloe walks over to the painting area. She takes an apron off the peg, without being reminded and manages to put it on without any assistance.	Showing initiative and independence
Chloe picks up a sheet of light-purple sugar paper from the centre of the painting table and places it in front of her.	Chooses between purple and green
Tracy (teacher), who is sitting at the painting table, offers to write Chloe's name on the paper. Chloe nods and Tracy prints 'C-h-l-o-e', sounding each letter.	Doesn't take much notice of the teacher writing her name – is focused upon starting painting

Observation	Interpretation: observer's initial notes
Chloe is looking at the trays of red and yellow paint. She stretches out her right hand and puts it into the tray of yellow paint. She spreads her fingers and moves her hand backwards and forwards.	Seems to enjoy the sensation of the paint beneath her hand
Chloe then lifts her hand and places it down firmly on the piece of paper and raises it again. She looks at the clear hand print and smiles and then puts her hand back into the tray of paint. She then makes two more firm and clear prints on the paper.	Strong and definite movements, appears to gain satisfaction from this mark making

Is concentrating on what she is doing |
| Tracy speaks to her, asking if she likes the colour yellow and how many fingers are there on her hand, but Chloe just nods and does not answer. | Seems more interested in her hand painting than the questions |
| Chloe reaches to put her right hand in the red paint but then changes her mind and reaches out her left hand instead. She presses her hand into the paint tray and then onto the paper, applying less pressure than when using her right hand. | Realises here that she still has yellow paint on her right hand and solves the problem by using her other hand

Right hand is dominant |
| Chloe then rubs her hands together, looking quite intently at the red and yellow colours merging together. She then puts her right hand down on her paper again, choosing the remaining empty space on the page to place the print. | She seems quite absorbed watching the colours mix to form orange

Seems to be experimenting with the effect of the new colour |

Table 6.2   Analysis of observation of Chloe painting in relation to areas of learning

Observation	Analysis: links to areas of learning
Chloe walks over to the painting area. She takes an apron off the peg, without being reminded and manages to put it on without any assistance.	PSED
Chloe picks up a sheet of light-purple sugar paper from the centre of the painting table and places it in front of her.	PSED
Tracy (teacher), who is sitting at the painting table, offers to write Chloe's name on the paper. Chloe nods and Tracy prints 'C-h-l-o-e', sounding each letter.	Literacy
Chloe is looking at the trays of red and yellow paint. She stretches out her right hand and puts it into the tray of yellow paint. She spreads her fingers and moves her hand backwards and forwards. Chloe then lifts her hand and places it down firmly on the piece of paper and raises it	Physical development

(Continued)

Table 6.2　(Continued)

Observation	Analysis: links to areas of learning
again. She looks at the clear hand print and smiles and then puts her hand back into the tray of paint. She then makes two more firm and clear prints on the paper.	Expressive arts and design
Tracy speaks to her, asking if she likes the colour yellow and how many fingers are there on her hand, but Chloe just nods and does not answer.	Mathematics
Chloe reaches to put her right hand in the red paint but then changes her mind and reaches out her left hand instead. She presses her hand into the paint tray and then onto the paper, applying less pressure than when using her right hand.	Physical development
Chloe then rubs her hands together, looking quite intently at the red and yellow colours merging together. She then puts her right hand down on her paper again, choosing the remaining empty space on the page to place the print.	Understanding the world

Expressive arts and design |

Analysis and interpretation of observations

The next step is to analyse and interpret the narrative observations. The person who recorded the observation, typically the key person, will read through and annotate the observations (see the example in Table 6.1) and make initial interpretations of the observation.

The main questions, at this stage, will relate to what the observation is telling us about the child:

- What personality traits are revealed?
- What skills and abilities is the child showing?
- What is the child interested in?
- What is the child learning?
- What does this observation reveal that I didn't know before?
- Are there patterns of behaviour that can be seen in all the observations?

There is rarely one answer to any of these questions. In order to analyse the child's skills, in relation to the areas of learning in EYFS, the observer can also annotate the observation to highlight which areas were covered during the activity seen in the observation (see the example in Table 6.2) and how the child responded.

It is helpful for staff teams to work in pairs or small groups to discuss all the observations of the child and compare their interpretations. Following from discussions of the child's learning it is possible to move on and to identify possibilities for development and ideas for activities. These can be recorded on a PLOD chart, with a learning target and one or more activities for each of the areas of learning.

Curriculum in the early years is not only planned and implemented in settings, such as pre-school playgroups and Foundation Stage classes, but also in children's homes and communities. It is important, therefore, to share the observations and interpretations with parents in order to ensure that experiences are planned that the child will benefit from. Parents will be able to confirm whether what is seen from the child's play at nursery is similar to, or different from, their perceptions of the child in the home environment. They will also be able to comment on the ideas for activities and perhaps add some useful suggestions that can be incorporated on the PLOD chart.

Close observation: the Tavistock approach

The Tavistock approach to close observation of babies and young children is named after the London clinic where it was developed. The method was pioneered by Esther Bick (1964) for use in the training of psychotherapists. As originally conceived, the approach involves weekly, hour-long visits to a family home in order to follow the development of a baby or very young child throughout a year of their life (Miller et al., 1989). The observer aims to be neutral and non-participant yet fully tuned in to the inner thoughts and feelings of the child. No notes are taken during the hour but very close attention is paid to non-verbal signals and the features of any interaction between the child and parents, particularly the mother. A detailed account of the session is later written up in which, as far as possible, the complete sequence of events is recalled and described. The observation accounts are interpreted using psychodynamic theory and pay particular attention to the emotional responses of the observer.

Elfer (2005) suggests that a modified version of this close observation technique can be used in early years settings. The time and frequency of the observations may be reduced, for example, to recording just 10–20 minutes of interaction. The method is retained: paying close attention while observing and then producing a written record from memory in as much detail as possible.

CASE STUDY

Feeding Jake

This observation is of a 7-month-old baby, Jake, who has recently begun to attend part-time at a day nursery, being fed fruit purée by his key person, Jenny.

(Continued)

(Continued)

Jake is seated in the low high chair, wedged securely with a small cushion. He is awake and wide-eyed. He raises and lowers his arms in front of him and clasps and unclasps his hands. Jenny brings the small bowl of apple purée and places it on the tray of the high chair, in front of him. Jake smiles widely and opens his mouth. Jenny smiles in response, but Jake is looking at the food bowl and not back at her. He watches as Jenny dips the tip of the spoon in the purée, opens his mouth even more widely and wriggles his whole body in anticipation. Jenny places the spoon in his mouth, quite slowly and gently. Jake closes his mouth around the spoon, momentarily, and then opens it again and turns his head away. He waves his arms and moves his mouth, as though sucking the food. Jenny scoops a little more apple onto the spoon, then watches him and waits. Jake opens his mouth widely and Jenny feeds him another spoonful. They continue in this pattern for several more mouthfuls. Jake continues to move his arms, but does not reach for the spoon or the bowl. When Jake closes his mouth, and grips the side edges of the high chair with both hands, Jenny offers his trainer cup with some water and he drinks.

Watching, I like the way that even during the busy nursery lunchtime Jenny is not rushing to feed Jake but seems tuned in to his body language and she is prepared to go at his preferred pace. In interpreting the observation, I can detail aspects of his personal, social and emotional development and recognise his progress with weaning onto solid foods. I am also aware of the positive emotions that are aroused in me, when observing Jenny carefully and responsively feeding Jake, and from this I sense that the mealtime is pleasurable for both of them.

Observing in this way, even for a short time, is a very valuable as a way of getting to know the unique child, understanding the child's developing relationship with his or her key person and appreciating the quality of the care provided. Practitioners who have observed children using close observation techniques report increased feelings of empathy towards the children and an ability to recognise their own emotions. EYFS includes a requirement for providers to make arrangements for supervision of staff who have contact with children and families. Close observations could be a useful tool for supportive discussion of the well-being of children.

Three planes of analysis

When we observe, we do not observe the child in isolation, but also see the child's interactions with others and the environment. This is recognised in the work of Barbara

Rogoff (1995, 2003), who writes of the significance of three planes of analysis: personal, interpersonal and community. *Development Matters*, the non-statutory EYFS guidance (Early Education/DfE, 2012), echoes this in organising the characteristics of effective learning and the areas of learning and development under three headings. A Unique Child involves observing what the child is learning and can be equated with a personal or individual plane of analysis. Positive Relationships concern what adults could do to support development, linking with an interpersonal plane, while Enabling Environments consist of planning and provision within the institution and wider community.

Observations using three planes of analysis focus not only upon the individual child, but also upon the social and cultural context in which he or she is being observed. Fleer and Richardson (2009) have described how practitioners in Canberra, Australia, changed their approaches to observation and began using personal, interpersonal and community planes of analysis as lenses. A particular advantage of this approach is that, rather than just noting the actual level of development that a child has reached, it is possible to record what a child can achieve with assistance. This enables the observer to see the child's potential and to plan activities and experiences, therefore, that will be stimulating and challenging.

The observation of Chloe and the interpretations shown above (in Tables 6.1. and 6.2) centre upon her as an individual, the traditional focus for child observations, and thus correspond with a personal plane of analysis. It is possible to view this observation through an interpersonal lens and analyse the interaction between Chloe and the teacher. This raises questions about the nature of the teacher's communication: on the one hand, we can see that she is supportive, but not intrusive, available to give help when needed (such as writing names on paintings); on the other hand it is possible to critique her responses. Why did she ask closed questions about colours and numbers? How else could she have responded to Chloe's handprinting? Similarly, the third lens is brought to bear on the context and questions can be asked about the institution and learning community. Why is this type of activity valued?

Summary

In stressing that paperwork should be kept to a minimum, and yet retaining the emphasis upon planning that is based upon children's interests, the EYFS guidance provides practitioners with opportunities to think critically and creatively about the methods of observation that they choose. The methods described above have value for getting to know and appreciate children and are useful for formative assessment and curriculum planning. For summative assessments, at age 2 years and at the end of the Foundation Stage, it is important to conduct observations accurately and systematically in order to base decisions upon objective evidence of what each child knows and can do.

Whatever methods of observation are used the role of observant adults is to look and listen actively and make sense of what children are doing and saying. The purpose of all analysis and interpretation of observations should be to open up possibilities for the children. If this is done well, practitioners will promote children's competence in making and expressing meanings and thus stimulate their learning. Importantly, the practitioner should also gain interest and satisfaction from observations of children as Dewey (1933/1998: 256) noted: 'the persons who enjoy seeing will be the best observers'.

Key points to remember

- Observations are central to early years education and care. They were introduced mainly by Maria Montessori and Susan Isaacs and they are now widely used as a way of collecting information about children and consequently assessing children.

- Within EYFS, observations keep a central role and it is now requirement that early years practitioners use observations to support children's learning, plan their daily activities and communicate effectively with parents.

- There is a plethora of ways of how to observe children, interpret and analyse observations. The most common approach in the early years sector is the Possible Lines of Direction (PLOD), introduced by Pen Green Centre.

- This chapter suggests the three planes of analysis approach to observations as this takes into consideration children as individuals as well as children's social and cultural context; it goes beyond what children can do, to what children can achieve with support in a stimulating environment.

Points for discussion

- In your opinion, how do key historical figures such as John Dewey, Maria Montessori and Susan Isaacs influence your current practice in early years education and care?

- In your experience what types of observations work best for getting to know children?

- How can we ensure that our summative assessments of children are rigorous and made on the basis of sound evidence?

Reflective tasks

Ola is 2 years and 4 months old. The objectives of the observation are to investigate how Ola is behaving during storytelling time. Reflect on the following observations and try to use the three planes of analysis:

Observation 1: *4 March*

Is beginning to join in (sit down) with the group story time (picks up and opens a flap and joins in the group)

Observation 2: *10 March*

Ola sat on Janet's [the teacher] knee during story time with four other children. Janet read 'Jack and Stack' and Ola was looking at the pictures and was repeating words the story all the way through. She joined in lifting the flaps and accepted other children taking turns.

Observation 3: *14 March*

Ola points to pictures in the book with Janet:

'Cat,' she says, turns page.

' Dog,' turns page, 'kangaroo'.

Observation 4: *17 March*

After the story time with Teddy story, Ola is playing with Teddy's suitcase (that has books and toys from the story book). She is repeating the words from the book, she uses comb to brush Teddy, dresses Teddy.

- Can you create Possible Lines of Direction for Ola?
- Reflect on your own experience of the use of observation in early years education and care, and think: how do you make meaningful use of observation and how important do you consider observation to be as a strategy for learning?

Further reading

Elfer, P. (2005) 'Observation matters', in L. Abbott and A. Langston (eds), *Birth to Three Matters*. Maidenhead: Open University Press.

Fleer, M. and Richardson, C. (2009) 'Cultural-historical assessment: mapping the transformation of understanding', in A. Anning, J. Cullen and M. Fleer (eds), *Early Childhood Education*, 2nd edn. London: Sage.

Palaiologou, I. (2012) *Child Observation for the Early Years,* 2nd edn. London: Sage.

Useful websites

For more information on Pen Green Centre approach to observation and documentation visit: www.pengreen.org/pengreenresearch.php

To gain **free access** to selected SAGE journal articles related to key topics in this chapter visit: www.sagepub.co.uk/Palaiologou2e

Assessment in the Early Years Foundation Stage

Sally Howard, Laura Harkin, Angie Hutchinson and Ioanna Palaiologou

Chapter roadmap

Good-quality early years education and care has a positive impact on all children for their future learning and success. While it is recognised that the experiences and opportunities at home play a significant role in this framing and forming of life skills, positive attitudes and cognition, it is in the early years settings that practitioners can actively address learning and development needs. In order to do this efficiently and effectively, however, there needs to be a system to assess, monitor and address learning and development. It is suggested throughout this chapter that an in-depth understanding of why we assess children needs to be developed prior to assessing children. This chapter will focus on the assessment of these complex and varied attributes and briefly discuss how and why this is an important aspect of effective early years education and care in the current legislative context of England.

This chapter aims to help you understand:

- the role of assessment in early years education and care
- complications involved in assessing children in early years education and care
- the statutory requirements for assessment in the EYFS.

What is assessment?

Assessment in early years settings is the gathering of a range of evidence about children's learning and behaviours so that judgements can be made about their progress. These judgements can fall into two broad categories:

- judgements about how to design and implement the next steps for further development in learning; and
- judgements on what has been learned and achieved.

The first category is often termed *formative assessment* or *assessment for learning* and is an ongoing planned process that always includes a 'next step action'. Its main purpose is to bring about improvement in the child's knowledge, understanding and skills on a daily basis in an iterative way (Black and Wiliam, 1998). The second category tends to focus on what has been learned and achieved, forms a record of a child's attainment and achievement and is referred to as *summative assessment*.

These judgements can also contribute to the design of Next Steps Actions. This is not the prime purpose, however, and for this reason the term 'continuous summative' has been coined to indicate the difference and similarities between formative and summative assessment. These judgements in summative assessment are made against a previously agreed set of criteria and the outcomes are then primarily used to track progress over a specific period of time. This ranges from a class-level tracking system to 'whole school' tracking. Put simply, summative assessment is a summary of attainment at a given point in time (Harrison and Howard, 2009).

It is this process of tracking of attainment over time that makes it easier to see and respond to patterns or trends in relation to individual children and groups of children. These trends could signify a potential educational problem that requires specific intervention, such as the involvement of a specialist. Recording and monitoring these trends can also provide an ongoing record of the progress individual children are making in relation to specific points in time. The process of summative assessment may include specific tests, including diagnostic tests, or a range of structured activities to check for a child's understanding including the acquisition of certain skills. It might also include a spontaneous observation of a child engaged in self-directed play where they child spontaneously presents evidence of specific attainment. The focus for summative assessment is on what has been achieved and accomplished and forms part of a record of progress for each child. It is an important aspect of tracking children's progress to ensure good accountability to parents and other key stakeholders. If used wisely it can also contribute to enrich our understanding of children's learning and the early years team can use this understanding to provide 'scaffolding' to the children in order to reach the next levels of learning (Bruner, 1970).

The prime and specific areas of learning and development within EYFS, as described in the non-statutory guidance document *Development Matters* (Early Education,

2012), can become the starting point of continuous summative assessment. The structure is clearly explained in the statutory framework for the EYFS document (DfE, 2012) and is set out under three broad strands relating to what to look out for and what can be done:

- *A Unique Child:* which supports observing what a child is learning expressed as short statements
- *Positive Relationships:* which provides statements about what adults could do to enhance learning
- *Enabling Environments:* which outlines what adults could provide to children to enhance their experiences based on children's needs.

It is this clear structure that helps the caregiver/practitioner to recognise the relevant evidence against the nationally agreed goals.

These developmental statements are then used to make a permanent record of attainment for each child as they make progress. It is about recognising the relevant individualised progress, not at fixed periods, but as an ongoing process in the child's individualised way. The prime and specific areas of learning and development should be descriptors to be used as guidance for summary judgements, rather than an absolute grade of attainment. It is by using an agreed framework that those involved in the care and development of children's physical, social and cognitive development can use assessment in a constructive way:

> The development statements and their order should not be taken as necessary steps for individual children. They should not be used as a checklist. The age/stage bands overlap because they are not fixed age boundaries but suggest a typical range of development. (Early Education DfE, 2012: 6)

The gathering and recording of this information is part of the process that contributes to a structured and progressive plan relating to the provision of appropriate indoor and outdoor experiences.

Formative assessment, on the other hand, is primarily about the 'hour by hour', 'day by day' processes that expert teachers and carers use to explore and develop a child's thinking process and their skills as they unfurl. It focuses on the thoughtful response and actions that come about and actively involves the young learner as well as the teacher. It is through an assessment for learning approach that teachers can reflect and then actively enhance learning through planned and spontaneous opportunities. Recognising the iterative aspect of assessment for learning through dialogic learning is fundamental to this assessment process (Harrison and Howard, 2009).

It is generally recognised (Alexander, 2007) that through dialogic talking opportunities children can be 'challenged' to think by explaining what they are doing and try to articulate their reasons for doing this. It is by showing an interest and asking questions that children can be challenged to consider cause and effect and make tentative suggestions about connections between their different experiences, both at home and within the setting. It is this metacognitive aspect of assessment for learning that marks it out as different from summative assessment.

An example might be that during a 'bug hunt' in the outside area a child finds a spider and, while looking at the body and leg parts, excitedly states that he has seen spiders before and his sister was afraid of them. The practitioner asked him how he knew it was a spider and not an ant? This is an illustration of how through a planned experience a child was observed 'thinking' aloud through their actions, expressions and behaviours and then demonstrated a cognitive process involving cause and effect (and their knowledge of insects was also probed). From this the practitioner is then better able to guide and scaffold the learning onto the next stage of cognitive, physical or social development.

CASE STUDY

Example from formative assessment

The early years practitioners are using these observation sheets to gather information and these were the steps that they were followed:

1 On each play area there was a packet of blank observation forms stuck to the wall.
2 If a member of staff suddenly observed something relevant about a child (opportunistic assessment) they would complete a form and then put it in the child's folder (note the example in Table 7.1 is observing four children).
3 At the end-of-the-day briefing, this information would be used to structure the next day's activities or groups (or influence the planning for the following weeks).
4 Where there was appropriate learning goals evidence, this was also recorded on the child's profile.
5 This seems a very 'manageable' process to give good formative information, which practitioners and other adults in the setting used well. It resulted in excellent teacher assessment and was not onerous as it was often (but not solely) opportunistic. The reason it was good assessment for learning was because it informed next steps, and either activities were restructured to build on the learning or particular children were 'targeted' for specific activities and focused development.

Table 7.1   Example from formative assessment

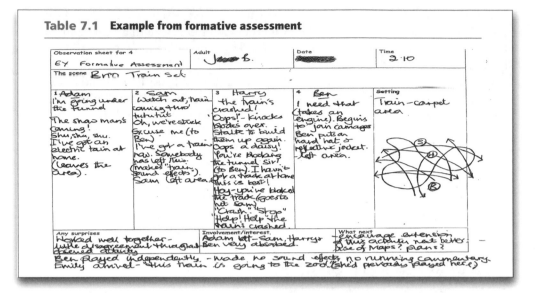

Observation sheet for 4			Adult	Date	Time
EY Formative Assessment			Jess b.	~~~~~	2.10

The scene Brio Train Set

1 Adam	2 Sam	3 Harry	4 Ben	Setting
I'm going under the tunnel. The shop man's coming! Shu, shu, shu. I've got an electric train at home. (Leaves the area).	Watch out, train coming thro' tututut Oh, we're stuck Excuse me (to Ben) I've got a train now. Somebody has left this. (makes "train" sound effects). Sam left area.	the train's crashed! 'Oops!'- knocks blocks over. Starts to build them up again. Oops a daisy! You're blocking the tunnel Sir. (to Ben). I haven't got a track at home this is best! Hey-you've blocked the track (goes to get Sam) "Crash" "Stop" "Help! Help the train's crashed.	I need that (takes an engine). Begins to join carriages Ben puts on hard hat & reflective jacket. left area.	Train -carpet area

Any surprises	Involvement/interest.	What next
Worked well together - little disagreement throughout - seemed absorbed.	Adam left- Sam, Harry & Ben very absorbed.	encourage extension of this activity next better. Use of Maps? plan s?

Ben played independently, -made no sound effects, no running commentary
Emily arrived - this train is going to the zoo (shed previous played here)

Assessment for learning requires the practitioner to design, in draft, a curriculum to cover a fixed period of time, then redesign this in a manner that enables the child to move forward in their learning appropriate to their individualised needs. Yet this process is not something an adult does to the child but a collaboration where the practitioner and the child are working together. This is when structured learning is at its most effective. It is a partnership between the learner, the practitioner and the home, yet it has to be recognised that in reality it is only the learner who can actually close the gap between what they can currently do and what is yet to be achieved, which is why capturing the child's intrinsic interests is the assessment foundation stone to build on (Sadler, 2008).

It is encouraging children to explore and using what is seen and what is happening that gives a practitioner an opportunity to assess language skills as well as problem solving and curiosity. Often children chat away to themselves as they become fully absorbed in an experience and this gives an insight into their thought process as well as their language acquisition. Consider a typical activity of 'water play' involving bubbles and different coloured water with a range of containers and funnels and tubes. Here is a wonderful opportunity for a child to show curiosity and manipulate objects to see how they work and explore what happens when different coloured water is added together. This is where assessment is a fully integrated aspect of learning.

There is a general agreement that *assessment for learning* is a term that has evolved over time and keeps evolving and building on Black and Wiliam's (1998) original statement that assessment for learning is

> all those activities undertaken by teachers, and or by their students, which provide information to be used as feedback to modify the teaching and learning activities in which they are engaged. (1998: 7)

Similarly, Cowie and Bell (1999, cited in Wiliam 2011: 37) have also stressed that formative assessment is a means of enhancing learning during the learning and it is this aspect of the assessment that has been present in quality early years settings (Sylva et al., 2004). This has now found further support in primary and secondary school settings (Shepard et al., 2005, cited in Wiliam, 2011), including a recent review by Looney (2011) for the OECD which clearly identifies formative assessment as a process to enhance learning through instruction rather, than merely an assessment tool.

It is well documented through a longitudinal study that successful early years educators use structured and unstructured play sessions to observe children's strengths in socialisation, manipulative skills and cognitive development so they can identify areas of priority for planned development (Sylva et al., 2004). It is by using the outcomes from these observations and discussions with the children that the previously planned curriculum can be restructured to give more appropriate learning experiences and opportunities (Harrison and Howard, 2009).

Why assess?

The EPPE findings (Sylva et al., 2004) clearly state the importance of quality experiences within a pre-school time period to enhance children's academic and socio-behavioural development. This extensive research identified specific factors that do, and do not, seem instrumental in good development for all children and in particularly addressing the needs of disadvantaged children. Boys were found to gain significant benefit from quality pre-school experiences in relation to girls, although both boys and girls benefit regardless of part-time or full-time experiences. It seems to be in relation to long-term duration, such as three years of quality experience as opposed to just one year.

Bailey and Drummond's (2006: 149–70) small-scale research on assessing who is at risk and why in early literacy found that while early years teachers are generally good at recognising which children are struggling with literacy skills development, they are less skilled at pinpointing the cause or how to intervene effectively. Bailey and Drummond suggest that in order to implement an effective assessment process that informs the early years pedagogy the early years team should have continuous professional development.

It is well recognised that better-quality provision has been associated with more staff being qualified and guided by qualified teachers, which is where the current guidance in the EYFS documentation can contribute to addressing the professional development needs of all persons involved in early years provision (Nutbrown, 2012).

The work undertaken by Siraj-Blatchford et al. (2002) found that when educational and social development were seen as complementary and equally important, children made all-round good progress. She identified such things as structured interventions between adults and small groups of children and sustained shared thinking opportunities to extend children's learning as beneficial because they require a deep understanding of child development. The Tickell Review (2011) draws on a wealth of evidence to state that the experiences children have in their early lives have a profound impact on their cognitive, personal and social well-being, not just while in formal education, but throughout their life. She found that those children in the lowest 20 per cent in terms of academic achievement and social well-being at the end of the Early Years Foundation Stage were six times more likely to be in the lowest 20 per cent at the end of Key Stage 1.

Central to effective learning and development is an agreed understanding that communication and language, personal, social, emotional and physical development are not just related but interconnected. It is because of this interconnection that early years providers, be they within a home setting or specialist environment, recognise that early experiences matter in terms of achieving an individual's lifelong potential (DfE, 2011: 9).

While there is still a debate about the distinct nature of development and learning, Davis et al. (2003) suggest that development is the outcome of experiences on an individual's genetic make-up and learning is an outcome of these experiences. It is the depth and breadth of understanding about how children learn, and how subject pedagogy can be structured, that underpins formative assessment. It is the means by which effective assessment can be embedded into daily practice so that a range of strategies and approaches are adapted to enable the child, and children, to become more effective and independent learners, rather than adopting an assessment approach that is bolted on as an additional activity.

The statutory requirements for assessment in EYFS

The Early Years Foundation Stage Profile (EYFSP) has had a beneficial impact on young children's attainment and achievement. There is consensus between providers and carers (Tickell, 2011), however, that there was a disproportionate amount of time spent filling out forms and other related paperwork, compared to time being available to actively engage with young children or even to observe them at play with their peers. As a result of this poor use of time the EYFS was radically streamlined on the recommendations of the Tickell Review (2011). This included reducing the number of early learning goals from 69 to 17. Other recommendations were made regarding efficiencies and greater effectiveness, such as a closer alignment with other primary health-care providers, such as the health-visitor two-year check. This now includes a summary of achievements and provides a key point for early identification of special educational and development needs. These issues can then be acted on in a timely manner and reduce the likelihood of potential problems later on in life.

In September 2012 the revised EYFS was implemented, to which all early years settings must adhere (DfE, 2012). The statutory guidance also forms part of the

Ofsted inspection and will be used to make judgements about the quality of care that providers are giving. EYFS sets out the learning and development requirements that are expected to influence the way activities and experiences should be organised for the benefit of the child's fuller development. It states that through the monitoring of the child's achievement, using the Early Learning Goals as assessment criteria, each child can be supported to attain the knowledge, skills and understanding that are considered most desirable and should normally be achieved by a child before the end of the academic year in which they are 5 years of age (DfE, 2012: 2). Requirements within EYFS provide 'best fit' judgements about typical development for age (Early Education/DfE, 2012: 3) and it is this baseline matching that can act as an early warning indicator should a child's progress appear slower than expected.

The documentation is based on a premise that children will grow and develop quickly if nurtured and supported in a manner that meets their physical, emotional and cognitive needs. EYFS acknowledges the unique nature of the child (Unique Child) and the complex contributing factors for success between the people and environments (Enabling Environments) that are likely to lead to a child's successful learning and development. It identifies seven areas of learning and development, which includes Early Learning Goals. In support of achieving successful outcomes it clearly identifies the details about the assessment requirements at different stages between the ages of 0 and 5 years of age as well as stating how a child's progress should be discussed with parents and or carers. Formal reporting to parents is required at two key points: first between 24 and 36 months of age (Progress Check at Age Two) and then at the end of the Foundation Stage in the EYFS Profile (EYFSP).

CASE STUDY

Assessment in my nursery class: the voice of an early years teacher

In a day nursery I supported as a Children's Centre teacher, I introduced ongoing observation and assessment and quickly linked this into the daily planning for further development. Practitioners began to look more closely at the aim of their observations and the rationale behind each observation. This had the effect of reducing the quantity of observations carried out within the setting and (yet) raising the quality dramatically. Practitioners found using these more focused observations helped them to focus on the child's needs and interests, and enabled them to plan the environment and future activities to develop children's learning further.

(Continued)

(Continued)

The case of Lewis

Lewis began his placement at the setting at 5 months old. Practitioners observed Lewis in all areas of learning and development and planned activities based on these observations. It soon became apparent to the practitioners that there was a lower than expected rate of progress in Lewis' speech development and an intervention was required. This was an ECAT setting (Every Child a Talker 2008). ECAT is a programme that has been designed and applied in several early years settings to support practitioners, parents and children with their communication and language skills in a supportive, stimulating environment in which children can enjoy exploring learning language.

All the practitioners had sound knowledge of language development and made this a focus in all of Lewis' activities. As he reached 2 years old and progressed into the toddler room, his gaps in speech sounds became more pronounced. Lewis' other areas of language development, such as his understanding of language, attention and most of his social skills, were all within the norms for his age range. These concerns were shared with his parents and together a formal 'concern form' was completed, in line with the setting's special educational needs (SEN) policy, and a series of activities were suggested for them to use at home with Lewis. At the SEN review it was decided to make an individual educational plan (IEP) to address Lewis' delay in language development. This included detailed plans for use in the nursery setting and at home. Although Lewis was only just approaching his second birthday his parents and the practitioners decided this was the best time to complete the Two Year Progress Check at Age Two as his parents were keen to approach other professionals for further support and guidance.

The practitioners found that the detailed observations and assessments they already had in Lewis' profile folder made completing the progress check a simple task; as all the information was already there and it was just a case of bringing it all together. Lewis' parents also found the assessment clear and easy to understand and commented that they liked the fact that it also celebrated his achievements. His mother stated that the approach would better inform the two-year-old health check as she had a detailed report backing up her concerns from the early years professionals who see Lewis daily, in a relaxed and familiar environment. She had been worried that his lack of speech when he met the health visitor could have been attributed to the fact that he was shy and reluctant to talk to a stranger. After completing the check, the professional practitioners were able to use the information to inform future planning in a more focused way to meet Lewis' specific needs. It also provided an efficient and effective means of sharing the information with other professionals, such as the speech and language therapists, if they needed to become involved.

Table 7.2   Lewis' progress check at age 2

Two-year Progress Check

Learning and Development Summary

Name: Lewis (age 2 years)

A Child Learning	Personal, Social and Emotional Development

A Child Learning

- **Playing and exploring:**

Finding out and exploring; playing with what they know; being willing to 'have a go'

- **Active Learning**

Being involved and concentrating; enjoying achieving what they set out to do; keeping on trying

- **Creating and thinking critically**

Having their own ideas; making links; choosing ways to do things

Lewis is playing and exploring at the engagement stage He is representing experiences through play and pretending objects are things from his experience

Personal, Social and Emotional Development

Self-confidence and self-awareness; making relationships; managing feelings and behaviour

Lewis is confident and feels secure when coming into the setting. He is confident to leave his parents. He shows staff what he wants to do and goes freely to staff when he wants something. Lewis plays alongside other children and makes sounds and gestures to communicate with adults and other children. Lewis is confident to follow nursery routines and shares toys most of the time though he does need reminding sometimes and shows others how to use toys. Lewis washes his hands when prompted and enjoys brushing his teeth after meal times. Lewis enjoys circle time and gets excited when he makes sounds of the colours, etc.

Self-confidence and Self-awareness

0–11	8–20	16–26	**22–36**	30–50	40–60+

Making relationships

0–11	8–20	16–26	**22–36**	30–50	40–60+

Managing feelings and behaviour

0–11	8–20	16–26	**22–36**	30–50	40–60+

Communication and Language

Listening and attention; understanding; speaking

Lewis does not have much speech and communicates through sounds and gestures. He is beginning to try to make the sounds of words for colours, etc. and is copying mouth movements. Lewis makes sounds and babbles. He enjoys joining in with songs, rhymes and again moves his mouth and tries to copy sounds. He also enjoys listening to stories and tries to join in with the other children, i.e. when making animal sounds. Lewis can understand and follow simple instructions.

Physical Development

Moving and handling; health and self-care

Lewis uses his whole body to get where he wants to be. He explores the outdoor environment with confidence and independence. He climbs up the climbing frame with confidence and can use all the bikes, etc. Lewis enjoys running around the garden and playing games. Lewis is also able to use his cutlery at meal times unaided and uses a cup with little spillage. Lewis is in nappies but will come to a member of staff when soiled. Lewis likes to run around but also comes to lie down after lunch and goes straight to sleep without any help.

Listening and attention

0–11	8–20	**16–26**	22–36	30–50	40–60+

Moving and handling

0–11	8–20	16–26	22–36	30–50	40–60+

Understanding

0–11	8–20	**16–26**	22–36	30–50	40–60+

Health and self-care

0–11	8–20	16–26	22–36	30–50	40–60+

Speaking

0–11	8–20	**16–26**	22–36	30–50	40–60+

Next steps to support his development:

An individual education plan has been put into place identifying targets to support Lewis' speech which can be done at nursery and at home:

- Modelling speech and words
- Naming objects and people
- Encouraging Lewis to say names rather than make noises and gestures

Parents' comments:

We agree with the summary of Lewis' profile and we will work with his key person and the nursery to help Lewis at home in these areas.

Source: Taken and modified from www.ealrylearningconsultancy.co.uk

The role of partnership in assessment

The case study above reiterates the key role of practitioners' support in assessing and structuring a child's learning and development. Working with the family and seeking the child's views, valuing their opinions and valuing the observations of practitioners is an important part of creating a rich picture of the child's capabilities. It is through observation of the child at play in isolation or interacting with their peers, and their engagement and response to adults' questions, that future learning opportunities can be structured. It is in collaboration with parents and carers that individual needs can be understood, such as identifying what the child likes doing and what they do not like doing. By asking about the sort of things that engage the child for sustained periods of time it is possible to understand and then build on the child's thinking and behaviours and attitudes in a constructive and beneficial way. This valuable information and engagement with parents, carers and others, including specialists such as health visitors, educational psychologists and social workers, is the collaborative assessment process that helps with the early identification of additional needs. For this information to be effective it has to be acted upon, otherwise it is just a summative measure at a certain point in time. This is the fundamental difference between formative and summative assessment. In the case of the Early Learning Goals this is an opportunity for formative observations to be used as evidence to make a summative statement. It is also a means of tracking the rate of progress over time and in this way informing practice as part of the process.

Organising and planning for assessment

Assessment is arguably the most useful tool in organising and planning early years practice (McClennan and Katz, 1992; Carr, 2001; Draper and Duffy, 2001; Drummond, 2003; Driscoll and Rudge, 2005; Elfer, 2005). In early years settings a number of different techniques of assessing and recording children's progress are used before this information is translated into the formal statutory requirement of EYFS. The most common ways of gathering information on children to assess their progress are the Learning Stories Pedagogical Documentation and the Ferre Laevers Scales of Involvement and Well-being.

Learning stories

Carr (1998, 1999, 2001; Car and Lee, 2012) has introduced *learning stories* as a means of ongoing observation and assessment in early years education and care. This process reflects the principles of the Te Whãriki Curriculum in New Zealand. As will be discussed in detail in Chapter 8, learning stories, or learning journeys, focus on documenting learning episodes in children's everyday worlds with a view to extending these episodes and furthering children's development. Early years practitioners gather information (stories) over time for either each child or for a group of children; a learning story becomes a window into understanding children's learning and development. These learning stories inform planning, help early years practitioners to share information with the parents and, most importantly, become a useful tool with which to discuss this planning with the children. Similarly to the EYFSP, learning stories are a way of communicating with children and parents, while being less formal and with no descriptive assessment scales. Learning stories are used widely in early years settings to collect information on individual children and then to inform the individual profiles. The next chapter offers a number of examples of how learning stories or journeys are used in early years settings.

Laevers Scales of Involvement and Well-being

Ferre Laevers at the University of Leuven introduced the *Scales of Involvement and Well-being* in 1976. The instrument was developed at the Research Centre for Experiential Education (Leuven University, Belgium). The aim is that these scales will measure and monitor children's involvement and engagement in activities as well as their well-being. Such an approach relies on the constant monitoring of children and helps practitioners to identify children who need extra care. As EYFS aims to help children to achieve the five outcomes of the Every Child Matters policy, the scales are becoming popular as they focus on children's well-being and involvement, and of course help to identify any additional needs for an early intervention. The scales aim to:

1 serve as a tool for self-assessment by early years settings
2 focus on quality, taking into consideration the child and its experience of the care environment
3 achieve appropriateness for the wide range of early years education and care.
   (Research Centre for Education, Leuven University, 2005)

After the scales have collected information about children through observations, early years practitioners can identify strengths and weaknesses. The results from the scales will enable practitioners to create the best possible conditions for children to develop. There are three steps in the process:

* Step 1 – assessment of the actual levels of well-being and involvement
* Step 2 – analysis of observations
* Step 3 – selection and implementation of actions to improve quality of practice in the early years setting.

Laevers (2005: 5) claims that this approach to the assessment of children can lead to significant changes in the setting as well as in the professional development of early years practitioners: 'Through the process [the practitioners] learn to take the perspective of the child in their approach and because of this to create optimal conditions for the social, emotional and cognitive development of the children.'

As EYFS suggests, assessment scales are provided for each area of development, thus the reasons for the popularity of the Laevers scales can be understood.

Pedagogical documentation

Reggio Emilia is an alternative and flexible pedagogical approach to a pre-defined and pre-described curriculum in which children, parents and teachers are working together through a variety of activities. Children express their ideas and lead the activities according to their interests. One of the main questions about the Reggio approach concerns the way in which children's 'making meaning' can be assessed. Instead of traditional assessment methods, such as scales, Reggio suggests, similarly to the Te Whāriki approach of learning stories, pedagogical documentation as an effective way of recording children's learning and development.

The concept of pedagogical documentation in Reggio is a way of collecting children's experiences during activities through materials, photographs, videos, notes and audio recordings. This information becomes visible to others (children and parents) through exhibits, DVDs, books, posters and pamphlets. The practitioners act as recorders/documenters for the children, helping them to revisit their actions and self-assess their own learning. In the Reggio setting documentation is an integral part of the procedure and it aims for a pedagogy in which children are listened to.

Rinaldi (2005: 23) stresses two important aspects of documenting children's activities:

1   [Documentation] makes visible the nature of the learning process and strategies used by each child, and makes the subjective and intersubjective process a common parsimony.

2   It enables reading, revisiting and assessment in time and in space and the actions become an integral part of the knowledge-building process.

Similarly to learning stories, the narrative of the documentation can be translated into assessment scales in order to create the profile of each child, as is statutory in EYFS. This is a creative and advocacy approach to children's assessment that can enable not only practitioners, but also children and parents to participate in the process.

The role of observation

As has been shown, there are different approaches to children's assessment. No matter which approach (or mixture of approaches) early years settings adopt, observations are central to all of them, as was shown in Chapter 6. There are a number of observation techniques available in early years education and care (participant observation, narratives, checklists, diagrammatic, sampling and media techniques) that can be used to record children's learning and development.

The systematic collection of information about children's learning and development in either a formative or a summative way is important, as it helps practitioners to:

- collect and gather evidence that can offer an accurate picture of children, their learning and development
- understand the reasons behind children's behaviour in certain situations
- recognise stages in child development
- inform planning and assessment
- provide opportunities for collaboration with parents and other services
- find out about children as individuals
- monitor progress
- inform curriculum planning
- enable practitioners to evaluate their practice
- provide a focus for discussion and improvement. (Palaiologou, 2012)

CASE STUDY

Assessment in my Reception class: the voice of an early years teacher

Assessing for my headteacher

For the first six weeks, focus in a Foundation Stage 1 class is very much on gathering on-entry evidence for the new children. The evidence is needed to give a baseline, to show where children's particular strengths and talents lie, to show what children enjoy and also to make explicit where children lack understanding. This helps to give a direction to the planning for the cohort for the subsequent weeks. Evidence is gathered from observations of children at play, both participatory and non-participatory, and should, according to EYFS, be collected when watching spontaneous and independent play, rather than when the children are engaging in an adult-initiated activity. This provides very rich data and teachers are discouraged from using checklists and from using the Development Matters document as a checklist. It is essential that the children's learning environment reflects all areas of learning, and there are numerous and varied activities on offer for the children to 'self-select'. The choices include activities that encourage dialogue between pupils as well as activities that

(Continued)

(Continued)

allow children to utilise their imaginations and creativity. This gives the children an opportunity to 'showcase' their talents and gives me, the observing practitioner, the opportunities I need to assess their current capabilities.

Pupil Progress Meetings are held at the end of each term. In preparation for this meeting I look at all of the observational evidence I have gathered. Each piece of evidence is given a level (age and stage) and from these pieces of evidence, I am able to assess within which band each child is working for each area of learning as a best-fit guide. If, for example, a child is consistently showing evidence of working within 30–50 months for problem-solving reasoning and numeracy then this is where I will assess the child as working. Once I have plotted each child's area of learning and each age and stage into a table, this gives me a clearer picture of all the children's attainment within my class.

The pupil-progress meeting held with my headteacher is to discuss not only progress, but attainment gaps and my plans for closing any gaps. This can be particularly challenging in FS1 (nursery-aged children) where the flexible offer means that different children may be at the setting for different sessions and days. During these meetings my headteacher will look at my data, and my analysis of each area, which will report possible relationships and reasons for low attainment, for example special educational needs, premature birth, an obvious lack of experiences in a child's first three years or vulnerable groups such as 'looked after' children.

My experience of assessing for Ofsted

When an Ofsted inspector visits an early years setting, they will be interested in seeing evidence of the progression of the children in your care. They will look at the on-entry data and current data to see what the value added aspects are. This relates to the progression that the children have made since they began attending the setting. The EYFS *Development Matters* document does make this challenging for the early years teacher, due to the wide range of differences within an overall 'normal' band of expectation. For example, a child may be working within the 30–50 months band for communication and language at the end of the Spring term and may still appear to be working within this band at the end of the Summer term. This does not mean to say that the child has made no progression, but progress has remained within the same band rather than the next phase. This is why it is important to ensure that all observation evidence within my files have sufficient levelled annotations so it is possible for another professional person, such as an Ofsted inspector, to see and understand the evidence in relation to progression over time.

Ofsted will also want to see evidence of the practitioner's recognition of gaps in learning along with the plans for intervention to address the next steps in

successful learning. In short, Ofsted will want to see a rigorous approach to assessment with tight tracking, clear evidence of progression and explicit verification that you, the teacher, are responsive to the needs of the individual child.

My experience of assessment and parents

Assessment information should always be shared with the parents/carers so that they understand and can support the child as best they can. Our observation files are available to parents at all times and it is this openness that helps provide continuity between home and school and enhances the partnership.

Often, parents want to help their children to reach their next stage of development, but are not sure how to, or lack the confidence to believe they are doing a good job already. To forge partnerships between home and school, I find it useful to hold 'stay and read' sessions. This is where parents are invited to stay during a literacy activity. They are able to see me teaching literacy, see how letter sounds are made and watch how I use focused praise to motivate. The parents can then copy my approach at home and support their child in literacy and a love of reading. These sessions are also a useful way to help parents with ideas for literacy-based activities and links to useful websites. I also hold 'Let's Talk About Learning' meetings where the child and the parent are invited to talk about strengths and interests and consider good ways of addressing weaker areas of learning. The child is encouraged to talk about what excites them and what they like best about coming to the setting and together we can discuss and agree a 'next step'. The children are actively involved in their own review and assessment. This approach also allows me as the teacher to encourage the child to actively think about what they promised in our meeting. For example, I had a very quiet child whose parent assured me that there was definitely a big voice in there! The child promised that during our circle times they would use their 'big voice' to contribute to our circle. A few reminders later and the child was consistently speaking clearly and forming confident, coherent sentences.

My perspective on assessing for the receiving teacher

As children move from FS1 to FS2, their new teacher will want to know who has received interventions, if there are any children with special educational needs, including those considered as gifted and talented, as well as those children with behavioural or emotional issues. Using annotated observational evidence it is possible to support your claims with evidence gathered over time as well as a summative record in the form of the 'tracker'. The tracker will give the new teacher an overview of different attainment

(Continued)

(Continued)

groups and areas of interest groupings, and an insight into current attainment. The introduction of the EYFS (2012) has given this transition point continuity as the children will continue to be assessed according to ages and stages through FS2 to the end of their Foundation Stage years.

And my own thoughts: I feel my priority should be to assess for the child, but as it is at the moment I do not have time to assess for my child.

Summary

This chapter focused on the assessment in early years education and care with a focus on the requirements of EYFS. Assessment is important in order to understand children's learning and development. Although it is welcomed, the two-stage assessment process within EYFS which includes the Progress Check at Age Two and the EYFS Profile at the end of the Foundation Stage year, does raise some concerns. The focus of these assessments appear to be on 'school readiness' as an overall aim of early years education and care rather than what is the best development progress for that individual child. A concern has been that this assessment information should support learning not drive a narrow curriculum by being limited to 'school readiness'. The EYFS Profile is intended to bring together a holistic picture of children's interests, ways of learning and their development. This collated information is very important in relation to effective transitions and enhancing learning potential through planned experiences (as will be discussed in Chapter 9). It can be a tool for all those involved in a child's education and care to discuss and celebrate a child's achievements, their rate of progress and their enjoyment and engagement in their learning and socialisation with their peers as well as adults.

Key points to remember

- Formative assessment is central to early years education and care in order to understand children's achievements and progress in learning and development.

- Assessment of children should become the starting point of planning activities and the environment around the children.

- Assessment of children should include parents' 'perspectives' of their children and it should be in dialogue with children's parents.

- There are two key types of assessment, summative and formative, and both need to take place in early years settings.

- Assessment is supported by conversations between parents/carers and early years practitioners.
- Observation of children is a key assessment tool.

Points for discussion

- What is the main difference between summative assessment and formative assessment in an early years setting?
- Think of at least two efficient and effective ways of assessing a child's social skills, physical and cognitive capabilities.
- How might a practitioner in an early years setting capture evidence for summative assessment?

★ Reflective tasks

- Reflect on the case study from the Reception-class teacher and discuss why there is not time to assess for the child first and foremost.
- Reflect on the EYFS assessment process and rate children's participation in their own assessment process.
- Reflect on the EYFS assessment processes and consider whether the impetus of the assessment is for developing the individual child or providing a record for the system.

Further reading

Carr, M. and Lee, W. (2012) *Learning Stories*. London: Sage.
Carr, M. (2001) *Assessment in Early Childhood Settings*. London: Sage.
Drummond, M.J. (2003) *Assessing Children's Learning*, 2nd edn. London: David Fulton.
Fiore, L. (2012) *Assessment of Young Children: A Collaborative Approach*. London: Routledge.

Useful websites

For more information on the Progress Check at Age Two visit: www.education.gov.uk/ childrenandyoungpeople/earlylearningandchildcare/a00191829/government-sets-out-reform-of-early-learning-and-childrens-centres

To gain **free access** to selected SAGE journal articles related to key topics in this chapter visit: www.sagepub.co.uk/Palaiologou2e

Using Learning Stories in the Early Years Foundation Stage

David Coates and Wendy Thompson

Chapter roadmap

The previous two chapters explained the role of observation and assessment requirements in EYFS. Learning stories were mentioned as having become a useful tool in gathering information to inform planning and assessment in the early years environment. This chapter aims to discuss the use of learning stories as a tool for observing and assessing children in EYFS.

This chapter aims to help you to:

- indicate how provision based on children's interests and motivations can be analysed and used to enhance children's learning

- illustrate how learning stories may be used to record progress within the Early Years Foundation Stage

- encourage analysis and reflection of children's learning

- consider the significant role of the early years practitioner in facilitating children's learning.

What are learning stories?

Learning stories can be described as approaches to observational assessments that explain the 'narrative' of children's learning. The 'narrative' in this context, taken from a social constructivist perspective, describes and analyses children's active involvement in activities (Carr, 2001). Learning stories allow practitioners to use multimedia tools to make learning visible, for example through the use of digital cameras.

In recording development and progress, relationships and actions become significant and illustrative of the progression in children's learning. The 'actions' described by Carr (2001) demonstrate children's readiness for learning through dispositions that include: children taking an interest; being involved; persisting with difficulty or uncertainty; communicating with others; and taking responsibility (see Table 8.1). Practitioners subsequently analyse the strategies applied by children, consider their levels of motivation and observe their abilities to recognise, select, edit, respond to or resist learning opportunities. Assessment, in this context, becomes more than just a record of the individual child's isolated skills and structured observation is a key to success (Anning et al., 2004: 73).

How can learning stories be used?

Practitioners working within play contexts search for and construct learning opportunities that will lead to more meaningful understanding and development (Anning and Edwards, 2006: 52). Carr (2001) describes this process as encompassing four elements of effective practice:

- describing
- documenting
- discussing
- deciding upon the next steps.

This process also avoids concentration on deficit models of children's development and learning as the learning story seeks to understand what a child *can do* and is, therefore, a more positive affirmation of his/her capabilities than are some forms of assessment (for example, standardised testing).

Stories are complex as they are collected in natural contexts and include reference to the environment in which the learning takes place, including the respective roles of peers and adults working within the same environment or activity (Anning et al., 2004: 73). They are particularly focused on what makes sense to the child. Broadhead (2001) noted that as children get older they show enhanced levels of mutual understanding, they begin to see other children as intentional agents and begin to accommodate their ideas. This supports the concept of a developed sense of 'memory in action' (Bruner, 1983) which highlights the complex nature of children's learning to adapt and respond within unfolding play scenarios.

This process of formative assessment is embedded within the statutory framework setting out the legal requirements for Learning, Development and Welfare of the 0–5 age

Table 8.1   Examples of how learning stories are recorded (adapted from Carr, 2001)

DATE: AREA OF PLAY ENVIRONMENT: CHILDREN INVOLVED:		
KEY DISPOSITION (Carr, 2001)	LEARNING STORY OBSERVATION	AREAS OF LEARNING (DCSF, 2008)
Taking an interest Finding an interesting topic, activity or role. Recognising the familiar, enjoying the unfamiliar. Coping with change.		Select from: Personal, Social and Emotional Development; Communication, Language and Literacy; Problem Solving, Reasoning and Numeracy; Knowledge and Understanding of the World; Creative Development; Physical Development.
Being involved Paying attention for a sustained period. Feeling safe, trusting others. Being playful with others or materials.		
Persisting with difficulty Setting and choosing difficult tasks. Using a range of strategies to solve problems when stuck.		
Expressing an idea or a feeling – in a range of specific ways. For example; oral language, gesture, music, art.		
Taking responsibility – responding to others, to stories and imagined events, ensuring that things are fair, self-evaluating and helping others.		
HOW DID PRACTITIONER/S FACILITATE LEARNING?	CHILDREN'S COMMENTS ABOUT THE ASSESSMENT	
WHAT LEARNING DID WE THINK TAKE PLACE? (Discussions with other practitioners if necessary)	HOW TO BUILD ON THE INTEREST/NEXT STEPS? (Discussions with other practitioners if necessary)	

phase in England, i.e. the EYFS (DfE, 2012). As explained in Chapter 7, the EYFS documents include guidance for assessment and monitoring standards to ensure the starting point is the 'unique child'.

Within EYFS, Observation, Assessment and Planning provides examples of describing and documenting in such ways as noting children's responses in different situations, as part of the daily routine, and finding out about their needs, what they are interested in and what they can do. This approach complements the methods used in documenting learning stories. The EYFS guidance continues with recommending analysis of the observations to help plan what next for individuals and groups of children. Practitioners are advised to create records that '[observe] what children can do to help identify where the child may be in their own development pathway' (DfE, 2012: 3) and it is also advised the early years practitioners ensure that the views of parents and practitioners are reflected in children's records (DfE, 2012).

The discussions between children and their peers and between children and practitioners form an integral part of learning stories. When documented they may be used as a tool for engagement in talk with both the children and their parents/carers. Examples of the strategies employed by practitioners, while engaging with children, involve using recall and drawing out patterns and connections in order to enhance children's learning. Thus, as Moss (2004) highlights, the practitioner is a 'co-constructor of knowledge' and values together with children; she/he is a cultured and curious person, which means an inveterate border crosser; and she/he is a researcher, with an enquiring and critical mind (Moss, 2004).

The learning story provides positive affirmation of children's capabilities as subtle actions and interactions are recorded and noted. The decision making stems from this analytical approach, which helps move forward children's thinking (Carr, 2001). This involves processes aimed at different levels. There is the immediate feedback given to children while they are engaged in activities; there is the process of thinking about the next stage in their learning, which will include sharing the results of observation with other practitioners and parents; finally, there is the modification to the learning environment to ensure children remain motivated and engaged. As Seifert (2006) emphasises, it is not sufficient simply to know or observe the behaviour of the children; it is what the practitioner does to ensure interest is sustained that is important. 'To call myself a teacher of the young, I must connect with them somehow, which means interacting, relating, and touching their lives in valuable ways' (Seifert, 2006: 9).

Personalised active learning

EYFS places emphasis on 'active learning', which occurs when children engage with people, materials, objects, ideas or events, and test things out and solve problems (DfE, 2012: 4). Personalised learning and the consideration of children's involvement in their learning, as well as the nature and quality of adult and peer interaction in children's learning, is also emphasised. A number of studies that examined play and learning indicated that children are capable of developing structured and purposeful play upon which educators can base future planning (Wood and Bennett, 2000). Moyles (2005: 9) describes the process of learning through play as providing opportunity 'for learning to live with not knowing' and allowing for 'independence in thought and action' where children are operating in an open frame of mind and are engaging in 'what if' situations. In this sense play is a process and not an activity in its own right (Smidt, 2006). This process allows children to create alternatives to reality, producing new combinations described by Bruner as 'memory in action' (Bruner, 1983).

The developmental potential of play can be maximised where children perceive the activity as play and subsequently approach it in a playful manner. Studies showed that children chose to distinguish play from other activities and to refer to certain indicative characteristics such as play being fun, noisy and spontaneous, occurring on the floor rather than at a table and also being free from rules (Howard, 2002; Howard et al., 2006; Westcott and Howard, 2007). The value of play as a learning medium in relation to enthusiasm, motivation, creativity and willingness to participate is inextricably linked to the way in which the player perceives the activity (Moyles, 1989). Playfulness is an internal state comprising of the personal qualities that children bring to an activity. It is important, therefore, to understand what children believe to be play, how such perceptions may have developed and how feelings of playfulness can be evoked. Wiltz and Klein (2001) found that regardless of classroom quality, self-selection and choice are important determinants of a child's perception of an activity as play. Children in a more teacher-directed and structured setting separated play from learning, describing teacher-directed activities as learning, and self-initiated activity as play and consequently not as learning (Howard et al., 2006). It could be argued that children are more intrinsically motivated and thus sustain interest and involvement when they perceive an activity as play and 'not work'. Children who are used to teacher involvement in play activity will be more likely to accept adult involvement and retain a sense of playfulness. This is important if practitioners are to be accepted as 'committed co-players' to facilitate learning (Rich, 2002). It is the role of the practitioner to recognise, intervene and facilitate where and when it is appropriate and 'encourage play that is emotionally, intellectually, physically and socially challenging' (QCA/DfEE, 2000: 5).

According to EYFS, children need sensitive, knowledgeable adults who know when and how to engage their interests and how to offer support at appropriate times. The role of the practitioner is considered crucial in:

- supporting children in their learning through playing and exploring, active learning and creating and thinking critically;
- helping children to develop in the context of relationships and the environment around them;
- respecting the unique context of each child and their family and reflecting individual communities and cultures. (Early Education/DfE, 2012: 4)

Appropriateness is key in this respect, as imposing these roles in an insensitive manner could destroy the play scenario. Practitioners need to focus on helping children to become resilient learners who enjoy learning and feel that they are able to succeed (Anning and Edwards, 2006: 54). They should create the conditions for learning through play (Members of the British Educational Research Association Early Years Special Interest Group, 2003).

CASE STUDY

Block play in the construction area (based on discussions with other practitioners)

Five children aged 4 years were involved – Alex, Harry, Chloe, Darshan and James.

The block play area was very popular and after practitioners' observations and discussions it was decided that the five children above often led the play. Other children entered the area and joined in at regular intervals, but the group of five showed sustained high levels of involvement, displayed sophisticated personal and social skills, negotiating for equipment, listening to others' points of view, and were engaged in problem solving. They also seemed very willing to take risks and failure in their stride and accepted it as a new challenge when things did not happen as they expected.

The children began their play by using large pieces of canvas placed on the floor that they decided would make a road. Initially it curled up at the corners, as it had been rolled up for storage. Alex immediately turned it over to make it lie flat.

Alex: Let's make a ramp. What do we need for a ramp?
       They all look around.
Harry: I know. This [*pointing to a basket*].

The children lifted the end of the canvas and placed a basket underneath the end, which made it slope for the cars to travel down. They then proceeded to play with the cars.

The next day the group made a replica of the model placing it at a higher level on top of a cupboard. Harry placed a long brick onto the cupboard and added a cylinder into the construction and rolled a car along to see what happened. The children looked carefully at the construction and then began to make minor adjustments to the height. Each time they made an adjustment they tried out the car and then adjusted it again until they felt happy with it.

Darshan: It's a big ramp.

They then decided to add a basket to the end of the construction to catch the car that fell out. The whole group felt happy with this new addition and began to take turns to roll the car down the ramp. They talked about fast, slow and how well

(Continued)

(Continued)

it worked. Throughout the sessions all of the children showed a sustained high involvement and excellent problem-solving skills.

Harry asked if they could look for something else to make a ramp. When a basket top was suggested Harry tried it:

Harry: It's no good. It's too rough. The cars don't move down it.

One of the practitioners took him to the resource room with Alex and James to find a suitable resource.

Harry found some pieces of thick carpet and brought them back to the classroom. He then tested them out:

Harry: It's no good. It's not strong.

The practitioners felt at this point that the challenge of finding the right material was a vital part of the learning process and knew the children were confident enough to try to discuss outcomes. Harry and James tested it independently and the material bent under weight.

The rectangular structure had a small opening housing the trucks and cars. The children began to discuss how to make a door for the cars to get in and out. Harry and Chloe spent long periods adjusting the bricks to allow the 'door' to open without the rest of the building falling apart. They eventually achieved this through a sustained period of trial and error and testing out their ideas.

Decisions made by practitioners

Early years practitioners working with children in the nursery school attempted to identify children's interests and motivations through careful observation and documentation. Practitioners felt that observation of the area and the dynamics of the group would be crucial to knowing how to proceed and support learning. The practitioners decided that daily discussions throughout the story would be the most significant factor in extending learning and that it was vital that the play be analysed before rushing to intervene. They accepted that the play could not be conceptually controlled.

> If children's perceptions of play are influenced by experience, the communication of the opportunities for learning in both child-initiated and teacher-directed activities, and teacher participation in a wide range of classroom activities could lead to adult acceptance during play. (Howard, 2002: 500)

For the children, adult involvement did not mean 'work' as they were used to practitioners being present and involved in their activities. By considering the children's perspectives the practitioners were able to motivate the children's learning by providing enjoyable and challenging experiences that the children believed were play.

Analysis of the learning story

The play experience allowed the children to explore and experiment, to discover the dynamics of cause and effect, to build imaginary worlds, to rehearse new roles and to practise new skills (Leyden, 1998). As Vygotsky (1978) noted, the play provided the children with an important mental system allowing them to think and act in more complex ways. The pretend play was social and it was essential that children agreed on the reference of pretence. The sharing of focus came about through inter-subjectivity (Smidt, 2006: 53). The 'road' made of canvas involved all children being engaged in an extremely complex cognitive act of shared meaning making.

Preparing a relevant environment implies that choices are being made by practitioners. The play-based provision may cause children to react to environmental stimuli in different and perhaps unexpected ways. Through play children can develop their higher-level thinking skills and problem solving abilities, while monotonous repetitious play, which is simply 'hands-on' and not 'brain-on' (Wood and Attfield, 1996) can offer little cognitive challenge for children. The practitioners in the nursery school picked up on and developed this child-initiated activity with the purpose of deepening children's thinking about what they were doing (Siraj-Blatchford and Sylva, 2004). It is the role of the practitioner to recognise, intervene and facilitate where and when it is appropriate, in order to promote challenging play experiences. Children, therefore, learn through play when they are in a 'healthy, safe and secure [environment], when their individual needs are met, and when they have positive relationships with the adults caring for them' (DfE, 2012: 13). In the nursery school the practitioners were seen and accepted by the children as 'committed co-workers' (Rich, 2002). A sense of playfulness was therefore maintained when the practitioners offered advice and discussed ideas with the children.

CASE STUDY

Outdoor play (based on discussions with other practitioners)

During this period the children had also been transferring their skills to outside play. They used large crates to make enclosures. Chloe displayed good spatial awareness of the amount of space needed and good problem-solving skills working out how to connect the crates.

In mark making, Alex, Harry and Chloe were also fitting shapes together to make objects and people, making cars, tractors and houses, and drawing people to put in them.

Decisions made by practitioners

An environment where open-ended play is valued and where there is a rich range of resources available to challenge children's thinking is important in this context. *Development Matters in the Early Years Foundation Stage* (Early Education/DfE, 2012) suggests the environment should allow children to explore, develop and be involved in learning experiences in order to help them make sense of the world.

The environment should include a balance and variety of experiences, which are multi-sensory and can be delivered with differentiated learning intentions for children, dependent on their needs. The provision of necessary time for sustained play and exploration is also considered an essential environmental attribute in the support of nursery children. The revised EYFS indicates how the environment should be developed to meet the needs of all children when it states:

> The ways in which the child engages with other people and their environment–playing and exploring, active learning and creating and thinking critically underpin learning and development across all areas and support the child to remain an effective and motivated learner. (Early Education/DfE, 2012: 4)

The skill lies in providing an environment resourced with challenge in mind and incorporating the facility to encourage sustained play and involvement.

The practitioners allowed the children's ideas to emerge as the children were given the freedom to explore boundaries in an unrestricted manner (DfES, 2006b) and cultivate their interests extensively and in depth. They utilised every opportunity to promote children's self-esteem, confidence, independence and imagination (CCEA et al., 2002: 1–2) and provided the scaffolding (Bruner, 1960) essential for children's learning. Through play children can develop their higher-level thinking skill and problem-solving ability. It is the role of the practitioner to recognise, intervene and facilitate where and when appropriate in order to promote challenging play experiences.

Sustained shared thinking

Practitioners have a crucial role as they should not simply be providing play activities, but should be supportive and interact with the children as they tackle the activities (Coates et al., 2008). The activities should be challenging and achievable and based on individual interests and experiences. One of the challenges for practitioners is to give children time to think about what they want and to express these wishes, rather than stepping in to 'help' by making decisions for them (Early Education/DfE, 2012).

Good outcomes for children are linked to adult–child interactions that involve 'sustained shared thinking', open-ended questions to extend children's thinking and formative feedback to children during activities. Practitioners should support and challenge the children's thinking by becoming involved with them in the thinking process. Sustained, shared thinking is a process that involves awareness of the child's interests and understanding, and collaboration in developing an idea or a skill (Early Education/DfE, 2012). Providing appropriate contexts for thinking, interacting with children and sharing children's small group interactions are just some of the ways in which this can be achieved. Children should be working within their zones of proximal development or ZPD (Vygotsky, 1978), characterised as the gap between learners' current or actual developmental level determined by independent problem solving and the learners' emerging or potential levels of development; these should be 'determined through problem solving under adult guidance, or in collaboration with more capable peers' (Vygotsky, 1978: 86). Vygotsky believed that whatever children can do with help today, they will be able to do by themselves tomorrow. The supporting practitioners give help to extend children's thinking and help children to make connections in learning (Early Education/DfE, 2012).

A rich learning environment offers cognitively challenging activities. It allows children to investigate in depth rather than moving from one task to another. This open-ended, flexible provision gives children the opportunities to follow their own interests, sustain their active involvement and pursue their own goals. It is generally understood that children from disadvantaged backgrounds fail to achieve as highly as their wealthier peers (Eyre, 2007).

Learning stories can help practitioners to provide a highly stimulating environment in an attempt to compensate for various deficits in the children's home circumstances (Clark, 2007). Eyre (1997) has highlighted the need for a stimulating environment to maximise a child's natural ability in the following model:

Ability + Opportunity/Support + Motivation = Achievement

The emphasis should be placed on play and oral language for the development of 'literacy, attention, concentration and memory skills, physical confidence and competence and the children's ability to build social relationships and co-operate with one another' (Walsh et al., 2006: 203). Practitioners should try to maximise learning opportunities that allow all learners to blossom. The classroom should be a place where all children can easily engage in activities and projects at their own respective level and pace (Smutny, 2001).

The environment should allow children to express elements of critical and creative thought. Such an environment would acknowledge both independence and collaboration with like-minded peers and supportive practitioners as necessary components. Opportunity to engage in open-ended exploration and knowledge-generation activities gives children the potential for autonomy and self-selection (Baczala, 2003) and is an essential feature of a nursery environment.

Group problem solving (extract from a group-learning story)

The group comprising Harry, Chloe, Darshan and James had been experimenting with masking tape and making enclosures within the home area and nearby book corner. They were very experimental, testing to see how far the tape would stretch before breaking, what it would stick to and how to cut it off at the right moment.

They needed to use scissors to achieve this and previously we had always asked the children to sit down or be still while cutting or using sharp tools. The practitioners had a discussion concerning safety versus learning opportunities. They decided to supervise the activity closely, so discussed and emphasised safe use of tools with the children concerned.

The children continued to enclose different sections of the home area each day and their methods became more sophisticated as they became more familiar with handling of materials. They used shorter pieces and stuck them together to make them stronger. There was a considerable amount of discussion and negotiation involved over equipment and the use of space and tools.

Developing the environment

The practitioners were providing an environment that supported children's learning and development. The children were confident in this environment which meant they were willing to try to 'find things out', being able to 'have a go' in a safe and secure environment where they knew that their efforts were valued (Early Education/DfE, 2012). The learning story shows how the practitioners were flexible enough to recognise and cater for the needs of every child while supporting groups in their learning.

Review of previous experience and building on interest through a learning story

The practitioners had already been discussing shapes during the week and one practitioner noticed the children were beginning to make shapes within the carpet area. With encouragement from the staff the children could discuss the properties of the shapes – sides, corners and curves. They knew how many corners and sides were needed for each shape. They also knew that circles had no corners and mastered the art of making one on the carpet. They used positional language to describe where they were putting the next shape. They began by making small shapes within the home area, working individually. James became much bolder and began to make large strips across a wide expanse of carpet. Darshan looked on at this point. He joined these up to make gridlines on the floor. He sustained a high level of involvement in this task, seeming totally unaware of the others. Staff continued to observe and noticed Darshan beginning to use long strips of the tape but at a higher level above the floor, attaching it to the bookcase and cupboard. This effectively blocked off the home corner so the children had great fun finding ways of getting through. Lots of positional vocabulary was used in this activity – for example 'over' and 'under'.

The next day Darshan and James moved to the home area and again began to experiment with the tape. Harry joined in, making waist-height gridlines across the home area. Darshan then noticed a musical instrument – a triangle, on the windowsill – and said, 'Should we stick this on?' James agreed. The tape was at waist level so they had a problem as the weight of the triangle made the tape sag on to the floor. They seemed to want the triangle suspended at waist height. At this point two practitioners had a discussion as to whether they should intervene and help the children solve the problem themselves. Given that the children were not getting frustrated and appeared just to be negotiating and discussing the problem they decided to observe only and intervene when it was thought necessary. The children persisted all afternoon using a process of trial and error in testing their theories. Eventually they discovered that sticking on extra lengths and putting the tape further over the windowsills enabled the triangle to be suspended at the height they wished. The sense of achievement was enormous.

Analysis of the learning story

This learning story is a good example of learners' advanced thinking skills and how the curriculum offered open-ended activities that 'encouraged higher level thinking skills such as analysis, synthesis, evaluation and problem solving, and promoted intellectual risk-taking' (Porter, 1999: 173). These children had the ability to create wonder from unpromising material (the masking tape). They felt safe to make mistakes and use trial and error to solve problems (Porter, 1999). The practitioners played a key role in developing the learning experience for the children, as they were happy not to be in complete control when they allowed the children to use resources in a unique manner (DfES, 2006a). They provided a high-quality environment, which provided an open use of resources, and encouraged the children to feel secure and confident to learn for themselves (DfES, 2002) and to pursue their own interests (Clark, 1997).

The practitioners allowed the children's ability to emerge as the children were given the freedom to explore boundaries in an unrestricted manner (DfES, 2006a) and to cultivate their interests extensively and in depth (Porter, 1999). They utilised every opportunity to promote children's self-esteem, confidence, independence and imagination (CCEA et al., 2002: 1–2) while providing the scaffolding essential to children's learning (Bruner, 1960).

Summary

This chapter has provided a theoretical approach to learning stories, while at the same time giving examples of how learning stories can be used in practice. Learning stories is a purposeful way of seeking to understand what children can do and their capabilities rather than using standardised assessment tools. Learning stories allow practitioners to focus on interventions that are process-oriented and not curriculum-focused (Bennett et al., 1997). The key is the formation of relationships that mutually influence both practitioners and children. The children were involved in activities that they perceived as play. Through these activities children could extend their interests, motivation and abilities (Seifert, 2006). Perceived playfulness in children can therefore be effectively supported by the skilful documentation and analysis of learning stories.

Key points to remember

Learning stories can help early years practitioners to:

- develop and monitor the application of effective pedagogy
- chart children's development and learning to ensure that the needs of all children are met
- work on flexible activities with children of similar aptitudes
- become active participants in children's play (this active involvement is crucial if the early years practitioners are to be able to analyse children's learning and development purposefully and accurately)
- identify the next steps in children's learning and development, and support them to further their development.

Points for discussion

- How do learning stories correlate with other forms of assessment and record keeping?
- Try to design and implement a learning story with a group of children. Reflect on this activity and try to investigate the advantages and disadvantages of using this technique for assessment of the children.
- Compare the learning stories with the pedagogical documentation described in Chapter 7. Can you see how these narrative documentations might help you to complete the assessment scales of EYFS?

> ⭐ **Reflective tasks**
>
> - Reflect on Ben's case study and try to explain how you will be able to follow the process of learning stories by:
>   - a describing what happens
>   - b documenting what has happened
>   - c discussing with the child, parents and early years practitioners
>   - d deciding upon the next steps.
>
> - Reflect on your own practice and try to investigate how the example in Table 8.1 can be used in your early years practice.
>
> - Reflect on how you can use learning stories as a way of involving children actively in their own learning.

Further reading

Carr, M. (2001) *Assessment in Early Childhood Settings*. London: Paul Chapman Publishing.
Carr, M. and Lee, W. (2012) *Learning Stories, Constructing Identities in Early Education*. London: Sage.
Clark, A., Moss, P. and Kjorholt, A.T. (eds) (2005) *Beyond Listening to Children: Children's Perspectives on Early Childhood Services*. Bristol: The Policy Press.

Useful websites

Learning stories:
www.aare.edu.au/99pap/pod99298.htm
Te Whāriki: He Whāriki Matauranga mo nga Mokopuna O Aotearoa. Early Childhood Education. Learning Media:
www.minedu.govt.nz/web/downloadable/dl3567_v1/ whariki.pdf

To gain **free access** to selected SAGE journal articles related to key topics in this chapter visit: www.sagepub.co.uk/Palaiologou2e

Effective Transitions into and out of the Early Years Foundation Stage

Ioanna Palaiologou

🚌 Chapter roadmap

Children's experiences when they are growing up are full of changes, such as changes in their own bodies, in family circumstances, moving house, the possible break-up of the family or loss of a family member, going from home to a playgroup or nursery and then from nursery to school. All of these changes in a child's life can be regarded as transitions. The EPPE project (Sylva et al., 2003) revealed that children do actually experience a number of these transitions during the first years of their lives, describing two types of transitions: the 'horizontal' and the 'vertical'. Traditionally, moving from home to school (a horizontal displacement) was considered as the most important transition in children's lives. It is now recognised, however, that children move vertically in their lives, for example, from home to playgroup with a member of the family; also, as it is increasingly common for both parents to work, they move from their home to that of grandparents, or to half-day nursery and half-day playgroup, or childminder care.

The statutory framework for the Early Years Foundation Stage is concerned with school readiness. It should be rather that early years settings and schools should be ready for the children by offering them rich experiences and stimulating learning environments. Within EYFS there is now an expectation that children are ready for entry to school in the key three prime areas: personal, social and emotional development, communication and language, and physical development. A progress check at the age of 2 years has also been introduced, an assessment undertaken by early years practitioners to ensure that children's learning and development needs are identified early. The summary of the progress check will be communicated if the child moves settings. There is also the EYFS Profile (EYFSP) report that aims to 'inform a dialogue between Reception and Year 1 teachers about each child's stage of development and learning needs and assist with the planning activities in Year 1' (DfE, 2012: 11).

In order to build effective and strong foundations in children's lives, however, it is important for early years practitioners to understand the importance of transitions in children's lives and try to accommodate these transitions. Early years settings and schools maintain a critical role in delivering a coherent approach both to the continuation of EYFS and when children are moving from EYFS to Key Stage 1. The smooth transitions into and out of EYFS are important for children's well-being and, therefore, for their development. This chapter deals with the key issues around transitions and discusses theoretical perspectives in trying to understand transition and its implications for early years practice.

This chapter aims to help you to:

- understand the theoretical aspects of transitions
- understand the impact of transitions upon children's well-being and development
- examine how effective transitions can be implemented into and out of EYFS.

Understanding transitions: theoretical perspectives

Through their lives children go through several transitions, such as: external transitions from home to the early years setting, from the early years setting to school, from school to childminders; or inner transitions such as their developmental growth and the changes that happen in their bodies. Transition is a complex concept as it is not only limited to changes in physical locations. Gorgorio et al. define transitions:

> not as a moment of change but as the experience of changing, of living the discontinuities between the different contexts … the construct 'transition' is, in our understanding a plural one. Transitions arise from the individual's need to live, cope and participate in different contexts, to face different challenges, to take profit from the advantages of the new situation arising from the changes. Transitions include the process of adapting to new social and cultural experiences. (2002: 24)

A number of theorists have examined the concept of transitions and their impact on children's lives. James (1980), for example, discussed transitions in relation to self and self-identity (inner transitions as psychological and developmental changes that happen in individuals), whereas Erikson (1975) discussed transitions in relation to physical moves from one place to another (external transition). Piaget (1976) linked transitions with cognitive development and claimed that transitions bring children in a disequilibrium situation that can have an impact on children's development. Vygotsky (1978) suggested that children try to construct knowledge through interacting with their social environment and are influenced by the culture, beliefs and values of this environment. In that sense transitions can be viewed as a process where children try to make sense of the world and the communities to which they belong.

Bronfenbrenner (1979) approaches transitions from an ecological perspective and defines transitions as an alteration to a person's ecological environment that brings changes in a person's self or social identity, changes in physical spaces, or both. He identified 'systems' – layers that we move into and out of throughout our lives. He claims, for example, that the microsystem (of home, playgroup, or childminder) of a child's life is rich in transitions, and these have an effect on a child's well-being. Bronfenbrenner emphasised, for the child's well-being, the need for links in between the systems:

> The developmental potential of a setting is increased as a function of the number of supportive links existing between the setting and other settings (such as the home and the family). Thus, the least favourable condition for development is one in which supplementary links are either non-supportive or completely absent, when the mesosystem is weakly linked. (1979: 215)

Consequently, for Bronfenbrenner, when a child is moving from home to an early years setting or a Reception class it represents not only a change in the layers of his/her environment, but equally a change in this child's identity from 'child' to 'pupil'. In that sense, early years practitioners should understand that in order to effectively accommodate young children they need to ensure that they provide an environment where there is emphasis on the inner changes that happens to children as well as the external changes.

Brooker (2002) extended the work of Bronfenbrenner and examined the role of culture in transitions. She researched children's, parents' and teachers' experiences in relation to social class, culture, religion, linguistics and other macro systemic factors. She found that children had to adjust to school life, classroom rituals, rules, codes of communication and interaction, but at the same time recognised that an imbalance between home and classroom life could emerge. A classic example she offers is that some parents might advise their children to do what the teacher tells them to do in the classroom, yet this can be in direct conflict with what the teacher is trying to achieve with the pupils when promoting independent and autonomous learning.

In an earlier study, Beach (1999) tried to investigate how people transfer knowledge and skills successfully from one context to another: for example, if a child is using strategies to cope with literacy skills such as synthetic phonics at school, whether this child uses the same strategies to effectively read at home or in real life situations. He argues that transitions are consequential in the sense that they have an impact on the person and his/her social context and claims that transition 'is the conscious reflective struggle to reconstruct knowledge, skills, and identity in ways that are consequential to the individual becoming someone or something new' (Beach, 1999: 30). He suggests a typology in an attempt to understand the inner and external conflicts of transitions:

- *Lateral transitions* which involve the moves between two activities (such as moving from an early years setting to Reception class). In lateral transitions the person is replacing one activity (the early years setting) with another activity (Reception class) and this move is involving progression.
- *Collateral transitions* where an individual is involved in two or more related activities and they move simultaneously to both; for example, the move from home to early years setting where children are asked to move to different activities in the setting. This type of transition does not have the element of progression.
- *Encompassing transitions* which take place within the boundaries of an activity that is itself changing and the individual has to adjust in order to participate in the activity. For example, children during role-play decide to change the play so individual children either have to adapt to the change or otherwise they will not be able to participate in the new activity that has emerged.
- *Mediational transitions* which are mainly related to educational activities. For example, we create an activity where children are playing post office and exchange money when they are not old enough to have their own money. In early years settings we can see mediational transitions with boys, for example pretending they hold guns and play war when in real life they are now allowed to have guns (especially common in Greek early years education where military service is compulsory for all young men at the age of 18), or girls where they pretend to wear shoes with high heels or to use make-up.

Beach's research on consequential transitions has a number of implications for early years education and care. Early years practitioners should create a learning environment where children effectively are prepared to move from home to the setting and vice versa, but at the same time effectively be prepared to move in between activities. The concept of mediational transitions also enables children to experience real-life situations in a safe and secure environment.

Beach's work demonstrated that transitions are a 'struggle', but at the same time he found that transitions have the potential to 'alter one's sense of self' (1999: 114). Evangelou et al. (2008) add that successful transitions can change children's sense of self through improved confidence and self-esteem. The uncertainty and anxiety that occurs from changes in one's life can be problematic, however, with Zittoun (2006) referring to problems that might occur in transitions as 'rupture'. He has described three types of rupture that can occur as a result of transitions:

- Change in cultural context that can be a result of a war, natural catastrophe such as an earthquake or flood, or a technological change that brings radical change in one's life. This can be seen to children who have experienced war or the violent death of a parent.
- Change to a person's 'sphere of experience', such as moving countries, houses or schools.
- Changes in relationships or interaction, for example a new key person, a teacher or a friend is moving to another city and leaves the nursery; or there is a divorce in the family or a bereavement with loss of a loved one.

Zittoun's idea of rupture in transitions has implication in early years settings as it can be seen that children's lives can be complex and changes do occur consequently that have an impact on children's lives. The importance of understanding the theoretical perspectives of transitions help us to understand the role of the social environment and the cultural environment, and invest in implementing 'personalised, flexible, comprehensive, multi-faceted and prolonged approaches to transition support which accommodate individual variability' (Crafter and Maunder, 2012: 16).

CASE STUDY

Saffinatu moves to England from Sierra Leone

Saffinatu is 4 years old and she has moved with her mother from Sierra Leone. Her father died from malaria and her mother then moved to England where she is now staying with extended family. Saffinatu's mother works for a domestic cleaning company so Saffinatu attends an early years setting every day from 8.00 a.m. to 3.30 p.m. When she first arrived in the setting she could not speak English and lacked confidence to interact with other children. Her key person observed that Saffinatu was demonstrating distress in the presence of other adults, such as parents of other children, and anxiety every time she was spoken to by a member of staff.

The early years practitioners in the setting worked with the Integrated Child Support Service 0–5 (ICSS) to implement a transition plan for Saffinatu.

(The Integrated Child Support Service 0–5 was previously the Early Intervention Team. For more information visit: www.southwark.gov.uk/info/200071/information_for_parents/2154/child_support_services/1).

The early years practitioners created a plan to support Saffinatu to achieve good levels in the EYFS Profile. The ICSS Transition Protocol was implemented and the Southwark Transition and Assessment Record (STAR) was developed.

Summary of Saffinatu's Transition Plan

Target 1: Encourage functional communication system with the mother and the extended family and the Team Around the Child (TAC) to reflect on what is best for Saffinatu in terms of promoting all prime areas: PSED, communication and language, and physical development.

Target 2: Create familiarity in terms of her culture, language, physical environment. Priority on building relationships with the mother and the extended family so they can be actively involved. Home visits to be encouraged.

Target 3: TAC to provide psychological support to Saffinatu and her family. Early years practitioners to create an environment where Saffinatu has a sense of belonging, with familiar items, such as toys, food and photos.

Target 4: Encourage Saffinatu to engage with activities and play indoors and outdoors.

The early years practitioners in the setting also used the Ecological and Dynamic Model *Ready Schools* framework (for more see the work of Pianta and Walsh, 1996; Pianta et al., 1999) and they developed steps of action:

Step 1: Encourage strong links with the family and the nursery with visits to home.

Step 2: Make connections with familiar contexts and if possible establish a continuation and connections in activities and other aspects of home and early years setting life.

Step 3: To give adequate time to adjust to the new environment.

The early years practitioners decided to use the Ecological and Dynamic Model of Transitions as it provides a framework that allows multi-agency collaboration, with a number of external agencies such as psychologists, social workers and health visitors working at a number of levels in the transition process.

Attachment and transitions

As will also be seen in Chapter 16, Attachment Theory as introduced by Bowlby (1969) has an impact on early years education and care. Attachment is the process where babies and parents or carers form a relationship and this leads to emotional bonds. Bowlby (1969) suggested that babies show stranger anxiety, a fear of unfamiliar persons or unfamiliar contexts, and this often causes stress to babies and young children. They also show separation anxiety at about the age of 6 months. This is a fear of being separated from care-givers (Vondra and Barnett, 1999). Babies appear to be upset when their parents or carers are leaving them and this can again cause distress. Early years practitioners who work with babies and toddlers are familiar with the signs of a child being distressed when the child initially arrives in the unfamiliar early years setting. Early years practitioners find the first few weeks in the early years settings the most difficult and challenging for children, who are anxious, distressed and disturbed until they settle down.

The dominant theory in the emotional development of children is that proposed by Bowlby (1960, 1969, 1973, 1980, 1986, 1999, 2005) and Ainsworth (Ainsworth, 1969, 1979, 1985, 1989; Ainsworth and Bell, 1970; Ainsworth and Bowlby, 1991; Ainsworth et al., 1971a, 1971b, 1978) regarding 'attachment'. All these studies proposed that when babies are born they are 'pre-programmed' to form close relationships with the mother/carer. This bond is attachment. The ideas of Bowlby and Ainsworth have influenced the way mother–child and carer–child relationships are perceived. Bowlby and Ainsworth have each described in detail the stages of attachment and how the formation of the relationship between the mother (or carer) and the baby takes place. They have also discussed the consequences of the separation of the child from the mother/carer.

Bowlby (1969) proposed four main stages in the development of attachment. First, he claims that when babies are born and at about the age of 2 months they are in an 'orientation' stage, where the infant shows orientation to social stimuli such as grasping, smiling and babbling. The babies will stop crying when they are picked up or when they see a face or hear a familiar voice. These behaviours increase when the baby is in proximity to a companion or another person, mainly the parent or the carer, although the baby cannot distinguish one person from another; for example, they cannot yet distinguish the mother from the father. Evidence of discrimination begins at about 4 weeks, when the baby is listening to sounds such as the mother's voice, and at about the age of 10 weeks the orientation becomes visual: the baby tends to recognise the face of the mother and smile towards her.

Second, when babies grow to about the age of 3–6 months, their orientation to signals is directed towards one or more discriminated figures. It has been observed that slightly older babies direct their orientation to the primary caregiver.

Third, when babies are 6–30 months old, their repertoire of responses to people increases to include visually following a departing mother, greeting her on return and using her as a base for explorations. It is at that age when babies treat strangers with caution and may evidence alarm or withdrawal expressed through intense crying.

At the final stage, and at about the age of 24–48 months, the child begins to acquire insight into the mother's feelings and goals, which leads to cooperative interaction and partnership (Bowlby, 1969).

What is important with attachment theory is that:

> [T]he infant and young children should experience a warm, intimate and continuous relationship with his mother (or permanent mother substitute), in which both find satisfaction and enjoyment. (Bowlby, 1951: 13)

Attachment theory has demonstrated that the transition from home to school and the separation from the mother/carer is an emotional journey for children, thus early years education and care needs to create an environment where the 'loss' of attachment to mother/carer is acknowledged and children are given time to adjust to the change from home to early years setting. The early years setting should create an environment that reflects warmth and enables children to have a sense of belonging. Activities such as encouraging children to bring photographs of their families or a display with photographs of children's family lives can become a comfort point for children.

Transitional objects

Winnicott (1986, 1987, 1995, 2005) started his career as a paediatrician; he tried to understand how children develop the concept of self into the context of the bonds they have with their parents. He investigated how children develop a healthy 'genuine self', as opposed to a 'false self', by looking closely at the relationships parents form with their children.

Winnicott uses the term 'self' to describe both 'ego' and self-as-object. He describes the self in terms of 'genuine' or 'true self', and 'false self'. For Winnicott, the 'genuine' or 'true self' is developed when the babies form their personalities by developing the capacity to recognise their needs and to express these. When babies are able genuinely to express their needs and their emotions, they are in the state of genuine or true self. For example, when a baby is hungry he or she usually cries. The mother responds to the crying by feeding the baby. Upon repetition of this behaviour the babies will realise that when they are hungry, they cry; the mother will feed them, thus their need will be met. A stable, consistent response or reaction by the mother to the baby's needs will help the baby to develop the genuine self. True self develops successfully only when the mother responds to the baby's spontaneous expressions and needs.

If the babies are growing up in an environment where their needs are not covered, however, they will build a 'false self'. Their real needs will not be expressed, which is a kind of mechanism for defending their 'true self' and is an unconscious process. Through the interactions with the mother or primary carer the babies are learning through experience and they begin to make sense of the world or, as Winnicot called it, acquire 'object reality'. The baby and carer enter what feels like a place of their own. Winnicott named that space a 'holding environment', which includes language and psychological and physical interactions between a mother and an infant. Thus, a holding environment is a space that is emotional and physical where the babies are protected without knowing they are protected. He claimed that for a child to form a healthy sense of self it is important for the child to know that the mother will be there when she is needed. Such a relationship with the mother makes the infant feel secure and protected; the child will then be well equipped to form a healthy self-concept.

The study of the 'holding environment' led Winnicott to develop his influential idea of the 'transitional experience'. He suggested that when children start becoming independent, for example when moving from the home to the outside world (such as to a nursery or a school), they need to represent their mothers when they are absent in order to feel secure. Children use objects such as teddy bears, blankets and dolls as transitional objects through which they facilitate a symbolic representation of the mother. In this way children can start enjoying the new environment into which they are moving (e.g. the nursery or the school) and become creative and independent; at the same time, the comfort provided by the transitional objects makes them feel protected.

The importance of transition objects has implications for children's transitions into and out of EYFS. This also raises the issue of respecting the objects brought with them from home by the children when they come to the nursery.

Steps towards effective transitions: early years settings readiness versus child's readiness

Develop a transition action plan

Although EYFS argues that early years education and care should prepare children to be 'ready' for school what will be argued here is that for effective transitions it is essential to prepare to receive children rather than to prepare children to 'fit' into the early years environment.

Early years practitioners have realised the significance of transitions in children's well-being and development. Thus, many early years settings and schools have developed 'transition programmes' consisting of a range of activities occurring throughout the year and constituting a process for preparing the children to accommodate 'horizontal' transitions. It is important, however, that early years settings develop action plans or transition programmes to also prepare children for 'vertical' transitions.

Many early years education settings have adopted the Southwark Transition and Assessment Record (STAR) and the Integrated Child Support Service 0–5 component Transitions Protocol (Southwark ICSS, see useful websites). STAR can become a useful tool for gathering information about individual children and it can provide early years setting with necessary information to support transitions and aid the sharing of information between settings and schools in order to meet the requirements of the EYFS.

An action plan is essential to make sure that the process of transition is implemented; it must not be forgotten or left too late in the hurry of the daily routine of the setting. All members of the staff should participate in this action plan as each has an important role to play. Within this action plan practicalities need to be considered, such as completing the Progress Check at Age Two and the EYFS Profile of the child for it to arrive at the new setting in time, determining who is going to work with the child (i.e. the key worker) and how many hours during the first couple of weeks a child will stay in the setting.

This action plan needs to involve the staff, children and parents. Brooker (2008) stresses the importance of this relationship and she describes it as 'a caring triangle'. She identifies three key processes for effective planning:

- understanding routines in the nursery and at home, such as sleeping habits, feeding habits (for younger children) or children's interests (for example, whether they like to play outdoors or with construction materials)
- enjoying relationships and having pleasurable interaction with other children: friendships in the nursery should be encouraged amongst children
- making links with the outside world: 'Enabling Environments' is a principle within EYFS, and the outside-of-the-class life of children is important; for example, little items such as a photograph of parents or a little toy help children to 'transfer' their own environment into the class setting, as will be explained later in this chapter.

Involve the children

During transitions it is important for children to be actively involved in the process. Throughout EYFS one of the key issues is to listen to the children, to ascertain how they feel about the setting, which activities they like to participate in and in which area in the setting they prefer to be. Observations are important in listening to children and involving them in the transitions. As was explained in Chapter 6, observations are a useful tool for assessment, while they also enable early years practitioners to listen to the children and understand their needs. Observations help recognise what the children like or dislike, especially where younger children (0–2) are concerned with their limited spoken language repertoire and thus they cannot always effectively express what they want.

CASE STUDY

From home to nursery

Harry is 18 months old. He is starting private nursery care for three days a week for not more than three hours per session. The parents have decided to send him to the nursery as he is the only child in the family and they have noticed that he is not interacting with other children of his own age. His mother is not working so she can be reached any time. Prior to the official starting date, there were a few visits to the setting so that Harry could familiarise himself with the place.

During the first 'official' day at nursery Harry and his mother enter through the main door and Harry immediately runs to the outdoor area. He takes out his little red car and starts playing with it. The early years practitioner invites him into the class, but he declines to enter. His mother says goodbye and she leaves. Harry seems fine when his mother has left, but he still does not want to go inside. He enjoys playing in the outdoors area on his own.

The early years practitioner leaves the door open in case he wants to come inside and join the other children. Harry is observing what happens in the classroom area, yet he does not want to come indoors.

Harry spent the first month in the outdoors area observing what was happening indoors, sometimes joining in with a nursery rhyme and making moves to accompany them, although still on his own outside. It took him a month to come inside the class, and the first activity he joined in with was singing.

In this case the early years practitioners did not force Harry to come indoors; they were 'listening' to Harry's needs. He was ready to be in the nursery, although he was not ready to be indoors with others. When he was indeed ready, he moved of his own volition. During this transition from home to nursery Harry was listened to and involved in the transition – he was not forced to be indoors, but was given appropriate time in which to feel comfortable to join in with indoor activities at the moment of his choosing.

Another key issue for effective transitions is to understand and respect the objects brought by children into the class from home. These objects, as Winnicott's theory on transitional objects has demonstrated – the little toys that children carry with them – offer emotional comfort to young children, who carry and regard them as symbols: the items symbolise the continuation from home to nursery. Examining the theory of attachment, and focusing on the work of Bowlby and Ainsworth, the importance of these objects carried by children during transitions is that they are essential for the children's well-being. In the above case study of Harry, he had a little red car with him for two months. For the first month it never left his hands. During the second month, when he was coming into the nursery, he wanted the toy for a while, and then, at the early years practitioner's suggestion, he left the car with the practitioner to 'sleep'. He always remembered to take it away with him, however, when he left the nursery. Harry was observed again after seven months. He was still bringing in his little red car, but as soon as he arrived in the nursery he immediately gave it into the safekeeping of the early years practitioner.

It is very important that practitioners make every effort to ensure that children feel both confident and supported when they are still new to the environment, making sure the vocabulary is appropriate and that the children understand what it means. Each setting uses different terms to describe certain items or activities; for example, in a nursery the staff may call the construction area something different from the term used in the Foundation Stage, so it is important to find out and clarify that everyone knows what items and locations are going to be called and therefore prevent confusion.

It is essential to explain what words mean – 'assembly', for instance, and 'corridor': words and concepts that adults use unconsciously yet that may not be familiar to children. Another example is the instruction 'Sit in a circle': 'But what is a circle?', 'How can I sit in a circle if there isn't one?'

As soon as children establish a relationship in the early years setting or school then they are ready to leave behind the objects they carry. Still, however, many children might feel the need to have them in their bags, such is the emotional attachment to these objects. Working in early years education and care it is important to respect the children's need to bring little objects from home and what these objects mean for the children. It is also essential to allow them to choose the materials they want to play with, to respect a child's daily routines and not to discourage constant links with home.

Involve the parents

Throughout EYFS the role of parents is highly emphasised. It is suggested that parents should be part of children's education and care and be encouraged to remain actively involved in all educational processes. The 'curriculum' of family life is vitally important because this is where young children spend much of their time. It is essential that we engage the parents in school life so that there is a 'joined-up' aspect to the child's experiences.

What it is important to understand when practitioners involve parents is that they themselves are also going through transitions. For example, they move between home and work and back again, changing 'hats' from parent to teacher, from daughter to mother, from son to father, and so on. As with early years practitioners, parents are as strongly influenced by the 'transition effect' as are their children. It also needs to be acknowledged that parents feel anxiety about their children's transitions. Of course, they see the effect of the stress in the children at home in ways that may not be reported to the early years setting or the school, especially if the relationship with staff has not been established. Perhaps a child has started bed-wetting, or using 'baby talk'; perhaps a child is misbehaving, unusually, or perhaps they spend a lot of time hiding under their bed. All these may be signs that a child is stressed and the cause of this could be their transition. It is imperative that the parents are involved in the process of preparing the child to 'go up'. As mentioned above, Bronfenbrenner (1979) has shown that the more practitioners can combine the interactions of settings that the child has in his life (i.e. not just 'him-and-school' or 'him-and-parents', but 'him-*and*-school-*and*-parents') the more effective the child's development will be. Since the child's family home is the most important setting (because this is where he/she spends most of his/her time and is most strongly emotionally influenced) it is important that the nursery or school communicates with the parents in a practical and positive way.

Building positive relationships with the parents helps effective transitions (for more on working with parents see Chapter 11). It is important to involve parents directly by making them feel really welcome in the setting or school by inviting them into the class, inviting them to sit with their children in the class and getting to know them (i.e. involving them not only in times of a crisis or trouble).

Documenting children's activities and sharing them with the parents helps to involve them indirectly (as has been shown in Chapters 6 and 11).

Familiar staff – the key person

As has been shown above, for young children attachment is important to their emotional and social development. EYFS has addressed this by identifying a key person for each child (see Chapter 16 for the role of the key person in EYFS). The children may be able to discuss with their key person fears and concerns they are experiencing, as they will know this person well and they will have started establishing a relationship with them. Children are sometimes happier talking to a toy or a puppet, however, than to an adult – and if the Foundation Stage and Year 1 teachers use this knowledge to bring questions and concerns out into the open, this will lead to conversations and discussions through which fears can be expressed.

Visits and cross-phase activities

One of the strategies that can be developed in order to smooth transitions is to set up a series of visits in either direction for specific age groups; for example, younger children might go to visit their future class, and the Year 1 children might visit the Foundation Stage settings. These visits can lead to a project such as a 'post office' area, where there are exchanges of letters between the Nursery and Foundation Stage, or between Foundation Stage and Key Stage 1. Visits and cross-phase activities are a helpful technique, not only to ease the transition process but also to provide enabling environments effectively.

CASE STUDY

'Our post office': an opportunity to visit a KS1 class

After a visit to a local post office, the children created a post-office area in a Foundation Stage class. In this area there were stamps, pens, envelopes, a set of scales and other material that one can find in a post office.

The children started writing letters and cards they wanted to post. The Foundation Stage teacher suggested posting letters to KS1 children. In this way they began a long and complex project where the two groups of children communicated with each other and provided a real opportunity for cross-phase working, which could be built upon during transition discussions.

Shared playtimes

There should be shared playtimes, when the younger children visit the older ones in the playground. In many settings the Foundation Stage children are separated from the rest of the school, so anything that can prepare them for, and assimilate them with, the older children is beneficial. One option is that, after visits, the children could be paired up so that the younger ones had a more experienced child to take care of them and become their 'body child'.

Use the outdoors

Many Foundation Stage classrooms and early years settings have their own outside space so that there can be freedom to move between the indoor and outdoor areas. The outside is vital for children, so every effort should be made by KS1 regularly to go outside for work to take place there. (see Chapter 10 for more information and examples of the use of outdoors)

Staff liaison and transfer of records

Transfer of records such as the Progress Check at Age Two and the EYFS Profile are an important aspect of the EYFS. Transferring children's official records helps staff to familiarise themselves with the children's needs and the ethos of EYFS, and to see how it can be transferred over to the National Curriculum.

Certain skills and abilities are to be expected after transition. If there is a lack of understanding, however, about a child's previous experience of learning – and, therefore, a lack of transition of methods – then the skills and abilities acquired by the child during EYFS might not be taken into consideration, with the result that learning opportunities are subsequently lost. Foundation Stage staff need to ensure that KS1 staff have attained the required understanding, in order to ensure that the delivery is appropriate until the children are settled. Otherwise, there is a clear danger that the children may become de-motivated because everything is so different. It is also important that the Foundation Stage staff have an understanding of the National Curriculum requirements in KS1 and can play their part in preparing children for the transition.

Summary

This chapter discussed the complex nature of transitions experienced by young children when leaving home for early years education and care. Transitions are changes that take place in individual's lives and these may be not only inner psychological transitions such as developmental growth or constructions of self-identity, but also external transitions such as moving physical spaces or moving countries and cultures. All these changes have an impact on children's social, emotional, personal and cognitive development. It is important that policy makers take on board the impact transitions can have in children's lives. It is also necessary to create environments in early years settings that take into consideration the impact of transitions on children's learning and development and ensure that the environment that is offered to children smoothes transitions and facilitates effective functioning of various contexts, cultures, religions and languages in which children live, learn and develop. Effective transitions in early years education and care should focus on supporting parents, children, practitioners and other key staff in creating effective environments to facilitate the transitions of children and not changing the child to 'fit' in the environment .

Key points to remember

- This chapter discussed the important role of transitions in children's lives. Transitions can become stressful for children and subsequently have an impact on children's well-being. Transitions cannot be avoided, but they can be effectively planned and organised so that the social and emotional effects of transition will not have a negative impact on children's well-being.

- This chapter offered some steps that can help children to experience effective transitions into and out of EYFS. There is great emphasis on involving the children themselves in the process, as well as involving the parents. Early years practitioners should become facilitators in the transition processes of children, involving all staff in the environment, and creating creative and stimulating activities for children.

Points for discussion

- Imagine that a child in your early years setting is going away for a month. Can you create an action plan to smooth the transition for when he or she returns? How can you prepare the parents and the child before their departure and how can you welcome the child back?

- Study the EYFS and the KS1 curriculum and try to identify the differences (and similarities) between these two curricula. How can you prepare children for KS1?

- What are the main challenges faced by early years practitioners when they try to implement 'enabling environment', organising visits and shared play, and liaising with other staff?

Reflective tasks

- Reflect on Saffinatu's case study. Using Bronfenbrenner's explanation of the ecological approach to transition discuss what inner and external changes Saffinatu is experiencing. Reflecting on Zittoun's types of rupture, what types can you identify in Saffinatu's life?

- Reflect on Beach's consequential transitions and discuss what types of transitions take place in early years education and care, and think how you can engage the families, other services and the children to overcome complexities of the transitions.

- EYFS emphasises children's school readiness and as High (2008: 1008) stresses, 'school readiness includes … the "readiness" of the individual child, the school's readiness for children and the ability of the family to communicate and support optimal early child development'. In that sense transitions are complex, influenced by a number of factors and reflect interactions and relationships among the child, nursery, school, family and community factors such as culture, religion and language. Consider what implications this might have for the experiences of children's transitions in relation to EYFS and how this impacts on your practice.

Further reading

Brooker, L. (2002) *Starting School: Young Children Learning Cultures*. Buckingham: Open University Press.

Brooker, L. (2008) *Supporting Transitions in the Early Years*. Maidenhead: Open University Press.

Dunlop, A.W. and Fabian, H. (eds) (2007) *Informing Transitions in the Early Years: Research, Policy and Practice*. Maidenhead: Open University Press.

Useful websites

Southwark Integrated Child Support Service 0–5:
www.southwark.gov.uk/info/200335/pupil_health_and_wellbeing/956/educational_psychology/5
Early interventions support children and families:
www.corechildrensservices.co.uk/what-we-do/early-interventions?gclid=CKLczrvQyLECFVJtfAodk
AoAXw
Early Intervention: the next steps (Allen, 2011):
www.preventionaction.org/prevention-news/allens-early-intervention-next-steps/5476
C4EO is a partner with NCB in a programme funded by the DfE aiming to:

- identify and work towards direct outcomes for children and families
- improve leadership and performance
- embed peer-to-peer support and challenge
- understand the requirements of a revised EYFS

www.c4eo.org.uk/themes/earlyyears/default.aspx?themeid=1

To gain **free access** to selected SAGE journal articles related to key topics in this chapter visit:
www.sagepub.co.uk/Palaiologou2e

Meeting EYFS Outcomes Outside of the Early Years Setting

Wendy Thompson

Chapter roadmap

One of the key principles of the Early Years Foundation Stage is that of 'Enabling Environments', instrumental in 'supporting and extending children's development and learning' (DCSF, 2008; *Statutory Framework*, p. 10). Outside classrooms, other environments can become helpful contexts for the learning goals of EYFS. Museums, archives, libraries and galleries all become not only an interesting educational context for children but also places that can promote a holistic approach to children's development.

This chapter aims to help you to:

- develop an understanding of how the Early Years Foundation Stage principles and areas of learning can be implemented outside of the early years classroom or setting, specifically with children of 30–60 months old
- reflect on opportunities for using the local environment as a starting point for initiating and extending learning opportunities for young children
- think about whether 'out-of-setting activity' and experiences can contribute towards children's motivation, interests and creative development
- consider the implications for developing partnerships with parents and widening participation to involve the community learning context.

What does 'out-of-setting' learning mean?

High-quality learning experiences can be found outside the classroom or setting and can prove to be a rich resource bank for children and their early years practitioners. If the latter are to provide experiences that motivate and encourage young children to achieve their full potential, and also empower and encourage parents and carers to do the same (DfES, 2005), then educational experiences need to be viewed holistically. The Qualifications and Curriculum Authority (QCA) provides (via its website) an overview of the 0–16 age phase curriculum, starting from the Early Years Foundation Stage (EYFS) to the end of Key Stage 4. This is titled the 'Big Picture of the Curriculum' and involves the entire planned learning experience, including learning outside the classroom or early years setting. In QCA terms this involves community participation, creativity and critical thinking.

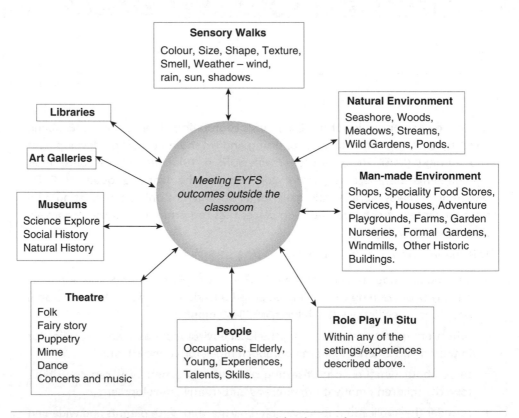

Figure 10.1 *Meeting EYFS outcomes outside the early years setting*

The Common Core of Skills and Knowledge (DfES, 2005) suggests practitioners should know how to motivate and encourage children to achieve their full potential, and should know how to empower and encourage parents and carers to help their children to achieve their full potential. Practitioners are encouraged to recognise that play and recreation, directed by young children, performs a major role in helping the children understand themselves and the world around them, as well as helping them to realise their potential.

The Children's Plan, *Building Brighter Futures* (DCSF, 2007), emphasises the need for young children to be involved in positive activities in order to develop personal and social skills, promote well-being and reduce behaviour that puts them at risk. Article 31 of the United Nations Convention on the Rights of the Child (UNCRC, 1992) emphasises that children should be able to participate fully in cultural and artistic life in order to develop talents and to promote respect for cultural identities.

Learning outside the classroom or setting can be interpreted in diagrammatic form (see Figure 10.1); in this context, it suggests opportunities for engaging in a wide range of experiences, in order to promote creativity and to stimulate interest and involvement. It is possible for aspects to overlap and interconnect in numerous ways.

Defining the boundaries between recreational and learning activities when working with young children is a difficult task. Proponents of an experiential learning model argue that young children are capable of demonstrating sophisticated levels of complex thinking when provided with an appropriate learning environment. Such an environment will encourage children to engage in reflective processes, problem solving and logical reasoning, and thus develop higher-order thinking skills and levels of creativity (Walsh and Gardner, 2005).

Young children and creativity

Creativity will be discussed in detail in Chapter 22, although the focus will be on constructing the pedagogy for creativity in the class. Here, creativity is approached in an attempt to investigate how it can be extended to out-of-class environments. Loveless (2005: 29) describes creativity as involving the interaction between people and their communities, in social processes and subjects, and in wider social and cultural contexts. Adult creativity can often lead to a product, such as a work of art or a solution to a problem, whereas very young children's creativity, by contrast, may produce no tangible product or result. Because of this, young children's creativity has been described as being 'fundamentally different [from] the creativity of adults' (Runco, 2006: 121). It may take the form of imaginative play and self-expression, or a new understanding of the world. The opportunity for widening children's experiences is thus essential.

If children do not fully utilise their imagination, explore possibilities, try new things, consider new actions, invent understandings and experiment they will not be able to discover who they are, what they are capable of and what is acceptable in their family, school, peer group and culture (Runco, 2006: 121).

Similarly, EYFS also emphasises widening children's experiences (DCSF, 2008). It states that children in the 30–60-month age phase are becoming more aware of their place within a community and are beginning to build a stronger sense of their own identity; also, of their place in a wider world. A competent learner needs an enabling environment that offers both outdoors and out-of-setting experiences. These will provide freedom for young children to explore, use their senses and be physically active and exuberant (DCSF, 2008: Card 3.3). In terms of wider contexts, EYFS suggests the need to develop multi-agency working, including working with librarians and local artists: 'When the setting values the local community it can encourage the different community groups to work together for the benefit of all' (EYFS, 2008: Card 3.4).

It is 'sustained engagement with experience' that leads to a different relationship with the world from that based on 'a succession of brief encounters' (Riley, 2007: 205). Sustained engagement can lead to new discoveries and different ways of viewing people, social situations and objects. Highly skilled and motivated professionals working within community learning environments (such as museums, libraries and galleries) may help to give depth to experiences and promote the type of learning that enables children's creativity to flourish. It is also possible for children to become active co-constructors of knowledge, if the adult positively enhances the learning experience (Riley, 2007). It is suggested that children are supported by adults who:

- highlight the critical features of the activity
- buffer the child's attention through distractions
- channel the child's activities to ensure success
- use errors to encourage learning
- enable procedures to be commented upon and explained. (Riley, 2007: 20)

In order to provide a focus for illustrating how EYFS outcomes can be met outside the classroom or setting, it is necessary to consider a beginning point or initial stimulus. The Museums, Libraries and Archives Council (MLA) will be selected, as it provides significant opportunities for developing higher-order thinking skills and creativity in young children.

Museums, Libraries and Archives Council and training opportunities

The MLA argues that it is best placed to serve communities and deliver local agendas to maximise local impact in neighbourhoods. Its aim is to provide new learning opportunities and to create partnerships across a number of sectors. The MLA offers a whole variety of initiatives and programmes in order to help individuals and settings develop accessible, inclusive and educational resources and services. As can be seen in Table 10.1, the MLA has created Generic Learning Outcomes applicable to working with a range of partners in EYFS such as early years professionals and early years teachers. As is shown in Table 10.1, the MLA Generic Learning Outcomes can be linked with EYFS learning areas.

Table 10.1   Museums, Libraries and Archives Generic Learning Outcomes

MLA Generic Learning Outcomes	Example of which EYFS learning areas are linked with MLA Generic Learning Outcomes
Knowledge and Understanding Knowing about *something* (for example a fact or information). Learning facts or information, which can be subject-specific, interdisciplinary or thematic. Making links and relationships between *things (or facts)* and using prior knowledge in new ways. Learning how museums, archives and libraries operate.	Knowledge and understanding of the world.
Skills Development Knowing how to perform an action. Intellectual, information management, social, emotional, communication and physical skills.	Personal social and emotional development. Communication, language and literacy. Physical development.
Attitudes and Values Feelings and perceptions. Opinions about selves and others. Positive and negative attitudes in relation to experience. Reasons for actions or personal viewpoints, empathy and capacity for tolerance.	Personal, social and emotional development. Problem solving, reasoning and numeracy.
Activity, Behaviour and Progression What people have done, do, or intend to do. Actions (observed or reported) and changes in behaviour. Progression towards further learning.	Personal, social and emotional development. Problem solving, reasoning and numeracy.
Enjoyment, Inspiration and Creativity Having fun, being surprised and inspired. Innovative thoughts and actions including creativity. Exploration and experimentation.	Creative development.

According to Salaman and Tutchell (2005: 1), museums and art galleries can offer unique opportunities to motivate children. Engagement with 'authentic' objects allows them to understand principles previously only available through books or verbal descriptions. They suggest that problem-solving activities can develop through a simple questioning approach: 'What does it look like? (Form) What is it for? (Function) What is it made of? (Material) Where does it come from? (Provenance)' (Salaman and Tutchell, 2005: 5).

The EYFS reminds us that children's engagement with people, materials, objects, ideas or events allows them the opportunity to test things out and to solve problems, stressing that children need the cooperation of adults to challenge and extend their thinking (DCSF, 2008: Card 4.2). The wider partnership, developed through early years practitioners working with experienced museum, gallery or library staff, should enable a dialogue to take place that will extend the knowledge base and enrich the interactions and experiences provided for children.

In order to build on experiences, the observation of children by professionals is essential. EYFS (DCSF, 2008: *Practice Guidance*, p. 11) urges practitioners to *look, listen and note* the progress children are making. In the context of museums, libraries, galleries and archives, the general advice given by Smidt (2005: 11) to practitioners regarding aspects to observe seems particularly apt:

- What is this child paying attention to or interested in?
- What experience does the child have of this?
- What does the child already know about this?
- What does the child feel about this?

Further analysis can connect observations to EYFS areas of learning and development, and thus provide a focus for future planning and resourcing, linked with what is already considered to be effective practice (DCSF, 2008).

Early Years Foundation Stage and areas of learning and development

The EYFS (DCSF, 2008) advocates key principles when planning experiences for children. These relate to the distinctive needs of individual children. EYFS stresses the importance of children developing secure relationships in positive and enabling environments, and being involved in active learning through play, exploration and critical thinking. It is suggested that it is possible to cover all six areas of learning of development when using out-of-setting learning contexts (DCSF, 2008):

- personal, social and emotional development (PSED)
- communication, language and literacy (CLL)
- problem solving, reasoning and numeracy (PSRN)
- knowledge and understanding of the world (KUW)
- physical development (PD)
- creative development (CD).

In fact, EYFS (DCSF, 2008) stresses that none of the six areas of learning can be delivered in isolation from the others, as all are equally important and interdependent. The actual focus during the out-of-setting event will, to some extent, depend upon children's needs and interests, and the type of stimulus offered.

For illustrative purposes only, personal, social and emotional development, communication, language and literacy, knowledge and understanding of the world, and creative development will provide the main focus for this chapter, as those areas specifically link with MLA experiences. Questions will be raised and group activities suggested to highlight the other two aspects of learning and development: problem solving, reasoning and numeracy, and physical development.

Within personal, social and emotional development the aspects of 'Disposition and Attitudes' and 'Sense of Community' are particularly significant, as the first is concerned with how children become interested, excited and motivated to learn. A sense of community relates to how children understand and respect their own needs, views, cultures and beliefs, and also those of other people (DCSF, 2008).

The communication, language and literacy aspects 'Language for Communication' and 'Language for Thinking' are significant in the context of out-of-setting learning. 'Language for Communication' is concerned with how children become communicators and the skills that develop as children interact with others and listen to and use language (DCSF, 2008). 'Language for Thinking' is concerned with how children learn to use language to imagine and re-create roles and experiences. It is also concerned with how talk is used to clarify thinking and ideas or to refer to events children have observed and are curious about (DCSF, 2008).

All of the knowledge and understanding of the world aspects are relevant. 'Exploration and Investigation' focuses on how children investigate objects and materials and learn about properties, change, patterns, similarities and differences; they question how and why things work. 'Designing and Making' is about the ways in which children learn about the construction process and the tools and techniques that can be used to assemble materials creatively and safely. 'ICT' is concerned with how children find out about and learn how to use appropriate information technology to support their learning. 'Time' concerns finding out about past and present events relevant to their own lives or those of their families. 'Place' focuses on how children become aware of and interested in the natural world and their local environment. 'Communities' is concerned with how children begin to know about their own and other people's cultures in order to understand and celebrate the similarities and differences between these in a diverse society (DCSF, 2008).

All of the creative development aspects are relevant. 'Being Creative – Responding to Experiences' and 'Expressing and Communicating Ideas' are concerned with how children respond in a variety of ways to what they see, hear, smell, touch or feel, and how they express and communicate their own ideas, thoughts and feelings. 'Exploring Media and Materials' is about children's exploration of and engagement (both independent and guided) with a widening range of media and materials. 'Creating Music and Dance' encourages children's independent and guided explorations of sound, movement and music. 'Developing Imagination and Imaginative Play' focuses on how children are supported to develop and build their imaginations through stories, role-playing, dance, music, design and art (DCSF, 2008).

Preparing children for the learning experience

Preparing children for an out-of-setting visit through describing the narrative in terms of the where, the why and what processes are involved in the event is especially important. This does not suggest taking away the elements of surprise and serendipity that may be an outcome of the experience; rather, it ensures that children know the fundamental features of what is likely to happen. Some children find unpredictable sequences and events particularly disturbing, and thus emotional security is essential for learning during out-of-setting contexts. To help alleviate distress a picture diagram of the events likely to happen throughout the day may help children to feel secure and in control of the situation.

Storytelling is also a useful technique for introducing the subject or theme attached to the event. This can be in the form either of published literature or of spoken stories, made up by the practitioner. Children particularly love made-up stories linked with actual places within their community. According to Riley, emotional development hinges on the ability to make meaning of experience in an often-bewildering world, and storytelling is one way of highlighting (within controlled boundaries) significant experiences:

> Stories provide a landscape in which children can confront and reflect on emotions and experiences too frightening to confront in daily life, feelings of anger, jealousy and confusion. And good stories are not over in an instant but continue to speak to the child and 'interact' with her developing experience. (2007: 59)

Made-up stories, developed alongside the child's ideas, can also promote the process of sustained shared thinking (Siraj-Blatchford et al., 2002) to a similar extent that sustained engagement with objects can promote deep-level thinking. Sustained shared thinking is embedded within the EYFS (2008) *Practice Guidance* and the Early Years Professional National Standards (CWDC, 2006: S16), where it is advocated as a way of helping to develop children's thinking skills and for providing a context for effective language development. Practitioners are encouraged to share a genuine interest in what seizes children's imaginations and ensure that mutual meaning making takes place. The imaginative story context is an ideal starting point for this process.

CASE STUDY

A seaside community

This case study is based on a seaside town in the north of England. There is a community library, natural history museum, art gallery, seashore, harbour and lighthouse within short walking distances of one another. A short journey by bus along the sea front passes a lifeboat station, a harbour, a castle and cliffs full of seabirds, a marina of yachts and a sea life centre. Any of the first three MLA sites (library, museum or art gallery) could be the starting point for learning outside the classroom, as could the stimulus provided by both the natural and man-made environment. This exemplar has been chosen as its MLA provision is not as extensive as that found in inner-city areas, yet is nevertheless a rich resource for meeting the needs of the local community. The community library offers story sessions, puppet performances and an extensive range of electronic resources, as well as providing children's literature. The art gallery offers both weekend and after-school workshops for children, and a dressing up and interactive area for young children. It also houses a number of large historical paintings of the town's sea front and its fishing industry. There is a museum within the locality that features earlier lifestyles and the changing role of the fishing industry within that community.

The art gallery has a variable programme of visiting exhibitions and the current display is focused on illustrations from 'children's fairy tales and fantasy'. A room has been set aside with games, fairy-tale books, dressing-up clothes, swathes of flimsy, colourful fabrics, and drawing and modelling materials specifically related to the theme. One of the larger fantasy illustrations, rich in detail, is an illustration of a children's fairy tale based under the sea, with both wonderfully imaginary and realistic sea creatures.

A group of 3- and 4-year-olds are visiting the art gallery; a musician has been invited to create musical sounds representing the feelings associated with the under-sea picture and the creatures depicted within it. The children are keen to contribute their ideas to the musician, suggesting sounds that depict the characters and how the characters are behaving, for example happy, sad, fierce or frightened. The children imagine whether the creatures will make high, low, loud or soft noises. Discussions surrounding the size and shape of the musical instruments and the type of noise they are able to make are all part of this dialogue.

After this discussion, an early years practitioner supports the musician by creating a musical story. The remaining early years practitioners encourage children to express their feelings by improvising physical movements and by selecting sea-coloured materials to swathe around themselves as they move to the music. A group of children eagerly takes part in the imaginative dance. One or two children choose to express themselves through pictures, rather than participate in movement and dance. Smidt's (2005: 11) observational questions are a useful tool to analyse and note individual responses: *What is this child paying attention to or interested in? What does the child feel about this?* Added to this, there would be questions about the child's use of vocabulary, their awareness of differences between objects and their creative responses to music and sound.

It is useful to refer back to the MLA Generic Learning Outcomes in Table 10.1 and reflect on the child's experience by questioning: What knowledge and understanding has been developed? What are the skills, attitudes and values that the child has demonstrated? How has the child shown their enjoyment, inspiration and creativity?

(Continued)

(Continued)

There are links with the learning outcomes for the EYFS (DCSF, 2008: *Statutory Framework*) from this out-of-setting experience:

- Personal, social and emotional development: seek and delight in new experiences; understand that people have different needs, views, cultures and beliefs that need to be treated with respect

- Communication, language and literacy: build up vocabulary that reflects the breadth of their experiences; use language to imagine and re-create roles and experiences

- Knowledge and understanding of the world: show curiosity and interest in the features of objects (musical instruments); look closely at similarities, differences, patterns and change

- Creative development: develop preferences for forms of expression; express and communicate their ideas, thoughts and feelings by using a widening range of materials, suitable tools, imaginative role play, movement, designing and making, and a variety of songs and musical instruments.

Continuing to build on the experiences encountered in this case study would depend upon both the children's responses and their interests. Reflection in thinking about the activities, behaviour and progression encountered in out-of-setting contexts is important to children and practitioners for developing effective, interesting and stimulating early years practice. It could be that the visit has been planned for a whole day, where during the afternoon the children are taken on a visit to the harbour and the nearby beach area. Children could look at the fishing boats, various types of fish, ice trays, lobster pots, buoys, nets and lighthouse. This offers extensive scope for developing the area of learning through knowledge and understanding of the world (DCFS, 2008: *Practice Guidance*, pp. 77ff.). It provides an opportunity to encounter creatures, plants and objects in their natural environment, and people in 'real-life' situations. It enables children to show curiosity about why things happen and how things work, and it provides opportunity for problem solving: for example, looking at the lobster pot one could ask, 'What do you think it is used for?' or 'How does it work?'

Developing creative and imaginative reasoning through questioning helps children to seek meaning from their experiences (DCSF, 2008: *Practice Guidance*, pp. 77ff.). According to Runco, the most important feature a practitioner can allow a child to develop is 'ego strength' (Runco, 2006: 128). This allows the child to believe in their own thinking and ideas, which is essential in developing creative thinking because the child has been able to withstand pressures to conform. It is important that early years practitioners should listen to children and value their ideas, whilst they should also encourage critical reflection by interpreting, analysing and helping to clarify children's ideas.

Being outdoors also gives children first-hand contact with the weather and the seasons; it helps them to understand how to behave by talking about personal safety, risks and the safety of others. It could be that the beach area offers opportunities for beach-combing for stones, shells, seaweed, driftwood, or for creating sand structures, thus continuing the morning's theme of homes and palaces for sea creatures.

Parents (or carers) as partners

Working with parents presents challenges, as Smidt (2006: 51) acknowledges, although it is important for the practitioner to rise to these challenges. Research has demonstrated how the home learning environment can have a significant impact on children's learning and development (Sylva et al., 2003). The Effective Provision of Pre-School Education (EPPE) Project found that home environments where children were involved in a range of activities – such as visiting the library or going on visits – were associated with higher intellectual, social and behavioural scores (Sylva et al., 2003). Providing a partnership with parents is thus crucial for continuity in the educational experience for children.

The EYFS *Practice Guidance* (2008: 6) suggests that early years practitioners have a key role to play in working with parents to support children through the shared identification of learning needs. The 'Parents as Partners' guidance acknowledges that parents are children's first and most enduring educators and that 'parents and practitioners have a lot to learn from each other' (DCSF, 2008: Card 2.2).

In a wider context, Smidt (2006: 51) questions whether parents can be taught to be 'good parents' as viewed from the practitioner's standpoint, as this implies the adoption of a model of parenting that is universal. What is considered essential for children's learning is to some extent culture-specific, and practitioners need to be careful not to impose their views without careful consultation and an opportunity to listen to the views of the parents. Within EYFS the need for effective communication with parents, as well as the need to respect the contribution made by parents and carers to the development and well-being of children, is emphasised. It is important to learn about and consider children within their respective family relationships and communities, including their cultural and religious contexts, and their place within the family (Zwozdiak-Myers, 2007).

Informing parents about the nature and value of out-of-setting learning is crucial to its success. Notice-boards within settings containing MLA website information and events relevant to young children are important for ensuring the development of an awareness for learning of community contexts. EYFS suggests that regular information should be provided about activities undertaken by children through visual displays, documentation and photographs. Newsletters informing parents about particular visits and linking these with the EYFS can help develop understanding and a transfer of knowledge. Seeking feedback from parents and asking for suggestions on ways to build on the children's experiences helps to promote a two-way flow of information, and it also shows that practitioners respect parental views. EYFS suggests that in a true partnership parents understand and contribute to the policies in the setting, thus influencing future planning and development (DCFS, 2008: Card 2.2).

To summarise, EYFS has four guiding principles that are grouped thematically and are crucially important in developing curricular opportunities for young children (DCSF, 2008: *Practice Guidance*, p. 5). Each aspect needs to be considered in order for out-of-setting learning to be successful and for the holistic needs of children to be met. Links have been made with MLA Generic Learning Outcomes:

- *A Unique Child* stresses the positive nature of the child, being a competent learner from birth who can be resilient, capable, confident and self-assured. It is the practitioner's role to build confidence or 'ego strength' (Runco, 2006: 128) and to ensure that a child is ready to face new challenges in out-of-setting contexts. MLA Generic Learning Outcomes: 'Attitudes and Values' and 'Skills Development'.
- *Positive Relationships* emphasises that children learn to be strong and independent from a basis of loving and secure relationships. It is the practitioner's role to provide out-of-setting learning that develops from a secure and consistent base. Developing opportunities for sustained shared thinking (Siraj-Blatchford et al., 2002) ensures that practitioners are alert to the learning needs of young children, and are sensitive to children's interests and motivational aspects. A two-way dialogue with parents/carers is essential in order to provide for the 'unique child'. MLA Generic Learning Outcomes: 'Activity, Behaviour and Progression' and 'Attitudes and Values'.
- *Enabling Environments* acknowledges that the environment plays a key role in supporting and extending children's development and learning. It is the practitioner's role to make the environment, within and outside the setting, both stimulating and motivating. MLA Generic Learning Outcomes: 'Enjoyment, Inspiration and Creativity' and 'Activity, Behaviour and Progression'.
- *Learning and Development* acknowledges that children develop and learn in different ways and at different rates, and that all areas of learning and development are equally important and inter-connected. It is the practitioner's role to map children's learning and development in order to ensure a broad and balanced curriculum, which builds upon children's experiences and provides for the unique child. Part of this process is through actively seeking partnerships with those professionals who are experts in their given field. MLA Generic

Learning Outcomes: 'Knowledge and Understanding of the World' and 'Skills Development'.

The definition of meeting EYFS, as explored in this chapter, considers that children gain much from out-of-classroom or out-of-setting experiences. This chapter has highlighted the importance of observing children and noting their interests and motivations in order to support their learning. It also stresses the importance of listening to children and encouraging them to express their views. According to Smidt (2006: 117), allowing children to express their thoughts and ideas can be contentious, as the 'language of education must express some stance' and invite those joining in either to agree or adopt a different stance. When children are allowed to reflect on what they think they are involved in 'metacognition'. This means that they are involved in understanding what it is they already know.

Katz (1998) implies that young children need opportunities to express, improve, transform, validate, develop, refine and deepen their own constructions of their worlds – the worlds of here and now, but also times past and times to come, and of people like and unlike themselves (Smidt, 2006: 117).

Practitioners are urged to promote a wider partnership with the community and with those professionals who have expertise in specific areas, in order to enrich children's experiences and to promote a deeper understanding of the world. The EYFS (DCSF, 2008: *Practice Guidance*, p. 10) adds force to the notion that high-quality early years experience provides a firm foundation on which to build future academic, social and emotional success. High-quality experiences can be found outside the classroom and add richness to the curriculum, as they provide a source of stimulation and motivation for young learners.

Summary

Although throughout this chapter the links are made with the first version of EYFS published in 2008, the key ideas of how EYFs can be met outside of the classroom are made explicit. Emphasis in the revised version of the EYFS (DfE, 2012; Early Education/DfE, 2012) is on enabling environments and the early years practitioners can take advantage of the local community and what their community can offer to children and their settings in a safe and secure way. Throughout the chapter it has been demonstrated how we can move children's experiences that lead to learning outside of educational buildings and take advantage of the opportunities offered by the community with children, families and the community as partners. More than ever early years education is encouraged to 'move out' of the class and in partnership with parents (as will be shown in Chapter 11) and with other services (as will be discussed in Part 3) to create a 'new way of thinking where intercommunicative actions are required' (Palaiologou, 2011).

Key points to remember

- This chapter explores how the six learning areas of EYFS can be met outside of early years settings. A number of independent organisations such as museums, libraries and archives can be used to promote children's learning and development alongside the EYFS requirements for learning.

- It is important for early years practice to include parents in activities outside of the classroom. Parents' participation can be of great help to the early years practitioners.

- Partnerships with local communities can enrich children's experiences and promote the six learning areas of EYFS.

Points for discussion

- When planning any out-of-setting activity a careful risk assessment needs to be carried out. Obviously, the intended location will have an impact on aspects that need to be considered. Your local authority will have specific guidelines regarding which compulsory checks need to be made. The key aspects include: pre-visit analysis and completion of risk-assessment documentation; parental consent forms; level of supervision (including ratios of adults to children); behaviour (including safety rules); health and hygiene rules (including food, toilet and hand-washing facilities); and first-aid provision and documenting incidents (including emergency procedures). The Teaching Resource Site (TRS) has information produced by the government and the Central Council of Physical Recreation (CCPR) on planning for out-of-setting contexts. Think about a location for a visit and consider the risk assessment that needs to be carried out in advance.

- Try to identify opportunities for meeting the communication, language and literacy, and personal, social and emotional development EYFS areas of learning and development outside of the setting.

- Think of an out-of-classroom experience that is possible within your own community. For example, this could include a farm museum, a traditional working windmill or a natural history museum. Focus on mathematics and look at the aspects of Numbers as Labels and for Counting, Calculating, Shape, Space and Measures; think about favourable conditions or opportunities for developing children's learning and development. This could be during the visit or back in the setting through the provision of role-playing or by other play experiences.

> ⭐ **Reflective tasks**
>
> - Reflect on the seaside community case study and, referring to Chapters 6 and 7, discuss ways how children's experiences and learning can be observed, documented and assessed in the light of the learning areas of the EYFS.
>
> - Reflect on the digital technologies children are using, such as iPads, laptops and iPhones, and how you can use these digital devices to enhance children's experiences outside of the classroom.
>
> - Study Section 3: The Safeguarding and Welfare Requirements in the Statutory Framework of the EYFS (DfE, 2012) and reflect on implications that outside-of-classroom experiences might have in your safety and welfare of children.

Further reading 📖

Griffin, J. (2000) Special issue: 'Learning outside the classroom', *Investigating: Australian Primary and Junior Science Journal*, 16 (4): 2.

Riley, J. (2007) *Learning in the Early Years*, 2nd edn. London: Sage.

Salaman, A. and Tutchell, S. (2005) *Planning for Educational Visits for the Early Years*. London: Paul Chapman Publishing.

Smidt, S. (2006) *The Developing Child in the 21st Century*. London: Routledge.

Useful websites 🖱

Inspiring Learning for All:

www.inspiringlearningforall.gov.uk

Describes what an accessible and inclusive museum, archive or library, which both stimulates and supports learning, looks like. It invites you to: find out what is learned by those using your services; assess how well you are achieving best practice in supporting learning; improve upon what you do. Learning is now high on local, regional and national agendas. Inspiring Learning for All will transform the way in which museums, archives and libraries deliver and engage users in learning;

Creative Partnerships:

www.creative-partnerships.com/

The government's flagship creative learning programme, designed to develop the skills of young people across England, raising their aspirations and achievements, and opening up more opportunities for their futures. This world-leading programme is transforming teaching and learning across the curriculum.

24-Hour Museum:

www.show.me.uk

This is the 24-Hour Museum's zone for children where places, counties and cities are listed, allowing for immediate contact with a huge range of museums and galleries. Designed for children aged 4 to 11 (or KS1 and KS2 in the English National Curriculum), this site is packed with online interactive resources produced by museums and galleries.

www.artscouncil.org.uk

www.farmsforschools.org.uk

www.inspiringlearningforall.gov.uk

www.kew.org

www.nationalparks.gov.uk

To gain **free access** to selected SAGE journal articles related to key topics in this chapter visit: www.sagepub.co.uk/Palaiologou2e

Part 3
Key Issues in Practice

11

Working in Partnership with Parents

Anna Knowles

🚌 **Chapter roadmap**

The EYFS identifies the need for 'partnership working between practitioners and/or carers' (DfE, 2012: 2). The building of a mutually responsive relationship with parents is central in supporting the well-being and development of the child. The need to work in collaboration with parents and carers was considered as a part of the government's Choice for Parents, the Best Start for Children strategy (HM Treasury, 2004). Prior to this, work with parents had lacked coherence and regularity. The strategy, which provided a foundation for EYFS, emphasised the need for partnership between practitioners and parents. This chapter will examine the challenges faced in engaging parents and the benefits of successful engagement. The term 'parent' will be used throughout the chapter to refer to any person who takes on a parental role, regardless of the biology of parenthood.

This chapter aims to help you to:

- understand the purpose and significance of working with parents and carers
- consider the ways in which we engage with parents to support children in early years education and care
- examine and reflect on the role of the early years practitioner in developing effective relationships with parents.

Building effective partnerships – a rationale

Building and maintaining effective partnerships with parents is essential in developing an awareness of the needs of the child. Wheal (2000) emphasises the parent as possessing a broad range of experiences, knowledge and ideas to offer the practitioner. Parents are experts on their child and should be regarded as such; they have an astute awareness of the specific behaviours and unique habits exhibited by the child. The sharing of parental expertise enables the practitioner to gain a solid understanding of the child, which can then be shared with staff across the setting. Prior to a child entering into early years education and care the parent builds the primary learning experience. Practitioners need an understanding of the content of this experience to enable a starting point for working with the child.

The combination of parental perceptions and the knowledge of the early years practitioner assists in ensuring positive outcomes for the child. The Reggio Emilia approach, as discussed by Thornton and Brunton (2007), emphasises the parent, practitioner and child relationship as a three-way process (Figure 11.1). The practitioner gains knowledge from the expertise of the parent and the parent learns from someone experienced in the practice of early years education and care. The child participates in interactions with both adults and is recognised as 'rich in potential, strong, powerful and competent' (Malaguzzi, 2001: 5). All individuals have equal importance in shared communications that embrace respect, listening and cooperation. Active participation is essential to the success of the relationships.

The established three-way relationship provides the parent with an opportunity to develop an understanding of what is happening in the early years setting and why. Consider how often you have seen a child race to the door to share a picture they have produced in nursery, to be greeted by statements and questions from a parent that attempt to enforce meaning or suppress creativity. Such responses derive from a lack of understanding of the unique ways in which children learn and develop. Practitioners

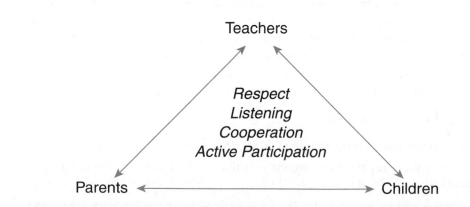

Figure 11.1 *The triangle of relationships (adapted from Thornton and Brunton, 2007)*

have the potential to support the parent in developing a new understanding for the way in which their child learns and the creative and imaginative processes involved.

The Department for Children, Schools and Families highlighted how parental involvement in children's education from an early age significantly affects educational achievements (DCSF, 2008). Outcomes in cognitive development are better when parents are involved in learning. Feiler notes the development of children as stemming from 'guided participation' of adults in the home and school environment, who work together (Feiler, 2010: 14). Providing parents with an understanding of early years education and care assists them in effectively supporting and extending their child's learning in the home environment. It should not be assumed that parents are unwilling to learn more about the ways in which their children learn. Whalley emphasises parental enthusiasm in her discussions of research conducted around parental partnerships at the Pen Green centre:

> We realised we had underestimated the enthusiasm which parents demonstrated for a deeper and more extended dialogue about their children's learning. We began to see that teaching and learning and curriculum issues, which had previously been the fairly uncontested domain of professional staff, needed to be opened up for wider discussion with parents in the early years community. (2007: 9)

Collaborative working with parents aims to promote the enthusiasm of parents. Effective partnerships stimulate shared verbal exchanges which derive from a reciprocal understanding of the child. Parent and practitioner should be attuned to the child's needs; this enables free and open discussion through mutually understandable communications.

Effective initial interactions

Initial interactions commence when a parent registers interest in a setting. It is important to reflect on the ways in which parents are engaged at this stage as early interactions form a basis for the partnership process. Practitioners should consider parental feelings about the process and allow time for partnerships to evolve.

The first face-to-face liaison with the parent is crucial in securing a successful future relationship. The practitioner's behaviour towards the parent should 'be a model of courtesy and respect' (Thornton and Brunton, 2007: 14). It is essential to adopt a sensitive, friendly and professional approach which takes account of the needs of the parent and, if present, the child. Affording time to initial meetings with parents undoubtedly presents implications in practice, but it is critical in ensuring the parent confidence in their relationship with the early years setting. Time also provides the practitioner with the opportunity to gain preliminary knowledge of the parent and this knowledge positively benefits future interactions.

The context of the initial liaison will vary; first meetings will generally either take place in the early years setting or the family home. Shaw (2009) discusses the diverse home circumstances existing for children in the twenty-first century. Visiting a parent and child in the home provides insight as it offers the parent the opportunity for initial liaison in a comfortable, familiar context and assists practitioners in building a picture of the child's primary environment. It is advisable that the visit be conducted by the child's potential key person along with another practitioner. One practitioner is able to spend time engaging the child while the other dedicates their time to listening and responding to the parent. Brief and objective observations of the child in their home environment may be noted down during or immediately following the visit. It is important not to spend too much time writing; a stronger foundation for future work is established when both the parent and the child feel sufficiently engaged during the visit. Some parents may not feel comfortable with a visit in their own home. This feeling must be respected and an alternative venue should be offered.

The practitioner is not provided with a second chance to make a good first impression so it is crucial, therefore, to examine practices for the initial engagement of parents. MacNaughton emphasises reflective practice as a skill that can be identified in quality practitioners. She advises 'looking back' at practices and 'rethinking them' (MacNaughton, 2005: 6). It is essential to reflect on our behaviour in initial meetings with parents; reflective questions can really assist this process and practitioners may choose to consider the following:

- How do I attempt to engage the parent and the child in the first meeting?
- Do both parent and child leave the meeting feeling they have received my attention?
- How do I emphasise a three-way process?
- Was the setting appropriate?
- Did I obtain necessary or useful information?
- What was effective about my engagement and what could be improved?

It is not possible for every early interaction to be a success, but reflecting on our conduct assists in finding ways forward for future work with parents.

Sustaining parental involvement and the sharing of practice

Effective sustained relationships continue throughout the child's time in an early years setting and enable practitioner and parent to work together to highlight a child's achievements, extend learning opportunities and exchange anecdotes in a relaxed manner. Practitioners should develop opportunities to engage parents in their practices and share experiences of the child.

Hobart and Frankel (2003) advise creating a welcoming environment for parents. They emphasise a need for consideration of both the building and the atmosphere created by the practitioner. If parents are to sustain involvement it is crucial this welcome is extended every time they enter the setting. Smiling and knowing a parent's preferred name, along with acknowledging each parent and child individually, is important.

The accessibility of the early years setting should be emphasised. Parents should be aware that they are able to stay to settle their child and join in with play. Open-door policies, if implemented, should be clearly explained. EYFS highlights that information should be made available for parents as to the 'range and type of activities and experiences' provided, along with how parents can share learning at home (DfE, 2012: 27). Organised 'stay and play' sessions provide an excellent opportunity for the sharing of activity through planned collaboration. The format for sessions will differ, but regularity and convenience are vital elements in securing attendance. Stay and play sessions can be particularly challenging for day-care settings where a high proportion of the parents drop their children off to attend work. Close liaison with parents is necessary to inform decisions around effective times for inviting parents in as it may be appropriate to consider a Saturday session. Alternatively, parents may have the time to stay and play for just five or ten minutes at the end of each day.

Parents should be empowered to share experiences and knowledge with the early years setting. Practitioners should embroil parents in discussions of their child and consider and respect their ideas. Inviting parents in to share a vocation or skill expresses appreciation of how their personal knowledge can enhance the learning of children. Valuing parental contributions is crucial to ensuring engagement and Leask emphasises this in her discussions of partnership with a Reggio Emilia pre-school:

> As parents in this setting we were initially quite surprised to realise that the teachers seemed to value our part in children's learning. The feeling of reciprocal respect and affection between the adults in the school, the children and the parents meant that we were more than willing to reciprocate in terms of attendance at meetings and participation in school activities. (Leask, 2001: 45)

Practitioners should be adapt at sustaining multiple interactions with a range of adults who hold a key role in the life of the child. Some children may not be dropped off and collected by a parent. Day-to-day interactions may take place with another significant person. It may be necessary to talk about the best way of maintaining a constant flow of information with parents who cannot always be present at drop-off and collection time. A regularly updated diary or shared learning journey can assist in forming regularity in the sharing of information. Sustaining partnerships with parents who do not attend the setting on a regular basis is possible. Early interactions and discussions should outline how this will happen. Parents should be encouraged to share their views on the most appropriate ways to retain contact with the setting; adoption of a flexible approach that encompasses the needs of the parent and child is essential.

CASE STUDY

Sustaining involvement with Jessica's mother

Jessica was 3 when she began attending sessions at a local authority nursery school. Her mother worked full-time and was unable to collect her on a daily basis. Jessica's

(Continued)

(Continued)

15 hours of care was carefully structured to suit the needs of Jessica, her parents and the setting. Jessica was collected by her father, grandparents or attended the after-session wraparound care, which meant her mother had little contact with Jessica's main key worker. Jessica's mother expressed her concern about this at the initial home visit. She was happy for Jessica's father and grandparents to maintain primary interaction with the setting, but felt unhappy that she was unable to do so. The role of the key worker was explained during the home visit. Jessica's mother expressed that she would engage with the key worker in any way possible. The key worker suggested maintaining contact with her through sharing Jessica's learning journey. Jessica and her mother could add pictures at home and write notes that could be shared in the nursery. Jessica became actively involved in this process, asking her key worker regularly if she could 'take the folder home to show Mummy what I've been doing'. The key worker jotted notes or anecdotes to support the observations of the activity and experience. One snowy weekend Jessica commented that she needed her mother to take photos to go into her learning journey folder. On printing out the pictures Jessica requested her mother write a narrative for her key worker: 'Write on them what I'm doing, Mummy, so Clare knows.' The setting was flexible in their approach to stay and play sessions and Jessica's mother was told that she could come in to stay and play, without notice, if she finished work early.

In this case, sustained involvement and interaction was effective despite the obvious difficulties in face-to-face contact. EYFS (2012) outlines that information about the role of the key worker should be explained to the parent (DfE, 2012: 27). The system of appointing a key person, and an explanation of their role, was crucial to interactions as it reassured Jessica's mother that she could maintain a flow of information with one person. Jessica's mother developed a good relationship with the key worker and Jessica's key worker was able to share and embed the work of the setting. Jessica is evidently crucial to the process, instigating the documenting of her learning and relishing the opportunity to share her experiences.

Sharing everyday practice

Smidt discusses the involvement of parents in the day-to-day running of the early years setting, advising this as 'one of the best ways of genuinely involving parents in the life of the nursery' (Smidt, 2007: 176). She suggests that parents should be clear as to their role. In providing clarity, the practitioner emphasises what is happening and why. This enables the parent a greater understanding of the aims and ethos of the setting and ultimately impacts on how a child's learning is extended in the home environment. Day-to-day activities may include assisting during sessions, visits or fundraising events, interviewing potential practitioners, supporting baking or sharing stories.

The sharing of practice specific to a child provides parents with the motivation to become involved in beneficial and meaningful collaborations with practitioners. Athey highlights that:

> Nothing gets under a parent's skin more quickly and more permanently than the illumination of his or her own child's behaviour. (2002: 209)

Digital photography and hand-held recording equipment have modified the ability to effectively share practice with parents. Annotated photographs and snippets of video supported by practitioner observation provide meaningful ways of sharing experiences of the child. Sending cameras home for parents and children to document their weekend allows the practitioner the opportunity for extending a child's interests and pursuits.

Children delight in the opportunity to share their achievements and parents can find this both stimulating and illuminating. Practitioners may send home children's work, a copy of an observation or the child's learning journey. Using journals or noted 'Wow' moments can effectively enable the sharing of experiences and ideas. Early years settings should offer opportunities for parents to note down or verbally relay significant events or information. Collaborations involving reading and writing should be sensitively approached. They involve knowledge of the capabilities of the parent and competence in reading and writing should never be assumed.

CASE STUDY

Collaborating to share experiences and achievements

Matilda was 18 months old when she began attending day care for two days a week. The setting explained to her parents that they used a 'child's voice' sheet to enable families to record and share what they had done at the weekend. Matilda's key worker explained that this information would be used to gain knowledge of her interests and weekend activities and that completed sheets would be displayed. The diary sheets were sent home on a regular basis and blank sheets made available for Matilda's parents to take away and record events or activities. The practitioners ensured value was placed on parental contributions through positively commenting on recorded experiences and making links to the nursery environment.

The setting effectively used display space as another means of communication with Matilda's parents. A mind map, which included a picture of Matilda in the centre, and links to the EYFS, was placed on the wall above Matilda's coat peg. Matilda's key worker recorded notes relating to observations of Matilda and her parents could contribute to this. When Matilda became ready for potty training her parents communicated this with the setting and this was noted as a shared aim on the mind map.

Using display space effectively can positively enhance partnerships; parents will frequently stop to discuss a photograph of their child that has been placed on the wall. A parent's information board serves as a tool for sharing information about the setting and should be placed on a display board directly visible to parents. Waiting areas, corridors and cloakrooms are all areas that are frequently accessed by parents.

Practitioners should provide parents with written feedback relating to their child's progress in the setting. EYFS outlines the progress check that should occur when a child is aged between 2 and 3 years. The framework advises providing parents with 'a short written summary of the child's development in the prime areas'. The written summary should highlight areas of progression and areas in which additional support may be required (DfE, 2012: 10). Parents should also be invited to the early years setting to discuss their child's learning journey or profile as this provides both practitioner and parent with the opportunity to work together to discuss next steps in the child's learning. It is also a chance to highlight strength areas and discuss any concerns.

When parents disengage

When parents disengage it is necessary to consider the reasons for this. Friendly verbal communications are useful in ascertaining why a parent, who has previously engaged successfully, ceases interacting with the setting. Factors such as alterations to work commitments or changes in the home or setting environment impact on engagement. Changes to a setting should be introduced sensitively in collaboration with the parents and new staff should be personally introduced.

Questionnaires serve as a tool in establishing effective ways to re-engage parents. However, they should be used in a sensitive way and the early years team should encourage parents to attend events in the setting. Some parents will prefer to complete questions with the support of a practitioner. Comments boxes are quick and easy ways to gain the views of parents as they allow anonymity for the parent and often provide honest feedback for the setting.

Disengagement is particularly concerning when it is associated with concerns around a child's welfare. Contact with external agencies, such as social services, may be necessary in such cases. It is beneficial to adopt a reflective approach in all instances of disengagement. The study of recent actions and events can enlighten the practitioner as to the reasons for a parent's sudden reluctance to interact and assist in re-establishing relationships.

Working with parents who find engagement a challenge

It is important to remember that not all parents will engage with a setting with confidence. Parents who find engagement a challenge may react in a variety of ways, ranging from total withdrawal to the exhibiting of violent behaviour. Arnold (2003) explored personal and interpersonal barriers to involvement. She identified the following feelings that prevented parents from feeling at ease in an education environment:

- anger, fear and anxiety
- not fitting in
- feeling undervalued
- feeling numb
- isolation
- tendency to run away/avoid authority
- inadequacy. (Arnold, 2003: 99)

Feiler emphasises that aspects preventing engagement are both 'diverse and complex' and advises that they include 'social deprivation, poverty, ethnicity and the experience of disability' (Feiler, 2010: 53). It is vital that practitioners are mindful as to the experiences and feelings that may prevent parents from becoming involved with the setting. Knowledge of such experiences allows practitioners to contemplate and plan appropriate opportunities for collaboration. It is essential to retain an approach that is sensitive, non-judgemental and structured around awareness of the family

The following case study examines how the staff at McMillan Nursery School worked to form partnerships with parents who had traditionally found collaborations a challenge. This is a large nursery school, built in 1939 at the same time as the large council housing estate which it serves. It has established relationships with families in the area, with some children having siblings, parents and grandparents who have all attended the school. Demographically the locality is one of the most deprived in the UK, with families facing a wide range of difficulties, including drug and alcohol abuse, domestic violence, unemployment, family breakdown, social isolation and mental-health issues. A high proportion of the children have special educational needs and many families are involved with external agencies such as social services. In addition, many parents have had negative experiences of school as teenagers, and qualifications in the area are low. Despite such challenges, the children are described as 'happy, clever, enthusiastic, independent, resourceful, imaginative, friendly, lively, active and energetic, and creative'. Parents are described by staff as 'passively supportive' of the school and demonstrate a reluctance to collaborate with the setting, but report that they are 'happy with their children's experiences at school' (Ofsted Inspection questionnaire, June 2010). Practitioners have explored a range of traditional methods to try to engage parents positively in their children's learning.

CASE STUDY

McMillan Nursery School: Encouraging parental involvement through the 'In the Woods' Forest Project

Andrew Shimmin

Consideration of the approach

The McMillan Nursery has been a Creative Partnerships 'School of Creativity' since 2008. Through this project members of staff were able to train as Forest School practitioners, qualified to lead activities in a woodland environment. The team decided that parental involvement would be a central feature of a planned Forest Project in an attempt to engage parents in children's learning. Staff hypothesised that for various reasons parents might be more inclined to become more deeply involved:

- Parents are historically enthusiastic about offsite visits, therefore might be more inclined to take part.
- Focusing on 'forest' activities might be less threatening to less confident parents than more traditional-'curriculum' oriented activities.
- Structuring a programme over six weeks would allow opportunities for longer-term engagement between parents, children and practitioners.

As a result, a programme was planned which involved a series of visits by the same small group of children and parents, led by Forest Trained practitioners. Parents were asked to commit to attending all sessions and were also invited to a parents-only pre-session. Staff explained and introduced Forest Practice, as well as safety and practical arrangements. A range of parents expressed interest in attending, including a significant number of fathers (traditionally a group less likely to become involved in nursery activities).

Initial visits focused on setting safety boundaries, introductions and establishing a group. Sessions consisted of a mix of practitioner-led activities and games and structured free exploration. Staff facilitated group reflection and planning from week to week and promoted group bonding. Parents were encouraged to express views and ideas; their contributions were valued and respected. Practitioners took early years practice models as a basis for a participant-led approach within Forest School structures. Foundation Stage practice was used to build confidence and self-esteem among both the children and their parents.

Outcomes

Some parents, fathers in particular, seemed confident outdoors. Other parents gave feedback on feeling nervous, worried or lacking in confidence initially. As sessions developed they described the development of confidence and group responsibility along with increased relaxation and enjoyment. Evident new friendships developed between both the parents and the children. Families who were supported by the centre's family support team described the experience as 'great fun' and relished the opportunity to talk about it. They suggested visiting the forest in the summer holiday to share the experience with other supported families, including parents with young babies and toddlers. Parents engaged with the experiences and feelings of their children, with one parent commenting: 'I've learned that going to the forest makes you more calm and carefree and I thought a lot of the children liked that feeling.'

Fun, enjoyment and time were crucial elements in the success of the project. Parents commented that they appreciated the time for them and their children to 'explore and spend quality time together'. The approaches explored in the forest were developed back at the nursery school and early years practitioners were able to set up and model shared explorations to support parents in their interactions with children. After the project a number of parents who had taken part volunteered to become governors and also signed up for further education childcare courses through the adult training provision at the Children's Centre.

Summary

It is essential to work progressively with parents who find collaboration a challenge, emphasising their valuable contributions develops confidence in their opinions and ideas. The case studies demonstrate how sensitive and well-considered interventions can encourage effective partnerships that positively benefit children, practitioners and parents.

Key points to remember

- This chapter examined the principles for engaging with parents and the creation and continuation of successful partnerships. Collaboration with parents has a positive impact on the achievements of children.

- Quality first interactions with parents and children provide a greater opportunity for sustained collaborations.

- Collaboration should be viewed as a three-way process between practitioner, parent and child.

Points for discussion

- Consider the messages parents receive from your early years setting in initial interactions. How do you ensure they are given time to discuss their concerns? How do you welcome and value their contributions?

- How can you encourage the parents of children in your setting to share a skill or talent with the children?

- How are parents welcomed on a day-to-day basis? Discuss how, as a team, you can enhance day-to-day interactions.

Reflective tasks

- You are visiting a family in the home environment for an initial 'introduction to nursery' visit. How will you ensure that you effectively engage with both the parent and the child? Consider the information you will need to retrieve that will be useful to your future work with the family.

- After analysing stay and play data you realise that a number of parents are still not accessing the session. You decide to research and deliver another session to attempt to engage these parents. Reflect on all of the possible reasons for low attendance at the stay and play session. Devise a parent questionnaire to inform your planning for a new session.

- You are working with a father who finds collaboration with practitioners a challenge. He tells you he had negative personal experiences of school and does not know how best to support his child in learning. List all the ways you will attempt to build the confidence of this father. How could you involve him in the day-to-day running of the nursery?

Further reading

Athey, C. (2007) *Extending Thought in Young Children: A Parent–Teacher Partnership*. London: Sage.
Feiler, A. (2010) *Engaging 'Hard to Reach' Parents*. Chichester: Wiley-Blackwell.
Whalley, M. (2007) *Involving Parents in their Children's Learning*. 2nd edn. London: Paul Chapman Publishing.

Useful websites

www.forestschools.com
www.foundationyears.org.uk
www.pengreen.org

To gain **free access** to selected SAGE journal articles related to key topics in this chapter visit: www.sagepub.co.uk/Palaiologou2e

Working Together to Safeguard Children

Jane Arnott

🚌 **Chapter roadmap**

Safeguarding and promoting the welfare of children is a key tenet of the Early Years Foundation Stage. It is stated that children thrive when they feel safe and secure and when they experience positive relationships with those who care for them. Children are vulnerable because of their age and their capacity to provide for themselves and their reliance upon others to meet their needs. The level of vulnerability also increases for children who have extra needs because of a disability or chronic illness, developmental delay or a behavioural or emotional problem. Research identifies that children with disabilities are three times more likely to experience maltreatment (Morris, 1999).

The aim of this chapter is to define the term safeguarding and to review the legislation so that you will be able to:

- develop an understanding of the terms safeguarding and child protection and how they impact on the developing child
- review the development of safeguarding and child-protection legislation
- reflect upon the processes within the work setting that support the safeguarding and protection of young children

The importance of safeguarding children

The reasons why children are maltreated constitute a complex interplay between the child, his/her family, the community and society. Bronfenbrenner's ecological perspective (1979) provides a useful overview of how the different elements of the child and his/her context are interrelated. Individual characteristics such as the child's personality and physical health will interact with factors such as styles of parenting and the family structure. The family structure is influenced by the neighbourhood and the resources that support or increase stress. The cultural context describes the beliefs, values and societal rules that influence the ways in which families and communities relate to one another.

Research by Sidebotham et al. (2006) identifies socio-economic deprivation and parental background, including poor mental health, as key indicators for child maltreatment. The impact of deprivation (which will be discussed more fully in Chapter 13) points to lack of social support, availability of childcare, poverty and the accessibility of alcohol. Many children, however, despite living within high-risk environments, do not experience maltreatment. The level of risk can be moderated by protective factors, such as warm and affectionate parenting, that can reduce the likelihood of abuse occurring as well as mitigate the impact on a child when it does.

A loving child–parent relationship enables babies and young children to regulate stress. Positive experiences, such as physical affection, lead to a biochemical response in the brain and the release of neuropeptides, which gives the child a sense of pleasure. These neuropeptides help neurons to grow and support normal brain development (Gerhardt, 2004). Sadly for some, these needs are not met and instead children experience maltreatment or abuse of some kind. The impact of the abuse interferes with the child's ability to regulate stress, triggering a different biochemical response in the brain with the release of cortisol. Sustained high levels of cortisol cause the brain to develop a different pattern of wiring and can lead to hyperactivity, anxiety, poor impulse and affect regulation. Research also demonstrates that development within the brain cortex is affected and the ability to problem solve and empathise with others is reduced (Barlow and Svanberg, 2009).

Statistics issued by the Department for Education (DfE, 2010) identified that for the year ending March 2010, 46,700 children were at risk of abuse, and 603,700 referrals were made to children's social services. This equated to a rate of 548.2 per 10,000 children aged less than 18 years of age being referred for suspected child-protection issues. What is more concerning about the statistics is research demonstrating that children who experience neglect are 2.6 times more likely to neglect their own children and twice as likely to physically abuse them. Adults who have experienced physical abuse as children are five times more likely to physically abuse their children (Kim, 2009). Furthermore, the long-term impact of child abuse is an increased likelihood of developing mental health issues, drug and alcohol abuse and difficulty in forming intimate adult relationships (Lazenbatt, 2010).

The meaning of childhood has been viewed differently across the centuries and there is plenty of evidence to show that the maltreatment of children is not a new phenomenon. Indeed, Charles Dickens gives some very vivid accounts of the appalling conditions and treatment of young children in his novels *Oliver Twist* and *David Copperfield*. What has changed, however, is the recognition that children have specific needs related to their age and development and that children and young people have a right to be safeguarded from harm in order to achieve 'optimum life chances and enter adulthood successfully' (DCSF, 2010: 1.20).

The Department for Children, Schools and Families (2010) defines a child as:

> anyone who has not yet reached their 18th birthday. 'Children' therefore means 'children and young people' throughout. The fact that a child has reached 16 years of age, is living independently or is in further education, is a member of the armed forces, is in hospital or in custody in the secure estate for children and young people, does not change his or her status or entitlement to services or protection. (DCSF, 2010: 1.19)

Safeguarding is a contentious area of practice for anyone responsible for the care of children. The public perception is that statutory agencies interfere unnecessarily in family life, but when a child death occurs they are all too readily accused of failing the child by doing nothing. Harlow and Smith (2012) acknowledge that safeguarding is challenging for any individual working with vulnerable families, but can have enormous rewards when outcomes for children improve through the efforts of partnership working with parents.

In 1995, the Conservative government brought together a series of research findings about child-protection practice. The document *Child Protection: Messages from Research* (Department of Health, 1995) identified that most child-protection referrals did not involve serious abuse or neglect. Instead, the referrals were largely made up of children who were thought to be at risk of harm due to parental failure to provide protective home environments because of substance misuse, inter-parental conflict and poor parenting capacity, disability, illness and poverty-induced stress. Furthermore the focus on risk of harm rather than needs of children meant resources were being targeted inappropriately (Barlow and Scott, 2010).

Throughout the Labour administrations from 1997 to 2010 a distinctive shift took place and the term 'safeguarding' came to replace that of child protection, refocusing the emphasis of protecting children away from reactive child-protection procedures to preventative and supportive services for families. This development was partly in a response to the United Nations Convention on the Rights of Children (United Nations, 1989) which helped to broaden the perspective of protecting children, but also the recognition that more support needed to be given to vulnerable families to help their children get a better start in life.

The Laming Report, which was published in 2003 after the death of Victoria Climbié, criticised the lack of communication and failure of effective interprofessional working to protect children and the lack of preventative resources. Every Child Matters (DfES, 2003) and the Children's Act 2004 provided the framework for developing more effective accessible services that would focus on the needs of children and young people. The definition of safeguarding children was understood as:

> The process of protecting children from abuse or neglect, preventing impairment of their health and development and ensuring they are growing up in circumstances consistent with the provision of safe and effective care that enables children to have optimum life chances and enter adulthood successfully. (HM Government 2006, cited in Barker, 2009: 21)

Safeguarding children describes two key components, that of protecting children from harm and preventing impairment of their health and development. The Children Act 2004 provides the legal framework for the Every Child Matters (ECM) programme for change (DfES, 2003), which focuses on improving the 'five outcomes' for all children, that is not just those in need, or at risk of significant harm. These five outcomes are outlined in the ECM and reiterated in the Children Act 2004 and are described as follows:

- be healthy
- stay safe
- enjoy and achieve
- make a positive contribution
- achieve economic well-being.

CASE STUDY

The Family Nurse Partnership Programme

The Family Nurse Partnership is an example of how professionals' support helps parents meet the needs of their children. The Family Nurse Partnership, a joint programme of the Department of Health and the then Department for Children, Schools, Families, offers intensive, nurse-led home visiting for vulnerable, young first-time parents in the United Kingdom. The original concept for this programme was created by David Olds, an American psychologist. Research studies of the Olds' programme (Olds et al., 1997, 2002, 2007) consistently demonstrated reduced rates of child maltreatment across multiple high-risk populations over significant periods of time.

The programme was introduced in England in 2006 as part of the Social Exclusion Action Plan (Cabinet Office, 2009). The programme is led by health visitors who work with families from early pregnancy until the child is 24 months of age. The main objectives of the programme are to build close, supportive relationships with families, promoting parenting, healthier lifestyles and to become self-sufficient (Cabinet Office, 2009).

In 2008, the tragic death of Baby Peter Connelly triggered further reviews of the safeguarding processes. The Laming Report (2003) concluded that the procedures in place to safeguard children were fit for purpose and emphasised the importance of placing children at the centre of the safeguarding process. Safeguarding involves all agencies working with children, young people and their families to ensure that measures are put in place to minimise risk of harm to children.

The Every Child Matters Strategy (DfES, 2003) introduced the Common Assessment Framework (CAF) in a response to the Laming Report (2003). The CAF process is not a referral process, but helps to identify the needs and resources a child may need. It also provides a framework to enable different agencies to work in a coordinated way to meet children's needs and protect them from harm (DfES, 2006c). The CAF focuses on three key areas which include the child's developmental needs, the parents' capacity and ability to respond to these needs, and the potential and capacity of the extended family and environment to support the child. For each assessment that is undertaken a lead will be identified to ensure the recommendations of the assessment are put into place. The CAF assessment is not suitable for cases where children might be suffering, or at risk of harm. In these cases, children are referred directly to social services to prevent delay.

The effects of abuse on children

Beckett (2010) identifies that one of the key roles of child-protection work is to stop or repair the harm done to children by their parents and carers. Furthermore, those working within child-protection roles need to understand the types of harm caused by child maltreatment and the carer's role in this behaviour in order to change any future outcome for the child.

Child abuse occurs across most cultures and countries and surveys suggest that at least 16 per cent of the population within Western cultures will experience some serious form of maltreatment during their childhood. Further research identifies that approximately 13 per cent of all men and 17 per cent of all women will experience two or more kinds of abuse before they are 18. In the vast majority of cases, children know their abusers, and abuse by a stranger makes up only 5 per cent of all abuse cases in the UK (Asmussen, 2010).

There are four main categories of harm or abuse: physical, emotional, sexual and neglect. *Physical* abuse may involve 'hitting, shaking, throwing, poisoning, burning or scalding, drowning, suffocating, or otherwise causing physical harm to a child' (DfES 2006b: 8). However, children may be physically harmed due to neglect that may lead to starvation or cold.

Neglect is described as

> the persistent failure to meet a child's basic physical and psychological needs and is likely to result in the serious impairment of the child's health or development. It may involve a parent or carer failing to provide adequate food, shelter or clothing, failing to protect a

child from physical danger or harm, or failing to ensure access to appropriate medical or care or treatment. It may also include neglect of a child's basic emotional needs. (DfES, 2006b: 38)

There are two other main categories of abuse. *Sexual* abuse involves forcing or enticing a child or young person to take part in sexual activities, whether or not the child is aware of what is happening. The activities may involve physical contact, including penetrative or non-penetrative acts. They may include non-contact activities, such as involving children in looking at pornographic material or watching sexual activities, or encouraging children to behave in sexually inappropriate ways (DfES, 2006b: 38). *Emotional* abuse is

the persistent emotional ill-treatment of a child such as to cause severe and persistent adverse effects on the child's emotional development. It may involve conveying to children that they are worthless or unloved, inadequate or valued only in so far as they meet the needs of another person. (DfES, 2006b: 38)

The definitions of abuse are important and need to be considered within the context of the child's age and development. The earlier a child experiences maltreatment the more deleterious this will be to his/her ability to grow in a fully integrated adult. Abused children may not retain or be able to access explicit memories for their experiences. They may recollect implicit memories of physical or emotional sensations, however, and these memories may produce flashbacks, nightmares, or other uncontrollable reactions (Applegate and Shapiro, 2005).

Beckett (2010) suggests that the harm that results from abuse can be viewed as bad information that becomes part of the individual's view of the world. This bad information becomes part of the working model of the world, as described by Bowlby (1980). It also influences how children position themselves within it. The child learns that those who should provide for their needs, including their security, are not available and more disturbingly are the source of threat and danger. The child develops strategies or faulty working models to cope with the anxiety. These strategies are often harmful as they distort the reality of what is happening; for example children may blame themselves for the abuse (Pezzot-Pearce and Pearce, 2007). Furthermore, the child's distorted view of the world if unchecked leads to the laying down of incomplete memories and dysfunctional behaviours which are triggered each time they face similar situations (Beckett, 2010). The internal faulty working models lead to low self-esteem, difficulty in relating to others, and will require the support of skilled therapists to repair the long-term damage.

Although the research demonstrates that children who have been maltreated or abused are more likely to develop problems in adulthood, research also demonstrates that some children appear to have a resilience that protects them from the impact of abuse (Bolger and Patterson, 2003). In a study by Collishaw et al. (2007), 55 per cent of adults with a childhood history of repeated abuse reported mental-health issues in adulthood while the remaining 45 per cent remained well. The conclusions of the study proposed that a significant minority of the abused population demonstrated resilience to the harm caused by childhood abuse and may potentially function at higher levels of adaptation than the population as a whole.

The research demonstrated that when the rates of adult adversity in the abused resilient group were compared to a subset of the population who were not abused, abused resilient individuals showed reduced rates of criminality (6.1 per cent to 19.3 per cent), poor health (3.1 per cent vs. 7.8 per cent) and relationship instability (7.7 per cent vs. 44.9 per cent). The research identified that factors contributing to resilience included a history of a warm and loving relationship with one's parents, positive peer relationships in adolescence, positive romantic relationships in adulthood and a more flexible personality style.

CASE STUDY

Tommy and Ben

Tommy and Ben are 3½-year-old twins and attend the nursery at the Children's Centre for four sessions a week. Tommy is painting and manages to spill water over himself and needs a change of clothes. When the member of staff helps Tommy to change his clothes she notices bruising across his back and left arm. Tommy is asked how he hurt himself and he says, 'Danny was cross and hit me.' Danny is Tommy's uncle.

Ben and Tommy's family have had a lot of difficulties in the last few months and the boys' attendance at the nursery has been erratic. Their father, Michael, has been made unemployed and their mother, Carrie, has been depressed after the death of her mother. Michael has been away from home doing work for a friend.

Danny is Michael's brother and visits the family when he is short of money. He has been in prison for theft. He drinks heavily and has been violent on occasions.

There is concern that the boys have looked very tired recently and appear to have lost weight, although there is no evidence of this.

The member of staff speaks to the nursery manager who is the safeguarding lead for the nursery and she calls Michael and Carrie to inform them of what has happened and that she will be ringing social services with her concerns.

The nursery manager contacts the duty team at social services to inform them of what has happened and makes a formal report.

The law states that those organisations caring for children and anyone working with children have a duty to keep them safe. Safeguarding, therefore, is everyone's business (Children Act 1989 and 2004). This will involve policies and procedures to be followed should a case of child abuse be suspected, training and awareness of safeguarding for staff, procedures for recording events and sharing of information and knowledge of other agencies involved in the safeguarding process. Any referral that will be made should be considered under the following three headings:

- Has suffered significant harm and /or;
- Is likely to suffer significant harm;
- Has developmental and welfare needs which are likely only to be met through provision of family support services (with agreement of the child's parent). (DCSF, 2010)

Safeguarding processes

One of the key recommendations within the *Working Together to Safeguard Children* document (DfES, 2006b) is the need for effective inter-agency working in order to assess the risk of harm and put into place resources to support families to successfully parent their children. The local Safeguarding Children Boards (DfES, 2006b) are the statutory bodies responsible for how local inter-agency safeguarding procedures function. The overall safeguarding framework has been identified in the *Working Together* document (DfES, 2006b) and includes the strategy meeting, the key worker, the initial case conference, the core group and the core assessment.

Referrals are requests for action from Children's Social Care in response to the perceived need of a child, as opposed to contacts where information is passed onto social services without the request for any action to take place. All referrals should be confirmed in writing within 48 hours of the verbal referral, and there should be confirmation from social services within a further 24 hours that this has been received (DCSF, 2010).

Once a child-protection referral has been made, a decision must be made within one working day about what action needs to be taken. The team has a duty to investigate the concerns under the terms of the Children Act 1989.

Initial assessment

A local authority is required to undertake an initial assessment under Section 47 of the Children Act 1989. This assessment must be completed within seven days of the referral. The level of risk is assessed under the Threshold Response Table in Section 47 of the Children Act 1989 and once the risk has been established a strategy discussion will take place.

Strategy discussion

The strategy discussion provides a forum to share information, and decide whether a Section 47 enquiry should be initiated or continued. The members of the group, who may include individuals from education, health and the local authority, will decide whether immediate protection is necessary and what will be shared with the family. Decisions will also be made about any legal action that may need to be taken.

The core assessment

The core assessment has to be completed within 35 days of the initial referral and should provide a more global picture of the child, the family and the protective or lack of protective factors.

Initial child-protection conference

Child-protection conferences should take place within 15 days of the strategy discussion. The conference draws together all relevant agencies and family members and is chaired by a professional who is not connected to the case in any way. The conference will decide whether the child is still at risk and will develop a child-protection plan. A key worker will be identified from the local authority and will ensure that the child-protection plan is realised.

The core group

The core group is made up of the key worker, family members and those professionals who will have direct contact with the family. The group will decide how the child-protection plan is to be implemented.

CASE STUDY

Outcome

Ben and Tommy's parents are shocked by the physical injuries to Tommy. He is seen by a hospital doctor who identifies physical maltreatment. Michael and Carrie had left the boys in the care of Danny, after he had been drinking, and with the full knowledge that he could be violent. Danny is arrested and charged with assault.

The key worker and health visitor are identified to work with the parents to develop adequate parenting strategies to protect the boys. Carrie is referred for counselling and the GP to address her mental-health issues. Michael will work with the key worker to look at back-to-work schemes.

Summary

Safeguarding is a complex topic and encompasses a broad range of concepts. This chapter has endeavoured to review some of the relevant safeguarding policy and psychological theory that underpin this area of early years education and care. This chapter has also identified the need for individuals working with young children to understand how the principles of safeguarding work and what can be put in place to protect children.

Key points to remember

- Safeguarding of children is of great importance and within EYFS is now statutory in its nature. All settings that care for children have a commitment for children's safety and security.
- Safeguarding is a wider term to describe protection of children from harm and preventing impairment of their health and development.
- Child abuse occurs across most cultures and countries and it can be physical, emotional, neglectful and sexual in nature.
- It is essential to be proactive in terms of putting strategies in place to avoid abuse of children, but equally important is to have strategies that will support children where there are safeguarding issues.

Points for discussion

- Can you identify the agencies that are responsible for safeguarding children?
- How would you contact these individuals?
- In your view what are the responsibilities of the key person in early years education and care?

Reflective tasks

- Reflect on the Family Nurse Partnership case study of how professionals support parents to meet the needs of their children. Can you identify any key actions or steps that need to be addressed in safeguarding children? What can you learn from the example? You might like to consider the following:

(a) physical needs – food, shelter, somewhere to sleep and play safely, access to medical and educational services

(b) emotional needs – loving parent(s)/carer(s) who can respond to the emotional needs of their child. This will include comfort, praise and setting boundaries to give the child confidence

(c) social needs – friends and family in order to develop relationships and to understand their place in the world and how the world works.

- Access the website below and read through the Every Child Matters outcomes that have been mapped against the United Nations Convention on the Rights of the Child (United Nations, 1989) www.yvpp.co.uk/?q=system/files/unicef.pdf

(a) Identify what you think a child needs to optimise their life chances.

(b) Describe how these needs might be met and who you think might be responsible for meeting them.

(c) Think about your place of work and what strategies are in place to enable children to achieve these outcomes.

(d) What other individuals and groups do you need to work with to ensure that these outcomes might be achieved?

Further reading

Barlow, J. and Scott, J. (2010) *Research in Practice: Safeguarding in the 21st Century: Where to Now?* Sheffield: Dartington Press, University of Sheffield.
Gerhardt, S. (2004) *Why Love Matters: How Affection Shapes a Baby's Brain*. London: Routledge.

Useful websites

Working Together to Safeguard Children:
www.education.gov.uk/publications/eOrderingDownload/00305-2010DOM-EN.pdf
The Common Assessment Framework
www.education.gov.uk/childrenandyoungpeople/strategy/integratedworking/caf/a0068957/the-caf-process
The Munro Report, 2010
www.education.gov.uk/publications/eOrderingDownload/Munro-Review.pdf

To gain **free access** to selected SAGE journal articles related to key topics in this chapter visit: www.sagepub.co.uk/Palaiologou2e

Children's Health

Jane Arnott

> ### 🚌 Chapter roadmap
>
> According to the EYFS, all children deserve the best possible start in life and the support to enable them to achieve their full potential. Children develop and grow rapidly in the first five years of life and research repeatedly demonstrates that healthy children are more likely to go on to enjoy a healthier adulthood (Department of Health, 2011a). Within EFYS, *A Unique Child* (DCFS 2008: Card 1.4) identifies health as a key constituent of children's well-being and embraces a holistic approach to the definition of health by incorporating the social, emotional, environmental, mental and spiritual dimension.
>
> The relationship between children's health and their development is well recognised and the need to protect and promote the health of children is identified in the Healthy Child Programme (HCP) (Department of Health, 2009). The HCP not only identifies the importance of an effective and high-quality child-health programme in contributing to a healthy society but recognises the complexity of this work and the need to address health inequalities to improve children's long-term health and well-being (Marmot, 2010).

The aims of this chapter are to help you to:

- develop an understanding of the Healthy Child Programme
- define the term 'health' and how it relates to children's growth and development
- explore the factors that influence the health outcomes of children
- reflect upon some of the key health challenges for children in the twenty-first century
- consider the roles and responsibilities of those working with parents to promote children's health and well-being.

Policy and initiatives

In 2003 the government published Every Child Matters (ECM) (DfES, 2003), which proposed the development of the Common Assessment Framework (CAF) (as discussed in Chapter 12) and five key outcomes to promote and protect child health. The five outcomes were identified as:

- be healthy
- stay safe
- enjoy and achieve
- make a positive contribution
- achieve health and well-being.

The aim of ECM was to develop and implement policy and practice arrangements that would enable all children and young people to make progress in the five outcomes identified above. The improvement of outcomes for children and young people introduced work processes that would be common across partner agencies within a framework of integrated strategy and governance. The publication of the ECM provided a more integrated approach to children's services.

In 2009 the Healthy Child Programme (HCP) was implemented with the objective of providing preventative services, tailored to meet the needs of children, young people and families (Audit Commission, 2010). The HCP provides a framework for all organisations responsible for commissioning services for pregnant women and 0–19-year-olds' health and well-being as well as frontline professionals delivering those services. The Healthy Child Programme, formerly known as the Child Health Promotion Programme, provides a universal public-health programme for all children and families and comprises a schedule of reviews, immunisations, health promotion, parenting support and screening tests. The HCP recognises the key role of both health and non-health professionals in promoting children's and young people's well-being and is therefore aimed at the full range of practitioners in children's services.

Health visitors have been identified to lead the 0–5 years' component of the HCP through the delivery of a range of evidence-based early interventions and packages of care. The HCP aims to provide an opportunity to identify families who are in need of additional support and children who are at risk of poor outcomes; a key aim is to reduce health inequalities. The HCP is also focused on prevention by incorporating early intervention where children are at risk of adverse outcomes.

The HCP identifies that since the publication of the *National Service Framework for Children, Young People and Maternity Services* (Department of Health, 2004) there has been an increase in knowledge about neurological development and in the evidence base supporting the efficacy of specific interventions, and a plethora of children's policies and developments in services to meet the needs and expectations of children and families. The universal programme which has developed out of this research is described in Table 13.1.

In February 2011 the Department of Health published the *Health Visitor Implementation Plan: A Call to Action*. The numbers of health visitors have been in decline in recent

Table 13.1   The development review according to ages:

Age	Review summary
After birth	Maternity services will support breastfeeding, caring for a new baby, the adjustment to parenthood
10–14 days	The health visitor will undertake new baby review
6–8 weeks	The baby will have several tests and a full physical examination by a health professional
8th week	The baby will be given their scheduled vaccinations
3 months	The baby will be given their scheduled vaccinations
4 months	The baby will be given their scheduled vaccinations
12 months	The second full review which includes language and learning, safety, diet and behaviour
12 and 13 months	Vaccination: MMR, Hib/MenC and PCV
$2\frac{1}{2}$ years	Developmental Review: The third full health and development review The review covers: • general development, including movement, speech, social skills and behaviour, hearing and vision • growth, healthy eating and keeping active • managing behaviour and sleeping habits • dental care • child safety • vaccinations Within EYFS it is expected all children between the ages of 2 and 3 years to have the Progress Check at Age Two. This should be a brief summary of child's learning and development in the prime areas (see example in case study in Chapter 7)
At school entry (4–5 years)	A pre-entry to school full health review. A child's weight and height will be measured and their vision and hearing tested

decades and there was no clear agreement of their role nationally. The *Call to Action* paper identified that there needed to be an increase in the number of health visitors of 4,200 by 2015. It also described a five-layered approach identified within the HCP and built upon the philosophy of 'progressive universalism' (Department of Health, 2011b), which means that the greater the need of the family and child, the greater the provision of services to support the family to enable the child to achieve their potential.

What is health?

One of the key questions we need to consider in this chapter is what we mean by health and how this relates particularly to children. Health has often been described as the 'absence of disease'. This is a common view, but is a limiting and negative perspective and is underpinned by a biomedical approach to health, which regards the body as a machine made up of a number of different parts. Malfunction (such as disease) is seen as an engineering problem, capable of being tackled by technical means. Essentially, for every disease there is a single and observable cause that can be isolated and treated. It also requires the expert to fix it – that is the professional. Some diseases cannot be understood by a single and observable cause, however, as many conditions will have a range of contributory factors, including lifestyle, genetic disposition, gender and age. Second, health is only possible if an individual is free of disease or disability and yet individuals, including children, live happy and fulfilling lives despite having a specific condition, diabetes mellitus or asthma being two such examples.

The social model of health is a broader concept and describes the complex interplay of the social, economic, environmental and personal factors that influence an individual's health and well-being. The World Health Organization (2003: 1) identifies the importance of the relationship between a child's environment and their health: 'Every child has the right to grow up in a healthy environment … to live, learn and play in a healthy place.' Seedhouse (1988) goes further and describes the definition of health as an important resource for living and 'equivalent to the state of the set of conditions which fulfill or enable a person (child) to fulfill his or her realistic chosen and biological potential'.

If we consider the underpinning philosophy of the EYFS (DCSF, 2008) and Healthy Child Programme (Department of Health, 2009), children should be supported to achieve their full potential and health can be viewed as a key resource to do this.

Dahlgren and Whitehead (1991) identify a series of layers that influence health and describe a social ecological theory of health which maps the relationship between an individual, the environment and potential disease (Figure 13.1). Individuals, and in this case children, are at the centre of the diagram and possess a fixed set of genes. The child is surrounded by influences on health that can be modified or changed to improve their health. The difference for children is that because of their age others are making health decisions and choices on the child's behalf. For example, the first layer describes personal behaviour and ways of living that can promote or damage health. In this layer we need to consider the choices made by the parent or carer which will affect the child; that is, the parent's choice to smoke or not, the diet provided or the warmth of the parenting the child receives.

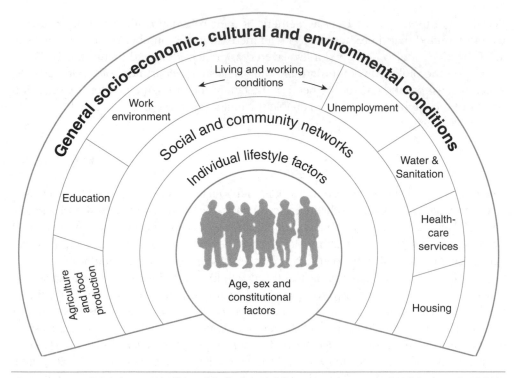

Figure 13.1   *Social model of health (adapted from Dahlgren and Whitehead, 1991)*

Passive smoking has been shown to have lifelong effects on children's health. Children who grow up with parents or siblings who smoke are 90 per cent more likely to smoke (NHS Information Centre for Health and Social Care, 2010) and for children who go on to be non-smoking adults the on-going risk to their health from childhood exposure to passive smoking is significant (Ferrence, 2010).

Research into obesity rates in children entering school demonstrates that just over one in five children in England start their school life overweight or obese (Dinsdale et al., 2012). Obese children are more likely to become obese adults, with the increased risk of developing diabetes, heart disease, musculor-skeletal problems and certain cancers. Furthermore, obese children are more likely to experience bullying and poor self-esteem, which may lead to under-performance at school (Department of Health, 2009).

Poor nutritional and lifestyle choices can lead to an increased risk of conditions such as rickets or iron deficiency. Iron deficiency is a common nutritional problem of early childhood and is related to poor nutrition and changeover to cow's milk before 12 months of age (Gregory, 1995). Iron deficiency is associated with lethargy, poor weight gain, developmental delay and frequent infections. Rickets is a condition that affects bone development in children and was a condition associated with vitamin D deficiency due to poverty. Children may suffer pain and soreness, being reluctant to walk and tiring easily. In the long term, they may have poor growth and development and could be shorter than average, more prone to fractures and with weak tooth enamel and increased risk of cavities. Research by Clarke et al. (2009), shows that the incidence of rickets is on the increase and across all social classes and is attributed to a diet low in vitamin D, overuse of sun screens and less outdoor play activity.

The social and community network layer describes the relationships between families, friends and communities which provides mutual support for members of the community. The more socially excluded a family is as a result of poverty, illness, disability, stigma and other factors, the greater the impact upon children's health. The Marmot Review identified that for children living in poverty there is a significant association between children's early cognitive development and educational attainment (Marmot et al., 2010). If we consider health from the socio-ecological perspective and see health as the means to realise potential, then poverty is a key factor to be addressed to improve health.

The next layer focuses on working and living conditions, housing, employment and access to health-care services, and the better the individual's circumstances and access to services, the greater the likelihood that their children will have better health outcomes. Poor housing stock has been attributed to a range of poor health and social outcomes (Graham, 2004). Individuals, and principally those who are very elderly or young or have some form of chronic illness, will be at particular risk. Families who live in damp, overcrowded housing are more likely to experience higher levels of stress, mental-health problems and physical ill health, including chronic respiratory conditions. Mayor (2004) identifies that the impact for children living in such conditions places them at greater risk of developing specific illnesses; one in 12 children will develop respiratory diseases, such asthma, bronchitis or tuberculosis, and there is a significantly increased risk of developing meningitis. The long-term effects for children living in overcrowded conditions affects their ability to learn, which can have a lasting impact on their ability to succeed in later life (Harker, 2006).

The outer layer highlights broader socio-economic, cultural and environmental forces such as economic development, shifts in welfare systems, political change, social forces and structures, which can impact positively or negatively upon the health of children. What is very clear to many commentators on children's health and well-being is cuts in family welfare benefits, unemployment and social exclusion impact more profoundly upon children (CPAG, 2008). Furthermore, Marmot argues that public-health priorities such as the rise in childhood obesity, increase in emotional and behavioural problems among children and young people, and the poor outcomes experienced by children in the most at-risk families demand a high level of commitment from government in terms of financial investment to support the reduction of these difficulties and improve health outcomes (Marmot et al., 2010).

Child-health promotion

Child-health promotion demands a partnership approach between parents and those members of the primary health-care team who work with families to monitor a child's health within the first five years of life. General practitioners, health visitors, midwives and members of the community nursing team are some of the individuals responsible for a range of activities in supporting families and children and these will include monitoring growth and development, and promoting breast feeding, healthy eating and immunisation uptake. Child-health promotion takes place across a wide range of settings, including the home, Sure Start and Children's Centres, nurseries and the general-practice setting. All parents are given a Personal Child Health Record (PCHR) before or after their child's birth and this record follows the child through their early years into school and provides a record of their growth, development and immunisation status. Parents are encouraged to take their PCHR with them to every contact with health professionals, including hospital appointments, and share with others who may care for the child; the childminder might be one example.

Growth and nutrition

Growth monitoring is an important part of the health and well-being assessment as it provides important data about a child's progress. Growth monitoring involves the periodic measuring from birth of a child's height, weight and head circumference which are plotted onto growth charts to allow health professionals to assess whether the measurements indicate normal growth, faltering growth that requires closer monitoring, accelerated growth, which may indicate a growth spurt, overfeeding, obesity or an underlying medical problem. In 2009, the UK–WHO growth charts were implemented as part of the HCP (McGraw, 2009). The charts are sensitive to the different growth patterns of breast feeding and bottle-fed babies, but are also sensitive to the different growth patterns of different ethnic groupings and reflects the diversity of factors that influence a baby's growth.

Growth in the first year of life is rapid, with a full-term infant trebling its birth weight and doubling its length by his/her first birthday. The growth of infants who breast feed exclusively exceeds that of bottle-fed babies in the first 6 months. After 6 months, however, bottle-fed babies gain more weight. Every child will require adequate nutrition to support this rapid growth and development as nutritional deficiency in the first few years of life not only impairs growth, but also leads to adverse neuronal development, immune suppression, impaired tissue and muscle function and reduced cardiac and respiratory reserve (RCPCH, 2012).

Breast feeding

Breast feeding has been shown to be the best source of nourishment for the early months of life and offers significant protective factors to the growing infant. The Department of Health, in line with the World Health Organization, recommends that mothers should be encouraged to and supported to breast feed (UNICEF, 2009). The UK continues to have one of the lowest breast-feeding rates in Europe. Breast-feeding rates are particularly low among very young mothers and disadvantaged socio-economic groups, potentially widening existing health inequalities and contributing further to the cycle of deprivation (Bolling et al., 2007).

Research demonstrates that breast milk is a complete food up until the age of 6 months. It is an important source of long-chain polyunsaturates (LCPs); these fatty acids have important roles in brain and retinal development. Breast milk helps to protect small infants from many types of bacterial and viral infections, partly because of the inherited immunity the baby gains from the mother, but because there is no need for preparation of breast milk as with formula feed, which increases the risk of gastrointestinal infection. Breast feeding promotes bonding between mother and baby and can reduce the risks of sudden infant death syndrome.

The Healthy Start government initiative (DH, 2011a) recognises that some babies and children will require vitamin supplements. The need for added vitamins may be associated with prematurity, small for dates, slow weight gain, culture and social inequalities.

Bottle feeding

As has already been identified, breast-feeding rates in the UK are low compared to other European countries. Within the first month of life the majority of babies are being fully or partially bottle fed, and by 10 weeks more than a half of babies are fully bottle fed. Babies should be given an approved infant formula, or a follow-on milk (after 6 months) until the first year of life. Most infant-feeding formula is based upon cow's milk that has been adapted to resemble the nutritional composition of mature breast milk. Infant formula can be divided into three groups:

- whey dominant (whey to casein ratio similar to breast milk)
- casein dominant (whey to casein ratio similar to cow's milk)
- follow-on formulas for babies over 6 months of age (higher iron content).

Whey-based formulas are the most similar to human-milk-protein composition. New and premature babies should be given these for the first 8 weeks of life as they will find the milk easier to digest. Whey formulas put less strain on the kidneys (low renal solute load), therefore reducing the incidence of dehydration. Casein is a larger protein molecule and it forms curds that are more slowly digested. It may cause digestive discomfort or constipation in some infants due to the longer digestive time. Scientific research has repeatedly demonstrated the importance of long-chain polyunsaturates (LCPs) in brain and retinal development and many manufacturers are now adding LCPs to some of their formula feeds.

Nutrition for older infants and children

Infants, toddlers and pre-school children between 0 and 5 years of age have high nutrient requirements relative to their size, as they are still undergoing rapid growth and development and are usually very active. Good nutrition is vital so that children optimise their growth and development potential; the development of good dietary habits will last throughout their lives and will prevent childhood and adult obesity. Weaning is recommended from 6 months of age (BDA, 2011), although the British Dietetic Association recognises that many babies start at around 4 months. Children between the ages of 1 and 3 years require about 1,200 calories a day, rising to about 1,600–1,700 calories depending upon the sex of the child (boys require more calories). A healthy balanced diet for 1–5-year-old children should be based on a balanced mixture of four different food groups identified below:

- bread, rice, potatoes, pasta and other starchy foods
- fruit and vegetables
- milk and dairy foods
- meat, fish, eggs, beans and other non-dairy sources of protein.

Immunisation

Immunisation is an important component of the Healthy Child Programme and protects children against a series of infectious diseases. It is not without controversy, however, and requires health professionals to utilise the best evidence to support parents in deciding to immunise their child. Immunisation is regarded as one of the most effective health-protection interventions (Health Protection Agency, 2004) and supports a utilitarian approach to the public-health perspective whereby the health of all is paramount and some risk to the health of individuals needs to be tolerated for the greater good. All vaccines are approved by the Joint Committee on Vaccination and Immunisation (JCVI), an independent expert advisory committee responsible for providing advice and scientific evidence to the UK health departments in the planning of immunisation schedules for children. Once recommendations from JCVI receive approval, they are funded centrally from government and vaccines are provided free to those who receive them.

Immunisation is usually given as an injection and describes the process of receiving the vaccine and becoming immune to the disease. Immunisation invokes an immune response; this is achieved through the administration of small doses of an antigen, such as dead or weakened live viruses, which are given to the individual to activate the immune system, or 'memory system'. Immunisation aims to achieve a level of herd immunity within a population. Herd immunity describes a form of immunity that occurs when a significant proportion of the population has been immunised to provide a level of protection for those who have not developed immunity to that specific disease. To achieve herd immunity about 95 per cent of the population need to be immunised (John and Samuel, 2000).

Table 13.2 illustrates the stages of immunisation programmes.

Table 13.2   Routine Immunisation Schedule UK, 2011

Age	Immunisation	
8 weeks	DTaP/IPV/HiB and PCV	Diphtheria, tetanus, acellular pertussis, inactivated polio vaccine, Hib and pneumococcal conjugate vaccine
12 weeks	DTaP/IPV/HiB and Men C	Diphtheria, tetanus, acellular pertussis, inactivated polio vaccine, Hib and meningococcal C

Summary

This chapter has discussed children's health. It has not covered physical development, which is one of the prime areas of the EYFS (and will be covered in Chapter 21). Children's health is important as children have particular needs and those who care for them need to be aware of these needs to promote better health outcomes. The points for discussion below enable you to reflect further on the key messages within this chapter. Further texts and websites have been identified to enable you to undertake some further research.

Key points to remember

- A key aspect of the EYFS is the promotion of healthy children, which is covered under the section *Safeguarding and Welfare Requirements*. It is recognised that children's health has great impact on children's development.

- The Healthy Child Programme (HCP) focuses on proactive actions to protect children's health, with developmental reviews at certain ages in children.

- The concept of health is complex and broad and children's health can be influenced by social, economical, environmental and personal factors.

Points for discussion

- Children from disadvantaged backgrounds are more likely to experience poorer health. How will this knowledge impact on the way care is delivered within your work setting?

- Are you aware of the different organisations and professionals who work with children and their families to improve children's health?

- Consider the role of the Family Nurse Partnership and Early Implementer Sites, and how they influence child-health outcomes – you can read about these initiatives in more depth by accessing the websites below:

  www.dh.gov.uk/prod_consum_dh/groups/dh_digitalassets/documents/digitalasset/dh_128402.pdf
  www.dh.gov.uk/en/MediaCentre/Pressreleases/DH_125655.

> ### ★ Reflective tasks
>
> - Spend a few moments thinking about the term 'health' and what it means to you. Can you think about how your definition would relate to children? Is it different? Who is responsible for promoting and protecting children's health? How does a child's age and development impact on their health?
>
> - What strategies will need to be put in place in your area of work to improve child health? How can you involve parents in this development?
>
> - If we consider the nutritional issues discussed above, what health-promoting strategies can be used to improve children's nutrition?
>
> - Who might you need to work with outside your organisation to implement these new strategies?
>
> You might like to access the following websites for ideas:
> www.healthystart.nhs.uk/
> www.nhs.uk/Change4Life/Pages/change-for-life.aspx
> parentsforhealth.org/balanced-diet
> www.mendcentral.org/whatweoffer/mend2-4

Further reading

Department of Health (2009) *The Healthy Child Programme: Pregnancy and the First Five Years of Life.* London: COI Department of Health.

Luker, K.A., Orr, J. and McHugh, G.A. (2012) *Health Visiting: A Rediscovery*, 3rd edn. Chichester: Wiley-Blackwell.

Marmot, M., Atkinson, T., Bell, J., et al. (2010) *Fair Society, Healthy Lives: The Marmot Review.* London: University College London.

Useful websites

Research into breastfeeding can be found at:
www.babyfriendly.org.uk
For further reading about the benefits of breast feeding see: www.unicef.org.uk/BabyFriendly
Weaning and nutrition for infants and children www.bda.uk.com/publications/statements/PositionStatementWeaning.pdfn
Obesity in children:
www.noo.org.uk/NOO_about_obesity/child_obesity/epidemiology

To gain **free access** to selected SAGE journal articles related to key topics in this chapter visit: www.sagepub.co.uk/Palaiologou2e

14

Inclusion in the Early Years

Alison Murphy

> **Chapter roadmap**
>
> Inclusion is often focused on children with additional learning needs. Inclusion encompasses a much broader spectrum, however, incorporating culture and language as well as disability.
>
> > Respectful educators will include all children, not just children who are easy to work with, obliging, endearing, clean, pretty, articulate, capable, but every child – respecting them for who they are, their language, culture, their history, their family, their abilities, their needs, their name, their ways and their very essence. (Nutbrown, 1996: 54)
>
> This chapter seeks to explore a number of aspects in relation to inclusive practice in early years education and care. Barriers to equal opportunities for children, families and early years practitioners will be explored and ways of removing such obstacles to equality of service identified. The role of the early years practitioner in facilitating inclusive practice and supporting children to fulfil their potential will also be discussed.
>
> The aims of this chapter are to help you to:
>
> - examine the issues relating to inclusive practice in the Early Year Foundation Stage
> - understand the role of the early years practitioner in facilitating inclusive practice and supporting children to fulfil their potential.

Defining inclusion

The revised EYFS identifies inclusive provision and practice as a core element of early years education and care in requiring 'equality of opportunity and anti-discriminatory practice, ensuring that every child is included and supported' (DfE, 2012: 2). Inclusion has multiple definitions and it can be problematic to achieve a definitive statement that encompasses all aspects. Many explanations of the term 'inclusion' focus around special educational needs or additional learning needs. In 1994, 92 governments and 25 international organisations formed the World Conference on Special Needs Education, held in Salamanca, Spain. The subsequent Statement and Framework for Action called for inclusive education to be standard, but again the emphasis was on the integration of children with SEN and disability. Their shared philosophy underlined the need for education for all and for learning to be adapted to the needs of the child.

> Regular schools with this inclusive orientation are the most effective means of ... achieving education for all; moreover, they provide an effective education to the majority of children and improve the efficiency and ultimately the cost effectiveness of the entire education system. (UNESCO, 1994: paragraph 2)

Looking at inclusion in a broader context, however, requires consideration of a number of issues that may prevent children from fully participating and accessing equality of opportunity. QCA (2000: 11) stated 'no child should be excluded or disadvantaged because of ethnicity, culture or religion, home language, family background, special educational needs, disability, gender or ability'.

Ethnicity and socio-economic status have long been recognised as impacting on children's ability to achieve, as well as other factors such as gender and having English as an additional language. DCSF (2010) statistics for attainment in the Foundation Stage 2008/9 indicated that ethnicity, gender and socio-economic status impact on attainment in the early years. Within these statistics, girls outperform boys, with 61.1 per cent of girls achieving six or more points in each of the attainment scales compared to 42.8 per cent of boys, a difference of 18.3 percentage points. Pupils from certain ethnic minority groups do not attain as well as others. Black African, Black Caribbean and Pakistani pupils achieve below average levels of development. In 2009, the same statistics revealed that 33.5 per cent of Pakistani pupils were classified as being in the lowest achieving 20 per cent of pupils. Family income can also impact on achievement: 55.0 per cent of pupils not eligible for free schools meals achieved a good level of development on the attainment scales compared with 34.5 per cent of pupils known to be eligible for free school meals, a difference of 20.5 percentage points.

There are many children who are at risk of being excluded, such as children who are looked after, young carers and children from families under stress. Children who do not feel included within the setting often suffer from low self-esteem and this can lead to underachievement and result in children being unable to achieve their full potential.

Inclusion is not just related to disability but is multifaceted. Inclusion is about feeling valued and part of a setting. Practitioners have the responsibility to ensure that policies and practices within the early years setting support the inclusion of all pupils and allow for the system to be manipulated, meeting the needs of each individual child.

Inclusion and children with special educational needs (SEN)/additional learning needs (ALN)

The provision of education for pupils with special educational needs in England is underpinned by the Special Educational Needs Code of Practice (DfES, 2001). This Code outlines the requirement for pupils with special educational needs to have their needs met and, that wherever possible, for this to be within mainstream provision. Also reinforced are the necessary steps that must be taken to acquire the views of the parents/carers and, whenever possible, the child. Each child should be given access to a broad and balanced curriculum encompassing all aspects of the Foundation Stage. All settings must appoint a SENCO (Special Educational Needs Coordinator) to adopt overall responsibility for policies, procedures and practices for pupils with SEN.

Recognising the need for early intervention with children in the Foundation Stage is essential. The Tickell Review advocated that practitioners should work alongside health visitors in identifying and supporting developmental delay as early as possible so that these children can achieve their full potential. Tickell (2011: 5) states: 'early identification of need followed by appropriate support is the most effective approach to tackling disadvantage and helping children overcome specific obstacles to learning'.

A multidisciplinary approach to ascertaining the child's unique needs and to scaffolding learning alongside the child and parent is fundamental to promoting inclusive practice in the early years; this was enshrined in the Children Act 2004 and Every Child Matters (DfES, 2003). The Foundation Stage guidance (DfE, 2012) requires practitioners to work alongside parents and to help families to access the relevant services and agencies as required, meeting the individual needs of the child. The focus within the EYFS should be initially around concerns within the three prime areas of learning, that is communication and language, physical development and personal, social and emotional development. Specific progress checks at 2 years of age should provide parents with a written summary of progress and a discussion to support this feedback. Practitioners must seek parental permission prior to sharing the information with other professionals and actively seek to help parental access to any support which they think the family might benefit from. At the end of the Foundation Stage, the EYFS profile must be completed for all children including those with special educational needs or disabilities. The assessment process may need to be adjusted for these children, with possible assistance from other specialists.

Children with additional learning needs may sometimes display challenging behaviour. All early years settings must have a policy on behaviour management and this should be implemented effectively. A designated practitioner who is responsible for behaviour management must be identified in every setting. This person should be prepared to help colleagues in dealing with behavioural issues, either through providing advice and support or accessing support from external agencies.

Equal access and equal participation in play is fundamental for children with additional needs and this should be reflected in the policy and practice of the setting. Barriers to achieving this goal include environmental obstacles such as lack of specific equipment, as well as social barriers such as practitioner attitudes. An environmental audit of the setting can identify whether all children are able to access the equipment and play situations set up. Attitudes may be more difficult to address but positive approaches to disability can facilitate strong working relationships between staff, parents and children in turn creating a more inclusive environment.

In summary, learning and play opportunities in early years education and care must be inclusive and meet the individual needs of all children within the setting. Additional needs should be identified as soon as possible to provide intervention and support in partnership with parents and other professionals. This inclusive response will ensure that children with particular difficulties in the three prime areas are identified earlier and support strategies are put into place to facilitate learning and development.

Good practice in EYFS with children with SEN/ALN

> *Unique child:* Identifying specific learning needs and developmental delay in the three prime areas as soon as possible.
> *Positive relationships:* Working in conjunction with parents and where necessary other professionals to meet individual needs.
> *Enabling environment:* Removing barriers to play and learning opportunities including physical and social barriers.

Ethnicity and inclusion

The UK has always been a multicultural society and the need to support the diversity reflected within our settings is preserved in legislation such as the Race Relations Act (1976), the Race Relations Amendment Act (2000) and the more recent Equality Act (2010). The Race Relations Amendments Act (2002) placed a duty on all educational settings to promote racial equality and develop policies and to support anti-discriminatory practice.

As stated previously in this chapter, certain groups of children from ethnic minority backgrounds do not achieve as well as other children. Equality of opportunity and anti-discriminatory practice is a key aim of the revised EYFS (DfE, 2012), providing inclusion and support for all children. The guiding principles of this document recognise that every child is unique and as such needs to experience positive relationships throughout the early years in enabling environments. Practitioners must be responsive to the needs of children from ethnic minority backgrounds; communication and language may be a focus initially if the child has English as an additional language. Another prime area, personal, social and emotional development, is also of primary importance in order to ensure that children from ethnic minority groups feel a sense of belonging when in the setting. When children feel valued and nurtured within early years education and care then they will be able to achieve their full potential.

In the past Gypsy, Roma and Traveller children have also experienced low attainment throughout all stages of education. According to the DCSF (2009a, p. 7), 'The gap between the educational attainment of Gypsy, Roma and Traveller children and all other children, which first appears in the Early Years, is one that widens steadily up to the end of statutory school age.' As far back as 1985, the Swann Report revealed Gypsy, Roma and Traveller children to be experiencing the worst degree of racism in schools. In 2009, the DCSF issued guidance that encouraged early years settings and practitioners to reflect on current practice with these groups of children (DCSF, 2009b). Examples of good practice cited in this document include making sure that the setting is welcoming and that Gypsy, Roma and Traveller children and their parents feel respected and valued; also, creating an environment that has culturally diverse resources and learning opportunities. There is a need for partnership between parents, the local community and organisations such as the Traveller Education Service to promote understanding and respect. This essentially is good practice for practitioners working with any ethnic minority groups.

Good practice in EYFS with children from ethnic minority groups

Unique child: Children from different ethnic groups bring their own distinctive cultures to the setting. These values, beliefs and ideas should be respected and valued by practitioner and children alike.

Positive relationships: The adult promoting and role modelling cooperation and respect for children and their families within the setting. Encouraging positive interactions among the children.

Enabling environment: Using culturally diverse resources in the setting and using these resources to facilitate meaningful learning experiences.

Language and inclusion

Gypsy, Roma and Traveller children usually speak English; however some may use Romani or Gaelic languages or European languages such as Polish or Slovak. As with other ethnic minority groups, therefore, practitioners may need to support these children's language needs by valuing their home language and encouraging their development of English as an additional language. The EYFS guidance (Early Education/DfE, 2012) requires providers to allow children to use and extend their home language through play and learning. In addition to this, opportunities must be provided to allow children to reach a good standard of English for entry into Year 1. When assessing children, practitioners must establish the child's competency in English. If the child does not have a competent grasp of the English language, then practitioners must work alongside parents/carers to identify if there are any concerns regarding language development, i.e. language delay.

Bilingualism or multilingualism should be seen as an advantage rather than a disadvantage. Baker (2001) identifies bilingualism as being advantageous in many ways, allowing children to experience two sets of traditions, literature and ways of thinking leading to more flexible and creative learning. He also recognises that bilingualism can break down barriers and create tolerance. It is important that children learning English as an additional language are not viewed from a deficit standpoint, but that their home language is nurtured alongside the development of English. Practitioners should have high expectations of these children and foster their self-esteem within the setting.

CASE STUDY

Suraya's story

Suraya is aged 4 years and 1 month, the oldest child in her family; she has two younger siblings. Her father works for the local authority and is fluent in English and her mother has limited English-language skills and communicates to her children in their home language. Suraya's home language is Bengali. She is one of the youngest children in a class of 24 children in her primary school on the outskirts of Cambridge. She started school in January 2012. The school does not have a bilingual assistant to support Suraya's language skills; however, they are committed to providing her with as much in-class support as possible to develop her use of the English language.

Poverty and inclusion

In March 2010 the Child Poverty Act was passed, legally binding the government to a commitment to eradicate child poverty in Britain by 2020. This ensured that the government and local authorities set targets with the aim of ending child poverty within the UK. Poverty has long been recognised as affecting children's attainment as well as their health and well-being. In terms of attainment, as seen at the start of this chapter, those children accessing free school meals did not achieve as well as other children in the Foundation Stage.

The independent review carried out by Frank Field (HM Government, 2010) identified the importance of early years education and care in terms of impacting on children's life chances. Field notes the success of Sure Start and initiatives such as Family Intervention Services in improving outcomes for children from some disadvantaged groups, although the report does concede that such provision is variable.

> Children learn best when they are healthy, safe and secure, when their individual needs are met, and when they have positive relationships with the adults caring for them. (DfE, 2012)

The PISA 2009 Report (OECD, 2010) identified that disadvantaged pupils can achieve when given the right support. Low expectations have been frequently cited by both researchers and policy makers as one of the most significant barriers to working-class educational achievement (DCSF, 2009b). In early years education and care it is essential to encourage each child to achieve and develop to their full potential; practitioners should have high expectations of the children in their settings. Likewise the children also need to be encouraged to raise their aspirations regarding what they are able to achieve. Parents/carers need to be involved with this process.

The individual needs and interests of the child must be taken into account. Those children coming from families who are living in poverty may have limited access to resources and opportunities to participate in visits and excursions. This must be taken into account when planning play and learning experiences. All children should be encouraged to value and respect each other and similarly practitioners should not be displaying inappropriate attitudes and practices that might lead to discriminatory behaviour.

Good practice in EYFS with children with EAL

> *Unique child:* Recognising the individual interests of the child.
> *Positive relationships:* Supporting parents/carers to develop partnerships with practitioners in facilitating learning and development.
> *Enabling environment:* Providing a range of resources and learning opportunities to stimulate aspirations.

Summary

The issue of inclusion is central to EYFS. The concept of inclusion is wide and it is influenced by a number of factors, such as politics, the economy, culture and education. This chapter has explored key issues of inclusion of children with SEN/ALN, which are covered by *The Special Education Needs Code of Practice* (DfES, 2001), including ethnicity, language and poverty. Referring back to the discussion about quality which underpins this book, a central aspect of quality for early years education and care is inclusion of all children no matter their socio-political, economical, cultural or religious background. Working with children and parents as well as with other professionals there is a need to develop practices where all are valued, listened to and respected equally as individuals, celebrating their differences and respecting these diversities.

Key points to remember

- Inclusive practice is fundamental to high-quality early years education and care.
- Each child is unique and as such has individual needs and capabilities; this should be reflected in the policies and practices of the environment.
- Working in partnership with parents and other professionals from a range of disciplines is important.
- The play and learning environment should reflect diversity.

Points for discussion

- If we consider an early years setting to be inclusive, discuss what sort of values we could expect to see in the setting. These values are fundamental in establishing a policy document on inclusion. For example, consider: Is every child's home language respected within the setting? And how is this respect demonstrated?

- Carry out an inclusion audit of an early years setting that you are familiar with. Consider the following:

  (a) Are all activities accessible, stimulating and challenging to children?

  (b) Are activities flexible and creatively designed to incorporate children's ideas as well as staff expertise?

  (c) Are early years practitioners developing respectful relationships with children who have SEN/ALN and empowering them to participate fully within the learning environment?

- Risk assessment is an important feature to consider, but are activities for children with additional needs risk-averse?

★ Reflective tasks

- Reflect on the policy of the setting you are familiar with and consider how it promotes racial equality. What strategies are used by early years practitioners to address issues of ethnic minority achievement and to promote race equality within the setting?

- EYFS (DfE, 2012: 6) states:

  For children whose home language is not English, providers must take reasonable steps to provide opportunities for children to develop and use their home language in play and learning, supporting their language development at home. Providers must also ensure that children have sufficient opportunities to learn and reach a good standard in English language during the EYFS, ensuring children are ready to benefit from the opportunities available to them when they begin Year 1. When assessing communication, language and literacy skills, practitioners must assess children's skills in English. If a child does not have a strong grasp of English language, practitioners must explore the child's skills in the home language with parents and/or carers, to establish whether there is cause for concern about language delay.

  Reflect on the above statutory requirements and consider ways where you can assess a child with English as a second language in an inclusive way.

- Reflect on the case study and consider:

  (a) What are the issues facing Suraya in this classroom?

  (b) How can the school support Suraya's development of the English language?

  (c) List key strategies that the class teacher can use to foster Suraya's learning.

  (d) How can the school involve Suraya's family in the process?

Further reading 📖

Knowles, G. and Holmstrom, R. (2012) *Understanding Families, Diversity and Home–School Relations*. London: Routledge.
Lindon, J. (2006) *Equality in Early Childhood*. London: Hodder Arnold.
Nutbrown, C. and Clough, P. (2006) *Inclusion in the Early Years: Critical Analyses and Enabling Narratives*. London: Sage.

Useful websites

To access information on government guidelines on 'Valuing People: Moving Forward Together' visit:

www.dh.gov.uk/en/Publicationsandstatistics/Publications/PublicationsPolicyAndGuidance/DH_4081016

To gain **free access** to selected SAGE journal articles related to key topics in this chapter visit: www.sagepub.co.uk/Palaiologou2e

Leadership in the Early Years Foundation Stage

Trevor Male

> ### Chapter roadmap
>
> The EYFS, both in its former and current modes, offers leadership challenges within early years education and care which are profound, but not wholly unique. This chapter will explore those challenges to help identify responses that are appropriate to early years settings.

The leadership context

The descriptor for state-sponsored or private provision for early childhood within England is now commonly referred to as 'early years settings'. This title tends to disguise, however, the complexity of relationships within the sector that generate significant challenges for those charged with leading and managing such provision. In practice a setting is a place where pre-school children are brought together on a regular basis and for which, as an organisation, there are certain legal, moral and societal expectations. The influences on how the setting is organised and run are multiple which, in turn, present those with responsibility with a wide range of behavioural opportunities. Together these expectations and influences present challenges that typically include:

- identification and consolidation of core purpose of provision
- reconciliation of personal (and institutional) values, ethos and mission with external influences and expectations
- clarification of leadership and managerial roles and responsibilities
- adoption of leadership structure, styles and behaviour that match the existing and emerging environment.

EYFS provides the framework of expectations for early years education and care, thus shaping the way in which these issues can be addressed and resolved. As can be seen from Chapters 1 and 2, the introduction of EYFS in 2008 was the first time that such a framework has existed. Four years later the revised EYFS (2012) has recognised the need for further change, yet we have still to reconcile the various policy decisions that preceded and have accompanied the introduction of this framework, which place the emphasis on those leading and managing early years settings as having overall charge. In this regard, this chapter refers to the impact of:

- legislation and regulation relating to Every Child Matters (ECM), which enhanced the notion of inter-agency work
- Early Years Professional Status (EYPS), with the emphasis on the leadership of learning
- other attempts to professionalise the workforce, including the National Professional Qualification for Integrated Centre Leadership (NPQICL)
- the expectations within EYFS.

The nature of the early years workforce, as those on whom the onus falls for reconciliation of these policy and legislative outcomes, also needs to be noted as a key factor in this scenario.

Where does leadership responsibility lie in early years education and care?

Leadership differs from management because it is about decision making, where management is the process by which decisions are enacted. There is still confusion, however, as to who is responsible for decision making in early years education and care, as Rodd indicates:

> leadership in the early childhood profession still has to be answered in a way that is meaningful and credible for practitioners [and there is an] apparent vagueness and haziness of what is meant by leadership in early childhood. (Rodd, 2006: 4–5)

Ultimately, leadership responsibility in any system will be aligned to those who are formally accountable. Within England, and under present circumstances, the main responsibility falls on the leader/manager of the early years setting, despite the fact so many others also have a leadership role. To understand this emphasis requires an understanding of the nature of leadership and, in particular, the difference between formal and informal leadership within social systems.

CASE STUDY

Susan's story

Susan is the head of an early years setting which had been a maintained nursery before being designated a Children's Centre as part of the Sure Start initiative. Since the transition the pattern of her activity across the year has changed and she now goes into the office at least twice a week during the school-holiday period, except when she has her own holiday. This has resulted in fundamental changes to her behaviour whereas in the past, as the headteacher of the nursery school, such attendance was entirely voluntary she now feels that she should be present throughout much of the 50-week working year. Interestingly there has not been any reconsideration of her terms and conditions of service and neither has there been a salary increase. When pressed to say whether her workload had gone up she indicated that changes had been made to the deputy's job that had seen the transference of some duties to the deputy, such as classroom observation and work on curriculum development, which has changed the nature of her own headship. In addition Susan gets additional support from a SEN worker for the Centre and a community liaison officer who organises and runs parent workshops and adult learning, thus relieving her of tasks that she would have previously done.

She perceives the major challenges of leading the Centre to be:

- governance
- funding
- sustainability
- keeping the ideal of the Centre being a community facility
- working to support the parents and children that come.

She considers the focus of attention should be balanced between social welfare and education in early years and sees her role as seeking to maintain that balance. It was easy to see how the social-welfare agenda could dominate early years provision, with major policy initiatives such as Every Child Matters being at the forefront of government policy. Clearly, in Susan's opinion, it is impossible to

(Continued)

(Continued)

educate children successfully without appropriate social support, but she considers this should be viewed as a means to an end rather than an end in itself. Her conclusion is for heads of Children's Centres to keep driving the learning agenda and to keep families directly involved.

The formal leader is not only accountable for outcomes and processes, but can also apply sanctions to other members of the organisation. The concept of leadership is much larger than this simple definition, however, and encompasses the way in which the leader is one who modifies the motivation of competences, motivation or behaviour of others (Bass, 1981). Leadership can be considered as a social interaction, therefore, and something more than describing the actions of formal leaders. Consequently in any system there are many leaders and many ways in which leadership can be demonstrated.

Much of the literature on leadership confuses this distinction, however, and contributions to the field of leadership in early years education and care do not often differ in this respect. Many actors in the field of early years education and care have leadership roles and responsibilities, therefore, with some also having formal accountability. In that regard much of the discourse is concerned with *headship* more frequently than the broader concept of *leadership*. In other words the contributions are focused on what the formal leader has to do as an individual, rather than what has to be done to create 'the conditions in which all members of the organisation can give their best in a climate of commitment and challenge' (Whitaker, 1993: 74). The institutional leader, in this instance typically the leader/manager of the early years setting, consequently has to create the appropriate conditions to support and enhance the key features of the EYFS statutory framework: the learning, development and safeguarding of pre-school children within their setting. To achieve this, the institutional leader (head) has the task of reconciling the expertise and efforts of all other adults also engaged in the support of pre-school children. These other actors range from those with proven expertise (such as the EYP, qualified teacher or professionals from other agencies) through to those with enthusiasm (such as parents or volunteer workers). Leadership in this context, therefore, is headship and will require a set of behaviours and leadership approaches that match the particular context. In this regard, and it has been demonstrated before, 'effective headship is situational and contingent on context and circumstance' (Male, 2006: 3).

Different leadership behaviours are required by others within the system, therefore, with notable contributions to be made by those with professional status, whether they be a qualified teacher, an EYP or a colleague from a related agency. To be successful in this quest the formal leader will need to ensure there are common values that are agreed and shared amongst the early years workforce and the community local to the setting (including parents). As has been suggested elsewhere, 'for an organisation or institution to provide an effective service there must be clarity of vision, particularly in regards to core purpose' (Male, 2012: 199). It is imperative, therefore, for the formal leader to establish and sustain a value set that corresponds to the society to be served and for those values to be reflected as the core ethos of the organisation and a framework for decision making (see Figure 15.1).

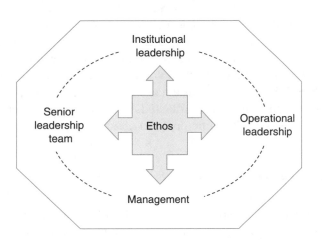

Figure 15.1   *Establishing the core ethos of an organisation*

Core purpose

The EYFS now provides the statutory framework and also offers non-statutory guidance which provides the minimum standard of acceptable provision, with these two elements becoming the frame of reference for accountability. The institutional leader of each early years setting will need to establish those minimum standards and ensure practitioners associated with the setting are sustaining such expectations. Given that many such settings may also have additional expectations (for example, it may have a direct sponsor or be a private profit-making institution) there may also be a need to determine difference and diversity in addition to societal expectations. In all instances, however, the legal imperative for formal leaders is to ensure compliance with the statutory framework while the moral imperative may be considered as ensuring the provision meets the social and emotional needs of young children within the context of their local community (see Chapter 10 for examples of engaging the local community) as well as being prepared for school as it is now a requirement in the EYFS. To that extent research into the field of leadership in early years education and care undertaken by Siraj-Blatchford and Manni (2007) led them to conclude the focus of leadership within the sector should be on learning:

> We have argued that *contextual literacy*, a commitment to *collaboration* and to the *improvement of children's learning outcomes* should be considered (by definition) to provide fundamental requirements for *leadership for learning*. (2007: 28, original emphasis)

Leadership for learning is something more, however, than the constructs of learning-centred leadership that grew from the notion of instructional leadership endemic in schools within the USA (see, for example, Southworth, 2002) and includes notions of working within the context of the current era and the community. This has led us to the conclusion that the wider elements of leadership are more accurately described in the construct of pedagogical leadership where the focus is on 'the centrality of relationships with others, such as the learners, parents, community and government, and the building of a learning community' (Male and Palaiologou, 2012: 107). In this context the core purpose of the formal leader is to ensure that the efforts of all contributors to the field of children's learning and care are coordinated, with the outcomes matching the statutory elements of EYFS as a bare minimum level of satisfactory provision.

Leadership in early years education and care

A key aspect of formal leadership in early years education and care is the recognition of the potential capability of other actors in the system to make a positive contribution to the setting. As has been discussed previously in this chapter, the workforce comprises a wide range of people, some of whom have advanced qualifications (for example, those with qualified teachers status and EYPs), others with lower-level specialist qualifications, and other employees. There were attempts by the Children's Workforce Development Council (CWDC) to classify the wide range of qualifications in a bid to determine those that are 'full and relevant' (Nutbrown, 2012: 6). At the time of writing, the ambition of putting an EYP into every early years setting by 2015 appears to be on target and over 70 per cent of the workforce holds a Level 3 qualification or higher.

The main actors in the leadership matrix, all of whose efforts need coordinating within early years settings, are:

- leaders/managers of early years settings
- professional staff within early years settings
- professionals from other related agencies
- qualified practitioners within the early years settings
- support staff within early years settings.

To be successful with both the legal and moral imperatives of early years education and care, leadership needs to be exhibited throughout the workforce and to be appropriate to situation and context. Leadership in this regard refers to dispositions and opportunities to 'take a lead' on something, or to show initiative (Nutbrown, 2012: 40).

Leadership within education and social systems is considered to be 'distributed, differentiated and diverse' in the new century (Southworth, 2006). This is because there are many more people playing a part in early years education and care, including teachers, EYPs, practitioners and professionals within other agencies. As a consequence we tend to find leadership in early years settings to be shared, with the personal accountability of the institutional leader being the key feature that distinguishes them from other members of provision in the sector. That part of the job is unlikely do go away as leaders/managers of early years settings have specific responsibilities in law. Operationally, however, the most effective settings are likely to be those where strategic decisions are investigated and determined collectively (Siraj-Blatchford and Manni, 2007).

This has led to calls for models of distributed leadership to be central to early years settings (Aubrey, 2007; Miller, 2011), although such calls seldom address the necessity to achieve an appropriate balance between leadership and management within settings or to filter influences external to the setting in the quest to provide education and care that is contextually relevant. As has been indicated previously, the key leadership role is the one held by the leader/manager of early years setting, while others also have significant leadership roles to fulfil. The roles of qualified teacher, EYP and room supervisor are the most notable within the setting, while the knowledge and expertise of professionals external to the setting are also significant. As will be discussed shortly, however, it is with the role of EYP where operational leadership may be needed if the provision is to be relevant to the needs of all children. In short, therefore, aspects of leadership behaviour need to be exhibited at all levels, but the key role of coordinating all efforts into an effective gestalt of leadership activity lies with the person charged with institutional leadership.

Leadership in the early years setting

The most effective settings will be those where internal structures and processes not only successfully support children's learning and provide safeguards relevant to need and context, but also deal more effectively with external initiatives that could affect day-to-day stability.

Internally there are generally some key elements of the organisation that need to be harmonised in order to provide the most effective environment. First, and as indicated in Figure 15. 1, there must be:

- a clearly defined culture that provides a frame of reference through which possible decisions are explored.

Furthermore, however, there also needs to be:

- a clear grasp of the difference between *leadership* and *management*;
- an effective *senior leadership team*; and
- the opportunity and support for *operational leadership*.

As has been stated above, leadership is commonly distinguished from management by means of determination. In other words, leaders make decisions and managers operationalise those decisions. Both terms are verbs, rather than nouns, however, so *leadership and management* are both legitimate activities for all members of an organisation. All settings need effective management systems which can effectively deliver policies and maintain good practice. These become the 'rules' of the organisation, the standard practices that allow for smooth operation on a daily basis. Effective institutional leaders are required, therefore, to establish management systems and practices that fulfil standard operational needs.

There are, of course, a range of leadership responsibilities emerging from the need to respond to different or unusual issues and the challenge for the institutional leader is to recognise that, although they cannot escape their individual accountability, they cannot complete all the leadership tasks that could accompany the job. Others are needed to share the load, and in terms of senior leadership it is the professionally qualified staff within the sector who would normally be identified as prospective senior leaders. The EYP is frequently prominent in this regard, with the inherent expectation that they are engaged in the 'leadership of practice' which distinguishes the role clearly from that of leader/manager of a setting (Miller, 2011: 20). Credence also needs, however, to be given to qualified teachers and other practitioners within the setting (particularly where the qualification is full and relevant). The critical stage of organisational development, however, is to build the capacity of the potential senior leaders so that not only are leadership responsibilities and actions shared, but the members become a *team*. The difference between a group and a team is well documented elsewhere (e.g. Katzenbach and Smith, 1993), but is usually determined as the willingness of members to give up on self-interest in favour of the group. Members of a team tend, therefore, to be prepared to give with no guarantee of getting anything back in return. Conversely, members of a working group can be identified as protecting their self-interest at a cost to overall ambition. Teams are generally considered as more desirable and are recognised as creating synergy, where the collective outcome exceeds the sum of individual inputs. A senior leadership team can only operate, however, where there are high levels of trust, in addition to mutual accountability.

The final piece of the internal structure jigsaw is the need for *leadership at the operational level* where individuals are empowered to take decisions that correspond to the shared value system that has been described above as a prerequisite for success. As I have described elsewhere, each practitioner will need to know what their fundamental priority is when the demands of practice present them with conflicting opportunities. The tools they need to determine their priority are the principles for action that are derived from the framework of values. The key issue is that the practitioner has 'the right to respond to the prevailing context, providing they do not contravene the ethical code that has been established for the organisation' (Male, 2012: 205).

Leading the early years settings in the wider context

The role of institutional leader in early years settings needs to become more team-focused, therefore, with individual behaviour moving to the periphery. This model does not deny that institutional leaders still have a major role to play in internal leadership and many modes will have to be adopted according to circumstance (see Figure 15. 2).

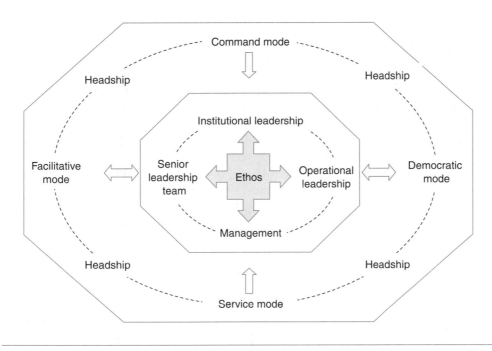

Figure 15.2 *Different modes of leadership behaviour within the organisation*

In this model it can be seen that the institutional manager adopts the headship role needed to sustain the internal structure through appropriate use of leadership style according to capability of their colleagues. Here reference is made to facilitative, demographic, support and command modes, although other contributors to the field of leadership theory have drawn attention to a greater number of styles (for example, Goleman, 2001). The main point to be made at this stage is that mode (or style) should be appropriate to context and situation. Recent analysis shows the workforce in early years education and care being composed almost completely of women, with such work being widely seen as low status, low paid and low skilled (Miller, 2011; Nutbrown, 2012). The predominance of women in the workforce has led some commentators to observe that there are distinctive features of leadership in this context that are mainly concerned with feminine attributes and behaviour (Moyles, 2006; Rodd, 2006; Aubrey, 2007; Whalley 2011). This is too simplistic an analysis, however, and it is more appropriate to recognise that a range of leadership attributes and behaviours are needed at different levels within the system, only some of which are based on traditional feminine leadership styles. It is entirely appropriate, for example, to adopt the 'command' mode in situations where there is little clarity of vision or relevant expertise available; similarly, it would be unwise to adopt a singular approach to decision making where there are professionally qualified and experienced staff with appropriate expertise available for consultation. The principal skill for the institutional leader in this respect is not to employ a pre-determined approach, but to choose a leadership style that is suited to the situation and context.

The key role of the institutional leader in the early years setting, however, is more likely to be one of managing the boundary and the quest to ensure the needs of children can be met. It has been suggested that the true art of institutional leadership has always been to manage the boundary with the external environment. Selznick (1983), for example, distinguishes institutional leaders from everyday managers by stating that leaders act on the boundary tensions between the core activities of an organization and the wider demands, challenges and opportunities of its environment. This work of boundary spanning involves protecting and supporting critical organisational functions while simultaneously attempting to accommodate external demands. Given the impact of EYFS (which includes the inherent relationships with external agencies), the demands of the local community and the continued emergence of policy initiatives, the institutional leader needs to be continually scanning the external environment to ensure their setting is remaining on task (see Figure 15.3).

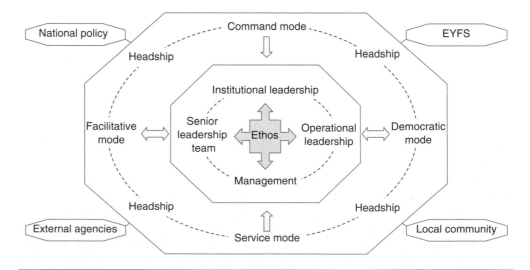

Figure 15.3   *Scanning the external environment*

A critical factor in this management of the 'boundary' is the role played by external agencies, who have a direct influence on the education and well-being of the child, as opposed to those agencies to which the setting is accountable (such as national inspectorates). Prominent in this regard are those working in health and social services as well as other educators who have been brought together under the ECM agenda into local collectives typically labelled 'Children's Services'. The notion of integrated services has led to the establishment of a new qualification, the National Professional Qualification for Integrated Centre Leadership (NPQICL), which was introduced in 2005 to support the professional development needs of leaders/managers of early years settings. As illustrated by Ang in her research of 359 practitoners who had been awarded NPQICL, 'working collaboratively and effectively with other professionals requires a higher level of professional sensitivity and commitment' which can present particular challenges and difficulties (2012: 296). A key aspect of such challenges is that 'there are many different visions, aims or expectations for early years education and care' (Jones, 2008: 18) and this is a field 'dominated by individual beliefs, values and perspectives that can have a strong emotional component' (Rodd, 2006: 110). As a consequence, people from other professions and agencies typically tend to 'view the situation from the perspectives of their own professions' (Miller, 2011: 83).

Bringing it all together

The issue of multi-agency and inter-agency working is the single factor that distinguishes leadership in early years education and care from other professions or occupations, and therefore discussions about 'feminine' leadership approaches for a workforce consisting almost wholly of women is of only marginal consequence in this respect. The centrality of multi-agency support mechanisms widens the responsibility for determining appropriate learning, development and care for young children (the core elements of EYFS) beyond any single institution or individual. Consequently the establishment and maintenance of core values that underpin actions is a task that sits uncomfortably between many actors. Leadership, as has been demonstrated above, is exhibited at a number of levels in any social system, but within early years education and care there is this added complex issue of the multi-agency support system.

Summary

This chapter has discussed the concept of leadership in relation to EYFS. There has been an increase in the literature on leadership in early years education and care since the introduction of both the EYFS in 2008 and the role of EYPS as leader of practice. The binding factor, however, is the focus on the child and the single accountable position within this system is the leader/manager of the early years setting. While that places significant responsibilities on individuals, leadership in early years education and care, however, has to be a collective effort, or 'connected effort' as Moyles concludes, that is child-centred. 'Connective leadership,' she suggests, 'is a new, integrative model of leadership that is vital to early childhood and care [as it provides] the basis of the ways in which practitioners work with children and families' (Moyles, 2006: 4). The starting point for such connected leadership efforts should be a value set that is meaningful not only for early years practitioners and the funding agency, but also to the service users and the local community (Male, 2012). Effective leadership in early years education and care, therefore, should be concerned with a collective approach that extends the capability of the child beyond the narrow confines of EYFS.

Key points to remember

- There is a difference between formal leadership and other leadership roles within early years education and care.
- Formal leaders have to coordinate the collective efforts of all contributors to the education and care of young children.
- The establishment and sustenance of core (and shared) values underpin successful leadership decision-making processes.

Points for discussion

- Do you agree that the statutory elements of EYFS are a bare minimum level of satisfactory provision?
- Does the leader/manager of early years setting have the key leadership role in early years education and care?
- Is learning the primary focus of leadership in early years education and care?

Reflective tasks

- Identify the key contributors to the education and care of young children in a setting known to you and consider who is the most significant figure in decision making.
- Think about the contribution each contributor makes to this setting and consider whether this is more focused on children's learning or their safeguarding.
- Consider whether there should be opportunities for every early years practitioner to exhibit leadership behaviours.

Further reading

Male, T. (2012) 'Ethical leadership in early years settings,' in I. Palaiologou (ed.), *Ethical Practice in Early Childhood*. London: Sage.

Rodd, J. (2006) *Leadership in Early Childhood*. Maidenhead: Open University Press.

Siraj-Blatchford, I. and Manni, L. (2007) *Effective Leadership in the Early Years Sector: The ELEYS Study*. London: Institute of Education, University of London.

Useful websites

National Professional Qualification for Integrated Centre Leadership:
www.education.gov.uk/nationalcollege/index/professional-development/npqicl.htm
Conceptualising Leadership in Early Childhood Education:
www.teacherscouncil.govt.nz/research/ece/concept-leadership-ece.pdf
Leadership in Early Childhood Education: Cross-cultural Perspectives:
http://herkules.oulu.fi/isbn9514268539/isbn9514268539.pdf

To gain **free access** to selected SAGE journal articles related to key topics in this chapter visit:
www.sagepub.co.uk/Palaiologou2e

Part 4

The Areas of Learning and Development in EYFS

Personal, Social and Emotional Development

John Bennett and Ioanna Palaiologou

Chapter roadmap

There is little doubt that the early years in a child's life are vitally important for personal, social and emotional development. To be as effective as possible, that development must take place in an environment that is safe, affectionate and encouraging for children, an environment that promotes positive feelings and social skills.

From the moment that children are born they are engaged in interaction with adults, in their growth to becoming both independent and social beings. The early stages of their lives are important for children's acquisition of social and emotional skills that will enhance their personal development and it is also clear that personal, social and emotional development can have a significant impact on academic achievement. The work of significant educational theorists, such as Vygotsky (1986), Piaget (1951) and Bandura (1977), alongside more recent studies into the development of the human brain and how social interaction and experience has an impact on the way in which the brain both works and continues to develop (Davison et al., 2009), confirms the critical role that early personal, social and emotional development has in future personal and academic success.

Personal, social and emotional development tend to be considered together, as they are linked and reinforce one another. This chapter aims to explore children's personal, social and emotional development; it aims to help you understand:

- personal, social and emotional development in the early years
- the role of the environment and its implication for children's personal, social and emotional development.

Personal, social and emotional development in EYFS

When the EYFS was reviewed in 2010/2011, a request was made as part of the call for evidence which asked what was the most important thing for settings and schools to do in relation to children's learning and development. Eighty-one per cent of the respondents to that request, the highest response, named personal, social and emotional development (PSED) as the most important thing (DfE, 2011). It is no surprise, therefore, that the revised EYFS statutory framework stresses the importance of PSED for young children's well-being, not just within the overarching principles it presents, but also as one of the three prime areas of learning and development (DfE, 2012). The framework considers PSED as 'crucial' within the EYFS. The four guiding principles of the framework support each child's PSED (DfE, 2012). This is most evident in the first two principles, those relating to the *unique child* and *positive relationships*. The principle that states that every child is unique cites the characteristics of resilience, capability, confidence and self-assuredness as ideals for children, all of which come through effective provision for PSED. The second principle, stating that in the early years 'children learn to be strong and independent through positive relationships' (DfE, 2012: 3), is clearly supported through positive social development. The importance of PSED in the EYFS is supported by the EPPE study (Sylva et al., 2003) which found that when early years settings view social development as being complementary and equal in importance, children make better progress in their processes of learning and development. The Effective Provision of Pre-school Education (EPPE) study also suggested the existence of strong links between the quality of early years education and care and the children's PSED.

As has been shown in Chapter 1, at policy level, the personal, social and emotional development of young children continues to be a key issue and a priority in the government's agenda. The strategies of the previous UK government, such as The National Childcare Strategy, Every Child Matters and the Safeguarding Children policies, aimed to protect children from harm and to promote children's well-being, and the principles embedded within those policies continue to resonate in the latest statutory framework for the EYFS.

The national EYFS guidance identifies the following three elements of PSED, each of which has an associated Early Learning Goal:

- *Self-confidence and self-awareness:* children are confident to try new activities, and say why they like some activities more than others. They are confident to speak in a familiar group, will talk about their ideas and will choose the resources they need for their chosen activities. They say when they do or don't need help.
- *Managing feelings and behaviour:* children talk about how they and others show feelings, talk about their own and others' behaviour, and its consequences, and know that some behaviour is unacceptable. They work as part of a group or class, and understand and follow the rules. They adjust their behaviour to different situations, and take changes of routine in their stride.
- *Making relationships:* children play cooperatively, taking turns with others. They take account of one another's ideas about how to organise their activity. They show sensitivity to others' needs and feelings, and form positive relationships with adults and other children. (DfE, 2012: 8)

Each of these elements is critical to the development of well-rounded, secure children, who feel accepted, both individually and as part of their community, and have the confidence to succeed or fail, knowing they have at least one supportive adult to help guide them.

The importance of personal, social and emotional development as key aspects of pedagogy in early years education and care should not be underestimated and has been emphasised in many places. The EPPE project showed that adults involved in an early years setting have a significant impact on children's well-being and this is clearly reflected in the latest EYFS guidance and the continued expectation that children in early years settings are linked with a key person (DfE, 2012). The Reggio Emilia pedagogy, for example, focuses on children's well-being and personal development, and expects that activities and the environment are organised around promoting children's well-being. As was discussed in Chapter 4 as well, a number of theorists researching effective pedagogy within the early years have linked pedagogy with children's social relationships (Dunn, 1993; Elfer et al., 2002; Howes, 1990, 1992; Hymel, 1983; Hymel et al, 1990; Rubin, 1982; Rubin et al., 1983). It is a positive factor that the EYFS addresses the key issues of PSED as being equally important to education as to children's learning. However, it can be argued that in pre-set goals and descriptive curriculum approaches such as EYFS, personal, social and emotional development can be seen as measured achievements, rather than as children's journeys towards self-awareness, well-being and building relationships.

Closely allied to the personal, social and emotional development of young children is their moral development, explored by theorists such as Piaget (1932), Kohlberg (1969) and Bandura (1977, 1986) and considered in relation to caring attachment by Gilligan and Wiggins (1987). While this area is not identified explicitly as an area of learning within the EYFS, it is important for all those working with young children to consider how they are supporting children's moral development. This is achieved through how they interact with the children, how they deal with children's behaviour and how they plan activities that allow children to explore right and wrong, through stories and circle time perhaps, which are both covered in this chapter. It is important to realise that young children will act on impulse and on their immediate needs, taking a toy from another child, for example, because they want to play with it. They need to be told why some behaviours are unfair or can hurt others, physically and emotionally. The language of emotions needs to be developed and children need to be guided in basic interactions, such as sharing and turn taking, particularly where resources are limited. Of critical importance is the way in which those who work with young children provide excellent role models with regard to how they behave, particularly towards others. Demonstrating positive social and moral expectations provides children with the examples to follow in their own actions.

The journey made by children on entering the world can be seen as a two-sided process, in which children simultaneously become integrated into their larger community and also develop as distinctive individuals. One side of social development is socialisation and the process by which children acquire the standards, values and knowledge of their community. The other side of social development is personality formation: the process through which children come to have their own unique patterns of feeling, thinking and behaving in a wide range of circumstances.

In order to effectively and successfully provide for young children's personal, social and emotional development, it is essential for adults working with them to have an understanding of the broad phases that most children go through in those areas, while acknowledging that 'developmental progression from birth to five across the prime and specific areas of learning will follow an individual path' (NCB, 2012: 18). As Ofsted noted in its review of the impact of the EYFS:

> Children's personal, social and emotional development was better where the providers visited were clear about the stages of learning and development and specifically planned activities to cover all aspects of this area of learning. (Ofsted, 2011: 6)

The assessment of development in these areas, and subsequent actions to meet the needs of the children in developing further, is supported through the non-statutory *Development Matters* materials, which offer practitioners prompts to make best-fit judgements about the stage children are working at (Early Education/DfE, 2012). The *Development Matters* materials also provide useful notes on what adults can do and provide in the development of positive relationships and enabling environments. The Statutory Framework for the EYFS, as demonstrated in Chapter 7, introduces children's summative assessment in all prime areas at two stages: the Progress Check at Age Two and assessment at the end of the EYFS, the EYFS Profile. Both of these summative assessments should reflect children's development and learning and the practitioners should use their own day-to-day observations to complete them and share the information with parents and carers or other services.

As was demonstrated in Chapter 6, observation of children by practitioners, rather than interaction, has increased in early years settings in recent years, prompted mainly by the previous assessment system in EYFS, which required judgements to be made against a significant number of criteria. While the assessment system has been slimmed down, the value of observation must still be recognised and it is extremely important that practitioners observe children when they are engaged in social situations, reflecting on their personal, social and emotional development and making decisions about what each child needs to progress in those areas. It is possible to do a considerable amount of that through interaction, but in taking the role of a non-participant observer the practitioner is able to focus purely on identifying features of the development of skills and attitudes that contribute to PSED.

The critical need to ensure the most effective personal, social and emotional development led the previous government to develop the SEAD programme (Social and Emotional Aspects of Development) specifically to support those working with young children in their efforts to develop social and emotional skills. The SEAD guidance for practitioners continues to provide a sound basis for work on these aspects (DCSF, 2008). That programme of development and training was aimed at birth to 36 months. The SEAL (Social and Emotional Aspects of Learning) materials, also developed by the previous government, provide similar resources for developing those aspects with children for 30 to 60+ months (DfES, 2005). Practitioners therefore have a wealth of useful support materials available to help ensure that effective personal, social and emotional development take place.

It is important for the early years practitioners to consider the elements of PSED from theoretical and practical perspectives, to develop the fullest understanding possible of what effective provision is for developing self-confidence and self-awareness, helping children to manage feelings and behaviour and supporting making relationships.

Self-confidence and self-awareness

When babies are born they have a very long way to go before becoming independent. If they are safely to survive, consistent care must be provided over an extended period of time. It is here that the social skills of infants come into play. Part of their development can be characterised as a process to differentiate themselves from others and to construct the concept of 'self' (or personal identity).

In the case of developing the self, babies have, as one of the major developmental points in this area, the gradually increasing awareness of a sense of themselves as distinct and separate entities, clearly differentiated from all other entities (human and non-human) that populate their everyday world. This process of articulation and definition of self begins in early infancy. At first babies do not recognise themselves. For example, when a baby is placed in front of mirror there is no reaction from them, as they do not recognise that the reflection is of them. At about the age of 18 months babies begin to have a clearer idea that this reflection is a representation of themselves.

The acquisition of the concept of identity is important for children's well-being. Selleck (2001) claims that the parent or carer in an early years setting plays an important role in this formation of infant identify. That role involves affirming responses, consistent care, ensuring that the child feels special, even when one of many, and acting in a way that builds the confidence of the child at every opportunity.

Adults helping children to develop a personal identity need to be aware that a baby's crying is a form of expressing how they feel (such as discomfort, stress, hunger or tiredness) and at the same time is a way of attempting to communicate with the parent/carer. The adult should respond accordingly, providing an appropriate response (relieving discomfort, stress, hunger or the need for rest).

Social communication, which adults need to be aware of, also develops through the 'social smile'. In the beginning of their lives, a baby's smile is a form of expressing their comfort, as it is related to their biological needs. When their biological needs are covered, they feel comfort, and the muscles in their faces relax and they appear to smile. They also appear to smile when the mother strokes and comforts them. At the age of between 6 and 10 weeks, however, infants start to show a clear preference for certain human beings and especially for familiar human faces.

A 'social smile' indicates the progress of babies in differentiating themselves as individual human beings and they respond to the face of another human being by smiling back to them. It is a major developmental stage in babies' lives towards the process of identity formation and towards the acquisition of a repertoire of social skills.

In the sequence of photographs in Figure 16.1 the social smile of a baby is captured. The baby is lying in his cot and an adult is approaching him. The baby looks at the adult's face and soon afterwards his lips form a smile (shown in the last photo) and the expression becomes one of happiness as the smile becomes more intense.

Gradually, when infants become more mobile and explore the world around them (alongside cognitive development), they begin acquiring self-recognition by becoming self-aware, an element central to children's emotional and social lives.

When working with young babies in an early years setting it is important to offer them opportunities to develop a concept of themselves. Activities such as nursery rhymes combined with physical movement mirrors in which babies explore their reflections and games such as when adults hide their faces with their hands in front of the baby (peek-a-boo!), are activities that sound simple yet actually help infants in their process of acquiring their concept of self.

Within this development of self-concept, and the understanding of personal identity, the critical areas of self-confidence and self-esteem must be fostered. In the early years the responses of others, whether they are parents, carers, staff in early years settings or other children, have an effect on the child's perception of self. All those who have responsibility for the development of young children should ensure that the interactions they have with those children are ones that enable children to feel they are secure

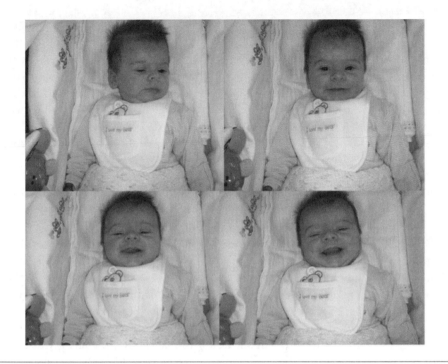

Figure 16.1 *A baby's social smile*

and accepted, that they have worth. These affirmations help children to develop a positive self-concept. The adults should engage in activities with the children which build self-confidence, critically through the use of praise and encouragement. The environment must also support this development and it is important that the interactions with other children are monitored and relevant, and appropriate interventions are made when necessary, for example, if another child is likely to cause upset that the child is unlikely to be able to cope with personally. Such interventions must be carefully considered, as an adult, through always intervening, will not allow the child to gain skills in dealing with difficulties personally or developing resilience to negative social situations.

Managing feelings and behaviour

Attachment

As was discussed in Chapter 9, a dominant and influential theory on the emotional development of children is that proposed by Bowlby (1960, 1969, 1973, 1980, 1986, 1999, 2005) and developed further by Ainsworth (1969, 1979, 1985, 1989), Ainsworth and Bell (1970), Ainsworth and Bowlby (1991), Ainsworth et al. (1971a, 1971b) and Ainsworth et al. (1978) regarding 'attachment'. All these studies proposed that when babies are born they are 'pre-programmed' to form close relationships with the mother/carer. This bond is called attachment. The ideas of Bowlby and Ainsworth have influenced the way mother–child and carer–child relationships are perceived. Bowlby and Ainsworth have each described in detail the stages of attachment and how the formation of the relationship between the mother (or carer) and the baby takes place. They have also discussed the consequences of the separation of the child from the mother or carer.

The *Development Matters* document, created to support assessment and planning for EYFS, clearly states that staff working with young children must be 'aware of the importance of attachment in relationships' (Early Education/DfE, 2012: 8).

This has considerable implications for early years settings. Owing to economic factors an increasing number of primary carers of children are entering the workforce so more children attend early years settings from a very young age. In the light of the attachment theory, it is necessary that the EYFS emphasises the importance of the role of the key person in relation to children for smooth transitions of children from home to early years settings. Prior to joining the setting young children need such emotional warmth as that provided by practitioners when they enter early years education and care in order to provide a form of substitute for the attachment, and they also need a continuous and stable relationship with the early years practitioners for their personal well-being.

Bowlby claims, 'If a community values its children, it must cherish their parents' (1951: 84). Not only do children form attachment with parents; parents form strong attachments with their children. Consequently, when children join early years settings, parents can feel guilty for not being with them and may experience anxiety as to whether their children will have an enjoyable time in the setting and make friends. It is essential to support the parents during this process and roles of the key person include continually reconfirming that children are forming stable relationships within the settings and reassuring the family about the care and support being provided.

Making relationships

An important aspect of the children's social development is how they form relationships with others, how they behave during these interactions with either other children or adults and how they make attempts to become part of the community and the wider social environment.

Children attempt from a very young age to make relationships. For example, small children are interested in the activities of others of a similar age, or they smile at other human beings (familiar faces in particular). Making relationships during early childhood is a major developmental task for children. It is essential to understand that children's perceptions and criteria for forming relationships differ in many ways from those of adults. Young children choose friends and to make relationships with other individuals on the basis of their pleasurable interactions with them. This does not mean that they are selfish. When children first begin to form relationships they lack abstract thinking, so are unable to conceptualise the meaning of mutual friendships. As they grow older and their cognitive development advances, however, they evolve into being able to form a more abstract relationship based on mutual consideration and psychological satisfaction.

For example, a child can be a friend with another child during outdoors play time as they have fun riding bikes, running or jumping; when in the class, though, each may be friends with another child as they enjoy playing in the construction area. Phrases such as 'You are not my friend' or 'I do not want to play with you' are common in early years settings. As Damon (1988) suggested, there are different levels at which children develop their friendships. Damon describes friendships in early childhood as a 'handy playmate', where children choose a friend on the basis that they do together those things each enjoys.

As children grow older and develop their own concept of self, self-awareness and an awareness of others' thoughts and feelings, they are able to form relationships involving mutual trust.

Sociometric status studies have shown that in early years settings children tend to fall into four major categories. Sociometric studies ask children to rate the other children in their respective group. Numerous sociometric studies (e.g. Rubin, 1982; Hymel, 1983; Rubin et al., 1983; Hymel et al., 1990; Howes and Matheson, 1992; Dunn, 1993; DeRosier et al., 1994; Black and Logan, 1995) have investigated how children form relationships within early years settings. It was shown that children in a classroom setting display the following tendencies:

- *Popular* children are liked by their peers. These children are very active, direct or lead activities, make suggestions and structure activities.
- *Rejected* children are those who are actively disliked by and receive many negative comments from their peers. Others do not want to invite them into their play. These 'rejected' children often demonstrate aggressive behaviours, such as hitting, biting, or kicking, none of which helps them.
- *Controversial* children get a large number of positive and negative comments from their peers.
- Finally, *neglected* children are seldom chosen to join in with activities, either positively or negatively. Their peers normally ignore these children, who then find themselves in isolation. Subsequently, neglected children do not participate in activities; they demonstrate isolated behaviour.

The degree of peer acceptance is a powerful predictor of current (as well as later) psychological adjustment. Rejected children, especially, are unhappy, alienated and poorly achieving children with a low sense of self-esteem. Practitioners and parents both view them as having a wide range of emotional and social problems. Research claims that peer rejection during middle childhood is also strongly associated with poor school performance, anti-social behaviour, and delinquency and criminality in adolescence and young adulthood (De Rosier et al., 1994).

With age, children come to develop a number of skills, such as perspective thinking and the ability to understand the viewpoints of others; therefore, they become better at resolving social conflicts and their relationships with others improve. Taking turns in activities helps children to develop social problem-solving skills, while serving one another during snack times helps them to develop a perspective of others. It is important to create activities within which children are offered opportunities to develop all of the necessary social skills and are encouraged to form relationships.

CASE STUDY

Friendships

Kayleigh and Leanne recently joined the nursery class at the same time and appeared to choose to play together all of the time. Each was assigned a different key worker.

Initially the girls were always placed in the same group, but over time both key workers identified ways in which the apparently strong bond between the girls was having an impact on their broader interaction and their development of essential social skills. For example, Kayleigh's key worker observed the girls playing with buckets, spades and large jelly moulds in the sand tray. Kayleigh always used the spade, while Leanne held the mould or bucket and when she asked to use the spade, Kayleigh said that was not her 'job'. Whenever another child came to try to join in Kayleigh told him or her it was just for her and her friend. Similarly, Leanne's key worker had heard Kayleigh tell another child that she could not play with Leanne, because Leanne was her friend only. Further observations confirmed that Kayleigh dominated and controlled the games she played with Leanne.

Although the key workers felt that there was no malice in Kayleigh's actions, they decided to make sure that the girls would be placed in separate groups at times, with the result that Leanne gained more independence and confidence and Kayleigh, after some initial difficulties and reassuring words and explanations from her key worker, began to share more readily and play happily with others. Over time, although the girls still tended to play together when not in separate groups, they also included others more readily.

Play and stories

The role of play in EYFS was explored in Chapter 5, where it was demonstrated how important play is for children's learning and development. This section examines the role of play in relation to children's PSED. When children enter their early years education and care they begin with non-social activity, and *solitary play* (i.e. unoccupied, onlooker behaviour). They later shift to a form of limited social participation, called *parallel play*, in which a child plays near other children using similar materials, but does not try to interact with or influence their behaviour (Barnes, 1971; Rubin, 1982; Rubin et al., 1983; Dunn, 1993; Smith, 1997).

As children grow older they reach a higher level of social interaction, characterised by two forms of true social interaction: *associative play*, in which children engage in separate activities, although they do interact by exchanging toys and commenting on one another's behaviour, and *cooperative play*, a more advanced type of interaction involving work oriented towards a common goal, such as acting out a make-believe scenario or working on the same product, for example, a sand castle or patchwork quilt (Barnes, 1971). All of these types of play co-exist during early childhood, as illustrated in Table 16.1.

Table 16.1 Examples of all types of play in early childhood

Play type	Examples
Non-social activity	**Solitary play** A child is sitting alone in the writing corner using the table as a motorway to play with his cars. He plays there for about six minutes. **Parallel play** Four children are sitting at a table, trying to put together some puzzles. Each child does a different puzzle. **Functional play** Simple, receptive motor movements with or without objects.
Unoccupied	A 3-year-old boy sits for a long time in a chair doing nothing. He was not obviously engaged in anything, but after close observation he is aware of other children and he watches them very carefully.
Associative play	**Constructive play** Children are sitting on the carpet playing with Lego. They try to make a farm with animals. Each has his or her own pieces, and the children exchange pieces and talk about what animals the farm will include. **Make-believe play** Two girls are in the dolls' house, pretending that they are friends and that they have invited each other for tea; they talk about their dolls as if these are real babies.
Comparative play	Four children are in the yard looking at some lentils that they planted in the morning. Suddenly, they see a tortoise and try to stop it because they think that the tortoise will eat the lentils. **Games with rules** Two boys and a girl are in the outdoor area and they want to play in the sandbox area. They make a motorway in order to race their cars. They set two rules: not to damage the motorway by shifting the sand with the cars, and, second, not themselves to step on the sand.

Furthermore, although non-social activity eventually declines with age, it is still the most frequent form of behaviour among 3- and 4-year-olds. Even among young children it continues to take up as much as a third of children's free-play time. The occurrence of both solitary and parallel play remains fairly stable between 3 and 6 years of age (Howes and Matheson, 1992).

Make-believe play is developed in parallel with representation. Piaget (1951) believed that through pretending children practise and strengthen newly acquired symbolic schemes. Make-believe play also allows children to become more familiar with social-role possibilities by acting out familiar scenes and highly visible occupations (for example, police officer, doctor or nurse). In this way play provides young children with important insights into links between themselves and society.

Piaget's view of make-believe play as being mere practice of symbolic schemes is now regarded, however, as too limited. More recent research indicates that play not only reflects, but also contributes to children's cognitive and social skills (Nikolopoulou, 1993).

Vygotsky offers a slightly different view of make-believe play. In accordance with his emphasis on social experience and language as vital forces in cognitive development, Vygotsky (1986) granted make-believe play a prominent place within his theory. He regarded it as creating a unique, broadly influential zone of proximal development, during which children advance themselves as they try out a wide variety of challenging skills:

> In play, the child always behaves beyond his average age, above his daily behaviour; in play it is though he were a head taller than himself. As in the focus of a magnifying glass, play contains all developmental tendencies in a condensed form and is itself a major source of development. (Vygotsky, 1978: 102)

During make-believe play, pre-school children act out and respond to one another's pretend feelings. Their play is rich in references to emotional states. Young children also explore and gain control of fear-arousing experiences when, for example, they play the role of a doctor or a dentist, or pretend to be searching for monsters. As a result, they are better able to understand the feelings of others and also to regulate their own. Finally, collectively to create and manage complex narratives, pre-school children must resolve their disputes through negotiation and compromise – skills they develop when they become older (Singer and Singer, 1990; Howes, 1992).

All of the points above highlight the need for those working with children in early years education and care to ensure that opportunities for make-believe play or role-play as it is commonly named, are an integral part of the planned provision, but also that the setting facilitates child-initiated role-play. Much of this can be achieved by having role-play areas and role-play resources. The areas can be set up to mirror social contexts, such as a shop, a school or a doctor's surgery, or they can simply be spaces where the children can play. The areas could also be set up as settings from stories the children are hearing and sharing, such as the bridge from *The Three Billy Goats*, *The Gruffalo* or the differing environments in *We're Going on a Bear Hunt*. Resources appropriate to each role-play setting should be added, including props and costumes, as well as toys such as teddies, dolls and puppets. All of these enable the children to role-play social interaction in pretend social spaces, which is essential practice and promotes social development in secure, non-threatening environments. The adult's role in this is very much as the facilitator, but stepping in and playing, also in role, can help to resolve disagreements to support social and emotional development, as well as to model social and emotional responses.

There are strong links between the two prime areas of learning of communication and language, and personal, social and emotional development. It is notable that a significant number of the statements related to what children do in EYFS at the various ages/stages in the *Development Matters* overview of PSED relate to talk, discussion and communication. The development of talk (which is covered in Chapter 17 and 18) obviously facilitates the building of relationships and the critical ability to communicate feelings in a more refined way, but the strong links between the two areas of learning go further than this.

The importance of stories in the EYFS cannot be underestimated. Stories provide young children with opportunities to explore personality, social situations, interactions, emotions and the broad range of personal, social and emotional experience, from the safety of being a listener. Stories communicate important messages about life and give children opportunities to empathise with the characters. Most children will naturally follow up hearing stories with self-generated activities related to them, engaging in imaginative play, both individually and with others. Adults can support this and also enhance the whole impact of stories through provision of areas to play in, props, puppets, soft toys and costumes. As well as telling stories and giving the children the chance for story-based play, adults should also engage the children in talk about the stories, developing understanding and exploring how characters act and feel. This is one way of helping to develop the language of emotions.

A further method for exploring emotions, which also supports social development, turn taking, and speaking and listening skills, is to introduce the children to circle time (Mosley, 2005). In the context of taking turns going around the circle, questions about feelings can be explored in many different ways, offering children insights into the way in which others feel and the chance to express their own perspectives. When done well, this type of activity can support many aspects of PSED, particularly increasing the children's understanding of emotional language and contributing to their skills in listening to others and identifying the feelings of others.

CASE STUDY

Emotional language development through story

Amrit and some of the other children had been listening to a nursery nurse reading the Michael Rosen book *We're Going on a Bear Hunt*. In the story the family do encounter a bear and run away from it. The nursery nurse asked the group to pretend that they were the children in the family and to say what they were feeling when they

(Continued)

(Continued)

found the bear. One of the children responded 'scary', one said 'scared' (a word used a lot in the story) and another said 'fightened' (which the nursery nurse repeats as 'frightened'), but Amrit said that he would feel 'funny'. The nursery nurse asked Amrit why he thought it was funny and he said that 'it isn't funny', but he would 'feel funny'.

Amrit did not yet have the language to fully express his emotions and reverted, therefore, to something he has heard others say, but wasn't entirely appropriate in this situation. Through the responses of the other children and the nursery nurse's repetition of appropriate words, Amrit started to learn the language associated with being scared.

In a later activity, the nursery nurse heard Amrit say that his cat was frightened by a dog in next door's garden. He was beginning to use appropriate language and the nursery nurse planned to consolidate that by using *The Gruffalo* (Donaldson, 1999) as another starting point for further discussion.

Resources and the environment

The quality and quantity of play materials has a major impact upon young children's personal, social and emotional development. In an interesting study, Smith (1997) showed that fights and disruptions increase in early years settings where children were confined to a relatively small space in which to play and where there were not enough toys to share around.

It is important to make sure that children have a variety of toys and play materials available to them. Construction materials, building blocks and puzzles tend to be associated with solitary play, but these are important materials to have available when children decide to engage in solitary activities. As has been demonstrated, all types of play co-exist in children's daily routine within the setting. Children choose what type of play they want to join in according to their needs at that time.

In order to encourage participation from all children, open-ended activities and relatively non-constructed objects (such as using fabrics or instigating face-painting) can facilitate both cooperative and imaginative play. Children will need to use their negotiation, problem solving, communication and listening skills, when participating in these activities, developing and practising these essential abilities.

Using realistic toys such as trucks, dolls, telephones and tea-sets helps children to act out everyday roles and this also promotes role-playing. Role-play requires complex interactions, especially when children try to re-create 'real' events that have happened to them. Additionally, role-play is essential for enabling children to express and articulate their feelings within a safe environment.

Classroom activities need to be adapted in order to increase the participation of all children present. Regular systematic observations of the different areas of the class are required; practitioners need to be prepared to change the organisation of their setting to ensure that children can move around and use all areas to the maximum.

In recent years the use of the outdoor environment has received considerable promotion as part of early years education and care. It is essential for PSED that outdoor activities are a planned part of the range of experiences young children have. Outdoor play can help promote social interactions, through a broader range of potential cooperative activities, such as sand play and large construction equipment. Some outdoor games and equipment, such as large play equipment, that need space and room for children to move freely, help children to develop respect for their peers by waiting to take turns or, for example, by playing in pairs. Emotional development is supported by the potentially greater freedoms afforded by being outdoors. Children can express their emotions in larger spaces and in louder ways than are often acceptable indoors. They can run and jump and shout and scream, if they wish, expressing pleasure and revelling in the freedom the outdoor environment provides.

The role of the adult in all of these situations is highly important. The adult can help children with activities, or can suggest activities where peer collaboration is required. The adult can monitor interactions among the children, and make sure that all children are encouraged to play with one another.

In a supportive setting or outdoor environment where the social behaviours of children are promoted, and in an environment where children feel safe to express their feelings, the children's developmental journey will be supported effectively.

Summary

This chapter has discussed a key aspect of children's development: personal, social and emotional development. Although PSED was studied separately here, it is necessary to stress that it is influenced by all aspects of development, such as cognitive development, language and physical development. In the following chapter it will be demonstrated how important PSED is in other aspects of children's development. It is a positive aspect of the EYFS that PSED is a statutory prime area for children's well-being.

Key points to remember

- This chapter looked at the personal, social and emotional development of young children. Although these three aspects of development are studied separately, they are interlinked, and they form the foundation for the other areas of children's cognitive development.

- When working with very young children it is important to understand their relationships with the family and with other children, and how they form relationships in the early years setting.

- The organisation of the early years environment and the materials and resources used play a crucial role in children's personal, social and emotional development.

Points for discussion

- Consider the implications of attachment when you are planning for the arrival of a new child into your setting. What strategies would you use to help with the transition? How would you allocate the key person? How would you plan for involving this child in the setting's daily activities?

- If personal, social and emotional development are not supported by effective planning in a setting, what might the impact of this be?

- How would you encourage a hesitant child to get involved in role-play activities?

Reflective tasks

- Reflect on the different definitions of social positions of children in the setting (i.e. 'popular', 'rejected', 'controversial' and 'neglected') and try to identify in which category the children in your group belong. How can you help a rejected child to form relationships with other children? How can you help a controversial child? How can you involve a neglected child?

- Choose one of the three elements of EYFS PSED and using the *Development Matters* materials and observation over time, track one child's progress in that area. Does the development match with what *Development Matters* shows as the developmental journey or are there differences? If there are differences, can you identify the factors that lead to those?

- If you were introducing circle time in an early years setting for the first time, how would you go about it? What would you need to do to prepare the children to take part? What environmental factors would you need to consider? What themes would you explore when first implementing this strategy?

Further reading

Dowling, M. (2010) *Young Children's Personal, Social and Emotional Development*, 3rd edn. London: Sage.

Papatheodoropoulou, T. and Moyles, J. (eds) (2009) *Learning Together in the Early Years: Exploring Relational Pedagogy*. London: Routledge.

Sheppy, S. (2009) *Personal, Social and Emotional Development in the Early Years Foundation Stage*. London: David Fulton.

To gain **free access** to selected SAGE journal articles related to key topics in this chapter visit: www.sagepub.co.uk/Palaiologou2e

Communication and Language

Claire Head

> ### 🚌 Chapter roadmap
>
> The revised Early Years Foundation Stage states that the prime area of communication and language development 'involves giving children opportunities to experience a rich language environment; to develop their confidence and skills in expressing themselves; and to speak and listen in a range of situations' (DfE, 2012: 5).
>
> Communication is a vital human experience that should place children at the heart of their social network from the moment they are born. Learning to communicate in a variety of ways, through non-verbal and verbal means, allows children to explore emotions, develop relationships and begin learning about their world. This process starts within the community of the family.
>
> This chapter aims to help you to:
>
> * appreciate that children need the right environment in order to develop effective communication skills. This includes interaction with adults who are genuinely interested in listening to children and in sharing conversations that help children to develop their language for thinking, responding and for expressing feelings
>
> * recognise that early childhood is a critical phase of brain development and the act of communication with the primary caregiver has a decisive influence on how the brain becomes 'wired' for life
>
> *(Continued)*

> *(Continued)*
>
> - understand that learning a language system is a complex puzzle with interlocking pieces and we need to help children to make use of all their linguistic resources.

The range of research evidence that will be explored in this chapter has one common uniting factor: babies and young children are ready to connect and communicate and wait only for encouragement and opportunity from the surrounding world. A recent research project ('Face to Face', March 2009–2011), aimed at promoting key messages for effective communication between parents and infants, reminds us that the word 'infant' derives from the Latin *infans* and means 'speechless' (*in* 'not' and *fari* 'to speak'). However, far from being 'speechless', babies and young children find many ways to express themselves and actively seek interaction with others. Indeed, language development and sensitivity to sounds begins before birth as research has shown that babies in the womb can identify the sound of the mother's voice (Karmiloff and Karmiloff-Smith, 2001).

Creating connections for communication

Hence, a key consideration for parents of young children *and* early years practitioners is how they can positively influence this rich period of potential development from birth to 3 years of age in order to help children to lay secure foundations for lifelong communication. How can adults 'tune in' to the child's voice and encourage children to share their ideas, questions, interests and feelings? Rouse Selleck reminds us that adults need to learn to listen to children: 'Although most infants do not learn to talk until their second year, their voices are there for us to hear from birth' (Rouse Selleck, 1995, cited in David et al., 2003: 80).

In Reggio Emilia (in Northern Italy) the approach to early education founded by Loris Malaguzzi (just after the Second World War) is based on a pedagogy of listening to the child's voice and recognising children can express themselves in many different ways. It is the teacher's task to seek and to hear the voice of the child and to find a way to hear the 'hundred languages of children'.

Extract from 'The Hundred Languages of Children'

No way.

The hundred is there.

The child is made of one hundred.

The child has

> a hundred languages
>
> a hundred hands
>
> a hundred thoughts
>
> a hundred ways of thinking
>
> of playing
>
> of speaking. (Malaguzzi, 1996)

Similarly, Bruce (2010) encourages adults to share music, rhyme, rhythm and move-ment with children in order to foster a sense of connection and shared experience. Both these approaches emphasise the primary role that communication and language experience plays as the starting point for immersion in a rich language and literacy context.

The revisions to the Early Years Foundation Stage indicate that a distinction should be made between the prime aspect – communication and language – and the specific aspect – literacy. The separation of the traditionally interrelated areas of reading and writing (literacy) and speaking and listening skills is prompted by research that high-lights the time-sensitive link between early brain development and the acquisition of communication and language skills that 'happen during an optimum window of brain development' and are 'experience expectant' (Tickell, 2011: Annex 8: 98).

Brain development relies on a complex interplay between the genes you have and your interaction with life experiences, which creates neural activity and builds neural connections (for more on brain development, see Chapter 21). Consequently, experi-ences in early years education and care can have a significant impact on the rest of life (Gopnik et al., 2001).

Creating meaning

Effective communication is fundamental to quality of life and learning. In order to become competent language users babies and children need opportunities to rehearse their communication skills in sociable contexts, encouraged by trusted and loving adults who value children's attempts to interact and make connections. The *Birth to Three Matters* framework embraces a positive image of the baby or child as a 'skilful commu-nicator' and emphasises the importance for children of 'making meaning with the famil-iar people in their lives' (David et al., 2003: 77).

Social interactionist theory about language development hinges on the idea that meaningful interactions with another human are crucial in order to motivate language acquisition. Bruner (1983) points out that the adult–child conversation begins when babies respond sensitively to a mother's facial expressions and the pair take turns in their exchange of utterances in an attempt to reach a shared meaning. Schaffer (1977) highlights the way that this sense of reciprocity is evident when children are feeding and mothers use pauses in sucking to cuddle and talk to their babies. He also noted that mothers and their babies were so attuned to each other that they rarely tried to 'talk' at the same time as they negotiated their interaction in a responsive and warm relationship. Similarly, Trevarthen and Aitken (2001) describe these early interactions as 'proto-conversations' as they provide a training ground for the more complex social exchanges that children experience as they mature.

Learning to talk necessitates language acquisition, but this cannot be meaningfully implemented without a growing awareness of social recognition and co-construction of meaning. This flourishes in the warm, regular and playful exchanges in the family home (Bruner, 1986). For example, my 20-month-old niece can certainly make her feelings known with one simple utterance '*bah!*' which is accompanied by a wagging finger when she is seriously displeased or her plans have been thwarted by another family member.

Learning to converse

Children need to learn the rules of interaction and how to sustain the conversation as well as recognising speech and attempting communication. Hart and Risley (1999) emphasise the importance of 'social reciprocity' in this process and describe the way that children successfully communicate when they are able to engage in meaningful exchanges, turn-taking, interpreting and responding in order to maintain the interaction. Responsive adults behave as if they were in a real conversation with the baby and leave gaps for the baby to reply in the form of whole-body movements, hand waving, excited noises or a smile (Trevarthen, 1979). This exchange is a sophisticated and sensitive process that requires inter-subjectivity to be successful as 'learning a language is about co-ordinating what you do with what other people do' (Gopnik et al., 1999: 101). Wells (1990) describe this inter-subjectivity established by caregivers as the probable foundation for 'all subsequent communicative development' (1985: 6). This innate ability that mothers seem to have to apportion meaning to their babies' early vocalisations and gestures, random coos and gurgles is more than indulging in baby talk; it is the first stage of scaffolding.

Motherese

However children acquire language, researchers have agreed that there is a common feature present in all languages when caregivers (and older siblings) interact with babies and toddlers, and this is known as 'motherese' or infant-directed speech (Snow and Ferguson, 1977). Motherese is characterised by short, grammatically simple sentences. The adult uses a higher-pitched voice and speaks at a slower pace, using repetitive and exaggerated expression. Most adults seem naturally attuned to this mode of interaction with young children and strengthen the supportive process by placing key words at the end of sentences, drawing attention to these through intonation and expression. Mothers who are in tune with their infants' subtle development instinctively increase the level of complexity in their speech in order to help children take the next step in learning about communication (Henning et al., 2005).

Evidence from research about babies who have not been provided with this early positive experience of interaction indicates that not only is language development affected but also, without the presence of a responsive adult, children's emotional, cognitive and social development is impaired. Goldschmeid and Selleck (1996: 11) describe the way that children discovered in state institutions (in Trieste, Italy, in 1954) had become 'withdrawn, passive and despairing' as they had received adequate 'physical care', but limited 'personal care' and attention, and had consequently given up trying to initiate relationships with others. Babies begin to perceive their own importance in the reflected gaze of their carers and this is a fundamental period in childhood when the sensitive responses of supportive adults can begin to build a child's fundamental sense of self-esteem (Winnicott, 1971).

Language acquisition and development

The way that parents interact with their children plays a pivotal role in language development. The form and frequency of parent interaction has a significant impact on children's vocabulary development, their ability to be articulate *and* it influences emerging literacy skills (Kokkinaki and Kugiumutzakis, 2000). We know from recent research aimed at supporting parents in communicating with their young children that 'talkative parents have talkative children' and that 'early parent talk predicts later language ability' (National Literacy Trust, 2010).

When considering how language develops, theorists are involved in an ongoing debate about the dominance of nature vs. nurture. Children are pre-programmed to acquire language and the brain is wired to support this process, particularly from birth to 5 years old (nature). Consequently this predisposition towards language acquisition indicates that nature has designed a clear path for children to follow. Conversely, opposing theorists maintain that the overriding influence on early language development is the language environment in which a child is raised (nurture).

Noam Chomsky (1957, 1965) suggested that all children are born with an inherent ability to acquire language and to decode sounds using their innate language acquisition device (LAD). This helps children to organise language according to appropriate linguistic rules, including using grammatical knowledge to construct new sentences and phrases. Chomsky later defined this as the 'Universal Grammar' (UG) theory, and he uses this inborn ability infants have to explain how they learn phonology and grammar at an early age, despite being exposed to some limited 'degenerate' language models in their environment (e.g. motherese). Critics of this innate theory have argued that environment and, crucially, interaction with others plays a more significant role in language development than Chomsky implies (Vygotsky, 1962; Bruner, 1983). Bruner (1983) felt that the reciprocal relationship between the adult and child involved in conversation was the critical factor in helping children to develop their language and to make meaning from the interaction. He refers to this process as the 'language acquisition support system' (LASS), as it acknowledges that successful interaction relies on the scaffolding that adults, who are in tune with children, are best able to provide and it is this type and level of conversation that helps children to move on a step in learning about language. Similarly, Lev Vygotsky (1896–1934) highlighted the relationship between dialogue (inner speech to self and interpersonal interaction) and cognitive awareness and maintained that: 'language and thought are inseparable' (Vygotsky, 1978).

Language for thinking

The Ofsted summary report 'The Impact of the Early Years Foundation Stage' in 2011 concluded that 'children's language for thinking was weaker than their language for communication' and attributed this to 'missed opportunities' by practitioners who did not seize the moment to extend children's thinking or did not create time for thinking (2011: 17). Good examples cited by the inspectors included a problem-solving activity devised by one practitioner involving a 'derailed' toy train. 'I wonder who broke the wheel,' the practitioner asked as children arrived in the setting and then engaged them in discussion to explore the situation.

The guidance material that accompanies the revised EYFS suggests that in order to foster positive relationships adults should 'provide opportunities for children to talk with other children and adults about what they see, hear, think and feel' (Early Education/DfE, 2012: 17). This means making the most of naturally occurring talking points and also planning opportunities for children to be creative, to express their feelings and to solve problems together.

CASE STUDY

Hug (based on a sequence of lessons with a mixed age 4–6 class)

One morning the teacher shared the story *Hug* by Jez Alborough with the children and they talked about how the central character (Bobo the baby monkey) felt when he needed a hug. This was followed up in circle time when the class teacher encouraged the children to think about times when they have needed a hug or given a hug to someone. The teacher used a toy monkey as a puppet to encourage children to extend their vocabulary by modelling words they could use to help express feelings.

Repeated readings of the story took place while children used small hand-held mirrors to look at and describe their own expressions to match each part of the story. The next day when the children arrived at school they discovered that Bobo the toy monkey had got stuck up a tree in the playground and the children spent most of the day talking about how this could have happened, how Bobo must feel and subsequently devising elaborate schemes to get him down!

Figure 17.1   *Toy monkey and* Hug *story book*

Talking and learning at home and school

After analysing samples of talk between children and adults in the home and school context, Gordon Wells (Bristol Language Development Project, 1984 in Wells, 1986) concluded that the home environment provided richer opportunities for children to engage in genuine and meaningful conversations with adults. Talk at home tended to be led by the child and supportive adults sustained and extended children's interaction, which in turn challenged their emerging linguistic skills. Conversely, at school most of the talk was teacher-directed and children asked fewer questions and conveyed ideas in a simpler manner when responding to their teachers. Wells noted that children who made the most progress in terms of vocabulary learning were those who interacted with adults, who 'pick up and extend the meaning expressed in the child's previous utterance' (Wells, 1990: 3). This process requires adults to show genuine interest in children's ideas and conversation and to remember that during this process of developing learning through talk 'Children are active constructors of their own knowledge' (Wells, 1986: 65). Adults need to actively try to help children make connections between new knowledge and prior learning by recognising misunderstandings and helping children to make the links through dialogic thinking in order to reach a shared understanding. Edwards and Mercer describe this condition of sympathetic co-construction as 'mutuality of perspective' (1987: 95).

Adults can use a range of strategies to maintain children's interest and attention and to extend interaction, for example recasting, expanding and labelling. This provides a scaffold for children and leads to increased collaborative discussion, particularly in the context of reminiscing about past events and seeking opportunities to use language in a familiar environment.

CASE STUDY

The flood

Read the conversation below (which took place one rainy afternoon between a mother and her 4-year-old son). Look for evidence of the following:

- context and purpose of the conversation
- mother following the child's interests and leads
- introduction of new vocabulary
- use of 'wh-' questions
- mother responding by recasting or expanding child's conversational phrases
- information about causes and effects, objects and actions.

(C: child, M: mother)
C: So tell me again, Mummy.
M: Tell you about what again?
C: You know, Mummy – the flood! It was horrible!
M: Oh, you mean in our old house.
C: Yeah – when the rain was *so* much.
M: Well, there was a storm and it rained so much all the water couldn't fit down the drains outside and – [C interrupts]
C: It couldn't go to the sea?
M: No, instead some of the water flowed into our house!

> C: Did you paddle? *[C laughs]* Where did it comed in – down the chimney?
> M: A few raindrops fell down the chimney but most of the water in our house seeped under the back door. Why do you think it seeped in?
> C: It sneaked in – yeah, through little holes. It found a way. Is it leaked? Did our house dribble? How did you get it away?
> M: It was tricky – can you remember what I told you before about the pump and the special machine?
> C: Yeah – the sucker pump and the me-de – fire *[de-humidifier]*.

Creating a climate for co-construction

The adult's role is crucial if we want children to be active participants in learning and develop language for thinking. The interaction between children and practitioners during some play activities can lead to 'sustained shared thinking' (Siraj-Blatchford et al., 2002). This occurs when the teacher intervenes in the child's learning by asking open-ended questions, which help to extend a child's thinking. Co-construction occurs when adults are able to follow a child's interests and thought process and let the child become a genuine equal in a meaningful experience.

Researching Effective Pedagogy in the Early Years (REPEY) reported on the five-year longitudinal Effective Provision for Pre-school Education (EPPE 1997–2004) Project which investigated the effects of pre-school education and identified the characteristics of effective practice in the early years (Siraj-Blatchford et al., 2002). The REPEY research was based on case-study evidence collated from 14 'effective' Foundation Stage settings. The following extract from the report illustrates one of the most significant findings:

> The children and practitioners in excellent centres engaged in the highest proportion of sustained shared thinking interactions, suggesting that the excellent settings promote intellectual gains in children through conversations with children in which adult and child co-construct an idea or activity. For the practitioners in the good settings the most commonly used interaction was monitoring, a distinct difference to practitioners in the excellent and in the reception class settings. (Siraj-Blatchford et al., 2002: 51)

One of the key characteristics of effective learning that underpins development across all areas in the revised EYFS is *creating and thinking critically*. Early years practitioners need to create a careful balance between child-led and adult-led learning by providing a wide range of activities that sustain children's interests and promote shared talking and thinking.

Dialogic teaching refers to the enhancement of children's critical thinking and communication skills as they explore ideas and talk together in a purposeful way. Alexander proposes that one of the most effective 'tools' in mediation and 'pedagogical interven-tion' is 'talk ... the most pervasive in its use and powerful in its possibilities' (2008: 2). In the Cambridge Review (2008), Alexander outlines the many advantages of the dialogic teaching approach, which is about talking to learn and emphasises the 'necessary rela-tionship between how teachers think about their practice and how pupils learn' (2008: 308). One of the key features of dialogic talk is its reciprocal nature, and for this to hap-pen children need time, space and the skills to listen to each other and exchange ideas in a spiral of learning.

The amount of 'talk' and the time given for 'talk' in the classroom often depends on the status and value the class teacher ascribes to talk. Browne suggests that the effectiveness of the practitioner's role when working with young children is related to his/her:

- own understanding of the value of talk
- attitude to talk
- organisation for talk
- own use of language
- awareness of strategies and activities that encourage speaking and listening. (2009: 11)

Communication difficulties

Teachers are often the adults who first notice when children experience difficulties with communication as a result of early language impairment and need to be ready to sup-port children's specific speech, language and communication needs (SLCN). Without secure oral language skills children experience barriers to learning and attainment in every area across the curriculum is affected (Communication Trust, 2011). Understanding how children acquire language and how this development can be supported is an aspect of teacher training that the Communication Trust is attempting to improve by raising teachers' awareness of the difficulties that the one in ten children with this 'invisible' disability face in school every day.

Kamini Gadhok, the Chief Executive of the Royal College of Speech and Language Therapists, has produced the following definition of speech, language and communica-tion needs (Gadhok, 2007):

- Problems forming sounds and words
- Problems formulating sentences and expressing ideas
- Problems understanding speech and language
- Problems using language socially
- Delays and disorders in the development of speech and language skills.

Communication and social and emotional development

Children's communication skills can be developed when playing with peers or siblings, particularly when involved in joint activities, negotiating their role in a game or attempting to resolve conflicts. Adults can encourage this social networking and experimental talk through planning activities that develop emotional literacy and teach children to be good listeners as well as helping them to get their point across.

In Interaction Matters, part of the EPPE project, Siraj-Blatchford (2003) explains that in order for children to move from simply exchanging information into conversing, adults need to help them by:

- explaining what is happening
- acknowledging feelings – helping children to define the problem
- suggesting practical solutions to conflict between children.

In Reggio Emilia pre-schools teachers encourage children to negotiate, debate differing viewpoints and discuss ideas and feelings with each other as well as with adults. This is how two children responded when asked about children's rights in their setting:

> Two friends have the right to argue. It's good for knowing when you're wrong. You can discuss but also argue. It's like hitting someone with your voice. (Two children from the Diana pre-school, ages 5 and 6, in Mallaguzzi, 1996: 36)

In order to promote communication and language development in the early years setting, these key elements can be considered when trying to create playful contexts for interaction, as in the following examples:

- Provide telephones and message pads in role-play areas
- Make use of puppets/persona dolls to model conflict resolution or problem solving
- Invite visitors to talk – children have to seek new words in order to ask questions when motivated by an interested adult
- Introduce games for sharing – for example, 'Teach your teacher and two friends how to play'
- Create a musical instrument/sound table – 'Describe the sound to your friend. Does it remind you of anything?'
- Set up a cosy corner/meeting area for socialising and news telling
- Install a 'show and tell' table and invite groups of children to discuss significant objects
- Send home mystery bags and encourage children to rehearse their description of the object inside ready to describe the next day at school.

Summary

This chapter discussed communication and language development and aimed to illustrate what is meant when these two terms are used in early years education and care. Communication and language development is considered important for children's development and learning, as well as critical when literacy is discussed, as will be shown in Chapter 18. Throughout the chapter it was emphasised that the role of the environment in communication and language development should be rich and stimulating and offer opportunities for children to explore these two key aspects of development in a playful way.

Points to remember

- Early years education and care should provide rich opportunities for children to share ideas, questions and feelings from birth as children do have voices from the moment they are born.

- Learning to communicate requires a meaningful, social environment where all children are valued and feelings are recognised and treated with warmth and respect.

- A number of theoretical perspectives, such as those of Chomsky, Vygotsky and Bruner, have explored the role of adults and the interactions between adults and children and how these interaction can benefit children's communication and language development.

- The partnership between home and early years setting is important for effective development of communication and language skills.

Points for discussion

- Consider a lesson or activity that you plan to introduce to a group of children in EYFS. Discuss ways in which you can introduce and explain new vocabulary and provide opportunities for children to talk and listen together during the session.

- Discuss how you can capture the 'child's voice' to inform observation and assessment records and to ensure that children become accustomed to celebrating and verbalising their learning and sharing their ideas and opinions with supportive adults.

- Robin Alexander outlines five underlying principles of dialogic talk: 'collective, reciprocal, supportive, cumulative and purposeful' (2004: 22). Have you witnessed practitioners engaged in this type of guided talk with children? Discuss the way it can support children's learning.

> ### ⭐ Reflective tasks
>
> - Try to observe some spontaneous interaction between a parent/carer or practitioner and a toddler. You will need to seek permission from the adult and may decide to record the short conversation that you witness. Reflect on the communication you observed. Did the adult demonstrate any sign of 'motherese'? Did the child respond? How did both parties maintain the conversation?
>
> - How can early years practitioners create time and opportunities for thinking in the school day? Reflect on activities you have observed that engage children in critical thinking and problem-solving activities. Consider how this challenges and encourages children to develop their communication skills.
>
> - Reflect on Bruner's idea of reciprocal relationship between the adult and the child and discuss how successful interactions can be cultivated in an early years setting.

Further reading 📖

David, T., Goouch, K., Powell, S. and Abbott, L. (2003) *Birth to Three Matters: A Review of the Literature*. London: Department for Education and Skills.

Evangelou, M., Sylva, K., Kyriacou, M., Wild, M. and Glenny, G. (2009) *Early Years Learning and Development Literature Review*. DCSF Research Report: University of Oxford.

Sylva, K., Melhuish, E., Siraj-Blatchford, I. and Taggart, B. (2004) *The Effective Provision of Pre-School Education (EPPE) Project: Final Report*. London: DfES.

Useful websites 🖱️

www.ican.org.uk
www.literacytrust.org.uk
www.talkingpoint.org.uk

To gain **free access** to selected SAGE journal articles related to key topics in this chapter visit: www.sagepub.co.uk/Palaiologou2e

18

Literacy

Claire Head and Ioanna Palaiologou

> ### Chapter roadmap
>
> The revisions to the Early Years Foundation Stage indicate that a distinction will be made between communication and language as a prime aspect and literacy as a specific aspect. The separation of the traditionally interrelated areas of reading and writing (literacy) and speaking and listening skills is prompted by research that highlights the time-sensitive link between early brain development and the acquisition of communication and language skills, as discussed in Chapter 17. Children's literacy skills should not be neglected during this critical period, however, but should be nurtured from birth so that young children are immersed in 'a climate of talk about reading and writing' (Tickell, 2011: 98).
>
> Literacy should be part of a child's development, not isolated from the society and culture in which that child grows up. The process of becoming literate requires collaborative acts of learning as children engage repeatedly in literacy events and experiences.
>
> This chapter aims to help you to:
>
> - appreciate that becoming literate (learning to be a reader and a writer) is a cooperative exploit and needs opportunities for practice in meaningful contexts
> - recognise that effective readers pursue understanding and this process requires more than simply decoding the text; it is also about interpretation of the words

in context, in order to gain the potential cognitive, social and emotional value literature has to offer

- understand that real writers depend on oral rehearsal before writing; they plan, draft and revise their work, and they need a real purpose and audience for their writing.

Literacy development in the early years

In early years education and care practitioners need to extend the basic notion of literacy to indicate competence that enables literate individuals to function independently and flexibly in a society – a view that underpins the EYFS.

Research and theoretical developments have changed our understanding of young children's movement into literacy. The term 'literacy' relates to both reading and writing and suggests the simultaneous development and mutually reinforcing effects of these two aspects of communication. It is important to remember that children's language acquisition, and consequently their emerging literacy skills, develops at different rates and ages. Ayoub and Fischer (2006) explain that a child's development follows a unique pathway rather than a set linear route and adults need to be sympathetic to this progression when introducing new skills. Macroy (2006) warns against the introduction of formal literacy instruction too early at a stage when children still need to play with language and explore its use in familiar contexts.

Emergent literacy

This refers to the phase when a child is in the process of becoming literate, between approximately aged 6 months and school entry. Marie Clay (1991) introduced this term (in 1966) to describe the growing knowledge and awareness that young children have about print before starting school. Literacy development is seen as emerging from children's oral language development and their initial, often unconventional, attempts at reading (usually based on pictures) and writing (at first, scribbling): hence the term 'emergent literacy' (Holdaway, 1979; Sulzby, 1985, 1989). Within an emergent literacy framework, children's early unconventional attempts at reading and writing are respected as legitimate beginnings of literacy. Clay (1991) emphasises the interrelationship between speaking, listening, reading and writing and the importance of viewing the child as an active, self-motivated learner from an early age who 'creates a network of competencies which power subsequent independent literacy learning' (Clay, 1991: 1).

Environmental print

Children are surrounded by print in the environment and this is often the first meaningful print that children recognise in a familiar context. For example, many children today recognise McDonald's food outlets from the two yellow arches that form its logo. Children's print awareness gradually expands and is not limited to learning from the situational context. Their knowledge of print is also enhanced as they are exposed to print in books, magazines, newspapers, letters and other printed materials (Goodman, 1980). These early experiences directly influence children's awareness of print and can thus be considered as steps towards becoming readers.

In this early 'logographic phase' children tend to remember and recognise whole words or shapes rather than attending to individual letters (Frith, 1985). Significant adults at home and school can help children to build on this awareness by talking about the meanings ascribed to the signs and symbols seen in everyday life; for example, children can usually recognise their favourite cereal box at the supermarket. Practitioners in school can provide meaningful print around the classroom and encourage children to engage with it to develop their reading and writing skills. 'Literacy walks' or 'looking for print walks' (in the local environment) are good ways to involve parents and to strengthen links between learning about print inside and outside the classroom.

Literacy learning

Literacy development begins much earlier than previously thought. Teale and Sulzby (1989) suggest that we should no longer speak of reading readiness or pre-reading but, rather, of literacy development. In preference to 'getting a child ready' to learn to read, the emergent literacy perspective emphasises the child's ongoing development. Whitehurst (1998: 23), in an attempt to define emergent literacy, starts with the assumption that 'reading is a developmental continuum starting early in life'. Thus, the definition of emergent literacy is 'a set of skills, knowledge and attitudinal precursors to formal reading and writing and the environment that supports these precursors' (Whitehurst, 1998: 34).

The main competences of emergent literacy include:

- awareness of language
- conventions of print
- emergent writing
- phonological awareness
- graphemes
- phoneme–grapheme correspondence
- attitudes such as interest in interacting with books
- environments such as shared book reading, alphabet play and treasure baskets.

Reading storybooks to young children both at home and in school (Heath, 1983; Neuman and Roskos, 1997), along with opportunities children should have to explore print, words, rhymes and songs, helps children]at a very early stage to begin to experiment with a more literate language.

With increased experience, children begin to focus on the information conveyed in print. They begin by using scribbles and progress through increasingly accurate representations of the relationship between letters and the sounds for which they stand. As children think about how to represent the sounds of words through their writing, they are building skills that will be useful for reading as well. These are the 'foundations for conventional reading and writing and should be celebrated and encouraged at home, in pre-schools, and in the early years of formal schooling' (Searfoss and Readence, 1994: 58).

Literacy from home to school

There are numerous references to the role of the home environment in children's relationship with literature and the influence of early literacy experiences on long-term attainment (Goodman, 1980; Ferreiro and Teberosky, 1983; Hannon, 1995). Neuman (1992, 1996, 1997, 1999) has investigated younger children's literacy by examining literacy materials in the home and early years settings and opportunities for parent–child storybook reading. She concludes that parents' reading proficiency influences conversational interactions with different text types, serving as 'a scaffold' for parent – child interaction. She suggests that parents play a critical role in children's early literacy learning in the context of access to print resources, and opportunities and interaction in storybook reading.

Research from the Sheffield Raising Early Achievement in Literacy Project (Hannon and Nutbrown, 2003) indicates that promoting family literacy helps to strengthen links between home and school and improves children's understanding of environmental print, books, early writing and oral language. The project, which began in 1995, focused on pre-school children and suggested that parents/carers could provide a model for their children by adopting three key roles:

- reading a paper and writing notes/shopping list
- providing opportunities for children to engage in literacy by making materials available or by drawing children's attention to environmental print
- providing encouragement and praising achievement.

Parents were supported through use of the ORIM framework which highlighted Opportunities, Recognition, Interaction and Models of literacy and showed parents how they could interact with their children by sharing everyday language and literacy events, for example noticing environmental print. The REAL (Raising Early Achievements in Literacy) project outcomes were very positive and reflected a marked improvement in the children's language, literacy and social development. For example, at the end of the first year of the project:

- 78 per cent of children shared books most days compared with 27 per cent in the initial survey;
- 63 per cent of children went on to engage in mark making compared with 17 per cent at the 'start point'
- all the parents reported that they were interacting more with their children and could see more opportunities to help their children learn
- practitioners felt more confident about working with parents, supporting parents and talking about children's literacy development. (PEAL, 2011)

The links in literacy development between home and school begin when practitioners recognise and value children's pre-school literacy experiences in the community and seek to strengthen this connection by building on familiar literacy practices at school.

Becoming a reader

Children begin to be aware of the fact that to hold a book is to 'read' the pictures. The initial 'literacy event' takes place when a child holds a book and looks at the pictures. Gradually, the child moves from being a 'naïve' reader to being a more 'expert' reader, and learns such things as how to open the book, how to turn the pages, how to pay attention to the text, and so on. Similarly, after these skills have been mastered children start pretending to read or tell stories. This is not simply children's make-believe play, imitating the teacher or the parent who reads a book: it is an actual literacy event.

In order to move on from this role-play reading stage, children need to develop phonological awareness and this begins with the ability to distinguish between different sounds in order to hear sounds that make up words and are meaningful (Williams and Rask, 2003). Phonemic awareness is developed in early years settings and at home through the sharing or rhymes and songs and by playing games with language that develop children's oracy skills. As discussed in Chapter 17, the development of communication and language skills, particularly the enrichment of children's vocabulary and their ability to express emotions, is an essential building block for later literacy competence. A number of researchers have established the link between secure phonological awareness and vocabulary development and the way that interaction between these two aspects supports early reading development and later literacy attainment (Goswami, 2001; Snow, 2006).

Teaching early reading

There is a time-honoured debate about the most effective methods teachers can employ to help children to become readers and contemporary discussion has centred on the teaching of phonics. In 2005, Jim Rose (former HMI Director of Inspection at Ofsted) was appointed by the Secretary of State for Education to carry out an independent review of the teaching of early reading, and his report (2006) underpins subsequent policy and practice in primary schools today. The final report made several recommendations about 'best practice' in the 'teaching of early reading and synthetic phonics' (2006: 7). It emphasised the importance of teaching phonics in a discrete, systematic and explicit way beginning during the optimum 'time-sensitive' period reached when most children approach 5 years of age. Advice for teachers was presented in a 'conceptual framework', referred to as the 'Simple View' of reading. This reminds teachers that the aim of reading is to gain meaning from the text and this is dependent on the successful coordination of two elements:

- *Decoding* – reliant on speech sound information: phonology. This requires linking sounds with letters to read words. Rose recommends a 'synthetic phonics' approach which starts with blending letter sounds to read whole words
- *Comprehension* – relies on broader language skills, including a growing understanding of vocabulary, grammar and an ability to make inferences to discern meaning.

Rose highlighted the prime role that phonics instruction should play in the teaching of early reading, but noted that phonic work should be 'embedded in a broad and rich language curriculum' (2006: 35). In order to support early years teachers in providing high-quality phonics instruction the Primary National Strategy (PNS) published *Letters and Sounds* (DCSF, 2007) guidance material. This offered teachers a six-phase phonics programme designed to secure 'fluent word recognition for reading by the end of Key Stage 1' with the acknowledgement that teaching spelling skills would continue beyond 7 years of age (2007: 3). This programme was founded on the principle that 'phonic work should be regarded as an essential body of knowledge, skills and understanding that has to be learned largely through direct instruction' (2007: 10). Learning the skills of blending for reading and segmenting for spelling is a process that requires systematic instruction and then application. This was reiterated in the Tickell Review (2011):

> Becoming literate is culturally constrained and relies on learning a body of knowledge including the alphabetic code (i.e. the teaching of systematic synthetic phonics) in the same way that the learning of mathematics largely relies on securing knowledge and understanding of symbolic representation for number. (Tickell, 2011: 98)

Consequently this approach to teaching the specific area of literacy can be found in the revised EYFS: 'Literacy development involves encouraging children to link sounds and letters and to begin to read and write' (2012: 5, 1.6).

What do good readers do?

'Phonics is necessary, but not in itself sufficient, to develop effective and enthusiastic readers' (UKLA, 2008: Section 3). We know that effective readers make use of decoding skills early in the reading process, but teachers also need to keep in mind the longer process that leads to becoming a lifelong reader and the importance of adults sharing their enthusiasm for reading with children and modelling what good readers do.

> Good readers are more than successful print scanners and retrievers of factual experience. They find in books the depth and breadth of human experience. (Meek, 1988: 17)

Through storytelling, discussion surrounding good-quality picture books and shared reading we can help children experience the cognitive, social and emotional value of stepping into the world of a book. Although cumulative, graded and easily decodable reading scheme books build children's confidence and provide opportunities to practise reading skills they may not provoke the same enthusiasm and interest as immersion in 'real books'. Teachers need to ensure children's reading diet is not limited by ability and that generating motivation to read remains a priority when planning the literacy curriculum. After decoding her school-reading-scheme book Campbell's 5-year-old granddaughter Alice states, 'Soon I will be able to read real books' (Campbell, 2000: 134). The children in the case study below provide a good example of how imagination, 'real book' knowledge and familiar experiences blend together as children become the storytellers after sharing a range of traditional tales.

CASE STUDY

Our version of 'Jack and the Beanstalk' by children and teachers from Childhaven Community Nursery School (April 2010)

We read 'Jack and the Beanstalk' last week and then this week we used masks to retell the story and then add in some extra bits. In our version Jack had a cow called Steeleymoo and two sheep to sell at the market, but he still only got three magic beans for them. After the beans had been thrown out of the window five butterflies flew into Jack's bedroom to tell him about the beanstalk, which was really huge. Also, when Jack got inside the castle, the Giant was having a cup of tea with Mrs Giant and Batgirl! The Easter Bunny also asked the goose to lay some chocolate eggs, but she said she 'could only make golden ones'. Oh well! At the end of the story Jack and his mum were so happy that they decided to invite the Three Little Pigs for tea – what a busy day it was. I think we might do some more storytelling next week.

Becoming a writer

The National Literacy Strategy describes emergent writing as 'mark making with intent' in the guidance given to teachers in *Developing Early Writing* (DfEE, 2001: 166). It is this desire to create intentional marks that highlights a young child's growing understanding that print carries meaning. Adults can encourage a child to talk about her writing and its ascribed meaning in order to develop the child's knowledge about both transcriptional and compositional aspects of writing. This is a tricky balance for teachers to achieve, as it is important to encourage and celebrate children's attempts at writing by responding to its content without becoming so focused on the transcription that children are reluctant to try this difficult skill again. Practitioners can foster early writing skills by creating a supportive climate for writing and by using a variety of teaching strategies, which encourage children to actively experiment, and 'have a go' at writing.

In his book entitled *Reading with Alice*, which reflects his own granddaughter's development at home and in early years settings, Campbell (1999) emphasises the importance of allowing children to emerge as readers and writers. He states that Alice's considerable progression in literacy took place as a result of her active involvement with reading and writing rather than through direct instruction in these skills. He expresses concern that some teachers are relying on worksheets in early years settings rather than engaging the children in literary activities that capture their interest. Figure 18.1

Figure 18.1 *Example of mark making – symbols for dance moves*

provides an example of a child (age 6) who was motivated to make her own meaningful marks when she needed to find a way to record complicated dance moves in a sequence that could be repeated and shared with friends.

An important element of the literacy learning process is when children make their first attempts to write. Sulzby (1992) suggests that at this age children should be 'encouraged or nudged' and not pushed to start their writing process. When children first spontaneously produce graphic representations, drawing and writing are undifferentiated. When children first experiment with a pencil, what they want to do is to leave their mark everywhere, for instance on a piece of paper or on a wall (Ferreiro and Teberosky, 1983; Morrow, 1992).

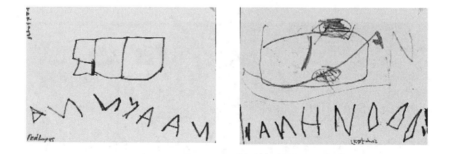

Figure 18.2   *Children's attempts to write*

Teaching writing

Although children do need to be taught the conventions of writing they also need to learn the context for writing. Children take part as 'active learners' and ideally should be exposed to the delights and challenges involved in the creative process (Graves, 1983). Children can be involved in the compositional aspects as the practitioner scribes: editing, filtering and refining suggestions from the class in a supportive relationship. When appropriate, the practitioner can draw attention to transactional aspects, including spelling, handwriting, punctuation, grammar and layout.

In order to help children understand the textual features of different forms of writing (different genres in varying contexts) practitioners need to discuss the reason and purpose for the writing. Riley and Reedy (2000) suggest that challenging children to answer the following questions when they encounter new text types will provide them with a model for their own writing and a deeper understanding of the way writing is organised in different genres:

- What is it? What is the text for?
- Why do you read it?
- Do we know who wrote it? (Riley and Reedy, 2000: 62)

Providing a real audience as well as spotting a real purpose for children's writing is an essential part of the practitioner's role as this motivates children to take their place in the literate society that surrounds them.

Opportunities to write

Providing opportunities to write is essential, as it will allow young children to appreciate and recognise the links between speech and print. Helen Dutton (1991, cited in Campbell, 2002) describes six main categories of writing that she noticed her children (aged 6) naturally engaged in during role-play:

- letters
- messages
- personal notes
- instructions
- factual descriptions
- stories.

This purposeful writing generated by structural play allows children to develop early writing skills. This can be supported and enhanced by adults who are ready to intervene sensitively to engage in 'teachable moments' that give meaning to children's literacy events (Owocki, 1999: 28).

Creating a rich literate environment

It is important to provide opportunities for children to read and write in different contexts and situations as part of play. Practitioners need to generate talk about classroom and environmental print by encouraging children to understand the purpose of these symbols in meaningful contexts. For example, signs and labels made in response to a real purpose will demonstrate the power that the printed word has to communicate (Figure 18.3).

Figure 18.3   *Please remember to water this plant every Monday*

Owocki (1999) advocates the setting up of literacy-enriched play centres in early years settings and reminds practitioners to evaluate their roles and to ask themselves:

- Do the children read and write during play? Are the materials meaningful?
- What functions does literacy serve in children's play? Are the children exploring a variety of genres and forms of written language?

Figure 18.4 shows a child's annotations on a story map of 'Little Red Riding Hood'. The child felt that the writing was necessary to help other children to play the game and re-enact the story as she intended with the playdough figures.

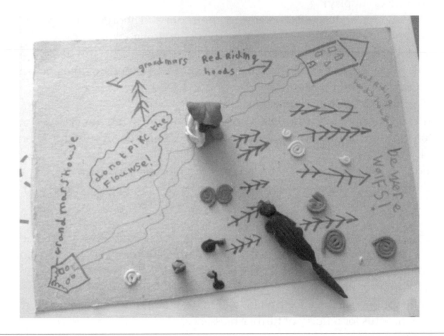

Figure 18.4 *Story map*

Literacy through play

Throughout this book the importance of play within EYFS is emphasised. Once again play maintains an important role in children's literacy development. Neuman (1997) examined the early years settings reflecting literacy-related situations in children's real-world environment. She found that literacy in play might become purposeful in an enriched literacy environment. She also found that literacy becomes part of children's play when literacy activities are in context.

In a study based on research in 35 kindergarten classrooms with 5–6-year-old children, Morrow (1992) concluded that many of the settings were not well designed to facilitate literacy behaviours. She observed that few literacy materials were easily available for children to use and practitioners did little to promote authentic literacy activities during play. In order for literacy events to take place during natural play sequences the children need to have literacy materials to hand: 'The inclusion in the play area of literacy materials is a starting point for the encouragement of literacy learning' (Campbell, 2002: 104).

An enriched literacy environment could include:

- pens, paper, books and other printed materials available in every area of the setting
- environmental print (the home languages of all the children who attend the setting should be on display)
- books – fiction and non-fiction around the room so children can explore different genres in appropriate settings, e.g. a recipe for making porridge alongside 'Goldilocks and the Three Bears' in the role-play area
- props, puppets, story sacks, dressing up clothes – to stimulate dramatic play
- sequence cards to retell stories
- writing area or mark making station
- Post box – to write to characters from stories or friends in other classes
- Calendars – to highlight important events, e.g. children's birthdays, school trips, book day
- Pigeon-holes – to encourage children to write messages to others
- Children's notice board – to celebrate attempts at mark making completed at home and school.

Successful role-play areas naturally stimulate literacy activities; however, practitioners need to continually 'feed' this creativity and to motivate the children to explore print. For example, providing props such as an old telephone and a messages pad can encourage lots of conversation and emergent writing. If the practitioner in that area models taking a telephone message for a child, and reads it aloud to the class, then this could act as the impetus for a flurry of further messages.

CASE STUDY

'The Garden Centre' – a teacher recounts

The most successful role-play area I established in my classroom, with the help of the children in my Reception/Year 1 class, was a 'Garden Centre'. The stimulus for this came from a visit to the local garden centre which was owned and managed by one of the parents of a child in my class. Once we returned to school the children were keen to re-create a mini version of this in our classroom and eagerly began planning its design and listing resources we would need. Here are just some of the activities that germinated from this seed!

- environmental print – signs, labels, notices
- growing sunflowers from seeds – linked to our science topic
- letters – thanking the garden centre staff and asking them technical questions about looking after plants

- seed-packet designs – children were encouraged to use real seed packets as a model
- instructions for planting – we devised a class list during shared writing
- watering plants rota – we found that our plants suffered if they were over-watered and so we had to monitor this
- measurement of school sunflower competition – we donated one seedling to each class in school with instructions for care and had a special assembly to see whose was the tallest at the end of the term
- related fiction, e.g. 'Jack and the Beanstalk', and non-fiction, e.g. 'From Seed to Sunflower' – read during shared reading and made available for the children to re-read
- price lists – accompanied by a till and 'money' so customers could shop
- descriptions of flowering plants – art work was accompanied by brief descriptions of each flower; The descriptions were separated from the pictures and children had to match them up again
- 'guess what this seed will grow into' competitions – related to work on seed dispersal
- reciting rhymes and songs related to plants
- stories about talking plants – stimulated by a large painting of two flowers which the children were able to stand behind and poke their heads through (seaside style) and talk in role to each other.

Summary

Although the areas of communication, and language and literacy have been explored separately, it is important to say that they are interrelated and communication and language maintains a key role in children's literacy learning. It is essential in early years education and care to create an environment to have wealth of opportunities where children are exposed to literacy and explore literacy through play. Play is central to literacy learning as it enables children to have experiences of literacy.

Key points to remember

- The threads of literacy; reading and writing are interwoven and build upon a child's early development as a communicator.
- Reading for meaning requires the child to employ decoding skills (converting printed words to spoken words) and linguistic comprehension.
- Literacy-enriched centres and a real audience and purpose for writing can make a difference to a child's literacy behaviour and his/her sense of becoming a writer.

Points for discussion

- How can practitioners use ICT to enhance children's literacy experiences and interaction with multi-modal texts?

- Given that children are surrounded by a host of television icons, videos, toys and related products at home and in society, do we need to incorporate work on these 'texts' into classroom life? Marsh and Hallet (1999) argue that this is essential and practitioners need to ensure children find their culture and lifestyle reflected, and provide experiences generated by children's interest and not always guided by adult agendas. Should popular culture be reflected in the classroom?

Reflective tasks

- Consider the range of environmental print and variety of sources that offer potential print encounters for children in the home or classroom. Reflect on the way that print helps people to function in everyday life. Perhaps you could compare this to your own experience of trying to read print in a foreign language on a visit to another country?

- The Rose Report (2006) and Letters and Sounds (DCSF, 2007) advocate a multisensory approach to teaching and learning phonic work. Reflect on phonic activities you have seen and consider how multisensory engagement (by touch, sight and sound simultaneously) enhances children's phonic knowledge and skills.

- Reflect on the most successful role-play area you have seen. How did it stimulate literacy activities? How did the practitioner 'feed' it and sustain children's interest?

Further reading

Bradford, H. (2009) *Communication, Language and Literacy in the Early Years Foundation Stage*. London: David Fulton.

Marsh, J. and Hallet, E. (eds) (2008) *Desirable Literacies: Approaches to Language and Literacy in the Early Years*, 2nd edn. London: Sage.

Riley, J. and Reedy, D. (2000) *Developing Writing for Different Purposes: Teaching About Genre in the Early Years*. London: Paul Chapman Publishing.

Useful websites

http://standards.dfes.gov.uk/phonics/report.pdf
www.familylearning.org.uk/early_years_foundation_stage.html
www.teachfind.com/national-strategies/best-practice-early-literacy-and-phonics

To gain **free access** to selected SAGE journal articles related to key topics in this chapter visit: www.sagepub.co.uk/Palaiologou2e

Mathematics

David Needham

Chapter roadmap

It could be argued that mathematical skills and knowledge provide a key role in equipping children for a rapidly changing world (Tipps et al., 2011). This chapter aims to explore why and how children from birth to 5 years develop their mathematical abilities as well as why this process should be both developmentally appropriate and meaningful for children (Seefeldt et al., 2012). When children make sense of the world they have a natural instinct for mathematical education. Daily first-hand experiences with numbers, shapes, space and measurement provides them with a rich diet of meaningful activities that stimulate their curiosity. As they explore and experience play children create, construct and develop their mathematical knowledge. This is simply part of the way in which they experiment and try things that are new for them. Mathematics is, therefore, something that has everyday relevance to the lives of children as they develop meaning from experiences. The chapter then focuses upon how individuals can contextualise and develop simple and practical learning opportunities when working alongside young children to help to develop their mathematical understanding.

(Continued)

(Continued)

This chapter aims to help you:

- consider the key role played by the successful development of numeric reasoning skills
- reflect upon how to develop an appropriate pedagogy for children in the Foundation Stage to achieve their learning goals within the areas of numeracy and mathematics
- develop an understanding of how young children construct and develop numeric skills
- appreciate how learning opportunities, though play and social interactions, enable children to develop their mathematical knowledge
- recognise factors that influence learning (such as the indoor and outdoor learning environments)
- consider how the existence of home–school links could support children's learning and development of mathematical skills and concepts.

Mathematical reasoning in context

It is easy to take for granted the multifarious numeric skills that help individuals, whatever their age, successfully to survive each day within any context. The processes of telling the time, spending money, mentally budgeting for the week, measuring, making comparisons, interpreting diagrams, reading timetables, undertaking simple calculations, looking at comparative relationships, applying logic and undertaking simple arithmetic are quite literally inculcated into the myriad daily decisions that people make. These processes, many of which are social (Munn, 1996a), seem almost instinctive as children learn and develop. Children need to make sense of what they see and what they do. It is a time when children are developing not just their reading skills, but also their mathematical skills. They experiment with what they see, particularly symbols, and this is at the centre of their development (Worthington and Carruthers, 2003). They go on to emphasise that 'our central argument is that children come to make their own sense of abstract symbols through using their own marks and constructing their own meaning' (2003: 70). Munn (1996b) further emphasises this link between literacy and numeracy through symbolic activity. She feels that 'their symbolic activity is related to their understanding of reading and to their identity as a reader' (1996: 31). In this way, as young children develop, mathematics is just one of the many ways in which they discover who they are and create ways of coping with the world in which they live (Devlin, 2000).

As children develop their symbolic activity and recognition it is more usual in these situations that more sophisticated numeric, reasoning and mathematical skills are required in order to solve a problem or to make a decision. Davis (1984: 1) views problem solving as having a fundamental role in work, social and private lives and he goes on to emphasise that learning about mathematics influences 'how one thinks through the analysis of mathematical problems'.

Although the use of numeric and mathematical skills to reason and solve problems will be for many individuals largely an unconscious process, it has a key role in everybody's life. Where good decisions are made, it follows that individuals are likely to do the right thing and be happier or more content with the outcomes from such decisions. For this reason children from a very early age need to make sense of numeracy and mathematics as they comprise an evolving life skill, almost like a language, that enables them to face both certain and uncertain situations with greater confidence. According to Nunes and Bryant (1996: 1) 'children need to learn about mathematics in order to understand the world around them'. Doing so helps them to explore, to become rational human beings, to take advantage of the opportunities that surround them and to develop their conceptual abilities to solve problems.

Mathematical skills as lifelong skills

Perhaps the best starting point is to consider what numeric and reasoning skills involve in order to appreciate the extent to which each contributes to problem solving in everyday life. It is frequently felt that as a way of thinking or as a form of language 'mathematics encompasses a wide range of ideas and activities' (Cooke, 2007: 2). As you think about mathematic or numeric skills you probably find that many different thoughts materialise: for example, you may think of some of the more abstract mathematical concepts, such as equations, fractions, algebra, geometry, data handling or even trigonometry. Alternatively, at its very basic level, it is easy to associate numeric skills with counting, measuring, size, patterns, relationships, recognising different shapes or undertaking simple calculations. The EYFS (DfE, 2012) emphasises that children should recognise and use numbers and quantities in order to count reliably as well as to solve practical problems such as sharing, halving or doubling. This links mathematics and language, so that children understand words such as 'more' and 'less' or 'greater' and 'smaller'. In doing so it implies mathematics is an enabler that contributes to the wider learning and development of young children.

For some children mathematics can seem difficult. There are probably many different kinds of reasons for this. In several ways mathematics is very different to many other curriculum subjects: it has its own signs and symbols; it involves developing an understanding of concepts that require progression in preparation for absorbing other concepts. Even simply the word 'mathematics' has been identified as a barrier, as it can communicate negative perceptions for learners (Skemp, 1989). If children are not confident they may feel challenged by the activities that they face. They may simply get stuck and not be able to think about how to move forward. Such a situation may create anxiety, which makes it more difficult for the learners to become unstuck.

It is in these situations that the role of the practitioner is often so important, in being able to identify and recognise that a difficulty exists and then support children, perhaps by providing them with more information or through simplifying or structuring the problem in a way that enables the situation to become a positive learning experience. The irony is that, according to Skemp (1989: 49), 'mathematical thinking is not essentially different from some of the ways in which we use our intelligence in everyday life'.

There is a strong link between how individuals think about mathematics and the pedagogy that might have provided the basis for their learning. For example, learning might take place by rote, to include learning how to count from 1 to 10 or by undertaking repetitious activities within the setting. Certainly, children might be able to undertake activities following processes of rote learning, while the real problem is that the learning simply assembles information and children may not really learn or comprehend what they are doing (Downs, 1998). Learning may simply transform a discipline into an area that depends upon memory rather than real understanding. By contrast, developing numeric and mathematical skills may be used as a way of solving problems so that children make clear connections between what they are learning and how they can use that information to reason, make decisions, or solve problems in everyday life (Cooke, 2007). The *Development Matters in the Early Years Foundation stage* document (Early Education/DfE, 2012) makes many suggestions about what adults can do as part of developing positive relationships, such as encouraging parents to:

- sing counting songs
- play games that relate to number order
- ask questions using mathematical language such as how many — ?
- talk with children about how to work out solutions to simple problems by using fingers or counting aloud
- discuss with children the methods they can use to solve problems.

Using the technique of problem solving as a basis for teaching mathematics is grounded in sound educational research. Hiebert et al. (1996: 12) argue that:

> [A]llowing [mathematics] to be problematic means allowing students to wonder what things are, to enquire, to search for solutions, and to resolve incongruities. It means that both curriculum and instruction should begin with problems, dilemmas and questions for students.

They argue that the curriculum should be designed so that instructions can 'problematise' the subject. This means that instead of children simply acquiring the skills and answering questions, they are resolving problems; this builds upon Dewey's (1938) notion of reflective enquiry.

CASE STUDY

Gardening

Elliot (2 years and 7 months old) joined the gardening activity. He became responsible for planting some beans. The group responsible for the gardening had to record in a notebook the development of the beans by drawing daily what happened to the beans.

Elliot started the planting with his group, and the practitioner introduced the notebook. The group had to put a symbol for who watered the beans and when, and to draw how the beans developed. Elliot was responsible for counting every day how many beans had grown. Then, with the assistance of the practitioner, the children started to fill in the notebook according to their daily observations. Every day, Elliot's group was asked to spend about five minutes checking on the beans, and then to record their observations in the notebook.

Elliot learned to count from 1 to 4, indicating how many beans had grown, to distinguish between small and big, and also to recognise 'more' or 'less' when he was watering the beans.

Developing mathematical knowledge

As young children grow and develop they need to develop strategies enabling them to interact with and make more sense of their own environment and setting. From 0 to 5 years of age children's learning is a continuum of development whatever the setting they are in. Initially, through this interaction learning takes place before children start their formal schooling. For example, even as early as 6 months old babies are able visually to identify small sets. Babies are also able to identify repetitions and identify size differences. This implies that they have some kind of basis on which they can make quantitative judgements.

There is also an issue concerning the sort of mathematics that children should learn about. Clements et al. (2004: 366) state that 'basic mathematics for preschool children can be organised into two areas: (a) geometric and special skills and (b) numeric and quantitative ideas and skills'. Schaeffer et al. (1974) identified the first three number skills understood by children as, first, the concept of 'more', second, their judgement of relative numbers (which involves recognition that one array has more than another) and, third, their pattern recognition of small numbers. The many different ways in which children learn in the home environment all contribute to the mathematical development of children. For example, parents may use:

- numbers in songs such as 'One, Two, Buckle My Shoe', words in numerical contexts and in everyday situations, such as when children do up their buttons
- shapes, space and measures as children play with water or sand so that they think about whether something is full, half-full or empty, or by drawing their attention to the shape of everyday objects such as a placemat or napkin.

Clearly, all of this early learning within the home environment has implications for the requirements of the curriculum once a child attends a nursery or goes to school. As Resnick emphasises:

> [T]here is a constructivist assumption about how mathematics is learned. It is assumed that mathematical knowledge – like all knowledge – is not directly absorbed but is constructed by each individual. This constructivist view is consonant with the theory of Jean Piaget. (1989: 162)

As a result, children bring into their first experience of education a depth of informal mathematical knowledge based upon the strategies that they have developed within their environment. Aubrey points out that:

> [Y]oung children construct their own knowledge and invent their own strategies in everyday situations and through their interactions with the environment. For connections to be made between this knowledge and the formal mathematical knowledge of school, however, analyses of children's strategies, including their errors, must be made, as well as detailed analyses of the mathematical content required to carry out these tasks. (1993: 29)

This has clear ramifications for the role of those who support learning for children in the Foundation Stage. Furthermore, as Aubrey (1993) emphasises, the competences brought by children into the classroom from their own backgrounds may 'pose some challenges to the conventional reception-class curriculum'. She highlights that Reception teachers need to be aware of the mathematical levels and abilities that learners bring into the school, as well as the need to be able to assess the learning that has taken place. Through this understanding of learning, practitioners can build upon the ongoing development of mathematical concepts.

Mathematics as a social activity

As has been seen, mathematics is a living subject. It lives because of the need for individuals to deal with numeric issues all around us. As children make sense of the world they begin to understand patterns and seek solutions that help them to explore and deal with everyday issues. For example, Resnick (1989: 162) indicates that: 'infants of about six months can discriminate the numerosity of small sets when these are presented visually. What is more, they can match sets cross-modally, recognising the same quantity where it is presented visually or auditorily.'

According to Schoenfeld (1992: 3), 'mathematics is an inherently social activity'. He also emphasises that as children learn about mathematics the process becomes empowering for the learner. In fact, Vygotsky (1978) mentioned the importance of understanding the social context of learning. Nowhere is the social aspect of learning about mathematics better underlined than the ways in which young children learn through the process of play during their early years. According to Wood and Attfield (2005: 1), 'early childhood education is underpinned by a strong tradition which regards play as essential for learning and development'. Although not all play is purposeful, playing can contribute to the learning and development of children as they grow. It provides an opportunity for them to be creative and to experiment; such behaviours can have widespread implications for the development of each individual. Many of the activities in which children engage while they play can be used to develop and support learning. As Wood and Attfield emphasise (2005: 13), 'if playing and growing are synonymous with life itself, then lifelong playing can be seen as an important aspect of lifelong learning'.

As will be demonstrated, play is therefore a good opportunity purposefully to develop social interactions with children in a way that provides a context for learning opportunities within the area of mathematics. For example, well-structured and planned play may provide situations in which the practitioner can set up a challenging learning environment for the child; it may extend their language and improve their understanding of key areas such as numeracy and mathematics. In doing so, play also provides the opportunity to set up creative and imaginative learning experiences for the child. While these experiences may challenge individuals, they will also satisfy their curiosity and encourage them to ask questions or want to learn more. Play also provides a creative pedagogy through which problem solving can be used as a base for learning.

Contextualised learning opportunities

There are so many different activities and opportunities through which children can interact with adults to develop their mathematical skills that it is not possible for this chapter to do them all justice. Instead, this section simply highlights a range of contextualised learning opportunities to provide a sample of the sorts of activities in which adults and children can engage.

The context for learning about mathematics may be provided by the home or other setting as well as the school. Research shows that both the home and the early years setting have the capability of making key contributions to the development of academic skills at the age of 5 years (Dickinson and Tabors, 1991). Winter et al. (2009) emphasise that children live in two very different worlds. They explain that children learn through their daily activities as they play with members of their family. Although this learning is subtle and hidden from view, it is a key element in learning mathematics. As children are learning in two very different environments, a strong argument can be made that in order to create synergy and make the most of how children learn in such contrasting contexts, home and setting should work closely together, so that the setting can take account of the learning experiences that children bring with them from home (Jones, 1998).

By exploring through interaction children intuitively learn about size and shapes (Price et al., 2003). At a very early stage, simply building a tower with blocks or making a house, having a range of toys with bright colours, or sorting sweets helps them to learn basic mathematical skills. Blocks are particularly useful in introducing children to shapes, sizes and colours. As infants become toddlers, there are many more social opportunities to interact with the child. For example, counting while handing objects over to a toddler, reciting songs that use numbers or using finger-play to reinforce numbers will help them to understand more about the notions of 'more' or 'less' such that they may start to compare numbers. It may also help children to say and use the names of numbers within an appropriate context, and encourage them to start counting objects independently.

Reading books with a mathematical bias help children to learn literacy skills alongside their development of mathematical terms and concepts in a context that they may enjoy.

Children are naturally curious, which stimulates them to ask many questions. For example, they might want to know how many cars are in the street, or how many people there are on a bus. By answering questions, it is possible to count with them or to provide them with some way of understanding greater, smaller, heavier or lighter. It may also provide an opportunity for them to understand the notion of shapes such as circles or squares or to be able to describe in their own words the shape of something. For example, when slicing up a cake or a pie it is possible to count each of the pieces out to the child. In a similar vein, when placing objects in front of the child, his or her understanding of adding and subtracting can be developed by adding objects to or taking objects from the pile. Measurement activities may also satisfy curiosity. If the child uses a sand pit or wants to play with water, measuring cups and spoons will enable him or her to understand which containers hold less.

'Story sacks' were initially developed by Neil Griffiths (1998). They provide a creative opportunity to develop materials to stimulate the interest of children and make their stories more 'real'. A story sack is a large cloth bag inside which is placed a children's book and other associated materials related in some way to the story. Items could be counted out, or may involve different shapes and sizes; they can be discussed in relation to the story, in order to make the story come alive. Story sacks provide a fresh approach to enjoying books, and also provide a learning opportunity for the reader and the child to interact using a range of tangible materials in a way that sustains their motivation to read. Materials provide an element of curiosity and at the same time make learning active. By providing materials focused upon numeracy, such as cards, games, activities or lines that promote mathematical development effectively, the story sacks become number sacks to be used to help children to learn key mathematical skills such as counting.

For children in the Foundation Stage role-play is an imaginative way in which to learn. According to Staub:

[C]hildren role-play extensively in their interaction with other children. By enacting a variety of roles and exchanging roles in interactive situations, children may learn to view events from a variety of points of view. (1971: 806)

Role-playing provides a situation where children can imitate behaviour and act out different situations. The home is a perfect setting for children to engage in role-play. The role of the facilitator is simply to adapt the setting and create a role-play area. For example, the child may help with some cooking and be involved in sorting ingredients; this helps them to learn about more or less, or how to compare the sizes or amount of ingredients. They may have a cooker as a toy or another item that can contribute to the role-playing situation. Role-play might include growing cress or sunflowers, counting plant pots, using money in a retailing role-play, sorting objects such as sweets or shells, weighing ingredients, or developing the notion of time.

CASE STUDY

Role-play

A group of 2- to 3-year-old children, after reading the story of 'Little Red Riding Hood', decided to do a role-play in front the rest of the group of children. They made a list of the things they would need: a cake and a basket with some food in it. Finally, they decided they would have to choose roles in their play.

First, they chose to prepare the basket with the foods that Little Red Riding Hood was to offer to her grandmother. The children decided to make a cake. They searched for a recipe and they 'wrote the recipe' on a big poster so everyone could see. They had opportunities to explore concepts such as 'more' or 'less', 'big' or 'small' and 'adding'.

They had opportunities to measure the ingredients for the cake, to add or to take away; for example, when they added two glasses of sugar, one glass of water, the flour, and so on. The practitioner decided to focus only on these three concepts during the process of baking the cake and the subsequent activities.

Second, the children decided to pack the basket by adding different objects. Again, they had the opportunity to explore the concepts 'big' and 'small', 'more' and 'less', and add how many objects were going into the basket.

Finally, the role-play took place. The children, after preparing Little Red Riding Hood's basket, chose their roles: who would be Little Red Riding Hood, the wolf, the trees, the grandmother, the hunter and the mother. During this activity, derived

(Continued)

(Continued)

from a fairy tale, the children had the chance to negotiate roles, responsibilities and plans, and to re-create roles and experiences. The whole project targeted children's problem solving and numeracy while other areas such as language and communication, social development and creativity were also developed.

The practitioner provided opportunities for the children that encouraged them to use the concepts of more/less, and big/small, as well as to count up to 5. A number of different materials were used to conceptualise the different concepts and to help the children interact with different materials and objects in order for them to understand the concepts in different contexts. Time was provided for children to initiate discussions from shared experiences.

Puzzles are good for helping children to develop their spatial skills within a different environment that enables them to achieve a range of purposes (Siraj-Blatchford et al., 2002). As children work with puzzles, they are actually putting bits together and solving problems at first hand. Puzzles help with coordination; children begin to recognise that individual parts all contribute towards a whole. Puzzles help children to understand that, by rotating pieces, they can find the way in which each piece fits. Then, piece by piece, the puzzle becomes a whole. A wide range of puzzles designed for different ages of children are available today. They may be 3D puzzles, pegboards, bead threading, as well as puzzles linked to different sounds and made of different materials. In fact it is not difficult to invent a puzzle or mathematical game (Clemson and Clemson, 1994). For example, they could be similar to those in a comic but with an educational content. They might involve:

- quantities
- comparing pictures and objects
- strategies
- songs
- displays.

The indoor and outdoor environments

Young children require an interesting environment with the capability of stimulating their learning and development. The key features of such an environment must be the early years setting, the materials and the toys available and any equipment required. While such an environment should prompt a child to explore in a challenging way, it needs to be safe and secure. According to Schroeder (1991: 129), 'the health and well-being of children, in comparison to adults, are often more severely affected by the quality of the physical environment'. An appropriate environment would offer children the opportunity to explore both outdoors and indoors. The children would also need to be supported and supervised by adults.

An indoor play area should be a place where children can be either active or quiet; it should be designed to support their active learning and development. The environment should contain resources and materials that enable children to play and to further their learning at their own pace. The nature of such resources or toys will depend upon the respective age of each child and, of course, their particular phase of development. The items should also be imaginative: natural materials such as shells and pine cones are as enjoyable and instructive as wooden spoons, containers and other simple household equipment; a brief glance at various commercial websites can identify toys such as teaching watches, cash tills with money, blocks and shapes, shopping games, puzzles, number games, electronic maths toys, match-it puzzles, jigsaws, thinking games, wooden toddler toys, manipulative toys and imaginative play sets. The list is almost endless. As Taylor et al. have written, 'toys can be used to promote children's cognitive, physical, motor, language, social and emotional development' (1997: 235).

Any outdoor space should offer children both shade and shelter, and within this area both natural and manufactured resources should be available for play. For example, items could help the child dig, swing, roll, move, stretch, or play with wheeled toys. The children can also play in a water area where concepts such as wet, dry, floating skimming, similarities and differences can be explored. The practitioners, with the help of the children, can create a fish market where children can have opportunities to act such roles as seller or customer, to count money, to think how the fish will be stored, and to count the fish for sale.

In such an environment children need at their own pace to make choices about how to explore and learn. Natural materials such as sand, soil, garden snail shells, a slatted tray and cardboard boxes can be very helpful for children's participation in meaningful activities such as those that encourage children to sort, group and sequence play. Resources designed to help their mathematical development might help them to collect, measure, make patterns or build as they play. Swings, seesaws, slides, tents or a climbing house help to support such an environment. The outdoor environment is an enabler for children to be energetic and to exercise while enjoying some concrete experiences. There are a range of outdoor toys designed to help children with the development of their mathematical skills, such as number bean bags, giant inflatable numbers, a numeracy octopus, shape wands, what-is-it boxes and scatter boards, as well as giant puzzles.

Planning for progression

The *Development Matters* document (Early Education/DfE, 2012) aims to help practitioners to support the learning and development of children to their current needs. In doing so they identify three areas that provide appropriate opportunities to support children in their learning and their development of mathematical skills. Positive relationships emphasise that children should be encouraged to develop mathematical concepts within the context of their own play, particularly in child-centred and child-initiated activities. According to the Mathematical Association (1955: v, vi), 'children developing at their own individual rates, learn through their active response to the experiences that come to them through constructive play, experiment and discussion, [and] children become aware of relationships and develop mental structures which are mathematical in form'.

The second area emphasised by the *Development Matters* is that of creating an enabling environment for children. It includes both an outdoor environment in which a physical activity can be used in order to discover about distances, shapes and measurement, as well as an indoor area where children have the chance to learn to count and calculate. Resources are a key feature of both of these environments.

Finally, *Development Matters* links positive relationships and enabling environments with the notion of the 'unique child' and the special way in which each and every child reflects the communities and cultures around them. This notion of individuality helps to emphasise that creative elements of mathematical development, such as songs, games and imaginative play, as well as activities that enable mathematical learning and problem solving to take place, need to be built into daily routines to provide a route for progression.

The importance of home–setting links as part of the planning process

The learning and development of young children should be a shared experience among parents and carers as well as early years settings. Parents may be concerned about how their children are getting on within the setting while, at the same time, practitioners may want to discuss with parents issues affecting learning. This may not always be easy, particularly for parents who might not be sure about how they could help the educational development of their children. According to Booth and Dunn (1996: 3), 'parents play a critical role in both their children's academic achievement and their children's socio-emotional development'. In their text they identify evidence that illustrates how such a relationship contributes to the success of children within the setting.

Parents or carers may feel that they require information to help them to complement the nature and type of activities engaged in by their child when at the setting. For some (particularly better-educated parents) this may be easier than for parents who were challenged by learning mathematics. The level and strength of participation may depend upon the resources available to parents, the strength of their belief in the need for participating with the setting, and attitudes towards education in general.

Summary

The *Development Matters* document (Early Education/DfE, 2012) identifies three different areas that help to develop learning in the area of problem solving, reasoning and numeracy. These are: (a) positive relationships, involving the provision of time, space and opportunities for children to explore and develop their learning and understanding; (b) enabling environments, whether indoors or outdoors, which are well resourced to promote and develop learning; and (c) viewing each child uniquely so that learning and development through play and activities are based upon regular daily routines in a way customized to culture and communities. Mathematics helps children to make sense of and better understand the world around them in their early years setting. It enables them simultaneously to develop their conceptual abilities and to solve problems. From the very earliest stage of development babies recognise patterns and make connections. Mathematics can seem difficult for some children because the area has its own language. It is important to develop strategies that help children to develop their mathematical knowledge and problem-solving abilities. As this development is undertaken it must be remembered that learning about mathematics is a social activity. There are a wide variety of ways in which mathematical knowledge can be developed, and this may be within the context of either indoor or outdoor play.

Points to remember

- Mathematical development of children starts from a very early age and it is important to explore maths in the context of everyday activities and recognise the importance of engaging children in lifelong learning skills.

- Play provides a creative way where children can develop a number of skills related to mathematical development. It is essential to create creative and imaginative learning experiences for children.

- The importance of effective home–setting partnership is essential in children's mathematical development.

- Although mathematics has been explored in a separate chapter, it is necessary to emphasise that communication, language and literacy skills are important elements and are interrelated in children's acquisition of mathematical skills and knowledge.

Points for discussion

- If children start in the early years setting with a range of numeric and mathematical knowledge constructed from their individual backgrounds, what are the implications for how early years practitioners organise their strategies for support?

- Based upon your experiences of working with early years children, identify concrete experiences or evidence of situations in which you have observed babies and children constructing mathematical knowledge.

- Think of concrete examples of where the learning of mathematics by children can be set up as a socially mediated activity. How does the social aspect of learning influence the richness of the learning activity? Are there any problems or issues that might arise as part of this social interaction?

Reflective tasks

- As has been emphasised throughout this chapter, mathematics is an ongoing journey and it requires lifelong skills. Reflect on your mathematical skills and try to identify what are the most important skills that are required for effective mathematical knowledge.

- Reflect on your own practice and discuss your role as early years practitioner and how you can interact with children during play situations to provide a context for learning opportunities within the area of mathematics.

- After studying Chapters 17 and 18, think how communication, language, literacy and mathematics are interrelated.

Further reading

Cooke, H. (2007) *Mathematics for Primary and Early Years: Developing Subject Knowledge*, 2nd edn. London: Sage.

Pound, L. (2006) *Supporting Mathematical Development in the Early Years*. Maidenhead: Open University Press.

Tucker, K. (2005) *Mathematics Through Play in the Early* Years. London: Paul Chapman Publishing.

Useful websites

Helium

www.helium.com/items/1117913

Helium is a site that provides a range of topical and first-hand content about diverse issues for readers, submitted by a wide variety of contributors. This particular part of the site is entitled 'How to help your young child to develop maths skills at home'. With more than 40 papers from parents and practitioners to read and review on the site, as well as plenty of advice, there is a plethora of suggested activities.

Edhelper

http://edhelper.com

Although there are parts of this website that require a subscription, there are a number of free areas with a series of number, shape, colouring, counting and matching activities, attractively presented and really useful for mathematically developing early years children.

Apples for the Teacher

www.apples4theteacher.com/math.html#geometrygames

Apples for the Teacher describes itself as a 'fun educational website for teachers and kids'. The site links itself to other pages, and has a huge number of downloads and links to puzzles, games and problem-solving activities. Activities range from measurement games and money games to those that help learners to make sense of the principles of number.

To gain **free access** to selected SAGE journal articles related to key topics in this chapter visit: www.sagepub.co.uk/Palaiologou2e

20

Understanding the World

Gary Beauchamp

Chapter roadmap

The fourth principle of the Early Years Foundation Stage (EYFS) is that children develop and learn in different ways and at different rates, with all areas of learning and development considered equally important and interconnected. In this context, understanding the world (UW) cannot be considered in isolation from other areas of learning and development when planning. Research has shown that 'the brain will learn from every experienced event, but because cognitive representations are distributed, cumulative learning is crucial. There will be stronger representation of what is common across experience ("prototypical") and weaker representation of what differs' (Goswami and Bryant, 2007: 4). In this situation it is important for early years practitioners to plan to reinforce key ideas across different areas of learning. In planning these experiences, however, it is essential that key ideas and concepts are presented in a recognisable form in a variety of contexts and formats so that children learn to recognise things which are common (for instance, the concept of a shape, for example of a ladybird, a 2D shape, and in patterns) when presented in different locations and materials, or even in different life forms. As Goswani and Bryant (2007: 4) conclude: 'there will be multiple representations of experience (for example, in motor cortex and in sensory cortices). This supports multi-sensory approaches to education.'

It is here that UW can offer unique and distinctive multisensory opportunities both to *introduce* new ideas (which can be reinforced in other areas) and to *reinforce* ideas (as introduced in other areas of learning). The key issue lies in recognising the distinctive opportunities offered by UW in a variety of learning contexts and interactions – including between children and teachers, among children themselves, and between children and their environment.

This chapter aims to help you:

- develop an understanding of the distinctive features of understanding the world within the context of the Early Years Foundation Stage (EYFS)

- develop an understanding of how these features integrate with, and enhance, other areas of learning

- enhance your awareness of the variety of learning perspectives offered by adopting a variety of curricular 'lenses'

- consider the role, and effective use, of information and communication technology (ICT) in learning.

The child: a unique actor in their own social world?

The EYFS acknowledges that 'every child is a unique child'. Nevertheless, although an individual child will learn in different ways and at different rates, what all children have in common is that they will need to develop 'positive relationships' in 'enabling environments'. Hence, it is essential to remember that 'learning in young children is socially mediated. Families, peers and teachers are all important' (Goswami and Bryant, 2007: 20). When the EYFS was reviewed, this was acknowledged in a call for 'a greater emphasis [to be] given in the EYFS to the role of parents and carers as partners in their children's learning' (Tickell, 2011: 5), resulting in the requirement for 'a strong partnership between practitioners and parents and/or carers' (DfE, 2012: 3).

In this situation, although a child is often focused on his or her own world, the role of practitioners is to broaden this focus to help them develop a variety of relationships and partnerships, both within and outside of the school or other setting. As well as providing opportunities to enhance social development, these partnerships should also be considered as vital parts of cognitive development as 'those settings which see cognitive and social development as complementary achieve the best profile in terms of child outcomes' (Siraj-Blatchford et al., 2002: 10). Indeed, there is evidence that enhancing cognitive development can be a catalyst to higher levels of parental involvement. A review of research concluded that 'parental involvement is strongly influenced by the child's level of attainment: the higher the level of attainment, the more parents get involved' (Desforges and Abouchaar, 2003: 4). Although the importance of this partnership will be discussed further in other chapters, it is important to explore here the specific contribution that UW can make due to its requirement to guide children in making sense of 'their physical world and their community through opportunities to explore, observe and find out about people, places, technology and the environment' (DfE, 2012: 5).

It is much easier to enhance professional and personal partnerships within a school or other setting as practitioners have direct access to other professionals and children. Conversely, especially for students on a teaching or other (e.g. observational) placement, it is much harder to develop partnerships with parents and carers as it may seem a higher priority to develop relationships with children. Nevertheless, it is vital that practitioners, and especially students, should not neglect opportunities to develop relationships with families (as mentioned in Chapter 11) and the community (as mentioned in Chapter 10) – even if this appears difficult on a time-limited placement. They should also take chances to understand the family background of the children and the needs of the community whenever possible. Even simple steps, such as being seen by, and making yourself available to talk to, parents at the beginning and the end of each day can be a starting point in achieving this. Further steps can include attending local community events, especially those with no connection to the school – such as a local carnival or village fete – to show your interest in the community.

In trying to develop an understanding of what parents and the community have to offer there should be 'a two-way flow of information, knowledge and expertise between parents and practitioners' (DCSF, 2008: Card 2.2). An essential first step is in seeing the knowledge and expertise of parents (and other members of their families), and indeed the local community, as an asset and as another resource that practitioners can use to enrich the learning experiences they offer to children. This is set in context by the ideas of Perkins (1993: 89), who makes the distinction between the person-solo, 'the person without resources in his or her surround', and the person-plus, 'the person plus [their] surround'. For all early years practitioners, part of their surroundings (and therefore a resource to be used) are the parents and carers of children in the setting, as well of others from the local community who may be able to offer specialist knowledge or skills – such as on religion or local history. Overall, we may conclude, as emphasised elsewhere in this book, that the involvement of parents in UW should be viewed as the opportunity it is, rather than a challenge.

Using a subject 'lens' to develop a variety of learning perspectives

Although each aspect of UW will be considered separately below, it is essential that practitioners are aware of how they fit holistically into a child's education. When looking at UW, and indeed other areas of learning, there is always a tension between ensuring subject rigour (for instance, correct science subject knowledge in exploration and investigation) and providing a broader topic-based or thematic curriculum (i.e. in covering a range of 'subjects'). Barnes (2007: 1) points out that 'our experience of the world is cross-curricular. Everything which surrounds us in the physical world can be seen and understood from multiple perspectives'. One of these perspectives may be that of a scientist, geographer or historian and it is here that the challenge begins in framing learning experiences for young children. This does not mean adopting a subject-based approach (this will come soon enough), but adopting a subject methodology or perspective: for example, history (as a body of knowledge) should not be taught as a subject, but an historian's approach to learning may be adopted – see more below. It is suggested that each subject gives a child a unique way of understanding the world and that viewing teaching ideas through, for example, a 'scientific lens' can offer new insights into how to develop effective learning opportunities. Eventually, it may well be that 'this operates at two levels (one for the teacher thinking of possible approaches to planning, the other for children thinking of ways to approach a problem), but the key idea is that you consider the possible benefits of approaching teaching and learning as, say, a musician or historian' (Beauchamp, 2012: 118–19).

The world

In essence, the requirement for children to 'explore similarities and differences in relation to places, objects, materials and living things' (DfE, 2012: 9) form the beginning of scientific enquiry as

> [t]he child's exploration of the world is the springboard from which the next step is taken, that of more systematic enquiry. Systematic enquiry may be described as 'scientific investigation' in later years. Nevertheless, the first step in any scientific enquiry is exploration, or 'play'. (de Boo, 2000: 1)

This play is not time-scaled; children will often repeat the same activity time and time again. This is not time wasted, as it allows the child to reinforce their understanding of what is happening: for example, every time I tip water from the jug it goes down; every time I put water on the sand it seems to change colour; every time the sun comes out the puddles disappear. Young children need opportunities to explore materials and objects in many different contexts. For example, modelling clay can be squashed, made into shapes, joined together with more modelling clay of a different colour, and there are still many other properties to be explored: Does it float? Can you paint it? Can it be used to stick things together? Will it mix with other materials? Or does it go hard like pottery clay? A curious child will surely come up with many more enquiries. This example is about exploring just one material, let alone how it works with others. It is therefore essential that practitioners provide opportunities to explore a range of suitable resources (water, different-coloured modelling clay, paint and so on). Some of these explorations can be anticipated and planned for, while others will be spontaneous and unexpected.

Both should be welcomed and encouraged. Indeed, as has been emphasised in Chapter 6, practitioners learn much from observing the spontaneous explorations of children and considering the extent, if any, to which they are worth replicating in planning for another occasion. Careful observation is the key both to assessment and in considering whether practitioners can help develop children's understanding by building on, and adding progression to, these spontaneous events by providing other resources and settings. Overall, the aim is to provide quality experiences that are meaningful and 'worthy of active involvement. If children are to continue their struggle to make sense of the world, then the world must be worth the struggle' (Fisher, 2002: 15).

One of the key features of active involvement is including children in planning. This is particularly true of exploration and investigation. Most topics can start with a 'brainstorming' by staff and children to ask the questions: 'What do we know already?' and 'What do we want to find out/would we like to learn?' The idea of children's having ownership of the direction of their learning is central, no matter how young the children. Obviously, early years practitioners need to retain an overview to ensure coverage of relevant skills, and to avoid repetition, but the central message is that practitioners do not always need to follow a predetermined and detailed scheme of work. As one early years practitioner interviewed while this chapter was being written put it, with this sort of planning 'You can't just pick it up and run with it'. In addition, ensuring suitable progression in these activities can present challenges. For example, the move away from schemes of work (with pre-defined assessment tasks and progression criteria) means that for each investigation and exploration practitioners need to consider how they are going to assess the outcomes and ensure that adequate challenges are built in to extend children's learning. When considering assessment, the importance of looking at situations through, for example, a 'scientific lens' is crucial, as this may offer unique insights. For instance, the processes of exploration and investigation (including the so-called 'process skills', identified by Harlen (2003) as observing, raising questions, hypothesising, predicting, planning, interpreting and communicating) are in themselves outcomes and are just as important as the end product of the investigation.

To assist early years practitioners in both teaching and assessment in UW, two skills are central: observation and questioning. Although there is guidance available on observation (see Further reading below) one teacher interviewed for this chapter noted that there was still a need to 'mould things to what we need to do for our children and it will be different for every school'. The use of questions is a more generic issue and, although good questions can increase the interactivity of teaching, much depends on practitioners developing listening skills (hearing what children actually say, and not what you think children were going to say!). All practitioners should also develop 'a repertoire of strategies to manage critical moments' (Myhill et al., 2006: 117) when children ask questions or make a comment and practitioners need to decide on how best to respond.

Technology

In the current climate of rapid technological change, it is very likely that young children have some understanding of technology, particularly information and communication technology (ICT), and a degree of 'tacit knowledge' (Hayes, 2006) of computers and electronic toys. They live in an age where ICT is a part of everyday life and many homes have access to the Internet. In a review of research into ICT in the early years in 2008, Aubrey and Dahl (2008: 4) suggested that

> ... most young children aged from birth to five years are growing up in media-rich digital environments in which they engage actively from a very early age. Family members are positive about this and actively promote the use of new technologies through on-going social-cultural practices of the home. They welcome ICT education outside the home and believe that it should be included in the curriculum from the earliest days. Young children are confident with new technologies and are very willing to explore new gadgets that they have not encountered before.

In addition, children's toys are becoming ever more sophisticated and children are 'surrounded by products of the information and communication age' (Feasy and Gallear, 2001: 5). Children will need to find out about a wide range of resources, including cameras, photocopiers, CD players, tape recorders and programmable toys, as well as learning how to use them. In this context, young children's 'openness to explore, or play, with new technologies is something that teachers need to both embrace and facilitate' (Beauchamp, 2012: 6)

This can take place both within and, increasingly with the advent of mobile technologies, outside of the classroom and can take many forms. Even the entry intercom and pelican crossing buttons are practical examples of technology that could be used during and after a walk around the locality. On this trip children could also be encouraged to look for other uses of ICT as well as other physical features – which can be used when exploring 'people and communities' (see later in this chapter). It may be best to consider ICT as a

> new tool that could and should be incorporated into existing early-years practice in developmentally appropriate ways, supplementing, not replacing, other important first-hand experiences and interactions and accompanied by quality adult input to help children learn about and through the technology. (O'Hara, 2008: 30)

As children explore ICT resources, all practitioners, parents and children need to consider when it is appropriate to use ICT and when it is not. In general terms, practitioners make informed choices about how and when to use ICT (if at all) based on the pedagogic demands of a subject and the age of the children concerned (Beauchamp, 2006). With young children, the demands of subject teaching do not apply, but the age of the children is central. While practitioners need to consider how to develop children's specific IT skills (such as moving a mouse), they are also concerned with how ICT can contribute to the learning environment: what it has to offer that other resources do not. The following features of ICT will influence this:

- *speed*: making processes happen more quickly than by other methods
- *automation*: making previously tedious or effortful processes happen automatically (other than changing the form of representation)
- *capacity*: the storage and retrieval of large amounts of material
- *range*: access to materials in different forms and from a wider range of sources than otherwise possible
- *provisionality*: the facility to change content
- *interactivity*: the ability to respond to user input repeatedly. (Kennewell and Beauchamp, 2007)

Some of these features will be more relevant to early years practitioners as they plan and prepare work (such as the ability to store large amounts of pre-prepared resources); others may be more useful in engaging the children in learning experiences (such as the speed things appear and the range of resources available from, for instance, the Internet); others still may be a feature of the learning experience itself (such as interactivity). They are all, however, also open to children as they work with ICT devices. It is necessary, therefore, to consider the role of ICT in early years settings and decide how, when and who should use it. To help with this, we should consider the variety of 'roles' that ICT can play, which will help in allocating these to different 'actors' (people in the classroom). Beauchamp (2011) has suggested a useful categorisation, as shown in Table 20.1.

Table 20.1   **The use of ICT**

Category of use	End product
(a) A ***passive tool*** for interactions: ICT provides structure and capability to complete a practitioner-directed task (such as 'writing up') or practitioner demonstration/modelling	• Practitioner-led demonstration (normally to whole class) or modelling of task with some limited opportunities for pupils to clarify with practitioner control of ICT • Minimal dialogue/discussion about nature of task
(b) The **object** of interaction: resources to interact about (e.g. video clip or pupil's work) where the practitioner usually provides the structure for interactions	• Dialogue/discussion about content of lesson
(c) A **participant** in interaction: a partner to interact **with** when **ICT** sets tasks and provides immediate feedback (such as a game, quiz or simulation)	• Completed task/discussion to complete task if more than one person
(d) An **active tool** for interaction: a medium to interact **through** (e.g. email/chat, annotation, mind-mapping) where **learners** usually provide the structure for interactions	• Dialogue/discussion/learning/co-construction of knowledge

Source: Beauchamp, 2011

When planning the use of ICT, these categories should not be considered as something that lasts through the whole lesson, or even a whole activity, but rather a learning activity could contain all (or indeed none) of these categories, lasting different periods depending on the learning outcome. In making a decision about how and when to use ICT, or technology in general, you are making an important decision about the locus of control in the setting and therefore who has control over of the direction of learning, you or the child.

CASE STUDY

A class of 4- and 5-years-olds were investigating the creatures that lived in the grounds of the setting. At the start of the session the teacher used the interactive whiteboard (IWB) to show pictures of some of the creatures they might find and some of the places in the grounds they may look – although they could look anywhere. [*Passive tool for interactions*] The class was split into groups and each group was given a digital camera and video camera suitable for their age – they had used them before so knew how they worked. The groups then went outside with an adult helper and explored the grounds of the setting, taking pictures and videos of what they found. When they returned, the teacher plugged in one of the digital cameras and showed on the IWB some of the creatures they had found. The class talked about these and tried to identify them. [*Object of interactions*] This was repeated with other cameras from different groups. The teacher then brought up a website on the IWB with an interactive game naming creatures that they had found. The pupils came to the IWB and tapped on the relevant creature and a sound signified if they were right or wrong. [*Participant in interactions*] At the end of the game, there was one creature they could not identify so the practitioner asked the class how they might find out what it was called. Several pupils suggested emailing a picture of the creature to someone who may know, so the whole class discussed what they should write and the teacher typed it in an email on the IWB in front of them. Having attached the picture, the teacher then sent the email and the pupils went out for play. In the playtime, the practitioner accessed the email (cunningly sent to themselves!) and sent a reply to the class. When they returned the practitioner opened the email in front of them and read them the reply before moving on to new activities. [*Active tool for interaction*]

In planning activities through an ICT 'lens' it may be appropriate to consider which of the above roles practitioners are intending ICT to play. The main consideration when using ICT is that children are required to 'select and use technology for particular purposes' (DfE, 2012: 9). The key question should perhaps always be: is this use of ICT-supporting learning, or is it just an end in itself? If it is the latter, don't use it!

People and communities – past and present events

It is always difficult for young children to understand the past when they cannot conceive that it directly affects them. Cooper (2002: 18) cites Marbeau's argument that 'history at first is the historicisation of a child's own existence' and contends that children 'build continuity into their existence by reciting it to others (and to themselves)'. This reflects a view of history which is based on evidence or an experience, and which is interpreted and then retold to others in a variety of forms (such as written or oral stories, photographs, movies or through art or song) – both separately and combined. To do this effectively, a cross-fertilisation with other areas of the EYFS is necessary, as well as within UW – such as activities in exploring and investigating, which may allow children to notice the effects of change over time (for example, when growing plants).

The key starting point for children is that they find out about past and present events relevant to *their own lives or those of their families*. There are many ways in which they can tell their own stories (including the use of ICT above), and much can be learned about diversity and culture in the process. It is necessary, however, to record a note of caution here as the very fact that these stories are so personal means that they should be handled with care – see 'Reflective tasks' below.

When planning activities within this aspect of UW, practitioners need to be aware of the historical processes of enquiry (the historical lens) so that appropriate foundations are laid for subject work as children grow older. Again, we are not considering teaching knowledge of the subject (historical 'facts', such as the year of a particular battle), but considering what skills need to be developed to allow children to become effective historians later in their school life. The following are suggested as processes of enquiry that are appropriate for historians:

- searching for evidence
- examining the evidence
- recording of accounts
- summarising historical narrative or argument. (Turner-Bisset, 2005)

You may well notice that these have much in common with processes in other areas that have already been identified. In considering 'time' activities, the importance of skilful questioning becomes most apparent as you untangle what happened first – often relating events to personal milestones, such as, 'Was this before or after you came into my class?' It should be self-evident that to develop the enquiring skills above, practitioners need to use open-ended questions that encourage children to seek their own answers to questions (both individually and with others), as well other questions that focus their attention on important details and processes. When planning learning activities, it is always helpful to consider how to develop the processes outlined above and how adequate progression in each can be ensured.

Some examples of relevant progression might be in:

- children's use of language (for example, 'yesterday', 'tomorrow' or 'next week' leading to 'past', 'now' and 'then') – 'learning about the past involves learning vocabulary which is to some extent specific to the history' (Cooper, 2002: 16)
- moving from considering events that affect themselves to those that affect others
- the ability to sequence ever-longer and more complicated series of events.

People and communities – families, communities and traditions

Work in this area is fundamentally about developing concepts of 'space' and 'place' (Palmer and Birch, 2004) and the position of families, communities and traditions within it. This development will be based on children's existing awareness of the world around them and their place in it; children are 'young geographers with a world inside their head' (Smeaton, 2001:15). These worlds may, however, vary tremendously based on the experience, or lack of it, children have already had before they come into an early years setting. In order both to broaden experience and to provide common ground (both literally and metaphorically), it is common for UW themes to begin with a trip. This could be in the local area or further afield, and the stimulus provides a focus for planning subsequent work – using the brainstorming approach with children, as discussed above ('What do you know already? What do you want to know?'). A shared experience of a new place can provide the basis for an open discussion without any loyalties to street, town or even country influencing views. It also ensures that all children have the same level of exposure to the location – for example, in a study of 'On the farm' it is important to determine whether all of the children have indeed been to a farm and experienced the sights (and smells!). In planning such trips it is important to remember that children's experience will be varied and we cannot take equality of previous experience for granted, even in the area around your school, especially in view of the large catchment areas of some settings (for more detail on using areas outside the classroom see Chapter 10).

One idea for using any area (including inside the setting) is to consider how it can be made 'strangely familiar' (Barnes and Shirley, 2007). This means encouraging the children to explore and express the uniqueness of the place by representing it through a range of curricular areas, specifically the arts such as poetry, painting and music. In this approach practitioners are again looking at the area of learning though a variety of 'lenses' (for instance, the musician, the film-maker or the dancer) to see how children can be engaged in their own learning, by presenting them with alternative perspectives and new challenges. The role of the early years practitioner is to act as a facilitator and pass control to the children, as well as providing relevant resources to choose from. In presenting their views of the local area (including their likes and dislikes) children can use sounds, shapes and materials collected from around the area, using video images, still photos (digital and paper), stories, dances, songs, art shows and even sculpture.

Such an approach also naturally leads on to, or better still incorporates, an exploration of the communities that make up the area. The end result can be shared with a variety of audiences (including the community) using traditional means (paintings), ICT (websites, slide shows and movies) and live performances (music, drama and dance).

In exploring communities, as we have already mentioned above, the knowledge of families, and key figures within the community, can also be very valuable, as these can often provide first-hand experience and life stories of growing up in, or moving into, the area and different communities. These stories may, however, be deeply personal and revealing, so it is important to allow time for discussion with visitors on what they will be saying before they meet with the children – see 'Reflective tasks' below.

Summary

Overall, we have seen that understanding the world has unique opportunities in its own right, as well as being inter-connected with other areas of learning and development. The activities that children undertake should contribute to forming effective relationships with others, both within and outside of the setting and the family, including the local community. The singular nature of UW also helps to build foundations for later work in the areas, especially science, geography, history and ICT. As stated above, however, this does not mean starting these subjects early, but using their subject 'lenses' to view activities to ensure their specific perspectives are taken into account. By doing this, practitioners are providing unique opportunities for 'igniting children's curiosity and enthusiasm for learning, and for building their capacity to learn, form relationships and thrive' (DfE, 2012: 4).

Key points to remember

- Understanding the world (UW) is a learning area of EYFS where early years practitioners can help children develop a set of skills to help them explore the world around them and also in laying the foundation for later work in science, history, geography or ICT.

- For young children to develop skills, learning could be viewed through a variety of subject 'lenses' as each of these offers a unique insight into the world. The way these skills are developed depends on good practice, such as the use of questioning and careful, systematic observation.

- UW can become the area in early years settings where a number of different, creative activities can be hosted.

- UW can be met both within and outside of the early years setting, using mobile technology if appropriate.

Points for discussion

- Can you identify the unique features, opportunities and approaches provided by UW that do not arise in other areas of learning?
- Is it ever appropriate to use ICT (such as an interactive whiteboard) in place of 'real' objects, such as plants and creatures? If so, when and why? If not, what do the real objects offer that ICT cannot?
- Can you see young children using ICT to explore the outdoors environment and how?

Reflective tasks

- Using the table below (adapted from Beauchamp, 2012), identify how ICT and different subject 'lenses' could be used in planning an understanding the world activity (such as a trip) of your choosing. Add more lenses as appropriate. Ensure you justify your choices by reflecting on the benefits for the children. A start is suggested:

Lens	ICT resource
The film-maker	<ul><li>Digital camera (still and movie)</li><li>Digital editing software – e.g. Movie Maker</li><li>IWB for showing end product</li></ul>
The musician	•
The poet	•
The dancer	•
The artist	•
The historian	•
The geographer	•
The scientist	•

- In this chapter there was a warning about how children could reveal personal details in some of the activities. In addition, it was stressed how important it was to know what visiting family or community members may say if talking to the children. Consider how you would deal with each of these situations in the following scenarios – remember to keep the interests of the child at the heart of your reflection:

(Continued)

(Continued)

(a) A child is telling their own life story to other children and reveals they had seen their parents killed in front of them before they moved to the country they are now in.

(b) When you invite a member of the community to come and talk to the children, they tell you that they intend to talk about an issue you consider inappropriate.

(c) Despite telling you they wouldn't, the person talks about it anyway when they speak to the class.

• Central to EYFS is the safeguarding of children. In exploring the world around children, in designing and making tools, both inside and outside the classroom, there will be times when you need to consider the safety of children as they discover things through using their senses. Can you identify any particular situations or types of activity you need to consider in order to keep children safe when planning UW?

Further reading

Beauchamp, G. (2012) 'ICT in the early years', in *ICT in the Primary School: From Pedagogy to Practice*. London: Pearson.

Cooper, H. (ed.) (2004) *Exploring Time and Place through Play*. London: David Fulton.

Palaiologou, I. (2012) *Child Observation for the Early Years*. London: Sage.

Price, H. (ed.) (2008) *The Really Useful Book of ICT in the Early Years*. London: Routledge.

Useful website

http://ictearlyyears.e2bn.org
Website of Homerton Children's Centre, which provides a wide range of resources for using ICT within the early years.

To gain **free access** to selected SAGE journal articles related to key topics in this chapter visit: www.sagepub.co.uk/Palaiologou2e

21

Physical Development

Ioanna Palaiologou

Chapter roadmap

One of the most important characteristics in a child's life is the physical activity that takes place during their early childhood. Bruner (1983: 121) emphasised the importance of physical activity in young children and he claimed that the physical activities of a child are part of their 'culture of childhood'. A number of theorists that have been explored throughout this book have discussed in detail the importance of the physical aspects of a child's life. Piaget, for example, states that children start their development from a sensory motor stage where they acquire sensory schemata. Currently, the importance of physical literacy is being discussed more than ever, as is the integration of physical activity into curricular approaches as an essential aspect of children's overall, and therefore holistic, development (Parry, 1998; Bailey, 1999; Talbot, 1999; Almond, 2000).

The Early Years Foundation Stage (EYFS) sets the physical development of children as one of the prime areas of learning and development. Aspects of physical development are stated as being, moving and handling, and health and self-care (DfE, 2012a: 8).

This chapter aims to help you to understand:

- the importance of the physical and biological development of children
- the impact of physical development on children's health and well-being
- how physical development can be enhanced in early years settings.

Physical and biological growth

When children are born, they display a number of skills crucial to their survival. In the first few months of infants' lives reflexes play an important role in physical development; they help infants to build social relationships, essential to all other aspects of their development. Infants' reflexes, such as breathing, sucking, swallowing and blinking, help babies and parents to establish interactions. When babies grasp a parent's fingers, for example, parents respond and encourage these behaviours, and this is the start of an intimate relationship.

Around the age of 6 months babies begin losing these reflexes. Gradually, as the brain matures, the reflexes become voluntary control behaviours. This is a complex developmental task. For example, initially babies suck the bottle or the mother's breast as an automatic reflex, yet at around the age of 6 months they are able to combine their vision with arm movement, and eventually reach for the bottle or the mother's breast by themselves.

One of the aspects in the physical development of children, as stated in EYFS, is that of movement. The motor development of children is divided between 'gross' and 'fine' motor development. 'Gross' motor development refers to all spatial movements used by children to manoeuvre around their environment, such as crawling, sitting, walking and, eventually, running, jumping and climbing. 'Fine' motor development concerns all of the smaller and more intricate movements, such as grasping, building a tower with cubes, putting objects into boxes, drawing and writing.

During their early years children are undergoing rapid physical development. There are changes in the size and proportions of the body with both skeletal and hormonal growth. During this period children display tireless physical activity, thus it is essential for children to be provided with the space in which to move freely and safely, as well as with activities to encourage their developing movements. Hale (1994), among other researchers (Parry, 1998; Bailey, 1999; Talbot, 1999; Almond, 2000; Doherty and Bailey, 2003), emphasises the importance of an enriched and stimulating environment that helps children to engage with physical activity, because an active, supportive environment makes children feel comfortable and leads to their learning.

Children learn constantly by moving. They touch, feel, smell, move around and have fun 'translating movements into spoken language' in a variety of contexts (Hopper et al., 2000: 1). Physical activity is the best way for children to experience the world around them, practising skills, gaining in confidence by achieving, and making explorations through motor play such as running, walking, jumping, climbing, catching or throwing.

Much of children's play is characterised by movement and it is impossible to keep young children from running or force them to sit down for long periods of time. When children are given opportunities to move around freely at home or in early years settings they engage in constant motor play. Activities such as songs with movements, role-playing involving movement, climbing, jumping and balancing are among the favourite activities in early years settings. All of their play is characterised by constant movement.

Brain growth

Essential to physical development is the development of the brain. The brain regulates all areas of development. As has been shown in Chapter 4, neuroscientific evidence has an impact on pedagogy, and has helped us to understand the importance of brain growth in all aspects of children's learning and development.

The first years of a child's life are very important for brain development. A baby's brain develops at an astonishing rate in the first three years, such that by the age of 3 years a child's brain is as complex as it will ever be (Shore, 1997). The brain comprises billions of nerve cells (neurons) designed to send and retrieve information across organs and muscles. An important process in the growth of the brain is the development of synapses. All of the billions of neurons are rapidly connected to each other in the first years of life.

As can be seen in Figure 21.1, during the first 6 years there is a rapid development of synapses in the human brain. However, the number of new synapses decreases as children enter adolescence and then adulthood. Babies acquire more synapses than they will need. After the age of 3 years some connections are lost. For example, a typical 18-year-old has lost half of the synapses acquired in early childhood. Synapses in the brain that are unused disappear. It is inevitable that an individual wonders why we could do certain things when we were children that we cannot do now as adults. Shore (1997) argues that synapses are eliminated if they are not used, which has implications for the continuation of a stimulus environment. For example, if children fail to continue being physically active, they will become less interested in physical activity and it is less likely to become part of their adult lives. Kimm et al. (2002) found that by the age of 15 one in five English girls exercise for no more than 60 minutes a week. In Western societies teenagers spend more than five hours a day watching television, at computer screens and playing video games (Hardman and Stensel, 2003).

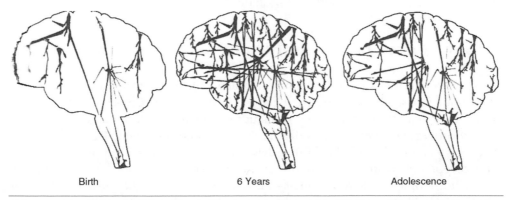

Birth   6 Years   Adolescence

Figure 21.1   *The development of synapses in early childhood (after Chugani, 1997)*

Growing up in urban apartment buildings, with fewer opportunities for physical development, movement and activity, may create a loss of those synapses responsible for physical activity. It is crucial that physical activity be promoted from a very early age; there is emphasis on continuing children's physical activity for their progression.

As illustrated in Figure 21.1, the first 6 years of a child's life are important for brain development. This period is considered as 'prime time' for neuron growth. Shore (1997: 26) suggests that the primary responsibility of parents and care providers is 'day to day care of young children's brains'. The care of the brain is accomplished through the creating of a stimulating environment. Early stimulation is important for helping children to achieve their developmental potential and for promoting infant brain growth. Providing a number of opportunities for physical and cognitive development will enhance the formation of synapses in the brain, then the continuation of stimulation will prevent the loss of these synapses.

The study of brain growth has given researchers an understanding of many aspects of children's development. Chapters 9 and 16, for example, discussed the importance of 'attachment' during early childhood. It is known that infants under stress, or infants who suffer from anxiety, are more likely to produce a hormone called cortisol (Hertsgaard et al., 1995; Nachmias et al., 1996). When this hormone is produced, the brain is threatened and reduces the synapses, leaving neurons vulnerable to damage. Gunnar (2001) found that when infants form secure relationships with their parents and their carers, the levels of cortisol are kept low. A warm and secure environment with parents and with other caregivers – an environment where the children are playing happily with stimulation – helps positively towards the physical development of their brain.

Studies into the development of the brain have offered an extensive knowledge and understanding of children's development, not only as regards the physical development of children, but other aspects, such as language (as shown in Chapter 17), numeracy (Chapter 19) and creativity (Chapter 22). Knowing about rapid brain growth in the infancy of a child helps early years practitioners to create environments where children are stimulated and their development promoted.

Cultural influences on children's physical development

Although children's physical development follows similar patterns and stages across the world, cross-cultural research demonstrates how the respective environment contributes to motor development. In a study conducted by Dennis (1960), babies in Iranian orphanages were observed. These babies were deprived; Dennis observed that they were spending a lot of time lying in cots with no toys available to them. After several observations he found that these babies delayed movement until they were 2 years of age. When they finally moved the experience of constantly lying on their backs led them to remain in a sitting position, rather than crawling as children normally do.

In a later study, Hopkins and Westra (1988) studied babies around the world and found that in some cultures there is an emphasis on children starting to move from an early stage. They found that in Western India, for example, the parents have a routine in which they exercise their babies daily. From the first months, parents exercise their babies by stretching each arm while suspending the baby, or holding the baby upside down by the ankles. However much these routines may surprise us, Hopkins and Westra found through interviewing the mothers that it is embedded in their culture for them to help their babies to grow physically strong, healthy and attractive.

In Kenya, Kipsigi parents deliberately teach children motor skills. In the first few months babies are rolled in blankets to keep them upright then seated in holes dug into the ground. Walking is promoted by frequently bouncing babies on their feet (Super, 1981). It was observed that these babies walk earlier than do babies in economically more developed societies.

Levels of physical activity vary by culture. A study of Puerto Rican and Euro-American mothers revealed that children's physical activities were rated more highly by Puerto Rican mothers, while the Euro-American mothers characterised physical activity as undesirable (Harwood et al., 1995).

When working with children from different cultural backgrounds, it is important to understand cultural differences. As it is important to work in partnership with parents, their values and beliefs need to be understood and channels of communication need to be developed, so the parents will feel comfortable with the level of their children's physical activity in the early years setting.

In the modern Western world there is a trend to emphasise academic development of children, whereas there is far less emphasis on physical activity. Children are supported and encouraged when they try to be physically active during early childhood, but this is limited later when formal schooling is starting and the focus on the children's academic progress is more intense.

It is noticed that there is a lack of physical activity among children when they grow older. The World Health Organization (1999) states: 'in many developed countries, less than one third of young children and people are sufficiently active to benefit their present and future health'. It is a positive point that EYFS clearly views physical activity of children as being important for children's development, a foundation on which children can build confidence and acquire habits leading to a healthy lifestyle. The revised EYFS (DfE, 2012) identified physical development as a prime area for children's learning and development, and the two key aspects are: moving and handling, and health and self-care. The Progress Check at Age Two aims to assess children's physical development as a means of early identification of 'any areas where the child's progress is less than expected' (DfE, 2012: 10). The age 2 progress check can become an indicator of any areas of concern that the child 'may have developmental delay' (DfE, 2012: 10) and strategies can be put in place in order that children can be offered opportunities to be psychically active, both indoors and outdoors, as a significant factor in brain muscle fibre development as well as their overall physical development.

Health and well-being

Within EYFS, central to physical development is helping children to learn what healthy living is and to sustain attitudes towards healthy living. Chapter 13 explored the medical approach and requirements for what constitutes a healthy child. In this section we focus on health and physical development. As discussed above, children are physically active during early childhood, but they do not sustain this level of activity as they grow older. Hardman and Stensel (2003) state that three modern trends – obesity, physical inactivity and an ageing population – are the main 'diseases' of the twenty-first century and high-light the importance of physical activity.

Obesity has increased rapidly over the past two decades. More and more children are overweight. There are a number of factors involved in the increase of obesity, such as eating habits, poor nutrition and lack of physical activity. A number of researchers, however, link obesity with physical inactivity rather than with overeating (Prentice and Jebb, 1995; Baur, 2002; Kimm et al., 2002). Given that most children are brought up in urban settings with a lack of space in which to move around, children tend to adopt alternative ways to play, such as with computer and video games. It is important to create opportunities for young children to be able to be physically active. The activities around physical development (PD) should appeal to children and be enjoyable for them. Contextualised activities, such as catching and throwing in games situations, or more complex activities like singing, dancing and swimming (where movements by children are required), promote their physical development.

Doherty and Bailey (2003) suggest that activities designed to promote physical development within educational settings should be characterised first and foremost by enjoyment. Children should want to take part in these activities and have fun. Such activities should be continued throughout the curriculum and not only during early childhood. By promoting physical activities across all ages a 'firm foundation base of movement experience' (DCSF, 2008) is established from a very young age.

Doherty and Bailey (2003) also suggest that children should, on a daily basis, become involved in physical activities if the aim is to develop physical activity as a lifelong habit for health and well-being. Children should have the freedom to choose the activities and the materials, according to their personal interests and physical skills.

Children's physical development and brain growth are important in order to sustain good health and well-being in children's lives. Young children should acquire habits of healthy living from an early age. There are many factors influencing a child's health and well-being, such as nutrition, emotional health, the structure of the family and the structure of their communities, which combine to contribute to children's physical, biological, mental and sexual health.

The physical activities of children help them to sustain a healthy lifestyle. In their study, Biddle et al. (1998: 4–5) highlight the benefits of physical activity. They claim that physical activity leads to psychological well-being, the increase of self-esteem, contributes to children's moral and social development, and prevents obesity, chronic disease and risk factors. Thus, it is essential that children in their daily routine are provided with opportunities to be physically active, that they have adults who are supportive and who facilitate children to move and, of course, most importantly, that children are given time to be physically active and to be able to play within the early years.

Whitehead extends this idea by introducing the concept of 'physically literate' children. He claims that children who are physically active, become physically literate:

> The characteristics of a physically literate individual are that the person moves with poise, economy and confidence, in a wide variety of physically challenging situations. In addition the individual is perceptive in 'reading' all aspects of the physical environment, anticipating movement needs or possibilities and responding appropriately to these with intelligence and imagination. Physical literacy requires a holistic engagement that encompasses physical capacities embedded in perception, experience, memory, anticipation and decision making. (2000: 10)

Whitehead emphasises the importance of a challenging environment where children are offered opportunities to move in a way that stimulates them and where, at the same time, they can experience enjoyment. He also suggests that physical activities are linked with other areas of development. For example, when children are having a dance activity or play in the water area, they are not only physically active but they are engaged in a number of cognitive activities such as language development ('let's put our hands up', 'let's move around in a circle', 'let's move in a line') or problem-solving activities ('let's throw objects in the water that float or objects in the water that sink'). Central to this is the creation of an environment that promotes physical activities.

The role of the environment

Before exploring the role of the environment in children's physical development it is important to understand what a 'healthy environment' means. Nutbeam (1998: 362) characterises a healthy environment as 'a place or social context in which people engage in daily activities, in which environmental, organizational and personal factors interact to affect health and well-being'.

A healthy environment has many forms and is influenced by cultural values and practices. In some families, for example, the home environment is redesigned and furniture is moved so children can move freely and have space to play; in other families children have rules about what they may touch and where they can go to play. It is not necessarily the case that one situation is 'wrong' and the other is 'right'. Physical activity and the space around children are related to the families' values. In the second situation it could be argued that in this way children learn about rules, learn about what is right and what is not, learn about safety from a very young age, and learn about their limitations.

A classic study conducted by Levine (1996) showed the diversity of strategies used in the world to provide healthy and safe environments for children. He observed different tribes and different cultures around the world and he offers a case from Kenya. In Kenya, babies and young children spent a lot of time outdoors as mothers are involved in their daily chores. Leaving young children outdoors without supervision seemed to hold many risks, as they could burn themselves in cooking fires, fall off cliffs or into lakes, or suffer snakebite. He found, however, that the parents in one village studied protected their children by carrying them on their backs and allowed them to be outdoors, without supervision, only when they were old enough to understand rules and the dangers around them.

Cultural aspects have an impact on physical development in terms of choosing outdoor or indoor environments. In the following case studies from three different curricular approaches, it can be seen how the indoor and outdoor environments are used to promote children's physical development.

CASE STUDY

Arts to promote physical development: example from Reggio Emilia

In the Reggio approach the artistic development of children is central. Gandini (1997) describes activities such as drawing, painting, sculpting and singing as fundamental methods for children's learning, at the same time as they enhance the physical development of children (i.e. gross motor development and fine motor development). Gandini describes the arts as essential not only to children's cognitive development, but as a major part of children's physical development.

The arts can help children more with their personal, social and creative development. Children, after a visit to a museum or gallery, can use materials to express themselves and experiment with water, painting, sculpting, etc., and all these activities require sophisticated and complex movements. Consequently, their physical development is shaped in a contextualised environment. Children's movements are viewed as creative; there are no constraints in time and space, and children can take as much time or space as they need in which to express themselves.

CASE STUDY

Physical development in a Te Whāriki class

The Te Whāriki curriculum has been introduced in New Zealand's early years settings. Emphasising multiculturalism and allowing children the freedom to choose materials and activities, it promotes children's having ownership of their own learning. This curriculum approach views children as 'competent and confident learners and communicators, healthy in mind, body and spirit, secure in their sense of belonging and in the knowledge that they make a valued contribution to society' (Ministry of Education, 1996).

A Te Whāriki class, similarly to the EYFS, is underpinned by five goals: well-being, belonging, contribution, communication and exploration. In a Te Whāriki class children move between freely indoors and outdoors, and choose which materials to play with. In the sand area they can make castles, whereas in another area they can make solid objects, such as chairs, using a number of tools that develop their fine motor skills.

Outdoors, children are offered opportunities to practise climbing, running and jumping, either individually or in small groups. The Te Whāriki outdoors environment is rich in real objects and thus encourages and motivates children to engage in physical activity through play.

They create tunnels from car tyres for children to crawl through, swings and water points, where they can 'splash about'.

Inside the class, singing is accompanied by physical movement, such as children imitating waves by using their bodies and their hands. The children have the opportunity to move constantly and to use a number of materials. In a corner of the room there are several clothes for dressing up, and this way the children's motor skills are developed.

Physical exploration of different materials meets one of the main principles in the Te Whā⁻riki approach: Kotahitanga ('holistic development'), where the child is viewed as a 'whole'. It is emphasised that the child learns in a holistic way by taking into consideration not only the child's physical, social, emotional and cognitive development, but also the cultural context and the spiritual aspects of the children's environment.

CASE STUDY

The Forest School: using the outdoor environment

In the 1950s, throughout the Scandinavian countries (especially in Sweden and Denmark) the concept of Forest Schools was developed. Central to Forest Schools is the idea to inspire children from a very young age to have positive experiences by interacting with nature. There is the ecological view that if children love nature from a very young age they will grow up respecting nature and try to protect it from pollution. Moreover, the Forest Schools approach is based on the argument that when children spend time in nature, in the fresh air, they grow healthy, are at minimum risk from disease and become stronger. It is also believed that the Forest Schools approach helps children with their social relationships, as this approach increases children's understanding and respect for others. Finally, in the Forest Schools children have opportunities to promote their physical development, and also to learn a number of skills, and to develop cognitively in a pleasant, natural, enjoyable and low-stress environment.

Increasing numbers of early years settings across the UK have adopted this innovative approach. A typical Forest Schools project is to take a group of children to a woodland area or a forest. Children can stay in the woodlands or forest anytime from one day up to a few days with adults, depending upon the ages of the children. During their time in the forest, children have the opportunities to play games, to create materials from wood by cutting timber, to build fires, to observe nature and record their observations, and to cook their own food. Prior to such a visit children normally agree on a certain project that they will carry out when they are in the woods.

Summary

This chapter discussed the importance of physical development for children's holistic development. Children's play is characterised by movement, and it should be encouraged. The physical activity of children is important to all aspects of their learning. Additionally, brain growth in early childhood is rapid. The formation of synapses between neurons is happening far more rapidly in the first few years of a child's life than later. This has implications when an environment is created for young children. Children's concepts of healthy living and well-being are strongly related to the enjoyment of physical movement. If adults want children to acquire healthy living styles then physical activity has to become a lifelong habit. Only when they are pleasurable will children wish to carry out physical activities.

Key points to remember

- Physical development of children is a prime area of the EYFS and the two important key elements are moving and handling, and health and self-care. More than ever, emphasis is placed on children's physical activity as a way of children acquiring healthy habits.

- Physical development is influenced by a number of factors, such as culture and the social and economic context in which children are growing.

- Early years education and care should offer numerous opportunities to children to enhance their physical development. Opportunities for physical development should be embedded in the daily life and activities of the early years setting and it should underpin all the activities, as was demonstrated in the case studies.

Points for discussion

- Look at the plan in Figure 21.2. Consider that this is the room you have been given in which to work with 2-year-old children. How are you going to design the environment so that you can promote children's physical development? In your new design you need to consider whether there is sufficient space for children to move around, what equipment you will have, and how you will redesign and resource your room. Do children have access to outdoor areas so they can move in and out?

- Bilton (2003: 38) suggests that when organising work in the outdoor environment the following should be considered:

  o layout of the environment

  o the amount of space available

  o the use of fixed equipment

  o the weather element

  o the need for storage.

Can you think of any other aspects when you organise activity in the outdoor environment? What activities can you plan that will offer appropriate physical challenges to children?

(Continued)

(Continued)

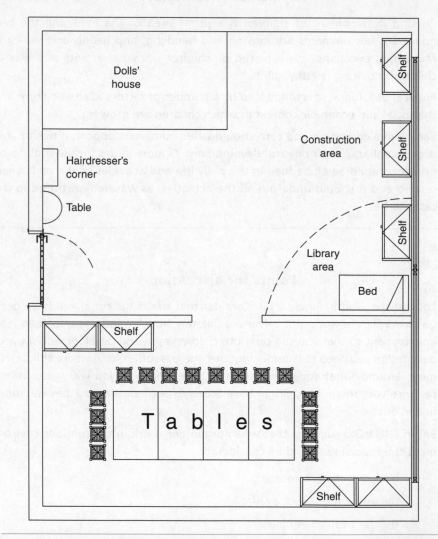

Figure 21.2 *Floor plan of a nursery*

• Compare a Reggio Emilia, a Te Whāriki and an early years setting within EYFS. Where do they differ and where are they similar in promoting the physical movement of children?

Reflective tasks

- Consider an early years setting you are familiar with and reflect on the daily activities. Are children engaged physically (fine or gross motor skills)?

- More than ever emphasis is placed on health and healthy environments. In your view what is a healthy environment and how can you promote that in your setting?

- Reflect on the case studies and think how indoors and outdoors are used in an early years setting within EYFS.

Further reading

Bilton, H. (2010) *Outdoor Learning in the Early Years*. London: Routledge.
Knight, S. (2011) *Forest School for All*. London: Sage.
Nurse, A. (2009) *Physical Development in the Early Years Foundation Stage*. London: David Fulton.

Useful websites

Forest Schools:
www.forestschools.com/index.php
Institute of Outdoor Learning (IOL):
www.outdoor-learning.org
Outdoor play in Europe:
www.eoe-network.org
This is the official website of the European Institute of Outdoor Adventure Education and Experiential Learning (EOE).

To gain free access to selected SAGE journal articles related to key topics in this chapter visit: www.sagepub.co.uk/Palaiologou2e

Creative Development

Nick Owen, Laura Grindley and Michiko Fujii

> 🚌 **Chapter roadmap**
>
> Although the revised EYFS (DfE, 2012) replaced the creative development area of learning with the expressive arts and design prime area, with emphasis on exploring and using media and materials, and being imaginative, it is still important to creativity for children to engage in arts, music, movement, dance and role-play.
>
> This chapter aims to show that 'being creative' in early years settings is a rich, extensive and common form of human expression and explores how we can promote creative practice in early years education and care. This chapter will highlight a particular model of expressive arts activities – the Midas Touch Creative Learning Project – to identify the necessary mindset and skills required to optimise children's creative learning experiences.
>
> The activities that will be discussed will reflect the principle that creative practice is not a domain exclusive to arts practice and the importance of collaboration will be stressed: it is suggested that instead of interpreting creativity solely as an attribute of individuals, creativity arises from the gravitational pull of relationships; it is thus a situational and contextual phenomenon, as opposed to an individual or psychological one. Collaboration stresses the need for the co-intentional imaginations

of adults and children to embrace, together, attitudes of improvisation, keeping an eye open for the off-chance, taking the occasional, unassessed risk and accepting the generation of and pleasure in 'mess'.

This chapter aims to help you to:

- understand that creative practice can be developed in all areas of early years settings and is not exclusive to arts practice

- undertake activities that form the basis in an early years setting of an action research project, which aims to address a 'creativity challenge'

- appreciate the contextual factors that have informed the development of contemporary creative practice in early years settings.

Developing creative practice: what's all the fuss about?

The notion of developing children's creativity has never been far off the political agenda in recent years. The educational establishment has frequently been jolted by politicians to come up with more and better methods to make sure not only that children are more creative, but that creativity is part of the daily routine, especially within the early years environment.

More jobs, more wealth, more growth, more prosperity: the drive towards creative nirvana is fuelled by the political expediency of economic growth, an element clearly identified in the 1999 NACCCE report on creativity and cultural education, *All Our Futures*. That report produced an almost canonical definition of creativity – 'imaginative activity fashioned so as to produce outcomes that are both original and of value' (Robinson, 1999: 30) and subsequently many educationalists have applied themselves in recent years to thinking how to get more creative bang for the always-limited educational buck. Do we achieve it by amending learning outcomes, rewriting the Foundation Stage curriculum, training practitioners to be more creative and building new Children's Centres? Or do we do it by being completely child-centred in our outlook – an outlook that privileges the ideas of the children over the ideas of adults, one that interprets all children's views and attitudes as the sacrosanct voice of the pure, unadulterated human being and witnesses the holy grail of creativity in the play and expression of very young children, for whom the world is a perpetual mystery? How can we promote creative development without stifling it?

Ironically, there are two easy routes to stifling creativity in young children.

- *Route one*: say 'no' to everything they suggest, muse on, play with and are curious about. Be sure to block initiative, stifle unacceptable behaviour and generate fear about the consequences of their actions. Worry them about their appearance, their status in other people's eyes, and what their attitudes and behaviour might rather say about *you* than it might about *them*.

- *Route two*: say 'yes' to everything they suggest, muse on, play with and are curious about. Be sure they understand there are no such things as boundaries of any sort, that all kinds of behaviour in any circumstances are completely acceptable. Encourage them to think that all of their ideas are perfect and require no further modification from any other source at all. Offer free, unconditional, unending praise for any kind of behaviour and have an unending supply of house points for every time they do something you deem creative.

Creativity development in early years settings – if it is to encourage and challenge children's experiences of creativity – needs to inhabit a place, however, somewhere in between the extremes set out by those two approaches and steps can be taken to ensure that a child stands the best possible chance of undertaking and completing the creative development journey. Making a child 'more creative' is not as tangible as letting their hair grow longer or passing an examination; it is about offering time and space to understand and experience the processes involved – which need personal qualities of application, struggle and testing, alongside the social qualities of cooperation, collaboration and mutual criticism. To accomplish all of that needs the presence of an element far more important than a paintbrush, a guitar or a pair of ballet shoes: it needs *you* – another human being.

Creative relationships in the early years

Understanding creativity has been introduced into many early years settings in recent years through Anna Cutler's work on the Four-Phase Stepped Progression model of creative learning. This model has, as its name implies, four phases, which suggest what we might look for when it comes to encouraging our children's creativity and approaches to learning. These are simply entitled *Input*, *Doing*, *Showing* and *Reflecting* (see Figure 22.1).

Cutler (2005) lists seven features of creativity required for creative learning within the Doing phase of the model: the ability to identify and /or to make problems, the ability to think divergently (opening the mind to new, surprising, unusual and perhaps uncomfortable ideas), attributes such as being open to experiences of fascination and curiosity, the ability to take risks, to play with and to suggest. These would occur in a climate marked by an absence of fear and in which children find pleasure in their endeavours for their own sake, as opposed to an anxious educational agenda that might be hovering over their shoulders. Briefly, the key questions characterising these seven features can be summarised as follows:

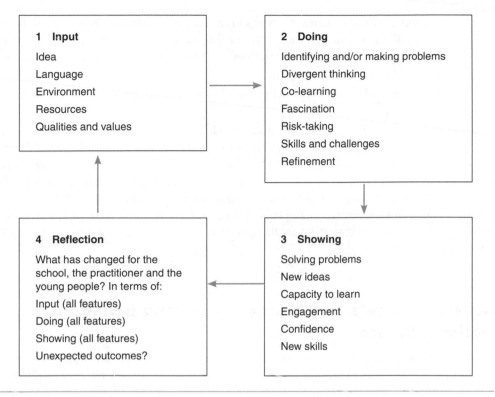

Figure 22.1 *A four-phase stepped progression model of creative learning (Cutler, 2005)*

Identifying problems: Does this project seek to challenge any issues? What kinds of problems might the project bring up and will these be an important part of the experience for everyone? How will such issues be handled?

Divergent thinking: How does the project offer different and original ways of thinking, different perspectives and opportunities for the novel use of the imagination? What unusual elements or ideas can be put together, and how can people try them out?

Co-learning: How do practitioners work with children and staff in a situation where all participants are learning something new together, or where early years practitioners are learning with the children from doing things together?

Fascination: How is this generated by the activity? Is it sustained beyond the project hours?

Risk-taking: Is the project able to offer something beyond the comfort zone of the individuals concerned? Is the project offering opportunities for risk-taking in practice?

Skills and challenges: Does the programme or project effectively use the skills of those involved and stretch them? Or are they kept within what they can do (and so risk boredom) or thrown in the deep end without the resources to get themselves out (and so risk fear)?

Refinement: How does the activity allow for practice, repetition and fine tuning?

While this is a significant description of the climate needed to bring forth creative practice, Cutler's work also makes it clear that creativity is not solely a feature of individuals alone: it is a shared, constructed and collaborative experience. It makes more sense to talk of 'our' creativity than 'my' or 'your' creativity, for instance, so when it comes to our own thoughts about how we make our own children more creative, and how to prevent their creativity being stifled, then starting with ourselves – and how we are creative *with* our children (not *on* them or *to* them or *at* them) – is indeed an excellent place to start.

Towards creative relationships: constructing pedagogies for creative practice

Craft (2002) envisages creative practice as something of which all individuals are capable: a function such as breathing or digestion, which we carry out unconsciously and automatically in order to get us through our daily lives. Creativity is not the exclusive preserve of the rich, famous, artistic genius; it is a phenomenon that we all share, irrespective of age, class, gender, race, ability or impairment. It is a frighteningly democratic and democratising process and thus might, one would think, be an easy enough matter to identify when '*little-c creativity*' *or* '*possibility thinking*' (as Craft, 2002, refers to it) is present:

> Little-c creativity ... focuses on the resourcefulness and agency of ordinary people ... it refers to an ability to route find, successfully charting new courses through everyday challenges ... It involves being imaginative, being original/innovative, stepping at times outside of convention, going beyond the obvious, being self-aware of all of this in taking active, conscious, and intentional action in the world. It is not, necessarily, linked to a product outcome. (Craft, 2002: 56)

However, were it such a simple matter to identify the subconscious, automatic – and perhaps invisible – nature of creativity, there would be no need for chapters like this or the myriad texts attempting to explain how creativity can be encouraged in early years education and care.

What is offered here is a methodology of how creative practice within early years settings can be developed from the most unlikeliest of sources: mess, scrap and rubbish.

Creative learning through recycling: the Midas Touch Project, St Helens

The Midas Touch Project was set up as a four-week pilot in March 2010 in St Helens, Merseyside, funded by the Find Your Talent programme, a national pilot scheme to encourage children and young people to participate in cultural activities, both in and out of educational settings.

Midas Touch was a transformative learning programme for very young children and their families and carers that aimed to enhance their sense of awe and wonder in their everyday lives. Using recycled, 'ordinary' objects as tools of play, work and learning, the Midas Touch programme aimed to uncover the unusual within the usual, the strange in the familiar, and the beauty within the unsuspecting. It relied on the metamorphosis of recycled, discarded and apparently worthless objects, their incorporation into challenging learning experiences and the documentation of children's learning for its affects and effects.

The Midas Touch Project was based on the *Remida* approaches of Reggio Emilia in Italy, where an early years practitioner (Pedagogue, Laura Grindley) and an artist (Atelierista, Michiko Fujii) worked collaboratively to enhance children's learning and promote the idea that waste materials can be resources. The team also wanted to adapt some key principles from the Reggio Emilia approach. These were:

- Children must have some control over the direction of their learning.
- Children must be able to learn through experiences of touching, moving, listening, seeing and hearing.
- Children have a relationship with other children and with material items in the world that children must be allowed to explore.
- Children must have endless ways and opportunities to express themselves.

Another vital factor within the project was the role of the adult, whether that be a practitioner or a parent/carer. The role of the adult within Midas Touch was to be the listener, the observer and a compass. Children were able to explore their interests through processes that did not necessarily lead to an end product. The adult could observe and listen to their children's interests, views and opinions and act as a compass by guiding their learning through appropriate questions, which would not impose their own views and opinions, but extend the child's learning. The project provided an opportunity for the practitioner and the child to go on a learning journey together which led to the opportunity to engage in sustained shared thinking. This led to a better understanding of the children in their care by making clear their interests, opinions and schemas of play, which in turn would help to better support a child's learning.

Planning, reflection and documentation were essential elements of the four-week pilot project. These elements are very important in the EYFS requirements. Each week involved suggesting a loose theme relating to the objects used: plastics, wood and metal, natural materials, and blacks and whites. The majority of the planning was emergent and reflective, looking at observations and reflections from the previous week. This meant that materials were introduced to extend learning and interests, such as a variety of mark-making media and real tools. Children's learning was observed and documented in such ways as taking photographs, recording videos and making written observations. This documentation was used to enhance learning opportunities while at the Midas Touch Project but also made into books and wall displays to share with children, parents/carers, practitioners and the community.

CASE STUDY

Midas Touch case study: The Gunpowder Plot

Along with three other Reception class children, five nursery children and two teachers, Adam and Levi attended several Midas Touch sessions. During Session One, Adam and Levi were particularly keen to explore the Midas Touch environment. We laid out an assortment of plastic objects which the two boys searched through extensively, tipping and emptying different containers and spreading all the objects they could find onto the floor. It seemed that they were not used to this amount of freedom and wanted to explore everything that the space had to offer.

The following week, however, we shifted the focus slightly by introducing wood and metal objects and tools in addition to the smaller plastic objects. Upon their return, Adam and Levi were drawn to a box of bike parts and began to think about different ways to attach or join the metal parts together. They discovered a box containing real tools, such as a hammer and pliers. It was clear that they were particularly keen to use these tools, having never had the opportunity to use them before. They continued to use these throughout the rest of the project. In particular, they were drawn to the hammer which they would share and interact with in a number of ways. The hammer became a tool for construction, role-play, mark making and noise making.

Adam and Levi returned to the work area that they had been exploring the previous week. Taking turns, they picked up a hammer and began to bash it against the wooden sleepers and planks, listening to the different sounds they made. Michiko had brought some charcoal and mark-making tools out for some of the other children and Adam picked up a piece of willow charcoal. He found a piece of tree bark and began to blacken it with the charcoal. He and Levi then proceeded to smash pieces of charcoal with the hammer and the piece of tree bark.

Michiko suggested that they move into the back space so that they could have more room and Adam asked if he could have more charcoal. He and Levi hammered away in their work area. They listened to the noises, explored the marks and then realised that the charcoal released a kind of dust as it was hit by the hammer.

'I've found smoke!' Adam exclaimed. 'It's gunpowder!' He then said to Michiko, 'You brought gunpowder ... let's make some more!' The two boys continued to hammer away throughout the session and then took turns to clean up the mess, which they actually seemed to really enjoy.

Our identified EYFS focus for each session was as it is described by the Reception teacher:

> I loved the approach. I believe it's how children should learn in an ideal world – exploring their own ideas. We are there to scaffold that learning. (Reception teacher)

Laura, Michiko and the Reception teacher worked together over the four-week project to allow Adam and Levi to explore the space and materials in a way that they were not used to normally. The teacher identified a number of potential risks or hazards within the space, but despite this she recognised the benefits of allowing the boys to explore freely. Laura, Michiko and the teacher brushed aside any preconceived ideas or judgements about the boys and engaged with them equally at their level throughout the four sessions.

Despite her fears, the teacher trusted Michiko and Laura to work with Adam and Levi. Laura and Michiko took the teacher's approval as an unspoken sign of trust and support, which encouraged them to support Adam and Levi's development even further. All three wanted the boys to have an experience that would enhance their confidence, communication and creativity as well as working towards achieving the identified EYFS goals.

What got in the way?

Although 'The Gunpowder Plot' was a one-off observation of creative play, when creating similar experiences it is likely there will be constraints that stand in the way. It seems that we now live in a risk-averse society where we are stopping children from experiencing and exploring due to our fear of risk. Letting children experience things first-hand, however, not only satisfies their curiosity but allows them to risk-assess for themselves.

Consumerism and curriculum also play a part in holding back these kinds of experiences for children. In early years settings we are often left with very little time

(Continued)

(Continued)

for truly open-ended play and give children less opportunity to explore with open-ended resources. It seems that we are all too ready to open an educational catalogue and buy shiny, bright new toys and prescriptive resources that unintentionally limit children's creativity.

> If our ultimate goal is to ensure that children grow up as engaged, self-confident, responsible, and resilient individuals who feel they have some control over their destinies and are alive to the consequences of their actions, childhood needs to include frequent, unregulated, self-directed contact with people and places beyond the immediate spheres of family and school, and the chance to learn from their mistakes. (Gill, 2008)

Overcoming obstacles

After the end of the first session, Laura and Michiko recognised that Adam and Levi had had a lot of fun tipping and piling materials onto the floor. They decided to introduce different tools in the second session as a way of encouraging the boys to focus their attention in a way that was more constructive. As the theme for Session Two was wood and metal, the idea of introducing tools fitted in nicely.

Sure enough, the boys were drawn to certain real tools as they began to investigate a corner where different metal and wooden parts were laid out. This interest was recognised by Laura, Michiko and the teacher and, rather than preventing Adam and Levi from exploring their interests further, the three adults sat by the two boys and supported them as they pursued their interest over the four weeks. The Midas Touch space became an 'enabling environment' where a mutual level of trust was agreed between adults and children. Materials were organised throughout different parts of the project space to encourage different types of activity for different needs and interests.

Outcomes

After the Midas Touch project had finished, we returned to the school a few months later to catch up with Adam, Levi and the teacher. We brought our book of photos and learning journeys and spent some time talking about our experiences with the hammer, the real tools, the charcoal and the scary gunpowder!

The teacher discussed her perceptions of the project and also showed photographs which demonstrated ways she had tried to extend the approach back in school. For Levi and Adam it was a chance to revisit the experience by looking at photos and talking about what we had done.

Adam, on working with wood and real tools:

> I was making ... church, drawing on it and then putting it on and banging it and then it goes everywhere. That's what I did with the charcoal. Levi did the same as me. He let me have the hammer, didn't he? And we swapped. The teacher took pictures. When I banged it [the charcoal] it went everywhere ... gunpowder. And I cleaned up.

On what was important to him:

> The hammer.

The teacher, on noticing outcomes:

> Levi's dad is absolutely beaming and he's just asked me at the door [after the reunion with the two boys], 'How did it go? Did he enjoy himself?' His dad came on numerous occasions and said what a difference it's made to him, they've seen the difference at home. He seems much more confident.

On the future:

> The nursery teacher and I both know the principles of early education and we agree with them 100 per cent. But putting them into a school setting when you've got your constraints, we find it difficult. So for us to actually come in [to the Midas Touch] and operate in that system, it was lovely. So we've decided we are going to definitely try and, within the boundaries, adopt those principles ... your way.

Summary

This chapter has addressed the complexities of trying to approach creativity. Our views about creativity are often influenced by our personal experiences and attitudes towards creative practice. It is important in order to meet the EYFS prime area of expressive arts and design to develop a theoretical understanding of creativity when we plan activities to promote creativity in early years education and care. As has been demonstrated with the other prime areas of development identified in the EYFS, creativity can be a solitary activity, yet a social activity at one and the same time. It is argued that when creativity is seen as a social activity with play as a tool then children are able to produce outcomes that are beyond adults' expectations.

Key points to remember

- 'Being creative' in early years education and care is a rich and extensive concept and it requires the encouragement and challenge of children's experiences of creativity.

- Early years settings should create opportunities for children to be able to explore different materials and ideas, and to be able to engage in self-expression so that they have the best possible chance to embark upon a creative development journey.

- Creativity is a social activity and as such it is a shared, constructed and collaborative experience.

Points for discussion

- What are your personal experiences and perceptions of, and attitudes towards, creativity? Considering the example of Cutler's work, can you remember whether you were given opportunities to explore creativity in a shared, constructed and collaborative way?

- Within the statutory framework for the Early Years Foundation Stage, creativity is not explicitly referred to as one of the specific areas in which providers must support children. Why do you think this is?

- How do staff and parents in your setting accept the importance of 'mess'? What sources of 'mess' or 'scrap' are used in your setting and what role do you think they have in promoting creative learning?

Reflective tasks

- One of the conflicts that early years practitioners report is that an overemphasis on the creative nature of learning conflicts with the requirements to raise standards. But are they to be mutually exclusive? Does your setting perceive a conflict between a creative curriculum and a standards-raising agenda? And what reasons are given, if any, for this conflict?

- How are recycled materials used in your setting for creative learning purposes? Can you identify how you might use those resources to better inform your practice? How would you go about documenting the learning that arises from this type of work?

- The open-ended approach to learning demonstrated by the Midas Touch Project has several risks associated with it. How does your setting respond to risk? Is it one where more time is spent on creating new learning opportunities or on cutting costs? Does your management team spend more time during meetings generating new ideas or discussing performance metrics? What might constitute a risk-tolerant or risk-averse culture in your setting?

Further reading

Abbott L. and Nutbrown, C. (2001) *Experiencing Reggio Emilia: Implications for Pre-school Provision.* Buckingham: Open University Press.

Bruce, T. (2004) *Cultivating Creativity in Babies, Toddlers and Young Children*. London: Hodder & Stoughton.

Sefton-Green, J. (2008) *Creative Learning.* London: Creative Partnerships.

Useful websites

Creative Partnerships, national creative learning programme:
www.creative-partnerships.com
Sightlines, the national agency for Reggio Emilia schools:
www.sightlines-initiative.com

To gain **free access** to selected SAGE journal articles related to key topics in this chapter visit:
www.sagepub.co.uk/Palaiologou2e

References

Chapter 1   Historical Developments in Policy for Early Years Education and Care

Baldock, P., Fitzgerald, D. and Kay, J. (eds) (2013) *Understanding Early Years Policy*, 3rd edn. London: Sage.

Board of Education (1905) Reports on Children under 5 Years of Age in Public Elementary Schools, by Women Inspectors. Cd 2726. London: HMSO.

Board of Education (1908) Report of the Consultative Committee upon the School Attendance of Children under 5. Cd 4259. London: HMSO.

CACE (1967) The Plowden Report: Children and their Primary Schools. London: HMSO.

Chitty, C. (2004) *Education Policy in Britain*. Basingstoke: Palgrave Macmillan.

Cleave, S., Jowett, S. and Bate, M. (1982) *And So to School: A Study of Continuity from Pre-school to Infant School*. Windsor: NFER–Nelson.

Cohen, L., Manian, L. and Morrison, K. (2004) *Research Methods in Education*, 5th edn. London: RoutledgeFalmer.

DES (Department of Education and Science) (1965) *Circular 10/65: The Organisation of Secondary Education*. London: Department of Education and Science.

DES (Department of Education and Science) (1972) *Education: A Framework for Expansion*. Cmnd 5174. London: HMSO.

Department for Education (2012) *Early Years Foundation Stage (EYFS) Pack – May 2008*. Available at: www.education.gov.uk/publicationDetail/Page 1/DCSF-00261-2008#downloadableparts (accessed September 2012).

DfEE (Department for Education and Employment) (1997) Tomorrow's Future: Building a Strategy for Children and Young People. London: Department for Education and Employment.

DfES (Department for Education and Skills) (2001) *Neighbourhood Nurseries Initiative (NNI): Prospectus*. London: Department for Education and Skills.

DfES (Department for Education and Skills) (2004) *Choice for Parents, The Best Start for Children: A Ten-Year Strategy for Childcare*. London: HMSO.

Galton, M., Simon, B. and Croll, S. (1980) *Inside the Primary School*. London: Routledge & Kegan Paul.

Gillard, D. (2011) *Education in England: A Brief History*. Available at: educationengland.org.uk/history (accessed January 2012).

Glass, N. (1999) 'Sure Start: the development of an early intervention programme for young children in the United Kingdom', *Children and Society,* 13: 257–64.

Hadow Report (1926) *The Education of the Adolescent*. Report of the Consultative Committee. London: HMSO.

Hadow Report (1931) *The Primary School*. Report of the Consultative Committee. London: HMSO.

Hadow Report (1933) *Infant and Nursery Schools*. Report of the Consultative Committee. London: HMSO.

Halsey, A. and Sylva, K. (1987) Introduction to the special 'Plowden Twenty Years On' edition. *Oxford Review of Education*, 13 (1): 3–11.

Holmes, E. (1911) *What Is and What Might Be*. London: Constable.

Isaacs, S. (1930) *Intellectual Growth in Young Children*. London: Routledge.

Isaacs, S. (1933) *Social Development in Young Children: A Story of Beginnings*. London: Routledge.

Lewis, J. and Lee, C. (2002) *Changing Family Structures and Social Policy: Child Care Services in Europe and Social Cohesion*. TSFEPS Project: National Report (UK): European Research Network.

Ministry of Health and the Board of Education (1929) *Circular from the Minister of Health and the President of the Board of Education to Maternity and Child Welfare Authorities and Local Education Authorities*. Circular 1054 (Ministry of Health). Circular 1405 (Board of Education).

Plowden, B. (1987) *'Plowden' Twenty Years On*. London: Carfax.

Pre-School Learning Alliance (2012) *A History of the Pre-School Learning Alliance*. Available at: www.pre-school.org.uk (accessed January 2012).

Taylor Report (1977) *A New Partnership for Our Schools*. Report of the Committee of Enquiry. London: HMSO.

Townshend, Mrs (1909) *The Case for School Nurseries: School Attendance of Children Below the Age of 5*. London: The Fabian Society.

Chapter 2   The Implementation of the Early Years Foundation Stage

Alexander, R., Rose, J. and Woodhead, C. (eds) (1992) *Curriculum Organization and Classroom Practice in Primary Schools: A Discussion Paper*. London: DES.

Allen, G. (2011) *Early Intervention: The Next Steps*. London: The Cabinet Office.

Anning, A. (2009) 'The co-construction of an early childhood curriculum', in A. Anning, J. Cullen and M. Fleer (eds), *Early Childhood Education: Society and Culture*. London: Sage. pp. 67–79.

Anning, A. and Edwards, A. (eds) (2006) *Promoting Children's Learning from Birth to Five: Developing the New Early Years Professional*. Milton Keynes: Open University Press.

Athey, C. (1990) *Extending Thought in Young Children*. London: Paul Chapman Publishing.

Bertman, P. and Pascal, C. (2002) *Early Years Education: An International Perspective*. www.inca.org.uk (accessed September 2008).

David, T. (1993) 'Educating children under *five* in the U.K.', in T. David (ed.), *Educational Provision for Our Youngest Children: European Perspectives*. London: Paul Chapman Publishing.

DCSF (Department for Children, Schools and Families) (2007) *The Children's Plan: Building Brighter Futures*. London: HMSO.

DCSF (Department for Children, Schools and Families) (2008) *The Early Years Foundation Stage: Setting the Standards for Learning, Development and Care for Children from Birth to five*. Nottingham: DCSF Publications. (Comprises the *Statutory Framework, Practice Guidance*, Cards and other resources.)

Devereux, J. and Miller, L. (eds) (2003) *Working with Children in the Early Years*. London: David Fulton.

DfE (Department for Education) (2011) *The Munro Review of Child Protection: Final Report – A Child-Centred System*. London: The Stationery Office.

DfE (Department for Education) (2012) *Statutory Framework for the Early Years Foundation Stage: Setting the Standards for Learning, Development and Care for Children from Birth to Five*. Runcorn: DfE.

DfES (Department for Education and Skills) (2003) *Every Child Matters*. Nottingham: DfES Publications.

DfES (Department for Education and Skills) (2004a) *Every Child Matters: Change for Children*. Nottingham: DfES Publications.

DfES (Department for Education and Skills) (2004b) *Choice for Parents, The Best Start for Children: A Ten Year Strategy for Childcare*. London: HMSO.

DfES (Department for Education and Skills) (2007) *Practice Guidance for the Early Years Foundation Stage: Setting the Standards for Learning, Development, and Care for Children from Birth to Five*. Nottingham: DfES Publications.

Field, F. (2010) *The Foundation Years: Preventing Poor Children Becoming Poor Adults*. The Report of the Independent Review on Poverty and Life Chances. London: Cabinet Office.

Goldschmied, E. and Jackson, S. (1994) *People Under 3: Young Children in Day Care*. London: Routledge.

Hennessy, E., Martin, S., Moss, P. and Melhuish, P. (1992) *Children and Day Care: Lessons from Research*. London: Paul Chapman Publishing.

Masmot Review (2010) *Fair Society, Healthy Lives*. London: The Masmot Review.

Mortimore, P., Sammons, P., Stoll, L., Lewis, D. and Ecob, R. (eds) (1998) *School Matters*. London: Open Books.

Moss, P. (2000) 'Foreign services', *Nursery World*, 3733: 10–13.

Moss, P. (2001) 'Britain in Europe: finger or heart?', in G. Pugh (ed.), *Contemporary Issues in the Early Years*, 3rd edn. London: Paul Chapman Publishing. pp. 25–39.

Moss, P. and Pence, A. (eds) (1994) *Valuing Quality in Early Childhood Services: New Approaches to Defining Quality*. London: Paul Chapman Publishing.

Moyles, J.R. (1989) *Just Playing? The Role and Status of Play in Early Childhood Education*. Milton Keynes: Open University Press.

Moyles, J. (ed.) (2007) *Early Years Foundations: Meeting the Challenge*. Maidenhead: Open University Press.

Moyles, J., Adams, S. and Musgrove, A. (2001) *The Study of Pedagogical Effectiveness: A Confidential Report to the DfES*. Chelmsford: Anglia Polytechnic University.

Nutbrown, C. (1999) *Threads of Thinking*. London: Paul Chapman Publishing.

Nutbrown, C.(2012) *Foundation for Quality: The Independent Review of Early Education and Childcare Qualifications*. London: DfE

Ofsted (2008) Early Years Foundation Stage (EYFS). www.ofsted.gov.uk (accessed September 2008).

Ofsted (2011) *The Impact of the Early Years Foundation Stage*. London: Ofsted.

Palaiologou, I. (2012) *Child Observation for the Early Years*, 2nd edn. London: Sage.

Penn, H. (1997) *Comparing Nurseries: Staff and Children in Italy, Spain and the UK*. London: Paul Chapman Publishing.

Penn, H. (2000) *Early Childhood Services: Theory, Policy and Practice*. Oxford: Oxford University Press.

Penn, H. (2008) *Understanding Early Childhood: Issues and Controversies*. Maidenhead: Open University Press.

Pugh, G. (ed.) (1996) *Contemporary Issues in the Early Years: Working Collaboratively for Children*, 2nd edn. London: Paul Chapman Publishing.

QCA/DfEE (Qualifications and Curriculum Authority/Department for Education and Employment) (2000) *Curriculum Guidance for the Foundation Stage*. London: QCA.

Smith, C. and Vernon, J. (1994) *Day Nurseries at the Crossroads: Meeting the Childcare Challenges*. London: National Children's Bureau.

Sure Start Unit (2002) *Birth to three Matters: A Framework to Support Children in Their Earliest Years*. Nottingham: DfES Publications.

Sylva, K., Melhuish, E., Sammons, P. and Siraj-Blatchford, I. (2001) *The Effective Provision of Pre-School Education (EPPE) Project*. The EPPE Symposium at the British Educational Research Association Annual Conference, University of Leeds, September.

Tickell, C. (2011) *The Early Years: Foundations for Life, Health and Learning*. An Independent Report on the Early Years Foundation Stage to the Majesty's Government. www.education.gov.uk/tickellreview (accessed July 2012).

United Nations (1989) *The Convention on the Rights of the Child*. Geneva: Defence International and the United Nations Children's Fund.

Whitebread, D. and Bingham, S. (2011) 'School readiness: a critical review of perspectives and evidence'. TACTYC Occasional Paper No. 2. TACTYC.

Chapter 3   The National Picture

ACCAC (2000a) *Desirable Outcomes for Children's Learning Before Compulsory School Age*. Cardiff: ACCAC.

ACCAC (2000b) *National Curriculum for Wales: Key Stage 1*. Cardiff: ACCAC.

CCEA (Council for Examinations and Assessment in Northern Ireland) (2007) *The Northern Ireland Curriculum: Primary*. Belfast: CCEA.

CCEA, DENI, DHSSPS (2006) *Curricular Guidance for Pre-school Education*. Belfast: CCEA.

Centre for Early Childhood Development and Education (2006) *Síolta: The National Quality Framework for Early Childhood Education*. Dublin: CECDE.

Dahlberg, G., Moss, P. and Pence, A. (2007) *Beyond Quality in Early Childhood Education and Care: Languages of Evaluation*, 2nd edn. London: Routledge.

DENI (Department for Education in Northern Ireland) and DHSSPS (Department of Health, Social Services and Public Safety) (1998) *Investing in Early Learning: Pre-School Education in Northern Ireland*. Belfast: The Stationery Office.

DENI (Department for Education in Northern Ireland) (2010) *The Early Years (0–6) Strategy*. Belfast: DENI. www.deni.gov.uk/english__early_years_strategy_.pdf. (accessed 30 April 2012).

DENI (Department for Education in Northern Ireland) (2012) *A Review of the Pre-school Admissions Arrangements*. Belfast: DENI. www.deni.gov.uk/review_of_pre-school_admissions_arrangements_-_with_actions_included.pdf (accessed 28 April 2012).

DES (Department of Education and Skills) (2010). *A Workforce Development Plan for the Early Childhood Care and Education Sector in Ireland*. Dublin: DES.

Donaldson, G. (2010) *Teaching Scotland's Future*. Edinburgh: Scottish Government.

Early, D., Maxwell, K., Burchinal, M., Alva, S., Bender, R., Bryant, D. et al. (2007) 'Teachers' education, classroom quality, and young children's academic skills: Results from seven studies of preschool programs', *Child Development*, 78 (2): 558-80.

Education Scotland (n.d.a) 'About Education Scotland: Remit', retrieved 25 April 2012 from www.educationscotland.gov.uk/about/remit/index.asp.

Education Scotland (n.d.b) 'What is the Curriculum for Excellence? Process of change', retrieved 25 April 2012, from www.educationscotland.gov.uk/thecurriculum/whatiscurriculumforexcellence/howwasthecurriculumdeveloped/processofchange/timeline.asp.

ETI (Education and Training Inspectorate) (2010a) *The Chief Inspector's Report 2008–2010*. Bangor: ETI. www.etini.gov.uk/index/support-material/support-material-general-documents-non-phase-related/the-chief-inspectors-report/chief-inspectors-report-2008-2010.pdf (accessed 30 April 2012).

ETI (2010b) *An Evaluation of the SureStart Programme for 2 Year Olds*. Bangor: ETI. www.etini.gov.uk/index/surveys-evaluations/surveys-evaluations-pre-school-centre-and-nursery-school/surveys-evaluations-pre-school-centre-and-nursery-school-2010/an-evaluation-of-the-surestart-programme-for-2-year-olds.pdf (accessed 27 April 2012).

Harland, J., Kinder, K., Ashworth, M., Montgomery, A., Moor, H. and Wilkin, A. (1999) *Real Curriculum: At the End of Key Stage 2. Report 1 from the Northern Ireland Curriculum Cohort Study*. Slough: NFER.

HM Inspectorate of Education (2002) *Count Us In: Achieving Inclusion in Scottish Schools*. Edinburgh: Her Majesty's Inspectorate of Education.

HM Inspectorate of Education (2005a) *A Climate for Learning. A Review of the Implementation of the 'Better Behaviour – Better Learning' Report*. Edinburgh: Her Majesty's Inspectorate of Education.

HM Inspectorate of Education (2005b) *Improving Achievement in Gaelic*. Edinburgh: Her Majesty's Inspectorate of Education.

HM Inspectorate of Education (2009) 'About us', retrieved 25 November 2009 from www.hmie.gov.uk/AboutUs/AboutHMIE/WhoWeAre.

HM Inspectorate of Education (2011) *Gaelic Education: Building on the Successes, Addressing the Barrier*. Edinburgh: Her Majesty's Inspectorate of Education.

HM Inspectors of Schools (1999) *Improving Science Education 5–14: A Report*. Edinburgh: Scottish Executive Education Department.

Humes, W.M. and Bryce, T.G. K. (2003) 'The distinctiveness of Scottish education', in T.G.K. Bryce and W.M. Humes (eds), *Scottish Education: Post Devolution*. Edinburgh: Edinburgh University Press.

Hunter, T. (2009) 'From policy to practice: the reality of play in Foundation Stage classes in Northern Ireland', unpublished MA thesis. Belfast: Stranmillis University College.

Jenkins, E.W. (2000) 'The impact of the national curriculum on secondary school science teaching in England and Wales', *International Journal of Science Education*, 22 (3): 325–36.

Learning and Teaching Scotland (2010) *Pre-Birth to Three: Positive Outcomes for Scotland's Children and Families*. Edinburgh: Scottish Government.

Macnab, D.S. (2003) 'Implementing change in mathematics education', *Journal of Curriculum Studies*, 35: 197–215.

Maynard, T. and Waters, J. (2007) 'Learning in the outdoor environment: a missed opportunity?', *Early Years*, 27 (3): 255–65.

Moss, P. and Pence, A. (eds) (1994) *Valuing Quality in Early Childhood Services: New Approaches to Defining Quality*. London: Paul Champan Publishing.

NAfW (2001) *The Learning Country: A Paving Document*. Cardiff: NAfW.

NAfW (2001a) *Laying the Foundations: Early Years Provision for Three Year Olds*. Cardiff: NAfW.

NAfW (2003) *The Learning Country: The Foundation Phase: 3–7 Years*. Cardiff: NAfW.

National Council for Curriculum and Assessment (2009) *Aistear: The Early Childhood Curriculum Framework*. Dublin: NCCA.

NIAO (Northern Ireland Audit Office) (2009) *The Pre-School Education Expansion Programme*. Belfast: HMSO.

OECD (2010) *PISA 2009 Results: What Students Know and Can Do*. www.oecd.org/edu/pisa/2009 (accessed March 2012).

OFMDFM (Office for the Minister and Deputy First Minister) (2006) *Our Children and Young People – Our Pledge*. Belfast: OFMDFM.

Pianta, R., Barnett, S., Burchinal, M. and Thornburg, K. (2009) 'The effects of preschool education: What we know, how public policy is or is not aligned with the evidence base, and what we need to know', *Psychological Science in the Public Interest*, 10 (2): 49–88.

Scottish Executive (2000) Standards in Scotland's Schools Act. Edinburgh: HMSO.

Scottish Executive (2007) *Building the Curriculum 2: Active Learning in the Early Years*. Edinburgh: Scottish Executive.

Scottish Executive (2010) *Building the Curriculum 5: A Framework for Assessment*, retrieved from www.ltscotland.org.uk/curriculumforexcellence/buildingthecurriculum/guidance/btc5/ index.asp (accessed July 2012).

Scottish Government (2008a) *Building the Curriculum 3: A Framework for Learning and Teaching*. Edinburgh: Scottish Government.

Scottish Government (2008b) *Early Years Framework*. Edinburgh: Scottish Government.

Scottish Government (2011) *Continuing to Build Excellence in Teaching: The Scottish Government's Response to 'Teaching Scotland's Future'*. Edinburgh: Scottish Government.

SOED (Scottish Office Education Department) (1994) 5–14 Practical Guide. Edinburgh: SOED.

Sheehy, N., Trew, K., Rafferty, H., McShane, E., Quiery, N. and Curran, S. (2000) *The Greater Shankill Early Years Project: Evaluation Report*. Belfast: The Greater Shankill Project and CCEA.

Siraj-Blatchford, I., Sylva, K., Laugharne, J., Milton, E. and Charles, F. (2005) *Monitoring and Evaluation of the Effective Implementation of the Foundation Phase (MEEIFP) Project Across Wales*. Final Report of Year 1 Pilot – Roll Out Age 3–5 Years, November 2005. An Evaluation Funded by the Welsh Assembly Government 2004–2005. Cardiff: WAG.

United Nations (1989) *The Convention on the Rights of the Child*. Geneva: Defence International and the United Nations Children's Fund.

WAG (2006) *The Learning Country 2: Delivering the Promise*. Cardiff: Welsh Assembly Government.

WAG (2008a) *Foundation Phase Framework for Children's Learning for 3–7 Year Olds in Wales*. Cardiff: Welsh Assembly Government.

WAG (2008b) *Learning and Teaching Pedagogy: Foundation Phase Guidance Material*. Cardiff: Welsh Assembly Government.

WAG (2011a) Foundation Phase child development profile. wales.gov.uk/docs/dcells/publications/ 110517foundassessmenten.pdf (accessed March 2012).

WAG (2011b) End of Foundation Phase Assessment exemplification of outcomes. wales.gov.uk/ docs/dcells/publications/110323endofphaseen.pdf (accessed March 2012).

WalesOnline (2012) 'Welsh Government launches new five year Welsh language strategy'. www. walesonline.co.uk/news/wales-news/2012/03/01/welsh-government-launches-new-five-year-welsh-language-strategy-91466-30439565 (accessed March 2012).

Walsh, G. and McMillan, D. (2010) 'War and peace in Northern Ireland: childhood in transition', in M. Clark and S. Tucker (eds), *Early Childhoods in a Changing World*. Stoke-on-Trent: Trentham.

Walsh, G., McGuinness, C., Sproule, L. and Trew, K. (2010) 'Implementing a play-based and developmentally appropriate curriculum in NI primary schools: what lessons have we learned?' *Early Years: An International Journal of Research and Development*, 30 (1) : 53–66.

Walsh, G., Sproule, L., McGuinness, C. and Trew, K. (2011) 'Playful structure: a novel image of Early Years pedagogy for primary school classrooms', *Early Years: An International Journal of Research and Development*, 31 (2): 107–19.

Walsh, G., Sproule, L., McGuinness, C., Trew, K., Rafferty, H. and Sheehy, N. (2006) 'An appropriate curriculum for the 4–5 year old child in Northern Ireland: comparing play-based and formal approaches', *Early Years: An International Journal of Research and Development*, 26 (2): 201–21.

WG (2010) 'Minister responds to PISA results'. wales.gov.uk/newsroom/educationandskills/2010/101207pisa/?lang=en (accessed March 2012).

WG (2012a) Mid-year estimates of the population 2010. wales.gov.uk/topics/statistics/headlines/population2011/110630/?lang=en (accessed March 2012).

WG (2012b) Annual population survey. www.statswales.wales.gov.uk/TableViewer/tableView.aspx?ReportId=5502 (accessed March 2012).

WG (2012c) 2001 Census of Population: first results on Welsh language. wales.gov.uk/topics/statistics/headlines/pop-2007/hdw200302133/?lang=en (accessed March 2012).

WISERD (2012) *Evaluating the Foundation Phase*. www.wiserd.ac.uk/research/evaluating-the-foundation-phase (accessed March 2012).

Chapter 4   Pedagogy of Early Years

Alexander, R. (2000) *Culture and Pedagogy. International Comparisons in Primary Education*. Malden, MA: Blackwell.

Bandura, A. (1977) *Social Learning. Theory*. New York: General Learning Press.

Bronfenbrenner, U. (1979) *The Ecology of Human Development*. Cambridge, MA: Harvard University Press.

Bruner, J.S. (2006) *In Search of Pedagogy Volume II: The Selected Works of Jerome S. Bruner*. Oxford: Routledge.

Bruner, J.S. and Haste, H. (1987) 'Introduction', in J.S. Bruner and H. Haste (eds), *Making Sense: The Child's Construction of the World*. London: Methuen.

Brownlee, J. (2004) 'Teacher education students' epistemological beliefs: Developing a relational model of teaching', *Research in Education*, 72: 1–17.

Cannella, G.S. (2005) 'Reconceptualizing the field (of early care and education): if 'Western' child development is a problem, then what do we do?', in N. Yelland (ed.), *Critical Issues in Early Childhood Education*. Maidenhead: Open University Press.

Carr, M. (1995) 'Dispositions as an outcome for early childhood curriculum', paper presented at the 5th European Conference on Quality of Early Childhood Education, La Sorbonne, Paris (7–9 September), available at: http://eric.ed.gov/ERICWebPortal/recordDetail?accno=ED407055 (accessed 3 May 2012).

Dahlberg, G. and Moss, P. (2005) *Ethics and Politics in Early Childhood Education*. London: RoutledgeFalmer.

Dahlberg, G., Moss, P. and Pence, A. (2007) *Beyond Quality in Early Childhood Education and Care: Languages of Evaluation*. London: Routledge.

DfE (2012) *Statutory Framework for the Early Years Foundation Stage: Setting the Standards for Learning, Development and Care for Children from Birth to Five*. Runcorn: Dfe, available at: www.education.gov.uk/publications/standard/AllPublications/Page1/DFE-00023-2012 (accessed 1 May 2012).

DfES (2004) *Every Child Matters: Change for Children in Schools*. Nottingham: DfES, available at: www.education.gov.uk/publications/eOrderingDownload/DFES-1089-200MIG748.pdf (accessed 1 May 2012).

Fox, N.A and Shonkoff, J.P. (2011) 'Violence and development: how persistent fear and anxiety can affect young children's learning and behaviour and health', in Bernard van Leer Foundation (ed.), *Hidden Violence: Protecting Young Children at Home*. Early Childhood Matters No. 116. The Hague: Bernard van Leer Foundation.

Hyun, E. (1998) *Making Sense of Developmentally and Culturally Appropriate Practice (DCAP) in Early Childhood Education*. New York: Peter Lang.

Katz, L. (1993) *Dispositions: Definitions and Implications for Early Childhood Practice*. Champaign, II: Clearing House of Early Childhood and Parenting (CEEP), available at: http://ceep.crc.uiuc.edu/eecearchive/books/disposit/part1.html (accessed 2 May 2012).

Malaguzzi, L. (1993) 'History, ideas and basic philosophy', in C. Edwards, L.Gandini and G. Forman (eds), *The Hundred Languages of Children*. Norwood, NJ: Ablex.

Moyles, J. (2010) *The Excellence of Play*, 3rd edn. Maidenhead: Open University Press.

Moyles, J., Adams, S. and Musgrove, A. (2002) *SPEEL: Study of Pedagogical Effectiveness in Early Learning*. London: DfES. Report No. 363.

Moss, P. (2008) 'Meeting across the paradigmatic divide', in S. Farquhar and P. Fitzsimons (eds), *Philosophy of Early Childhood Education: Transforming Narratives*. Malden, MA: Blackwell.

NAEYC (1996) *Developmentally Appropriate Practice in Early Childhood Programs Serving Children from Birth through Age 8*. Position Statement, available at: www.naeyc.org/files/naeyc/file/positions/position%20statement%20Web.pdf (accessed 2 May 2012).

Papatheodorou, T. (2006) *Seeing the Wider Picture: Reflections on the Reggio Emilia Approach*, available at: www.tactyc.org.uk/pdfs/Reflection_Papatheodorou.pdf (accessed 2 May 2012).

Papatheodorou, T. (2009) 'Exploring relational pedagogy', in T. Papatheodorou and J. Moyles (eds), *Learning Together in the Early Years: Exploring Relational Pedagogy*. London: Routledge.

Papatheodorou, T. (2010) 'Being, belonging and becoming: some worldviews of early childhood in contemporary curricula', *Forum on Public Policy Online*, Vol. 2 (September), available at: http://forumonpublicpolicy.com/spring2010.vol2010/spring2010archive/papatheodorou.pdf (accessed 4 May 2012).

Papatheodorou, T. (2012) 'Introduction: early childhood policies and practices', in T. Papatheodorou (ed.), *Debates on Early Childhood Policies and Practices: Global Snapshots of Pedagogical Thinking and Encounters*. London: Routledge.

Papatheodorou, T. and Loader, P. (2009) 'The Reggio Emilia Artists' Project: Changing Culture-Changing Pedagogy', paper presented at the 19th EECERA conference, Strasbourg France.

Piaget, J. (1952) *The Origins of Intelligence in Children* (trans. M. Cook). New York: International Universities Press.

Pre-school Learning Alliance (2011) 'Alliance voices concerns about meaning of "school readiness" as Government unveils its early years reforms', available at: www.pre-school.org.uk/media/press-releases/245/alliance-voices-concerns-about-meaning-of-school-readiness-as-government-unveils-its-early-years-reforms (accessed 5 May 2012).

Rinaldi, C. (2001) 'The pedagogy of listening: the listening perspective from Reggio Emilia', *Innovations in Early Education: The International Reggio Exchange*, Vol. 8, No.4, available at: http://academic.udayton.edu/JamesBiddle/Pedagogy%20of%20Listening.pdf (accessed 2 May 2012).

Rogoff, B., Mosier, C., Mistry, J. and Goncu, A. (1993) 'Toddlers' guided participation with their caregivers in cultural activity', in E.A. Forman, N. Mimick and C. Addison Stone (eds), *Contexts for Learning: Socio-Cultural Dynamics in Children's Development*. New York: Oxford University Press.

SCDC (Scientific Council on the Developing Child) (2010) *Early Experiences Can Alter Gene Expression and Affect Long-Term Development*. Working paper No. 10, available at: http://developingchild.harvard.edu/index.php/resources/reports_and_working_papers/working_papers/wp10 (accessed 2 May 2012).

Schön, D. (1983) *The Reflective Practitioner: How Professionals Think in Action*. London: Temple Smith.

Schweinhart, L.J. (1994) 'Lasting benefits of preschool programs', *ERIC Digest* (ERIC Clearinghouse on Elementary and Early Childhood Education, ERIC Identifier: ED 365478), available at: www.ericdigests.org/1994/lasting.htm (accessed 2 May 2012).

Shonkoff, J.P. and Phillips, D. (eds) (2000) *From Neurons to Neighborhoods: The Science of Early Child Development*. Washington, DC: National Academy Press.

Siraj-Blatchford, I., Sylva, K., Muttock, S., Gilden, R. and Bell, D. (2002) *Researching Effective Pedagogy in the Early Years*, Research Report 356. Norwich: DfES.

Sylva, K., Melhuish, E.C., Sammons, P., Siraj-Blatchford, I. and Taggart, B. (2004) *The Effective Provision of Pre-school Education (EPPE) Project, Technical Paper 12*. London: DfES/Institute of Education, University of London.

Trevarthen, C. (2011) 'How is meaning made before words – and why does it matter so much?' Lecture at Anglia Ruskin University, 28 March.

UNCRC (1989) *United Nations Convention on the Rights of the Child*, available at: www2.ohchr.org/english/law/crc.htm (accessed 2 May 2012).

UNCRC (2006) *Convention on the Rights of the Child, General Comment No. 7 [2005]*, Implementing Child Rights in Early Childhood, fortieth session, Geneva, 20 September, available at: www2.ohchr.org/english/bodies/crc/docs/AdvanceVersions/GeneralComment7Rev1.pdf (accessed 2 May 2012).

UNDP (2000) *The Millennium Development Goals*, available at: www.beta.undp.org/undp/en/home/mdgoverview.html (accessed 2 May 2012).

UNESCO (1990) *World Declaration on Education for All and Framework for Action to Meet Basic Learning Needs* (adopted by the World Conference on Education for All: Meeting Basic Learning Needs, Jomtien, Thailand, 5–9 March). Paris: UNESCO, available at: www.unesco.org/education/wef/en-conf/dakfram.shtm (accessed 2 May 2012).

UNESCO (2000) *World Education Forum: The Dakar Framework for Action, Education for All: Meeting Our Collective Commitments* (adopted by the World Education Forum 26–28 April). Paris: UNESCO, available at: www.unesco.org/education/wef/en-conf/dakfram.shtm (accessed 2 May 2012).

US Department of Health and Human Services (2010) *Head Start Impact Study, Final Report*. Washington, DC: US Department of Health and Human Services, Administration for Children and Families, available at: www.acf.hhs.gov/programs/opre/hs/impact_study/reports/impact_study/executive_summary_final.pdf (accessed 2 May 2012).

Vygotsky, L.S. (1978) *Mind in Society*. Cambridge, MA: Harvard University Press.

Vygotsky, L. (2002) *Language and Thought* (ed. and rev. A. Kozulin). Cambridge, MA: The MIT Press.

Watson, J.B. (1930) *Behaviorism,* rev. edn. Chicago, IL: University of Chicago Press.

Woodhead, M. (2006) 'Changing perspectives on early childhood: theory, research and policy'. Background paper prepared for the EEA Global Monitoring Report 2007, Strong Foundations: Early Childhood Care and Education. Paris: UNESCO, available at: http://unesdoc.unesco.org/images/0014/001474/147499e.pdf (accessed 2 May 2012).

Chapter 5   Play in the Early Years Foundation Stage

Avgitidou, S. (1997) 'Children's play: an investigation of children's co-construction of their world within early school settings', *Early Years: An International Journal of Research and Development*, 17 (2): 6–10.

BERA Early Years Special Interest Group (2003) *Early Years Research: Pedagogy, Curriculum and Adult Roles, Training and Professionalism.* Southwell: BERA.

Bruce, T. and Ockelford, A. (2010) 'Understanding symbolic development', in T. Bruce (ed.), *Early Childhood: A Guide for Students*, 2nd edn. London: Sage.

Bruner, J.S. (2006) *In Search of Pedagogy Volume II: The Selected Works of Jesome S. Bruner, 1979–2006.* Oxford: Routledge.

DCMS (Department for Culture, Media and Sport) (2004) *Getting Serious About Play – A Review of Children's Play*. London: DCMS.

DCSF (Department for Children, School and Families) (2008) *The Early Years Foundation Stage*. Nottingham: DCSF Publications.

DfE (Department for Education) (2012) *Statutory Framework for the Early Years Foundation Stage. Setting the Standards for Learning, Development and Care for Children from Birth to Five*. Runcorn: DfE, available at www.education.gov.uk/publications/standard/AllPublications/Page1/DFE-00023-2012 (accessed July 2012).

Dowdell, K., Graya, T. and Maloneb, K. (2011) 'Nature and its influence on children's outdoor play, *Australian Journal of Outdoor Education*, 15 (2): 24–35.

Gill, T. (2007) *No Fear: Growing Up in a Risk Averse Society*. London: Calouste Gulbenkian Foundation.

Knight, S. (2009) *Forest Schools and Outdoor Learning in the Early Years*. London: Sage.

Lindon, J. (2001) *Understanding Children's Play*. Cheltenham: Nelson Thornes.

Little, H., Wyver, S. and Gibson, F. (2011) 'The influence of play context and adult attitudes on young children's physical risk-taking during outdoor play', *European Early Childhood Education Research Journal*, 19 (1): 113–31.

Moyles, J. (2010) *Just Playing?* Milton Keynes: Open University Press.

Pound, L. (2005) *How Children Learn: From Montessori to Vygotsky*. London: Step Forward Publishing.

Sandseter, E. (2009) 'Affordances for risky play in preschool: the importance of features in the play environment', *Early Childhood Education Journal*, 36 (5): 439–46.

Santer, J. and Griffiths, G. with Goodall, D. (2007*) Free Play in Early Childhood: A Literature Review*. London: National Children's Bureau.

Siraj-Blatchford, I. (2009) 'Conceptualising progression in the pedagogy of play and sustained shared thinking in early childhood education: A Vygotskian perspective', *Educational and Child Psychology*, 26 (2): 77–89.

Smidt, S. (2010) *Playing to Learn: The Role of Play in the Early Years*. London: Routledge.

Stephen, C. (2010) 'Pedagogy: the silent partner in early years learning', *Early Years: Journal of International Research and Development*, 30 (1): 15–28.

Sylva, K., Melhuish, E., Sammons, P., Siraj-Blatchford, I. and Taggart, B. (2004) *The Effective Provision of Pre-school Education (EPPE) Project: Final Report: a Longitudinal Study (1997–2004)*. London: DfES.

Tickell, C. (2011) *The Early Years: Foundations for Life, Health and Learning. An Independent Report on the Early Years Foundation Stage to Her Majesty's Government*. www.education.gov.uk/tickellreview (accessed July 2012).

Vygotsky, L. (1978) *Mind in Society*. Cambridge, MA: Harvard University Press.

Walker, J.C. (2005) 'Self-determination as an Educational Aim', in W. Carr (ed.) *The Routledge Reader in Philosophy of Education*. Oxford: Routledge.

Waller, T., Sandseter, E., Wyver, S., Arlemalm-Hagser, E. and Maynard, T. (2010) 'The dynamics of early childhood spaces: opportunities for outdoor play?', *European Early Childhood Education Research Journal*, 18 (4): 437–43.

Wood, L. and Bennett, N. (1997) 'The rhetoric and reality of play: teachers' thinking and classroom practice', *Early Years: An International Journal of Research and Development*, 17(2): 22–7.

Chapter 6　Observations: Recording and Analysis in the Early Years Foundation Stage

Bick, E. (1964) 'Notes on infant observation in psychoanalytic training', *International Journal of Psychoanalysis*, 45: 558–66.

Brunton, P. and Thornton, L. (2010) *Science in the Early Years*. London: Sage.

Carr, M. (2001) *Assessment in Early Childhood Settings: Learning Stories*. London: Paul Chapman Publishing.

Carr, M. and Lee, W. (2012) *Learning Stories: Constructing Learner Identities in Early Education*. London: Sage.

Department for Education (DfE) (2012) *Statutory Framework for the Early Years Foundation Stage. Setting the standards for Learning: Development and case for children from Birth to Five*. Runcorn: DfE, available at www.education.gov.uk/publications/standard/AllPublications/Page1/DFE-00023-2012 (accessed 4 April 2012).

Dewey, J. (1897/1974) 'My pedagogic creed', in R.D. Archambault (ed.), *John Dewey on Education: Selected Writings*. Chicago and London: University of Chicago Press.

Dewey, J. (1933/1998) *How We Think*. Boston, MA: Houghton Mifflin.

Early Education/DfE (2012) *Development Matters in the Early Years Foundation Stage (EYFS)*. London: Early Education, available at www.education.gov.uk/childrenandyoungpeople/earlylearningandchildcare/delivery/education/a0068102/early-years-foundation-stage-eyfs (accessed 4 April 2012).

Elfer, P. (2005) 'Observation matters', in L. Abbott and A. Langston (eds), *Birth to Three Matters*. Maidenhead: Open University Press.

Fleer, M. and Richardson, C. (2009) 'Cultural-historical assessment: mapping the transformation of understanding', in A. Anning, J. Cullen and M. Fleer (eds), *Early Childhood Education,* 2nd edn. London: Sage.

Goldschmeid, E. and Jackson, S. (2004) *People Under Three: Young Children in Day Care*, 2nd edn. London: Routledge.

Goodson, I.F., Biesta, G.J.J., Tedder, M. and Adair, M. (2010) *Narrative Learning*. London: Routledge.

Isaacs, S. (1929) *The Nursery Years*. London: Routledge & Kegan Paul.

Isaacs, S. (1930) *Intellectual Growth in Young Children*. London: Routledge & Kegan Paul.

Isaacs, S. (1933) *Social Development in Young Children*. London: Routledge & Kegan Paul.

Miller, L., Rustin, M., Rustin, M. and Shuttleworth, J. (1989) *Closely Observed Infants*. London: Duckworth.

Montessori, M. (1912) *The Montessori Method* (trans. A. E. George). New York: Frederick A. Stokes Company, available at http://web.archive.org/web/20050207205651/www.moteaco.com/method/method.html (accessed 4 April 2012).

Podmore, V. and Luff, P. (2012) *Observation: Origins and Approaches in Early Childhood*. Maidenhead: Open University Press.

Rogoff, B. (1995) 'Observing sociocultural activity on three planes: participatory appropriation, guided participation and apprenticeship', in J.V. Wertsch, P. del Rio and A. Alvarez (eds), *Sociocultural Studies of Mind*. Cambridge: Cambridge University Press.

Rogoff, B. (2003) *The Cultural Nature of Human Development*. New York: Oxford University Press.

Whalley, M. and the Pen Green Centre Team (2007) *Involving Parents in their Children's Learning,* 2nd edn. London: Paul Chapman Publishing.

Chapter 7 Assessment in the Early Years Foundation Stage

Alexander, R. (2008) 'Dialogic teaching: discussing theoretical contexts and reviewing evidence from classroom practice', *Language and Education*, 22 (3): 222–240.

Bailey, A. and Drummond, V. (2006) 'Who is at risk and why? Teachers' reasons for concern and their understanding and assessment of early literacy', *Educational Assessment,* 11 (3–4): 149–78.

Black, P. and Wiliam, D. (1998) *Inside the Black Box: Raising Standards through Classroom Assessment.* London: King's College London School of Education.

Burner, J.S (1970) 'The growth and structure of skill', in K. Connolly (ed.), *Mechanisms of Motor Skill Development*. New York: Academic Press. pp. 62–94.

Carr, M.(1998) *Assessing Children's Learning in Early Childhood Settings: A Development Programme for Discussion and Reflection.* Wellington: New Zealand Council for Education Research.

Carr, M. (1999) *Learning and Teaching Stories: New Approaches to Assessment and Evaluation.* www.aare.edu.au/99pap/pod99298.htm (accessed December 2007).

Carr, M. (2001) *Assessment in Early Childhood Settings.* London: Paul Chapman Publishing.

Carr, M. and Lee, W. (2012) *Learning Stories.* London: Sage.

Davis, D., Evans, M., Jadad, A., Perrier, L., Rath, D. and Zwarenstain, M. (2003) 'The case for knowledge translation: shortening the journey from evidence to effect', *BMJ,* 327 (7405): 33–5.

DfE (Department for Education) (2011) Early Years Evidence Pack, available at www.education.gov.uk/publications/standard/Earlyyearsandchildcareworkforce/Page1/DFE-00274-2011 (accessed 19 July 2012).

DfE (Department for Education) (2012) *Statutory Framework for the Early Years Foundation Stage. Setting Standards for Learning, Development and Care for Children from Birth to Five.* London: DfE.

Draper, L. and Duffy, B. (2001) 'Working with parents ', in G. Pugh (ed.), *Contemporary Issues in Early Years: Working Collaboratively for Children,* 3rd edn. London: Paul Chapman Publishing.

Driscoll, V. and Rudge, C. (2005) 'Channels for listening to young children and parents', in A. Clark, A.T. Kjorholt and P. Moss (eds), *Beyond Listening.* Bristol: The Policy Press. pp. 91–110.

Drummond, M.J. (2003) *Assessing Children's Learning,* 2nd edn. London: David Fulton.

Early Education/DfE (2012*) Development Matters in the Early Years Foundation Stage (EYFS).* London: Early Education.

Elfer, P. (2005) 'Observation matters', in L. Abbott and A. Langston (eds), *Birth-to-Three Matters.* Maidenhead: Open University Press.

Every Child a Talker (2008) *Every Child a Talker: Guidances for Early Language Lead Practitioners.* Nottingham: DCSF. www.education.gov.uk/publications/standard/EarlyYearseducationandchildcare/Page6/DCSF-00854-2008 (accessed 16 July 2012).

Harrison, C. and Howard, S. (2009) *Inside the Primary Black Box. Assessment for learning in primary and early years classrooms.* The Black Box Assessment for Learning series. London: GL Assessment.

Leavers, F. (ed.) (2005) *Well-begin and Involvement in Care Settings: A Process-oriented Evaluation Instrument.* Brussels: Kind and Gezint/Research Centre for Experiential Education.

Looney, J.W. (2011), OECD Education working paper No. 58 Integrating Formative and Summative Assessment: Progress Toward a Seamless System available at: www.oecd.org/edu.

McClennan, D. and Katz, L. (1992) 'Young children's social development: a checklist adapted from assessing the social development of young children: a checklist of social attitudes', *Dimensions of Early Childhood*, pp. 9–10

Nutbrown, C. (2012) Nutbrown Review. Foundation for quality. The independent review of early education and child care qualifications. Final report. DFE. Crown Copyright. www.education. gov.uk/nutbrownreview (accessed 19 July 2012)

Palaiologou, I. (2012) *Child Observation for the Early Years*. London: Learning Matters.

Rinaldi, C. (2005) 'Documentation and assessment: what is the relationship?', in A. Clark, P. Moss and A.T. Kjorholt (eds), *Beyond Listening to Children: Children's Perspectives on Early Childhood Services*. Bristol: The Policy Press. pp. 17–28.

Sadler, D.R. (2008) 'Formative assessment and the design of instructional systems', republished in W. Harlen (ed.), *Student Assessment and Testing*. vol. 2, ch. 14: 3–28. London: Sage. (Originally published in *Instructional Science*, 1989, 18: 119–44.)

Siraj-Blatchford, I., Sylva, K.,Muttock, S., Gilden, R. and Bell, D.(2002) *Researching Effecting Pedagogy in the Early Years*. DfES Research Report 365. London: HMSO.

Tickell, C (2011) *The Early Years: Foundation for Life, Health and Learning. An Independent Report on the Early Years Foundation Stage to Her Majesty's Government*. www.education. gov.uk/Tickellreview (accessed 16 July 2012).

Wiliam, D. (2011*) Embedded Formative Assessment*. Bloomington, IN: Solution Tree Press.

Chapter 8   Using Learning Stories in the Early Years Foundation Stage

Anning, A. and Edwards, A. (2006). *Promoting Children's Learning from Birth to Five*, 2nd edn. Milton Keynes: Open University Press.

Anning, A., Cullen, J. and Fleer, M. (eds) (2004) *Early Childhood Education*. London: Sage.

Baczala, K. (2003) *Guidance on Gifted and Talented (Very Able) Children in Foundation Stage*. Medway: Medway Council.

Bennett, N., Wood, L. and Rogers, S. (1997) *Teaching and Learning Through Play*. Buckingham: Open University Press.

Broadhead, P. (2001) 'Investigating sociability and cooperation in four and five year olds in reception class settings', *International Journal of Early Years Education*, 9 (1): 23–35.

Bruner, J. (1960) *The Process of Education*. Cambridge, MA: Harvard University Press.

Bruner, J. (1983) *Child's Talk: Learning to Use Language*. New York: W. W. Norton & Company.

Carr, M. (2001) *Assessment in Early Childhood Settings: Learning Stories*. London: Paul Chapman Publishing.

CCEA (Council for the Curriculum, Examinations and Assessment), NES (NES Arnold) and BELB (Belfast Education and Library Board) (2002) *Enriched Curriculum: The Beginning*. Belfast: CCEA.

Clark, B. (1997) *Growing Up Gifted*. New York: Macmillan.

Clark, B. (2007) 'Understanding intelligence and the gifted brain'. Paper presented at the 17th Biennial Conference of the World Council for Gifted and Talented Children, University of Warwick.

Coates, D., Thompson, W. and Shimmin, A. (2008) 'Using learning journeys to develop a challenging curriculum for gifted children in nursery (kindergarten) settings', *Gifted and Talented International*, 23 (1): 94–101.

DfE (Department for Education) (2012) *Statutory Framework of the Early Years Foundation Stage: Setting the Standards for Learning, Development and Care for Children from Birth to Five*. Runcorn: DfE.

DfES (Department for Education and Skills) (2002) *Schools Achieving Success*. www.dfes. gov.uk/ achievingsuccess (accessed 4 February 2008).

DfES (Department for Education and Skills) (2006a) *GTEU Early Years Bulletin*, February 2006, Issue 1. www.learningwithsouthglos.org/GiftedandTalented/acrobat/misc/EYsGTBull206.pdf (accessed 5 November 2008).

DfES (Department for Education and Skills) (2006b) *Improving Outcomes for Children in the Foundation Stage in Maintained Schools*. Nottingham: DfES Publications.

Early Education/DfE (2012) *Development Matters in the Early Years Foundation Stage* (EYFS). London: Early Education.

Eyre, D. (1997) *Able Children in Ordinary Schools*. London: David Fulton.

Eyre, D. (2007) *What Really Works in Gifted and Talented Education*. www.brightonline.org.uk/what_really_works.pdf (accessed 7 November 2008).

Howard, J. (2002) 'Eliciting children's perceptions of play using the Activity Apperception Story Procedure', *Early Child Development and Care*, 172 (5): 489–502.

Howard, J., Jenvey, V. and Hill, C. (2006) 'Children's categorisation of play and learning based on social context', *Early Child Development and Care*, 176 (3&4): 379–93.

Leyden, S. (1998) *Supporting the Child of Exceptional Ability*. London: David Fulton.

Members of the British Educational Research Association Early Years Special Interest Group (2003) *Early Years Research: Pedagogy, Curriculum and Adult Roles, Training and Professionalism*. www.bera.ac.uk/pdfs/BERAEarlyYearsReview31May03.pdf (accessed 4 February 2008).

Moss, P. (2004) *Dedicated to Loris Malaguzzi, The Town of Reggio Emilia and Its Schools*. www.sightlines-initiative.com/fileadmin/users/files/ReFocus/library/articles/PDFs/townofrepmoss.pdf (accessed 4 February 2008).

Moyles, J. (1989) *Just Playing: The Role and Status of Play in Early Childhood Education*. Milton Keynes: Open University Press.

Moyles, J. (ed.) (2005) *The Excellence of Play*. Miadenhead: Open University Press.

Porter, L. (1999) *Gifted Young Children*. Buckingham: Open University Press.

QCA/DfEE (Qualifications and Curriculum Authority/Department for Education and Employment) (2000) *Curriculum Guidance for the Foundation Stage*. London: QCA.

Rich, D. (2002) 'Catching children's stories', *Early Education*, 36: 6.

Seifert, K.L. (2006) 'The cognitive development and the education of young children', in B. Spodek and O.N. Sarecho (ed.), *Handbook of Research on the Education of Young Children*. Hillsdale, NJ: Lawrence Erlbaum Associates.

Siraj-Blatchford, I. and Sylva, K. (2004) *The Effective Pedagogy in the Early Years Project: A Confidential Report to the DfES*. London: London University Institute of Education.

Smidt, S. (2006) *The Developing Child in the 21st Century*. London: Routledge.

Smutny, J.F. (2001) 'Teaching young gifted children in the regular classroom', *ERIC Digest* www.ericdigests.org/2001-2/gifted.html (accessed 7 November 2007).

Vygotsky, L.S. (1978) *Mind in Society: The Development of Higher Psychological Processes*. Cambridge, MA: Harvard University Press.

Walsh, G., Sproule, L., McGuinness, C., Trew, K., Rafferty, H. and Sheehy, N. (2006) 'An appropriate curriculum for 4–5-year-old children in Northern Ireland: comparing play-based and formal approaches', *Early Years*, 26 (2): 201–21.

Westcott, M. and Howard, J. (2007) 'Creating a playful environment: evaluating young children's perceptions of their daily classroom activities using the Activity Apperception Story Procedure', *The Psychology of Education Review*, 31 (1): 27–33.

Wiltz, N. and Klein, E. (2001) 'What do you care? Children's perceptions of high and low quality classrooms', *Early Childhood Research Quarterly*, 16 (2001): 2009–236.

Wood, E. and Attfield, J. (1996) *Play, Learning and the Early Years Curriculum*, 2nd edn. London: Sage.

Wood, E. and Bennett, N. (2000) 'Changing theories, changing practice: early childhood teachers' professional learning', *Teaching and Teacher Education*, 16 (5): 635–47.

Chapter 9   Effective Transitions into and out of the Early Years Foundation Stage

Ainsworth, M.D.S. (1969) 'Object relations, dependency, and attachment: a theoretical review of the infant–mother relationship', *Child Development*, 40: 969–1025.

Ainsworth, M.D.S. (1979) 'Attachment as related to mother–infant interaction', *Advances in the Study of Behaviour*, 9: 2–52.

Ainsworth, M.D.S. (1985) 'Attachments across the life span', *Bulletin of the New York Academy of Medicine*, 61: 792–812.

Ainsworth, M.D.S. (1989) 'Attachment beyond infancy', *American Psychologist*, 44: 709–16.

Ainsworth, M.D.S. and Bell, S.M. (1970) 'Attachment, exploration, and separation: iIllustrated by the behaviour of one-year-olds in a strange situation', *Child Development*, 41: 49–67.

Ainsworth, M.D.S. and Bowlby, J. (1991) 'An ethological approach to personality development', *American Psychologist*, 46: 333–41.

Ainsworth, M.D.S., Bell, S.M. and Stayton, D.J. (1971a) 'Individual differences in the strange situation behaviour of one-year-olds', in H.R. Schaffer (ed.), *The Origins of Human Social Relations*. New York: Academic Press. pp. 15–71.

Ainsworth, M.D.S., Bell, S.M., Blehar, M.C. and Main, M. (1971b) 'Physical contact: a study of infant responsiveness and its relation to maternal handling'. Paper presented at the biennial meeting of the Society for Research in Child Development, Minneapolis, MN.

Ainsworth, M.D.S., Blehar, M.C., Waters, E. and Wall, S. (1978) *Patterns of Attachment: A Study of the Strange Situation*. Hillsdale, NJ: Erlbaum Associates.

Beach, K.D., (1999) 'Consequential transitions: a sociocultural expedition beyond transfer in education', *Review of Research in Education*, 24: 101–39.

Booker, L. (2002) *Starting School: Young Children Learning Cultures*. Buckingham: Open University Press.

Bowlby, J. (1951) *Child Care and the Growth of Love*. Harmondsworth: Penguin.

Bowlby, J. (1960) 'Grief and mourning in infancy and early childhood', *The Psychoanalytic Study of the Child*, 15: 9–52.

Bowlby, J. (1969) *Attachment and Loss, Volume 2. Separation: Anxiety and Anger*. New York: Basic Books.

Bowlby, J. (1973) *Attachment and Loss, Volume 2. Separation: Anxiety and Anger*. (International Psycho-analytical Library No. 95). London: Hogarth Press.

Bowlby, J. (1980) *Attachment and Loss, Volume 3. Loss: Sadness and Depression*. (International Psycho-analytical Library No. 109). London: Hogarth Press.

Bowlby, J. (1986) 'Citation Classic: *Maternal Care and Mental Health*', www. garfield.library. upenn.edu/classics1986/A1986F063100001.pdf (accessed November 2008).

Bowlby, J. (1999) *Attachment and Loss, Volume I*, 2nd edn. New York. Basic Books.

Bowlby, J. (2005) *The Making and Breaking of Affectional Bonds*. London: Routledge Classics.

Bronfenbrenner, U. (1979) *The Ecology of Human Development*. Cambridge, MA: Harvard University Press.

Brooker, L. (2008) *Supporting Transitions in the Early Years*. Maidenhead: Open University Press.

Crafter, S. and Maunder, R. (2012) 'Understanding transitions using a sociocultural framework', *Educational and Child Psychology*, 29 (1): 10–18.

DfE (Department for Education) (2012) Statutory Framework for the Early Years Foundation Stage: Setting the Standards for Learning, Development and Care for Children from Birth to Five. Runcorn: DfE.

Erikson, E.H., (1975) *Life History and the Historical Moments*. London: WW Norton.

Evangelou, M., Taggart, B., Sylva, K., Melhuish, E., Sammons, P. and Siraj-Blatchford, I. (2008) 'What makes a successful transition from primary to secondary school?', Secondary Education 3–14 Project (EPPSE 3–14). Department for Children Schools and Families Research Report No. DCSF-RR 019. London: DCSF.

High, P.H., (2008) 'School readiness', *Pediatrics*, 123(e): 1008–15.

Gorgorio, N., Planas, N. and Vilella, X. (2002) 'Immigrant children learning mathematics in mainstream schools', in G. de Abreu, A. Bishop and N.C. Preseh (ed.), *Transitions between Contexts of Mathematical Practice*. Dordrecht: Kluwer Academic Press. pp. 23–52

James, W. (1980) *The Principles of Psychology: Volume 1*. Mineola, NY: Dover Publications.

Piaget, J.J. (1976) *The Grasp of Consciousness: Action and Concept in the Young Child*. London: Routledge & Kegan Paul.

Pianta, R.C. and Walsh, D.J. (1996) *High Risk Children in Schools: Constructing Sustaining Relationships*. New York: Routledge.

Pianta, R.C., Cox, M.J., Taylor, L. and Early, D. (1999) 'Kindergarten teacher's practices related to transition to schools', *Elementary School Journal*, 100: 71–89.

Sylva, K., Melhuish, E., Sammons, P., Siraj-Blatchford, I., Taggart, B. and Elliot, K. (2003) *The Effective Provision of Pre-school Education (EPPE) Project: Findings from the Pre-school Period: Summary of Findings*. London: Institute of Education/Sure Start.

Vondra, J.I. and Barnett, D. (1999) 'Atypical attachment in infancy and early childhood among children at developmental risk', *Monographs of the Society for Research in Child Development*, 64 (Series No. 258).

Vygotsky, L. (1978) *Mind in Society: The Development of Higher Psychological Process*. Cambridge, MA: Harvard University Press.

Winnicot, D.W. (1986) *Holding and Interpretation: Fragment of an Analysis*. New York: Hogarth Press.

Winnicot, D.W. (1987) *The Child, the Family, and the Outside World*. New York: Addison-Wesley.

Winnicot, D.W. (1995) *Maturational Processes and the Facilitating Environment: Studies in the Theory of Emotional Development*. New York: Stylus.

Winnicot, D.W. (2005) *Playing and Reality*. London: Routledge.

Zittoun, T. (2006) *Transitions: Development through Symbolic Recourse*s. Greenwich, CT: Information Age Publishing.

Chapter 10   Meeting EYFS Outcomes Outside of the Early Years Setting

CWDC (Children's Workforce and Development Council) (2006) *Early Years Professional National Standards*. Available at www.cwdcouncil.org.uk resources/ handbooks (accessed 2 June 2009).

DCSF (Department for Children, Schools and Families) (2007) *The Children's Plan: Building Brighter Futures*. London: HMSO.

DCSF (Department for Children, Schools and Families) (2008) *The Early Years Foundation Stage: Setting the Standards for Learning, Development and Care for Children from Birth to Five*. Nottingham: DCSF Publications. (Comprises the *Statutory Framework, Practice Guidance*, Cards and other resources.)

DfE (Department for Education) (2012) *Statutory Framework of the Early Years Foundation Stage: Setting the Standards for Learning, Development and Care for Children from Birth to Five*. Runcorn: DfE.

DfES (Department for Education and Skills) (2005) *The Common Core of Skills and Knowledge*. Nottingham: DfES Publications.

Early Education/DfE (2012) *Development Matters in the Early Years Foundation Stage (EYFS)*. London: Early Education.

Katz, L.G. (1998) 'Introduction: What is basic for young children', in S. Smidt (ed.), *The Early Years: A Reader*. London: Routledge.

Loveless, A. (2005) 'Thinking about creativity: developing ideas, making things happen', in A. Wilson (ed.), *Creativity in Primary Education*. Exeter: Learning Matters. Chapter 2.

MLA (Museums, Libraries and Archives Council) www.mla.gov.uk (accessed 26 May 2008).

QCA (Qualifications and Curriculum Authority) www.qca.org.uk (accessed 3 June 2008).

Palaiolgou, I. (2011) 'Transdisciplinarity in early years: a case for Doxastic pedagogy'. Paper presented at British Early Childhood Education and Care Conference, Birmingham, February 2011.

Riley, J. (2007) *Learning in the Early Years*, 2nd edn. London: Sage.

Runco, M. (2006) 'The development of children's creativity', in B. Spodek and O.N. Saracho (eds), *Handbook of Research on the Education of Young Children* Hillsdale, NJ: Lawrence Erlbaum Associates. pp. 121–31.

Salaman, A. and Tutchell, S. (2005) *Planning for Educational Visits for the Early Years*. London: Paul Chapman Publishing.

Siraj-Blatchford, I., Sylva, K., Muttocks, S., Gilden, R. and Bell, D. (2002) *Researching Effective Pedagogy in the Early Years*. DfES Research Brief No. 356. London: DfES.

Smidt, S. (2005) *Observing, Assessing and Planning for Children in the Early Years*. London: Routledge.

Smidt, S. (2006) *The Developing Child in the 21st Century*. London: Routledge.

Sylva, K., Melhuish, E., Sammons, P., Siraj-Blatchford, I., Taggart, B. and Elliott, K. (2003) *The Effective Provision of Pre-School Education (EPPE) Project: Findings from the Pre-School Period*. Research Brief No. RBX15-03. London: Department for Education and Skills, available at: www.ioe.ac.uk/projects/eppe (accessed 24 June 2008).

TDA (Training and Development Agency) Qualified Teacher Standards and ITT Requirements. www.tda.gov.uk (accessed 26 May 2008).

TRS (Teaching Resource Site) www.teachernet.gov.uk (accessed 3 June 2008).

UNCRC (1992) UK Ratification of the Convention on the Rights of the Child. Available at www.direct.gov.uk/en/Parents/ParentsRights/DG_4003313 (accessed 18 June 2008).

Walsh, G. and Gardner, J. (2005) 'Assessing the quality of early years learning environments', *Early Childhood Research and Practice,* 7 (1), available at: http://ecrp.uiuc.edu/v7n1/walsh.html (accessed 2 June 2009).

Zwozdiak-Myers, P. (ed.) (2007) *Childhood and Youth Studies*. Exeter: Learning Matters.

Chapter 11   Working in Partnership with Parents

Arnold, C. (2003) *Observing Harry: Child Development and Learning 0–5*. Maidenhead: Open University Press.

Athey, C. (2007) Extending Thought in Young Children: A Parent–Teacher Partnership. London: Sage.

DCSF (Department for Children, Schools and Families) (2008) *The Impact of Parental Involvement on Children's Education*. Nottingham: DCSF Publications.

DfE (Department for Education) (2012) *Statutory Framework for the Early Years Foundation Stage. Setting the Standards for Learning, Development and Care for Children from Birth to Five*. Runcorn: DfE.

Dunhill, A., Elliot, B. and Shaw, A. (2009) *Effective Communication and Engagement with Children and Young People, Their Families and Carers*. Exeter: Learning Matters.

Feiler, A. (2010) *Engaging 'Hard to Reach' Parents*. Chichester: Wiley-Blackwell.

HM Treasury (2004) *Choice for Parents, the Best Start for Children: A Ten Year Strategy for Childcare*. London: HMSO.

Hobart, C. and Frankel, J. (2003) *A Practical Guide to Working with Parents*. Cheltenham: Nelson Thornes.

Leask, J., quoted in Abbot, L. and Nutbrown, C. (2001) *Experiencing Reggio Emilia – Implications for Pre-school Provision*. Maidenhead: Open University Press.

MacNaughton, G. (2005) *Doing Foucault in Early Childhood Studies*. Oxford: Routledge.

Malaguzzi, L., quoted in Abbot, L. and Nutbrown, C. (2001) *Experiencing Reggio Emilia – Implications for Pre-school Provision*. Maidenhead: Open University Press.

McMillan Nursery School Hull (2011) *The McMillan ABC: The 100 Letters of the Alphabet*. Hull: Blurb.

Pugh, G. and Duffy, B. (2006) *Contemporary Issues in the Early Years,* 4th edn. London: Sage.

Shaw, A. (2009) 'Engaging with children, young people, families and casers at home and in other settings', in A. Dunhill, B. Elliott and A. Shaw (eds), *Effective Communication and Engagement with Children, Young People, Their Families and Casers*. Exeter: Learning Matters.

Smidt, S. (2007) *A Guide to Early Years Practice,* 3rd edn. London: Routledge.

Thornton, L. and Brunton, P. (2007) *Bringing the Reggio Approach to Your Early Years Practice*. Oxford: Routledge.

Whalley, M. (2007) *Involving Parents in their Children's Learning,* 2nd edn. London: Paul Chapman Publishing.

Wheal, A. (2000) *Working with Parents, Learning from Other People's Experiences*. Trowbridge: Cromwell Press.

Chapter 12   Working Together to Safeguard Children

Applegate, J.S. and Shapiro, J.R. (2005) *Neurobiology for Clinical Social Work Theory and Practice*. New York: W.W. Norton.

Asmussen, K. (2010) *Key Facts About Child Maltreatment*. London: NSPCC.

Barker, R. (ed.) (2009) *Making Sense of Every Child Matters: Multi-professional Practice Guidance*. Bristol: The Policy Press.

Barlow, J. and Scott, J. (2010) *Research in Practice: Safeguarding in the 21st Century Where to Now?* Sheffield: Dartington Press, University of Sheffield.

Barlow, J. and Svanberg, P O. (2009) *Keeping the Baby in Mind: Infant Mental Health in Practice*. Hove: Routledge.

Beckett, C. (2010) *Child Protection: An Introduction,* 2nd edn. London: Sage.

Bolger, K. and Patterson, C. (2003). 'Sequelae of child maltreatment: vulnerability and resilience', in S.S. Luthar (ed.), *Resilience and Vulnerability: Adaptation in the Context of Childhood Adversities*. New York: Columbia University. pp.156–81.

Bowlby, J. (1980), *Volume 1. Attachment and Loss Attachment.* London: Pimilico.

Bronfenbrenner, U. (1979) *The Ecology of Human Development.* Cambridge, MA: Harvard University Press.

Cabinet Office (2009) *Social Exclusion Task Force, Family Nurse Partnership.* Available from: http://webarchive.national archives.gov.uk/+/http:/www.cabinetoffice.gov.uk/social_exclusion_task_force/family_nursepartnership.aspx (accessed 29 April 2012).

Collishaw, S., Pickeles, A., Messer, J., Rutter, M., Shearer, C. and Maughan, B. (2007) 'Resilience to adult psychopathology following childhood maltreatment: evidence from a community sample', *Child Abuse and Neglect,* 31: 211–29.

DCSF (Department for Children, Schools and Families) (2008). *The Early Years Foundation Stage.* EFYS Pack (May). Nottingham: Department for Education.

DCSF (Department for Children, Schools and Families) (2010) *Working Together to Safeguard Children: A Guide to Inter-Agency Working to Safeguard and Promote the Welfare of Children.* London: DCSF.

DfES (Department of Education and Skills) (2003) *Every Child Matters.* London: The Stationery Office.

DfES (Department for Education and Skills) (2006c) *The Common Assessment Framework for Children and Young People: Practitioners' Guide.* London: DfES.

DfES (Department for Education and Skills) (2006a) *What to Do If You Are Worried a Child is Being Abused: Summary.* Nottingham: DfES.

DfES (Department for Education and Skills) (2006b) *Working Together to Safeguard Children: A Guide to Interagency Working to Safeguard and Promote the Welfare of Children.* London: The Stationery Office.

DfE (Department for Education) (2010) Statistical Release: Children in Need in England … (Children in Need – Final) Year Ending 31 March 2010. London: DfE.

Department of Health (1989) *Introduction to the Children Act.* London: HMSO.

Department of Health (1995) *Children Protection: Message from Research.* London: Department of Health.

Gerhardt, S. (2004) *Why Love Matters: How Affection Shapes a Baby's Brain.* London: Routledge.

Harlow, J. and Smith, M. (2012) 'Safeguarding children: debates and dilemmas for health visitors', in K. Luker, J. Orr and G. McHugh (eds), *Health Visiting: A Rediscovery*, 3rd edn. Chichester: Wiley-Blackwell.

Kim, J. (2009) 'Type-specific intergenerational transmission of neglectful and physically abusive parenting behaviour among young parents', *Children and Youth Services Review*, 31 (7): 761–7.

Laming, Lord H. (2003) *The Victoria Climbié Inquiry: Report of an Inquiry by Lord Laming*, CM5730. London: The Stationery Office.

Lazenbatt, A. (2010) *The Impact of Abuse and Neglect on the Health and Mental Health of Children and Young People.* London: NSPCC.

Morris, J. (1999) 'Disabled children, child protection systems and the Children Act 1989', *Child Abuse Review*, 8: 91–108.

Olds, D.L., Eckenrode, J., Henderson, C.R. Jr et al. (1997) 'Long-term effects of home visitation on maternal life course and child abuse and neglect: fifteen-year follow-up of a randomized trial', *JAMA,* 278: 637–43.

Olds, D.L., Kitzman, H., Hanks, C. et al. (2007) 'Effects of nurse home visiting on maternal and child functioning: age-9 follow-up of a randomized trial', *Pediatrics,* 120: 832–45.

Olds, D.L., Robinson, J., O'Brien, R. et al. (2002) 'Home visiting by paraprofessionals and by nurses: a randomized, control trial', *Pediatrics,* 114: 1560–8.

Pearce, J.W, and Pezzot-Pearce, T.D. (2007) *Psychotherapy of Abused and Neglected Children*, 2nd edn. New York: Guilford Press.

Sidebotham, P.D. and the ALSPAC Study Team (2006) 'Patterns of child abuse in early childhood: a cohort study of the "children of the nineties"', *Child Abuse Review*, 9: 311–20.

United Nations (1989) *The Convention on the Rights of the Child*. Geneva: Defence International and the United Nations Children's Fund.

Chapter 13   Children's Health

Audit Commission (2010) *Giving Children a Healthy Start*. London: Audit Commision.

Bolling, K., Grant, C., Hamlyn, B. et al. (2007) *Infant Feeding 2005: A Survey Conducted on Behalf of The Information Centre for Health and Social Care and the UK Health Departments by BMRB Social Research*. London: The Information Centre.

British Dietetic Association (2011) wearing yaw child. BDA Specialist Paediatric Group.www.baa. uk.com/foodfacts/wearing yaw child.pdf.

CPAG (Child Poverty Action Group) (2008) Budget Measures and Low-income Households: Evidence for the Treasury Select Committee. Available at: www.cpag.org.uk/info/briefings_ policy/CPAG_evidence_Treasury_Select_Committee_0508.pdf.

Clarke, N. M.P. and Page, J.E. (2009) 'Vitamin D deficiency: a paediatric orthopaedic perspective', *Paediatrics*, 24 (1): 46–9.

Dhalgren, G. and Whitehead, M. (1991) *Policies and Strategies to Promote Social Equity in Health*. Stockholm: Institute for Futures Studies.

DCSF (Department for Children, Schools and Families) (2008) *The Early Years Foundation Stage. EFYS Pack* May. Nottingham: DCSF.

Department of Health (1991) *Report No. 41: Dietary Reference. Values for Food Energy and Nutrients for the UK. Report of the Panel on Dietary Reference Values of the Committee on Medical Aspects of Food Policy*. HMSO. London.

Department of Health (2009) *The Healthy Child Programme: Pregnancy and the First Five Years of Life*. London: Department of Health. Available from: www.dh.gov.uk/en/PublicationsandStatistics/ Publications/PublicationsPolicyAnd Guidance/DH_107563 (accessed 10 April 2012).

Department of Health (2004) *National Service Framework for Children, Young People and Maternity Services: The Mental Health and Psychological Wellbeing of Children and Young People*. London: Department of Health.

Department of Health (2011a) *Delivering a Healthy Start for Pregnant Mums, New Mums, Babies and Young Children*. London: COI Department of Health.

Department of Health (2011b) *Health Visitor Implementation Plan: A Call to Action: 2011–2015*. London: Department of Health.

Dinsdale, H., Ridler, C. and Rutter, H. (2012) *National Child Measurement Programme: Changes in Children's Body Mass Index Between 2010/2011*. Oxford: National Obesity Observatory.

Ferrence, R. (2010) 'Passive smoking and children', *British Medical Journal*, 340: 1680.

Graham, H. (2004) *Understanding Health Inequalities*. Maidenhead: Open University Press.

Gregory, J.R., Collins, D.L., Davies, P.S.W., Hughes, J.M. and Clarke, P.C. (1995) *National Diet and Nutrition Survey: Children Aged 1.5–4.5 years*. London: HMSO.

Harker, L. (2006) *Chance of a Lifetime: The Impact of Bad Housing on Children's Lives*. London: Shelter.

Health Protection Agency (2004) Annual Report and Accounts 2004. England and Wales. London: HPA.

John, T.J. and Samuel, R. (2000) 'Hend immunity and herd effect: new insights and definitions', *European Journal of Epidemiology*, 16(7): 601–6.

Marmot, M., Atkinson, T., Bell, J. et al. (2010) *Fair Society, Healthy Lives. The Marmot Review.* Marmot Review Team. London: University College London.

Mayor, S. (2004) 'Cardiovascular disease threaters the developing countries', *Journal of Epidemiology and Community Health,* 58: 801.

More, J., Jenkins, C., King, C., and Shaw, V. (2010) *BDA Paediatric Position Statement Weaning Infants into Solid Foods. paediatric Specialist Group.* London: British Dietetic Association.

Mc Graw, M.E. (2009) 'Delivery of the Paediatrc Curriculum of the Royal College of Paediatrics and Child Health', *Disease in Childhood*, 94: 254–7.

NHS Information Centre for Health and Social Care (2010) *Statistics on Smoking: England, 2010.* Leeds: NHS Information Centre for Health and Social Care.

RCPCH (Royal College of Paediatrics and Child Health (2012) Position Statement: Breastfeeding. www.rcpch.ac.uk/child-health/standards-care/nutrition-and-growth/nutrition-and growth#Breastfeeding (accessed 22 April 2012).

Seedhouse, D. (1988) *Ethics: The Heart of Health Care.* Chichester: John Wiley.

UNICEF (2009) The UNICEF UK Baby Friendly Initiative. Developing a breastfeeding strategy – evidence and appendices London: UNICEF and the World Health Organization.

World Health Organization (2003) *Health Environments for Children.* www.who.int/features/2003/04/en (accessed 10 April 2012).

Chapter 14   Inclusion in the Early Years

Baker, C. (2001) *Foundations of Bilingual Education and Bilingualism,* 3rd edn. New York: Multilingual Matters.

DCSF (Department for Children, Schools and Families) (2009a) *Building Futures: Developing Trust. A Focus on Provision for Children from Gypsy, Roma and Traveller Backgrounds in the Early Years Foundation Stage.* Nottingham: DCSF Publications.

DCSF (Department for Children, Schools and Families) (2009b) *The Extra Mile: How Schools Succeed in Raising Aspirations in Deprived Communities.* Nottingham: DCSF Publications.

DCSF (Department for Children, Schools and Families) (2010) *Inclusion Development Programme: Supporting Pupils with Behavioural, Emotional and Social Difficulties.* London: DCSF.

DfE (Department for Education) (2012) *Statutory Framework for the Early Years Foundation Stage. Setting the Standards for Learning, Development and Care for Children from Birth to Five.* Runcorn: DfE, available at www.education.gov.uk/publications/standard/AllPublications/Page1/DFE-00023-2012.

DfES (Department for Education and Skills) (2001) *The Special Educational Needs Code of Practice.* London: DfES.

DfES (Department for Education and Skills) (2003) Every Child Matters. Nottingham: DfES.

Early Education/DFE (2012) *Development Matters in the Early Years Foundation Stage (EYFS).* London: Early Education.

Field, F. (2010) The Foundation Years: Preventing Poor Children Becoming Poor Adults. The Report of the Independent Review on Poverty and Life Chances, Available at: www.bristol.ac.uk/ifssoca/outputs/ffreport.pdf (accessed 25 October 2011).

Nutbrown, C. (1996) *Respectful Educators: Capable Learners – Children's Rights in the Early Years.* London: Paul Chapman Publishing.

OECD (2010) *PISA 2009 Results: What Students Know and Can Do. Student Performance in Reading, Mathematics and Science (Volume 1).* PISA, OECD Publishing-doi: 10.1787/9789264091450-en.

QCA (Qualifications and Curriculum Authority (2000) *The Curriculum Guidance for the Foundation Stage.* London: QCA.

Tickell, C. (2011) *The Early Years: Foundations for Life, Health and Learning. An Independent Report on the Early Years Foundation Stage to Her Majesty's Government.* www.education. gov.uk/tickellreview (accessed July 2012).

UNESCO (1994) *The Salamanca Statement and Framework for Action on Special Needs Education.* Paris: UNESCO.

Chapter 15   Leadership in the Early Years Foundation Stage

Ang, L. (2012) 'Leading and managing in the early years: a study of the impact of a NCSL programme on Children's Centre leaders' perceptions of leadership and practice', *Educational Management Administration & Leadership*, 40 (3): 289–304.

Aubrey, C. (2007) *Leading and Managing in the Early Years.* London: Sage.

Bass, B. (ed.) (1981) *Stodgill's Handbook of Leadership.* New York: Free Press.

Goleman, D. (2001) *The Emotionally Intelligent Workplace.* San Francisco: Jossey-Bass.

Jones, C. (2008) *Leadership and Management in the Early Years: From Principles to Practice.* Maidenhead: Open University Press.

Katzenbach, J. and Smith, D. (1993) *The Wisdom of Teams: Creating the High Performing Organization.* Maidenhead: McGraw-Hill.

Male, T. (2006) *Being an Effective Headteacher.* London: Paul Chapman Publishing.

Male, T. (2012) 'Ethical leadership in early years settings', in I. Palaiologou (ed.), *Ethical Practice in Early Childhood.* London: Sage.

Male, T. and Palaiologou, I. (2012) 'Learning-centred leadership or pedagogical leadership? An alternative approach to leadership in education contexts', *International Journal of Leadership in Education*, 15 (1): 107–18.

Miller, L. (2011) *Professionalization, Leadership and Management in the Early Years.* London: Sage.

Moyles, J. (2006) *Effective Leadership and Management in the Early Years.* Maidenhead: Open University Press.

Nutbrown, C. (2012) *Review of Early Childhood Care Qualifications: Interim Report.* Available at www.education.gov.uk/nutbrownreview (accessed March 2012).

Rodd, J. (2006). *Leadership in Early Childhood.* Maidenhead: Open University Press.

Selznick, P. (1983) *Leadership in Administration: A Sociological Interpretation.* Berkeley, CA: University of California, Berkeley Press.

Siraj-Blatchford, I. and Manni, L. (2007) *Effective Leadership in the Early Years Sector: The ELEYS Study.* London: Institute of Education, University of London.

Southworth, G. (2002) 'Instructional leadership in schools: reflections and empirical evidence', *School Leadership & Management,* 22 (1): 73–91.

Southworth, G. (2006) 'A new flame', *LDR*, 20: 19–21 (Nottingham: National College for School Leadership).

Whalley, M. (2011) *Leading Practice in Early Years Settings,* 2nd edn. Exeter: Learning Matters.

Whitaker, P. (1993) *Managing Change in Schools.* Buckingham: Open University Press.

Chapter 16   Personal Social and Emotional Development

Ainsworth, M.D.S. (1969) 'Object relations, dependency, and attachment: a theoretical review of the infant–mother relationship', *Child Development*, 40, 969–1025.

Ainsworth, M.D.S. (1979) 'Attachment as related to mother–infant interaction', *Advances in the Study of Behaviour*, 9: 2–52.

Ainsworth, M.D.S. (1985) 'Attachments across the life span', *Bulletin of the New York Academy of Medicine*, 61: 792–812.

Ainsworth, M.D.S. (1989) 'Attachment beyond infancy', *American Psychologist*, 44: 709–16.

Ainsworth, M.D.S. and Bell, S.M. (1970) 'Attachment, exploration, and separation: illustrated by the behaviour of one-year-olds in a strange situation', *Child Development*, 41: 49–67.

Ainsworth, M.D.S. and Bowlby, J. (1991) 'An ethological approach to personality development', *American Psychologist*, 46: 333–41.

Ainsworth, M.D.S., Bell, S.M. and Stayton, D.J. (1971a) 'Individual differences in the strange situation behaviour of one-year-olds', in H.R. Schaffer (ed.), *The Origins of Human Social Relations*. New York: Academic Press. pp. 15–71.

Ainsworth, M.D.S., Bell, S.M., Blehar, M.C. and Main, M. (1971b) 'Physical contact: a study of infant responsiveness and its relation to maternal handling'. Paper presented at the biennial meeting of the Society for Research in Child Development, Minneapolis, MN.

Ainsworth, M.D.S., Blehar, M.C., Waters, E. and Wall, S. (1978) *Patterns of Attachment: A Psychological Study of the Strange Situation*. Hillsdale, NJ: Erlbaum.

Bandura, A. (1977) *Social Learning Theory*. New York: General Learning Press.

Bandura, A. (1986) *Social Foundations of Thought and Action: a Social Cognitive Theory*. Englewood Cliffs, NJ: Prentice–Hall.

Barnes, K.E. (1971) 'Preschool play norms: a replication', *Developmental Psychology*, 5: 99–103.

Black, B. and Logan, A. (1995) 'Links between communication patterns in mother child, father child, and child peer interactions and children's social status', *Child Development*, 66: 951–65.

Bowlby, J. (1960) 'Grief and mourning in infancy and early childhood', *The Psychoanalytic Study of the Child*, 15: 9–52.

Bowlby, J. (1969) *Attachment and Loss, Volume I. Attachment*. London: Hogarth Press

Bowlby, J. (1973) *Attachment and Loss, Volume 2. Separation: Anger and Anxiety*. (International Psycho-analytical Library No. 95). London: Hogarth Press.

Bowlby, J. (1980) *Attachment and Loss, Volume 3. Loss: Sadness and Depression*. (International Psycho-analytical Library No. 109). London: Hogarth Press.

Bowlby, J. (1986) 'Citation Classic: *Maternal Care and Mental Health*', www.garfield.library. upenn.edu/classics1986/A1986F063100001.pdf (accessed November 2008).

Bowlby, J. (1999) *Attachment and Loss, Volume I. Attachment*, 2nd edn. New York: Basic Books.

Bowlby, J. (2005) *The Making and Breaking of Affectional Bonds*. London: Routledge Classics.

Damon, W. (1988) *The Moral Child*. New York: Free Press.

Davison, J.D., Sherer, K.R. and Goldsmith, H.H. (2009) *Handbook of Affective Sciences*. New York: Oxford University Press.

DCSF (Department for Children, Schools and Families) (2008) *Social and Emotional Aspects of Development: Guidance for Practitioners Working in the Early Years*. Nottingham: DCSF Publications.

DfE (Department for Education) (2011) *The Early Years Foundation Stage (EYFS) Review: Report on the Evidence*. London: DfE.

DfE (Department for Education) (2012) *Statutory Framework for the Early Years Foundation Stage: Setting the Standards for Learning, Development and Case from Birth to Five.* Runcorn: DfE.

DfES (Department for Education and Skills) (2005) *Excellence and Enjoyment: Social and Emotional Aspects of Learning (Guidance).* Nottingham: DfES Publications.

DeRosier, M.E., Gillessen, A.H., Coie, J.D. and Dodge, K.A. (1994) 'Group social context and children's aggressive behavior', *Child Development*, 65: 1068–80.

Donaldson, J. (1999) *The Gruffalo*. London: Macmillan.

Dunn, J. (1993) *Young Children's Close Relationships: Beyond Attachment.* London: Sage.

Early Education/DfE (2012) *Development Matters in the Early Years Foundation Stage (EYFS).* London: Early Education.

Elfer, P., Goldschmied, E. and Selleck, D. (2002) *Key Persons in Nurseries: Building Relationships for Quality Provision.* London: National Early Years Network.

Gilligan, C. and Wiggins, G. (1987) 'The origins of morality in early childhood relationships', in J. Kagan and S. Lamb (eds), *The Emergence of Morality in Young Children*. Chicago, IL: University of Chicago Press.

Howes, C. (1990) 'Can the age of entry into child care and the quality of child care predict adjustment in kindergarten?', in *Developmental Psychology*, 26: 292–303.

Howes, C. (1992) *The Collaborative Construction of Pretend.* Albany, NY: SUNY Press.

Howes, C. and Matheson, C.C. (1992) 'Sequences in the development of competent play with peers: social and social pretended play', *Developmental Psychology*, 28: 961–74.

Hymel, S. (1983) 'Preschool children's peer relations: Issues in sociometric assessment', *Merrill-Palmer Quarterly*, 19: 237–60.

Hymel, S., Rubin, K., Rowden, L. and LeMare, L. (1990) 'Children's peer relationships: longitudinal prediction of internalizing and externalizing problems from middle to late childhood', *Child Development*, 61: 2004–21.

Kohlberg, L. (1969) 'Stage and sequence: the cognitive-developmental approach to socialization.', in D.A. Goslin (ed.), *Handbook of Socialization Theory and Research*. Chicago, IL: Rand McNally.

Mosley, J. (2005) *Circle Time for Young Children*. London: Bloomsbury.

NCB (2012) *'Know How': The Progress Check at Age Two.* http://media.education.gov.uk/assets/files/pdf/k/know%20how%20materials.pdf (accessed April 2012).

Nikolopoulou, A. (1993) 'Play, cognitive development, and the social world: Piaget, Vygotsky and beyond', *Human Development*, 36: 1–23.

Ofsted (2011) *The Impact of the Early Years Foundation Stage.* Manchester: Ofsted.

Piaget, J. (1932) *The Moral Judgment of the Child*. New York: The Free Press.

Piaget, J.(1951) *Play Dreams and Imitation in Childhood*. London: Routledge & Kegan Paul.

Rosen, M. (1989) *We're Going On a Bear Hunt*. London: Walker.

Rubin, K.H., (1982) 'Non-social play in preschoolers: necessarily evil?', *Child Development,* 53: 651–7.

Rubin, K.H., Fein, G.G. and Vandenberg, B. (1983) 'Play', in E.M. Hetherington (ed), *Handbook of Child Personality and Social Development,* 4th edn. New York: Wiley. pp. 693–744.

Selleck, D. (2001) 'Being under 3 years of age: enhancing quality experiences', in G. Pugh (ed.), *Contemporary Issues in the Early Years*, 3rd edn. London: Paul Chapman Publishing.

Singer, J.L. and Singer, D.C. (1990) *The House of Make Believe*. Cambridge, MA: Harvard University Press.

Smith, P. K (1997) *Play Fighting and Fighting: How Do They Relate?* Lisbon: ICCP.

Sylva, K., Melhuish, E., Sammons, P., Siraj-Blatchford, I., Taggart, B. and Elliot, K. (2003) *The Effective Provision of Pre-school Education (EPPE) Project: Findings from the Pre-school Period: Summary of Findings.* London: Institute of Education/Sure Start.

Vygotsky, L.S. (1978) *Mind in Society: The Development of Higher Psychological Processes*. London: Harvard University Press.

Vygotsky, L.S. (1986) *Thought and Language*. London and Cambridge, MA: The MIT Press.

Chapter 17   Communication and Language

Alborough, J. (2001) *Hug*. London: Walker Books.

Alexander, R. (2008) *Introducing the Cambridge Primary Review*. Cambridge: University of Cambridge, Faculty of Education.

Browne, A. (2009) *Developing Language and Literacy 3–8*. London: Sage.

Bruce, T. (2010) *Early Childhood: A Guide for Students*, 2nd edn. London: Sage.

Bruner, J. (1986) *Actual Minds, Possible Worlds*. Cambridge, MA: Harvard University Press.

Bruner, J. (1983). *Child's Talk: Learning to Use Language*. Oxford: Oxford University Press.

Communication Trust (2011) *Let's Talk About It: What New Teachers Need to Know About Communication Skills*. London: The Communication Trust.

Chomsky, N. (1957) *Syntactic Structures*. The Hague: Mouton.

Chomsky, N.A. (1965) *Aspects of the Theory of Syntax*. Cambridge, MA: MIT Press.

DfE (Department for Education) (2012) Statutory Framework for the Early Years Foundation Stage. Setting the Standards for Learning, Development and Care for Children from Birth to Five. Runcorn: DfE.

David, T., Goouch, K., Powell, S., and Abbott, L. (2003) *Birth to Three Matters: A Review of the Literature*. London: Department for Education and Skills.

Early Education/DfE (2012) *Development Matters in the Early Years Foundation Stages (EYFS)*. London: Early Education.

Edwards, D. and Merces, N. (1987) *Common Knowledge: The Development of Understanding in the Classroom*. London: Methven/Routledge.

Gadhok, K. (2007) Speech, language and communication needs – a definition. National Literacy Trust website. www.literacytrust.org.uk/talk_to_your_baby/news/2528_ Speech_Language_ and_communication_needs (accessed July 2012).

Gopnik, A., Meltzoff, A.N. and Kuhl, P.K. (1999) *The Scientist in the Crib: What early learning tells us about the mind*. New York: Harper Collins Publishers.

Goldschmeid, E. and Selleck, D. (1996) *Communication Between Babies in Their First Year*. London: National Children's Bureau.

Gopnik, A., Sobel, D.M., Schulz, L.E. and Glymour, C. (2001) 'Causal learning mechanisms in very young children: Two-, three-, and four-year-olds infer causal relations from patterns of variation and covariation', *Developmental Psychology*, 37 (5): 620–9.

Hart, B. and Risley, T.R. (1999) *The Social World of Children: Learning to Talk*. Baltimore, MD: Paul H. Brookes Publishing Inc.

Henning, A., Strian., T. and Lieven, E.V.M. (2005) 'Maternal speech to infants at 1 and 3 months of age', *Infant Behaviour and Development*, 28: 519–36.

Karmiloff, K. and Karmiloff-Smith, A. (2001) *Pathways to Language: From Fetus to Adolescent*. Cambridge, MA: Harvard University Press.

Kokkinaki, T. and Kugiumutzakis, G. (2000) 'Basic aspects of vocal imitation in infant–parent interaction during the first 6 months', *Journal of Reproductive and Infant Psychology*, 18 (3): 173–87.

Malaguzzi, L. (1996) 'The hundred languages of children', translated by Lella Gandini. Reggio Children, Preschools and Infant–Toddler Centres, Istituzione of the Municipality of Reggio Emilia.

National Literacy Trust (2010) Talk to Your Baby Face to Face Project. Literature Review. www. talktoyourbaby.org.uk (accessed October 2010).

Ofsted (2011) The Impact of the Early Years Foundation Stage. Ofsted document. Available at www.ofsted.gov.uk/resources/impact_of_early_years_foundation_stage (accessed September 2012).

Schaffer, H.R. (ed.) (1977) *Studies in Mother–Infant Interaction*. London: Academic Press.

Siraj-Blatchford, I., Sylva, K., Muttock, S., Gilden, R. and Bell, D. (2002) *Researching Effective Pedagogy in the Early Years*. London: Department for Education and Skills, Research Report 356.

Siraj-Blatchford, I., Sylva, K., Taggart, B., Sammons, P., Melhuish, E., and Elliot, K. (2003) *The Effective Provision of Pre-school Education (EPPE) Project: Intensive Case Studies of Practice Across the Foundation Stage*. London: DfEE/Institute of Education.

Snow, C.E. and Ferguson, C.A. (1977). *Talking to Children*. New York: Cambridge University Press.

Tickell, C. (2011) The Early Years: Foundations for Life, Health and Learning. An Independent Report on the Early Years Foundation Stage to the Majesty's Government. www.education.gov. uk/tickellreview (accessed July 2012).

Trevarthen, C. (1979) 'Communication and cooperation in early infancy: a description of primary intersubjectivity', in M. Bullowa (ed.), *Before Speech: The Beginning of Interpersonal Communication*. Cambridge: Cambridge University Press.

Trevarthen, C. and Aitken, K.J. (2001) 'Infant intersubjectivity: research, theory and clinical application', *Journal of Child Psychology and Psychiatry*, 42 (1): 3–43.

Vygotsky, L.V. (1962) *Thought and Language*. Cambridge: Cambridge University Press.

Vygotsky, L. (1978) *Mind and Society: The Development of Higher Mental Process*. Cambridge, MA: Harvard University Press.

Wells, C.G. (1986) *The Meaning-Makers: Children Learning Language and Using Language to Learn*. Portsmouth, NH: Heinemann Educational.

Wells, G. (1990) *The Meaning Makers*. London: Hodder & Stoughton.

Winnicott, D. (1971) *Playing and Reality*. Harmondsworth: Penguin.

Chapter 18   Literacy

Ayoub, C. and Fischer, K. (2006) 'Developmental pathways and intersections among domains of development', in K. McCartney, and. D. Phillips, (eds), *Blackwell Handbook of Early Child Development*. Oxford: Blackwell.

Campbell, R. (2000) *Literacy from Home to School: Reading with Alice*. Stoke-on-Trent: Trentham Books.

Campbell, R. (2002) *Reading in the Early Years Handbook,* 2nd edn. Buckingham: Open University Press.

Clay, M.M. (1991) *Becoming Literate: The Construction of Inner Control*. London: Heinemann Educational.

DCSF (Department for Children, School and Families) (2007) *Letters and Sounds: Principles and Practice of High Quality Phonics*. London: DCSF.

DfEE (Department for Education and Employment) (2001) *Developing Early Writing*. London: DfEE.

Ferreiro, E. and Teberosky, A. (1983) *Literacy Begins Before Schooling*. London: Heinemann Educational.

Frith, u. (1985) 'Beneath the surface of developmental dyslexia', in K.E. Patterson, J.C Marshall and M. Coltheart (eds), *Surface Dyslexia*. London: Erlbaum.

Goodman, Y. (1980) 'The roots of literacy', in M.P. Douglas (ed.), *Reading: A Humanising Experience*. Claremont: Claremont Graduate School. pp. 42–68.

Goswami, U. (2001) 'Early phonological development and the acquisition of literacy', in S.B. Neuman and D.K. Pickinson (eds), *Handbook of Early Literacy Research*. New York: Guilford Press. p. 111.

Graves, D.H. (1983) *Writing: Teachers and Children at Work*. Exeter, NH: Heinemann Educational.

Hannon, P. (1995) *Literacy, Home and School: Research and Practice in Teaching Literacy with Parents*. London: Falmer Press.

Hannon, P. and Nutbrown, C. (2003) 'REAL Involvement for parents', *Literacy Today*, September, 24–25.

Heath, S.B. (1983) *Ways with Words*. Cambridge: Cambridge University Press.

Holdaway, D. (1979) *The Foundations of Literacy*. Portsmouth, NH: Heinemann Educational.

Macrory, G. (2006) 'Bilingual language development: what do early years practitioners need to know?', *Early Years*, 26: 159–69.

Marsh, J. and Hallet, E. (eds) (1999) *Desirable Literacies: Approaches to Languages and Literacy in the Early Years*. London: Paul Chapman Publishing.

Meek, M. (1988) *How Texts Teach What Readers Learn*. Stroud: Thimble Press.

Morrow, L.M. (1992) *Family Literacy: Connections in Schools and Communities*. Newark, DE: International Reading Association.

Neuman, S.B. (1992) 'Is learning from media distinctive? Examining children's inferencing strategies', *American Educational Research Journal*, 29 (1): 119–40.

Neuman, S.B. (1996) 'Children engaging in storybook reading: the influence of access to print resources: opportunities, and parental interaction', *Early Childhood Research Quarterly*, 11: 495–513.

Neuman, S.B. (1997) 'Guiding young children's participation in early literacy development: a family literacy programme for adolescent mothers', *Early Child Development and Care*, 32: 127–8.

Neuman, S.B. (1999) 'Books make a difference: a study of access to literacy', *Reading Research Quarterly*, 34 (3): 286–311.

Neuman, S.B. and Roskos, K. (1997) 'Literacy knowledge in practice: contexts of participation for young writers and readers', *Reading Research Quarterly*, 32 (1): 10–32.

PEAL (Parents, Early Years and Learning) (2011) 'Great first year for REAL'. www.peal.org.uk/latest_news/news_archive/success_for_real.aspx (accessed by 9 May 2012).

Owocki, G. (1999) *Literacy Through Play*. Portsmouth, NH: Heinnemann Educational.

Riley, J. and Reedy, D. (2000) *Developing Writing for Different Purposes*. London: Paul Chapman Publishing.

Rose, J. (2006) *Independent Review of the Teaching of Early Reading: Final Report*. London: Department for Education and Skills.

Searfoss, L. and Readence, J. (1994) *Helping Children to Read*. Boston, MA: Allyn & Bacon.

Snow, C.E. (2006) 'What counts as literacy in early childhood?', in K. Mccartney, and D. Phillips, (eds), *Blackwell Handbook of Early Childhood Development*. Oxford: Blackwell. pp. 274–94.

Sulzby, E. (1985) 'Kindergarteners as writers and readers', in M. Farr (ed.), *Children's Early Writing Development*. Norwood, NJ: Ablex. pp. 82–126.

Sulzby, E. (1989) 'Forms of writing and rereading example list', in J. Mason (ed.), *Reading and Writing Connections*. Boston, MA: Allyn & Bacon. pp. 51–63.

Sulzby, E. (1992) 'Research directions: transitions from emergent to conventional writing', *Language Arts*, 69: 290–7.

Teale, W.H. and Sulzby, E. (1989) 'Literacy acquisition in early childhood: the roles of access and accommodation in storybook reading', in D.A. Wagner (ed.), *The Future of Literacy in a Changing World*. Oxford: Pergamon. pp. 111–30.

Tickell,. (2011) *The Early Years: Foundations for Life, Health and Learning. An Independent Report on the Early Years Foundation Stage to Her Majesty's Government*, Annex 9. www education.gov.uk/tickellreview (accessed May 2012).

UKLA (United Kingdom Literacy Association) (2008) Submission to the Review of Best Practice in the Teaching of Early Reading. UKLA International Conference Report.

Whitehurst, G. (1998) 'Relative efficacy of parent and teacher involvement in a shared-reading intervention for pre-school children from low income backgrounds', *Early Childhood Research Quarterly*, 13 (2): 263–90.

Williams, M. and Rask, H. (2003) 'Literacy through play: how families with able children support their literacy development', *Early Child Development and Care*, 173 (5): 527–33.

Chapter 19   Mathematics

Aubrey, C. (1993) 'An investigation of the mathematical knowledge and competencies which young children bring into school', *British Educational Research Journal*, 19 (1): 27–41.

Booth, A. and Dunn, J. (1996) *Family–School Links: How Do They Affect Educational Outcomes?* Philadelphia, PA: Lawrence Erlbaum Associates.

Clements, D.H., Sarama, J. and DiBiase, A. (2004) *Engaging Young Children in Mathematics*. Philadelphia, PA: Lawrence Erlbaum Associates.

Clemson, D. and Clemson, W. (1994) *Mathematics in the Early Years*. London: Routledge.

Cooke, H. (2007) *Mathematics for Primary and Early Years: Developing Subject Knowledge*, 2nd edn. London: Sage.

Davis, R.B. (1984) *Learning Mathematics: The Cognitive Science Approach to Mathematical Education*. Norwood, NJ: Greenwood.

Devlin, K.J. (2000) *The Language of Mathematics*. New York: Henry Holt.

DfE (Department for Education) (2012) *Statutory Framework for the Early Years Foundation Stage* Runcorn: DfE.

Early Education/DfE (2012) *Development Matters in the Early Years Foundation Stage (EYFS)*. London: Early Education, available at www.early-education.org.uk (accessed 4 May 2012).

Dewey, J. (1938) *Logic: The Theory of Enquiry*. New York: Henry Holt.

Dickinson, D.K. and Tabors, P.O. (1991) 'Early literacy: linkages between home, school and literacy achievement at age five', *Journal of Research in Childhood Education*, 6 (1): 30–46.

Downs, S. (1998) 'Technological change and education and training', *Education and Training*, 40 (1): 18–19.

Griffiths, N. (1998) *Story Sacks*. Video. Bury: Story Sacks Ltd.

Hiebert, H., Carpenter, T.P., Fennema, E., Fuson, K., Human, P., Murray, H., Olivier, A. and Wearne, D. (1996) 'Problem solving as a basis for reform in curriculum and instruction: the case of mathematics', *Educational Researcher*, 25 (4): 12–21.

Jones, L. (1998) 'Home and school numeracy experiences for young Somali pupils in Britain', *European Early Childhood Education Research Journal*, 6 (1): 63–72.

Mathematical Association (1955) *The Teaching of Mathematics in Primary Schools*. London: Mathematical Association.

Munn, P. (1996a) 'Progression in literacy and numeracy in preschool', in M. Hughes (ed.), *Progression in Learning*. Bristol: Multilingual Matters.

Munn, P. (1996b) 'Assessment of literacy and numeracy acquired before school', in R. Duggan and C.J. Pole (eds), *Reshaping Education in the 1990s: Perspectives on Primary Schooling*. London: Routledge.

Nunes, T. and Bryant, P. (1996) *Children Doing Mathematics*. London: Blackwell.

Price, S., Rogers, Y., Scaife, M., Stanton, D. and Neale, H. (2003) 'Using tangibles to promote novel forms of playful learning', *Interacting with Computers*, 15: 169–85.

Resnick, L.B. (1989) 'Developing mathematical knowledge', *American Psychologist*, 44 (2): 162–9.

Schaeffer, B., Eggleston V.H. and Scott, J.L. (1974) 'Number development in young children', *Cognitive Development*, 5: 357–9.

Schoenfeld, A.H. (1992) 'Learning to think mathematically: problem solving, metacognition, and sense-making in mathematics', in *Handbook for Research on Mathematics Teaching and Learning*. New York: Macmillan.

Schroeder, H.E. (1991) *New Directions in Health Psychology*. Oxford: Taylor & Francis.

Seefeldt, C., Galper, A. and Stevenson-Garcia, J. (2012) *Active Experiences for Active Children: Mathematics,* 3rd edn. London: Pearson.

Siraj-Blatchford, I., Sylva, K., Muttock, S., Gilden, R. and Bell, D. (2002) *Researching Effective Pedagogy in Early Years*. London: HMSO.

Skemp, R.R. (1989) *Mathematics in the Primary School*. London: Routledge.

Staub, E. (1971) 'The use of role playing and induction in children's learning of helping and sharing behaviour', *Child Development*, 42 (3): 805–16.

Taylor, S.I., Morris, V.G. and Rogers, C.S. (1997) 'Toy safety and selection', *Early Childhood Education Journal*, 24 (4): 235–8.

Tipps, S., Johnson, A. and Kennedy, L.M. (2011) *Guiding Children's Learning of Mathematics*. Belmont, CA: Wadsworth.

Vygotsky, I. (1978) *Mind in Society: The Development of Higher Psychological Processes*. Cambridge, MA: Harvard University Press.

Winter, J., Andrews, J., Greenhough, P., Hughes, M., Salway, L. and Yee, W. (2009) *Improving Primary Mathematics: Linking Home and School*. Abingdon: Routledge.

Wood, E. and Attfield, J. (2005) *Play, Learning and the Early Childhood Curriculum*. London: Sage.

Worthington, M. and Carruthers, E. (2003) *Children's Mathematics: Making Marks, Making Meaning*. London: Sage.

Chapter 20   Understanding the World

Aubrey, C. and Dahl, S. (2008) *Parents as Partners in Education*. Coventry: Creative Partnerships.

Barnes, J. (2007) *Cross-curricular Learning 3–14*. London: Paul Chapman Publishing.

Barnes, J. and Shirley, I. (2007) 'Strangely familiar: cross-curricular and creative thinking in teacher education', *Improving Schools,* 10 (2): 162–79.

Beauchamp, G. (2006) 'New technologies and "New teaching": a process of evolution?', in R. Webb (ed.), *Changing Teaching and Learning in the Primary School*. Maidenhead: Open University Press. pp. 81–91.

Beauchamp, G. (2011) 'Interactivity and ICT in the primary school: categories of learner interactions with and without ICT', *Technology, Pedagogy and Education*, 20 (2): 175–90.

Beauchamp, G. (2012) *ICT in the Primary School: From Pedagogy to Practice*. London: Pearson.

Beauchamp, G. and Kennewell, S. (2008) 'The influence of ICT on the interactivity of teaching', *Education and Information Technologies*, 13 (4): 305–15.

Cooper, H. (2002) *History in the Early Years*, 2nd edn. London: Routledge Falmer.

DCSF (Department for Children, Schools and Families) (2008) *The Early Years Foundation Stage: Setting the Standards for Learning, Development and Care for Children from Birth to Five*. Nottingham: DCSF Publications. (Comprises the *Statutory Framework, Practice Guidance*, Cards and other resources.)

De Boo, M. (2000) Science 3–6: *Laying the Foundations in the Early Years*. Hatfield: ASE.

Desforges, C. and Abouchaar, A. (2003) *The Impact of Parental Involvement, Parental Support and Family Education on Pupil Achievement and Adjustment: A Literature Review*. Research Report No. RR 433. Norwich: HMSO.

DfE (Department for Education) (2012) *Statutory Framework for the Early Years Foundation Stage: Setting the Standards for Learning, Development and Care for Children from Birth to Five*. Runcorn: DfE.

Feasey, R. and Gallear, B. (2001) *Primary Science and ICT*. Hatfield: ASE.

Fisher, J. (2002) *Starting from the Child: Teaching and Learning from 3 to 8*, 2nd edn. Maidenhead: Open University Press.

Goswami, U. and Bryant, P. (2007) *Children's Cognitive Development and Learning* (Primary Review Research Survey 2/1a). Cambridge: University of Cambridge Faculty of Education.

Harlen, W. (2003) *The Teaching of Science in Primary School*, 3rd edn. London: David Fulton.

Hayes, M. (2006) 'What do the children have to say?', in M. Hayes and D. Whitebread (eds), *ICT in the Early Years*. Maidenhead: Open University Press.

Kennewell, S. and Beauchamp, G. (2007) 'The features of interactive whiteboards and their influence on learning', *Learning, Media and Technology*, 32 (3): 227–41.

Myhill, D., Jones, S. and Hopper, R. (2006) *Talking, Listening, Learning: Effective Talk in the Primary Classroom*. Maidenhead: Open University Press.

O'Hara, M. (2008) 'Young children, learning and ICT: a case study in the UK maintained sector', *Technology, Pedagogy and Education,* 17 (1): 29–40.

Palmer, J. and Birch, J. (2004) *Geography in the Early Years*, 2nd edn. London: Routledge Falmer.

Perkins, D.N. (1997) 'Person-plus: a distributed view of thinking and learning', in G. Salomon (ed.), *Distributed Cognitions: Psychological and Educational Considerations*. Cambridge: Cambridge University Press. pp. 88–110.

Siraj-Blatchford, I., Sylva, K., Muttock, S., Gilden, R. and Bell, D. (2002) *Researching Effective Pedagogy in the Early Years*. Research Report No. RR 356. Norwich: HMSO.

Smeaton, M. (2001) 'Questioning geography', in R. Carter (ed.), *Handbook of Primary Geography*. Sheffield: Geographical Association. pp. 15–17.

Tickell, C. (2011) *The Early Years: Foundations for Life, Health and Learning. An Independent Report on the Early Years Foundation Stage to the Majesty's Government*. www.education.gov. uk/tickellreview (accessed July 2012).

Turner-Bisset, R. (2005) *Creative Teaching: History in the Primary Classroom*. London: David Fulton.

Chapter 21 Physical Development

Almond, L. (2000) 'Physical education and primary schools', in P.R. Bailey and T.M. Macfadyen (eds), *Teaching Physical Education 5–11*. London: Continuum.

Bailey, P.R. (1999) 'Play, health and physical development', in T. David (ed.), *Young Children Learning*. London: Paul Chapman Publishing.

Baur, L.A. (2002) 'Child and adolescent obesity in the 21st century: an Australian perspective', *Asia Pacific Journal of Clinical Nutrition*, 11: 524–8.

Biddle, S., Cavill, N. and Sallis, J. (1998) 'Policy framework for young people and health-enhancing physical activity', in S. Biddle, J. Sallis and N. Cavill (eds), *Young and Active? Young People and Health Enhancing Physical Activity: Evidence and Implications*. London: Health Education Authority.

Bilton, H. (2003) *Outdoor Play in the Early Years*, 2nd edn. London: David Fulton.

Bruner, J. (1983) *Child's Talk: Learning to Use Language*. Oxford: Oxford University Press.

Chugani, H.T. (1997) 'Neuroimaging of developmental nonlinearity and developmental pathologies', in R.W. Thatcher, G.R. Lyon, R. Rumsey and N. Krasnegor (eds), *Developmental Neuroimaging: Mapping the Development of Brain and Behaviour*. San Diego, CA: Academic Press.

DCSF (Department for Children, Schools and Families) (2008) *The Early Years Foundation Stage: Setting the Standards for Learning, Development and Care for Children from Birth to Five*. Nottingham: DCSF Publications. (Comprises the *Statutory Framework, Practice Guidance*, Cards and other resources.)

Dennis, W. (1960) 'The effects of cradling practices upon the onset of walking in Hopi children', *Journal of Genetic Psychology*, 56: 77–86.

DfE (Department for Education) (2012) *Statutory Framework for the Early Years Foundation Stage: Setting the Standards for Learning, Development and case for Children from Birth to Five*. Runcorn:DfE.

Doherty, J. and Bailey, R. (2003) *Supporting Physical Development and Physical Education in the Early Years*. Buckingham: Open University Press.

Gandini, L. (1997) 'The Reggio Emilia story: history and organization', in J. Hendrick (ed.), *First Steps Towards Teaching the Reggio Emilia Way*. Englewood Cliffs, NJ: Merrill/Prentice–Hill.

Gunnar, M.R. (2001) *Quality of Care and Buffering Stress Psychology: Its Potential for Protecting the Developing Human Brain*. Minneapolis, MN: University of Minnesota Institute of Child Development.

Hale, J. (1994) *Unbank the Fire: Visions for the Education of African American Children*. Baltimore, MD: Johns Hopkins University Press.

Hardman, A. and Stensel, D. (2003) *Physical Activity and Health*. London: Routledge.

Harwood, R.L., Miller, J.G. and Irizarry, N.L. (1995) *Culture and Attachment: Perceptions of the Child in Context*. New York: Guilford Press.

Hertsgaard, L., Gunnar, M., Erickson, M.F. and Nachmias, M. (1995) 'Adrenocortical responses to the strange situation in infants with disorganized, disoriented attachment relationships', *Child Development*, 66: 1100–6.

Hopkins, B. and Westra, T. (1988) 'Maternal handling and motor development: an intracultural study', *Genetic, Social and General Psychology Monographs*, 14: 377–420.

Hopper, B., Grey, J. and Maude, T. (2000) *Teaching Physical Education in the Primary School*. London: Routledge Falmer.

Kimm, S.Y.S., Glynn, N.W., Barton, B.A., Kronsberg, S.S., Daniels, S.R., Crawford, P.B., Sabry, Z.I. and Liu, K. (2002) 'Decline in physical activity in black girls and white girls during adolescence', *New England Journal of Medicine*, 347: 709–15.

Levine, R.A. (1996) *Child Care and Culture Lessons from Africa*. Cambridge: Cambridge University Press.

Ministry of Education (New Zealand) (1996) *Te Whā-riki. He Whāriki Matauranga mo nga Mokopuna O Aotearoa. Early Childhood Education*. Learning Media. www.minedu.govt.nz/web/downloadable/dl3567_v1/whariki.pdf (accessed December 2008).

Nachmias, M., Gunnar, M., Mangelsdorf, S., Parritz, R.H. and Buss, K. (1996) 'Behavioral inhabitation and stress reactivity: the moderating role of attachment security', *Child Development*, 67: 508–22.

Nutbeam, D. (1998) 'Evaluating health promotion – progress, problems and solutions', *Health Promotion International*, 13: 27–43.

Parry, J. (1998) 'The justification for physical education', in K. Green and K. Hardman (eds), *Physical Education: A Reader*. Aachen: Meyer & Meyer.

Prentice, A.M. and Jebb, S.A. (1995) 'Obesity in Britain: gluttony or sloth?', *British Medical Journal*, 311: 437–9.

Shore, N. (1997) *Rethinking the Brain: New Insights into Early Development*. New York: Families and Work Institute.

Super, C.M. (1981) 'Behavioural development in infancy', R.H., Monroe, R.L. Monroe and B.B. Whiting (eds), *Handbook of Cross Cultural Human Development*. New York: Garland.

Talbot, M. (1999) 'The case for physical education'. Paper presented at the World Summit on Physical Education, Berlin, November.

Whitehead, M. (2000) 'The concept of physical literacy'. Paper presented to the HEI Conference, 'Meeting Standards and Achieving Excellence. Teaching PE in the 21st Century', Liverpool John Moores University, 11 June.

World Health Organization (1999) Health Promotion, Active Living: The Challenge Ahead. www.who.int (accessed September 2008).

Chapter 22 Creative Development

Craft, A. (2002) *Creativity and Early Years Education: A Lifewide Foundation*. London/New York: Continuum.

Cutler, A. (2005) *Signposting Creative Learning*. Kent: Creative Partnerships.

DFE (Department of Education) (2012) *Statutory Framework for the Early Years Foundation Stage: Setting the Standards for Learning, Development and Case for Children from Birth to Five*. Runcorn: DFE.

Gill, T. (2008) 'No fear – growing up in a risk averse society', *Children, Youth and Environments*, 18 (1) ISSN 1546–2250.

Robinson, K. (1999) *All Our Futures: Creativity, Culture and Education*. London: National Advisory Committee on Creative and Cultural Education.

Index